*"After all that has just passed, all the lives taken and all the
possibilities and hopes that died with them,
it is natural to wonder if America's future is one of fear.*

*Some speak of an age of terror. I know there are struggles
ahead and dangers to face. But this country
will define our times, not be defined by them.*

*As long as the United States of America is determined
and strong, this will not be an age of terror.
This will be an age of liberty here and across the world.*

*Great harm has been done to us. We have suffered great loss.
And in our grief and anger we have found
our mission and our moment.*

*Freedom and fear are at war. The advance of human freedom,
the great achievement of our time and
the great hope of every time, now depends on us.*

*Our nation, this generation, will lift the dark threat of violence from our people
and our future. We will rally the world to this cause by our efforts,
by our courage. We will not tire, we will not falter and we will not fail."*

*George W. Bush
President, United States of America
September 20, 2001*

GUARDIANS OF THE GARDEN CITY
The History of the San José Fire Department
Memorial Reprint Edition

This edition is dedicated to the victims of September 11, 2001,
their families, friends, the courageous fire fighters, law enforcement officers,
emergency assistance personnel, doctors, nurses, hospital workers, construction personnel,
all the other service personnel, victim assistance workers,
and the citizens who rose from the community
to stand as heroes.

The tragedy of the September 11, 2001 terrorist attack has reached the daily lives
of every American. Two hijacked airliners torpedoed into the World Trade Center towers in
New York City. Another assaulted the Pentagon. The fourth, headed for the White House,
crashed in Pennsylvania after its heroic passengers fought to reclaim the aircraft
from its hijackers. The cost in American lives was very high.

This infamous event has focused our attention on
thanking the unrecognized heroic public servants who place their own
lives in jeopardy daily to fill the needs of our communities.

FIRE FIGHTERS · LAW ENFORCEMENT AGENCIES · EMERGENCY MEDICAL TEAMS
SEARCH & RESCUE TEAMS · U.S. POSTAL WORKERS · MILITARY PERSONNEL

Printed by Smith & McKay Printing Co., Inc.

96 North Almaden Blvd., San José, California 95110-2490

(408) 292-8901 · Fax (408) 292-0417

www.smithmckay.com

 92

First printed in 1972, "Guardians of the Garden City" chronicles
the development and history of the San José Fire Department from
its humble beginnings in the mid-1800's through 1972.

Due to the requests of members of the San José Muster Team and others,
Smith & McKay Printing published this 2nd Edition including
a 9/11/01 Memorial Dedication.

This special section was added to the front of the book listing all of the current
San José Fire Fighters, those who have retired, and most importantly,
those gallant fire fighters who have made the ultimate sacrifice
while serving the citizens of San José.

Special thanks to the many contributors who helped fund this project
for the benefit of local community service organizations.

Although the publishers have exercised due diligence in their research efforts, should there be a fire fighter who has been overlooked by this listing,
or unintentionally listed incorrectly, please be assured that the selfless service of ALL the San José Fire Fighters is recognized and appreciated by this special memorial edition.
Because this is a reprinting, the history contained in this book ends in 1972 when the book was originally published.

A San José Fire Fighter's View
Who Worked at Ground Zero

By Battalion Chief Gerald Kohlmann

September 11, 2001...

As on-duty members started their morning routine and the on-coming shift was in the midst of their commute, they were all struck with the same unbelievable news... at 6:03 a.m. local time, an airliner had hit one of the World Trade Center Towers. Soon after, the second plane struck the second tower and it became clear that beyond the tragedy of the first crash; this was more than an accident, this was an attack. The San José Fire Department then began the process of contingency planning and emergency staffing augmentations.

This required the personnel of the off-going and on-coming personnel and placed city management in the Emergency Operations Center.

By noon, the activation orders came through requesting that the San José Fire Department provide four members to respond to Menlo Park and staff positions on California Task Force 3, one of 28 Federal Emergency Management Agency Urban Search & Rescue Task Forces. There were many San José Fire Fighters ready to respond, but the participation was limited to four personnel trained and approved to travel with CA-TF3. Still,

The 62 members of the California Task Force 3 at McGuire Air Base in New Jersey prior to the return flight to Moffett Federal Airfield.

other San José Fire Fighters responded to Menlo Park and helped prepare the Task Force for travel and one or two self-dispatched to New York to help in any way possible. The four members honored with the opportunity to be a part of the 62 member Task Force roster were; Captain Harry Jackson (Hazardous Materials), Fire Engineer David Lerma (Rescue), Captain Rod Villa (Rescue) and Battalion Chief Gerald Kohlmann (Plans).

For the next nine days, CA-TF3 waited for their turn to rotate into New York. That time was effectively used to tailor the content of the equipment cache and to obtain briefings about the situation and strategies for working at "Ground Zero." In the city of San José, further planning and procedure development occurred to address new threats (such as the anthrax letter threat) and to adapt to changing conditions. On September 19th at 1:30 a.m., CA-TF3 responded via military aircraft to McGuire Air Base in New Jersey and started on a 12 day mission to contribute to the country's recovery. During those 12 days, CA-TF3 developed and implemented two collapsed structure rescue teams to work with the FDNY in the event of any other attacks or building collapses. After completing this mission, CA-TF3 was assigned to work at the World Trade Center for three 24-hour shifts with half of the 62 member team staffing the day shift, and half staffing the night shift.

The magnitude of the damage was hard to imagine, and impossible to describe… nothing could have prepared anyone for the scale of the debris pile, the sight of destroyed fire and police apparatus and equipment, and the knowledge that at least 400 emergency responders lay in the rubble, beside those they went to rescue. Everyone worked hard, and many grew close to our comrades from the Fire Department of New York during their time working side by side and often stopping to talk about their friends they would probably never see again.

The people of the San José Fire Department contributed in many ways and performed magnificently during, and after, the time of immediate need. Whether they were assigned to the FEMA Task Force or taking independent action (often at great expense emotionally and financially), many found a way to contribute to the recovery of America. The feelings still flow through the fire stations of San José and those that gave their lives for the lives of others are fondly, and respectfully remembered. The lives that were lost caused many to recognize the lives of other fire fighters and emergency responders that are injured or die each year in the service of others. The cost will never be forgotten, and as time goes on, new lessons will be learned.

San José Fire Department members in the terminal at McGuire Air Base in New Jersey (left to right): Fire Engineer David Lerma (Rescue), Captain Rod Villa (Rescue), Captain Harry Jackson (Hazardous Materials) and Battalion Chief Gerald Kohlmann (Plans)

The San José Muster Team

By Battalion Chief Josh Weggeland, President

The Muster Team was formed in 1974 as a non-profit organization with the purpose of acquiring, restoring, displaying, operating and preserving historically significant fire apparatus and equipment, and participating in regional education and training programs. The team supports public fire safety and education programs and participates in community events including parades, fire prevention week, fire fighter recruiting, graduation and promotion ceremonies, funerals, toy delivery programs and of course, musters.

"Musters" are competitive events held throughout California in the summer months. The events are: hose cart, bucket brigade, motorized apparatus, steamers, and hand pumpers. Each of these timed events requires team members to move a prescribed volume of water from one location to another or to use apparatus and equipment to knock down a target with a charged hose line. Musters take place on weekends and include a wide variety of activities for the entire family. There is always a "kid's mini-muster", dinner dance, sightseeing trips, etc. Camping is available at each location or hotels may be utilized.

The team is managed by a group of active and retired fire fighters who fill officer positions and establish goals and objectives for the team. Officers are elected on an annual basis at a general membership meeting. Membership is open to active and retired San José Fire Fighters, non-sworn department employees and members of allied organizations.

The Muster Team maintains membership in several related organizations including:

- California Firemen's Muster Association (CFMA)

- California Chapter, Society for the Preservation and Appreciation of Antique Motor Fire Apparatus in America (SPAAMFAA)

- Antique Automobile Club of America (AACA)

Muster Team volunteers restoring a 1905 Model F Cadillac Chiefs Buggy

- Knox Motor Club of America

- Fire Museum Network (FMN)

The Muster Team assists the San José Fire Fighter's Burn Foundation, which provides support to the Santa Clara Valley Medical Burn Unit; a summer camp for youthful victims as well as providing toys and entertainment at Christmas.

Funding for Muster Team activities is primarily through items sold by the team throughout the year. These items include books, tee-shirts, belt buckles, jewelry items and fire apparatus trading cards. In addition, individuals may choose to support the Muster Team through our payroll deduction or directed gift programs.

The Muster Team building is presently located at 1661 Senter Road #D1, and open for visitors the first Tuesday of every month from 9 a.m. to 1 p.m. Stop by and see the collection! Our phone number is 408-998-6184.

Foreground 1929 REO, Background 1926 Seagrave

There are currently thirty-seven pieces of fire apparatus in the Muster Team collection. Included are a number of unique and extremely rare units such as the 1810 James Smith Hand Pumper, a 1905 Model F Cadillac Chief's Buggy, the 1914 Knox-Martin Tractor towing an 1899 American Steamer, a 1914 American LaFrance Type 31 Aerial Ladder Truck, a 1924 National Calliope, a 1937 American LaFrance Metropolitan Engine, a 1930's Merryweather hand drawn steam engine, and a Crosley powered miniature fire engine hand built in 1959 by department members.

Merryweather Steam Engine

Left 1890 Amoskeag Steamer   Center 1885 American Steamer   Right 1899 American Steamer & 1914 Knox Martin

Bruce Kegg with the Franklin Engine #3 which he restored to original condition. The 1890 Amoskeag steam fire engine can be viewed at the San José Fire Department Museum established by the San José Muster Team.

On June 5, 2002 a dedication ceremony was held to celebrate the return to San José of the restored Franklin Engine #3. An 1890 Amoskeag steam fire engine, this is one of San José's original steam pumpers. It was one of three steam engines that saved San José from burning to the ground during the San Francisco earthquake of 1906. The pumper was found in boxes in Lodi, California and was immaculately restored by Bruce Kegg who was honored at the dedication. Others recognized for their contributions were retired Battalion Chief Lawrence Campbell, retired Captain Sam Seibert, retired Captain Dennis Madigan and the John and Christine Davis family. In attendance at the dedication ceremony were San José Mayor Ron Gonzales and city councilmembers.

San José Fire Department

(As of June 2002)

FIRE CHIEF
Manuel P. Alarcon

ASSISTANT FIRE CHIEF
Dale E. Foster

DEPUTY FIRE CHIEFS
Lacy Lee Atkinson
Theodore A. Guerrero
John A. McMillan
Robert H. Piper
Dana C. Reed

DIVISION CHIEF
Nicolas Thomas

BATTALION CHIEFS
Thomas H. Afflixio
Michael A. Ayala
Jerry T. Buzzetta
James H. Carter
Kevin G. Conant
Rodney M. Davis
Henry G. De Groot
John P. Flatley
Gary S. Galasso
Donald C. Jonasson
Robert B. King
Gerald R. Kohlmann
José M. Luna, Jr.
Richard L. Mattish
Teresa L. Reed
Susan Salinger
David E. Schoonover
Gregory D. Spence
James C. Stunkel
George M. Vega
Darryl P. Von Raesfeld
Gary L. Weekley
Joseph P. Weggeland

FIRE CAPTAINS
Scott P. Ackemann
Daniel J. Addiego
David A. Allshouse
Karen M. Allyn

Daniel J. Alvarado
Steven F. Alvarado
Alan M. Anderson
Samuel Avila, Jr.
Kevan L. Banton
Jeffrey A. Barone
Oscar D. Bazurto
Donald K. Bellone
Alan J. Belluomini
R. Steven Bennett
Michael W. Blatz
James R. Blean
William C. Blean
Evan S. Bloom
Gary Bogue
Tim A. Borden
Robert W. Brown
Mario P. Busalacchi
Gary H. Bystrom
Rudolph J. Cabigas
Allison Cabral
Joseph L. Carrillo
John C. Castro, Jr.
Wesley J. Chacon
Galvin Charekian
David L. Churchill
Marvin M. Coffey
Ronald E. Cook
Joseph Crivello
Christopher J. Crowley
Philip G. Croyle
Dante Cruz
Michael L. Cunningham
Robert J. Dawson
Francois P. De Groen
Johnny D. Dellinger
Philip J. Demers
Juan F. Diaz
Brent T. Dickinson
John S. Diquisto
Paul A. Eden
John W. Emerson
Mark R. English
Rick M. Ezquerro
Cheryl A. Faltersack
Stephen L. Felder

Mark E. Filson
Barry E. Franchi
Joseph N. Fowles
Jan M. Gall
Ramon Gamino
Thomas A. Gianatasio
Steve L. Greenfield
José L. Guerrero
Anthony Guinnane
David M. Gutierrez
Gilbert J. Gutierrez
Mary F. Gutierrez
Robert V. Gutierrez
Greg E. Hemingway
Eric J. Hernandez
Martin E. Hoenisch
Angela Holston
Calvin Hom
Clifford G. Hubbard
David W. Huseman
Harry L. Jackson
Curtis Jacobson
David J. Jimenez
Richard K. Jones
Stanley Jones
Robert M. Juelson
Michael K. Kahn
Wade N. Katsuyoshi
Keith K. Keesling
Terry L. Kerns
Paul J. King
Richard C. Kirkham
Stephen A. Kleszyk
Scott R. Kouns
John R. Laurent
Ivan D. Lee
George J. Lucchesi
David Maas
Tony F. Magallon
Phillip J. Manley
Bryan P. Marks
Oscar J. Martinez, Jr.
Kenneth S. McCarthy
James B. McClure
Stewart A. McGehee
Glen P. McGuire

Benigno Mercado
Carlos A. Miller
Arthur C. Mitchell
Gary W. Moe
Mark B. Mooney
David E. Moore
David R. Moore
Richard J. Moore
Steve H. Moreno
Michele E. Morey
James V. Morphis
Robert W. Mueller
Colleen A. Mulholand
Edward D. Muñoz
Robert J. Naughten
William A. Newton
Robert A. Nice
Albert N. Olmos
Leslie P. Omans
Ralph R. Ortega
Steven R. O'Steen
Steve E. Padilla
Richard F. Palmer
Gaudenz C. Panholzer
Steven B. Perez
Russell D. Pfirrman
Joel B. Phelan
Anthony E. Pianto
Ronald E. Pomerantz
James B. Randall
Charles Rangel
Joseph W. Reich
Thomas A. Reischl
Matthew P. Rivera
Joseph D. Roberts
James D. Roszell
David S. Salazar
Jean-Pierre Santos
Robert Sapien
Edward J. Scanlon
Steven L. Schmidt
Paul A. Schuller
Craig G. Schwinge
Vincent A. Sciortino
Richard R. Seal
Randy R. Sekany

Michael H. Shaw
Lawrence J. Silva
John A. Skeen, Jr.
Mark J. Skeen
Matthew R. Smith
Steven L. Smith
Dana B. Snapp
Paul M. Sprague
Aloysius G. Souza
Todd B. Spellman
Dan R. Stapp
Floyd D. Stewart
Ray H. Storms
Patricia A. Tapia
William Greg Thornton
Richard J. Toledo, Jr.
Ruben L. Torres
Javier G. Valle
Wayne D. Van Gundy
Rodney D. Villa
James F. Voreyer
Debra L. Ward
Clarence R. Wells
John A. Wells
Thomas M. Westrup
Mike J. Willcox
Mitchell J. Wisinski
Michael J. Woodworth
James B. Wyatt, Jr.

ARSON INVESTIGATORS
James E. Acker
Enrique A. Carruth
Karen A. Gall
Jeffrey B. Weber

FIRE PREVENTION
INSPECTORS
Kenneth M. Alviso
Peter C. Araujo
Derrick Chapman
Thomas J. Conry
Charlotte L. Endicott
Flanoy D. Garrett
Felipe Gonzalez
Joe Grimaldo
Ronald S. Hackett
Russell G. Hayden
El-Hajj Malik, Sr.
Jack Carl Roberts
Carol A. Sippel
Oscar Tovar

FIRE ENGINEERS
Joseph Abasolo
Gregory W. Alameda

Bryan M. Aquino
Rudolph R. Arroyo
Javier A. Ascencio
Vernon Avery
José G. Avila
Richard H. Bailey, Jr.
Jesse D. Baliscao
Wilfredo Banuelos
Michael A. Bauer
Juan Bautista
Dennis Bell
Ruben Benavides
Linn W. Bergland
Steven P. Biakanja
Douglas B. Biddle
Glenn P. Bishop
Brett Blean
Shannon M. Blean
William Bodero
John L. Borsi
Patrick D. Bowers
Robert G. Britton
Scott L. Burke
Eric A. Bygdnes
Rafael A. Campos, Jr.
Larry E. Cantrell
Peter Caponio
Patrick H. Carder
Charles C. Carter
Dennis L. Caywood
José Chavez
Rodney W. Clark
Soren M. Coats
Kevin M. Collins
Terry J. Coman
Richard A. Constantine
William J. Cooley
Jess A. Coria
Jesus Corona
James E. Cowan
George F. Cravalho
Gordon E. Crowell
Mario Cuestas
Eduardo A. Cuevas
Russell V. Davis
Raymond E. Dellinger
Gerald E. Denis
Mark S. Dessert
Scott C. Diehl
Ralph J. Dillon
Hien Q. Doan
John S. Donald
David L. Dorman
Cleotis Doss, Jr.
Gerald L. Durk

Danny N. Eaton
Barry A. Ehlers
Lorin Engler
Trent N. Engler
Hector R. Estrada
Scott M. Fey
Michael D. Fields
Gary A. Flagg
Joseph M. Franco
James E. Froisland
Daniel J. Gallardo
Daniel C. Gamban
Roberto M. Garcia
Samuel G. Garcia
Kevin P. George
Alan G. Gerbino
Eric Giordano
Rudy Gonzalez
Steve F. Goytia
Edward J. Guillory
Gregory S. Hamane
Albert Hernandez, Jr.
James Hirano
Bryan W. Hodges
John M. Hodges
Kevin Holston
Roland L. Hooks
Richard D. Hopp
Antoinette Z. Igno
Cindy Jamison
Albert Jessel
Clint A. Johnson
Ernest R. Jones
Paul S. Kennedy
George D. King
Keith A. Kirmse
Julie I. LaBlanc
Gerry B. Laird
Ronald A. Landeros
Richard S. Laye
Edward S. Leglu
David C. Lerma
Robert R. Lilly
Grant D. Lind, Jr.
Daniel E. Lockwood
Victor Loesche
Martin Lomeli
Carlos Lopez
Eric Lopez
Peter D. Lovier
Ramon O. Luna
Gary R. Lynn
Brett Maas
Clayton D. Markel
Robert J. Martone

Ervin Mathews
George A. Matteucci
Teresa D. Mauldin
Thomas A. McClusky
Dennis M. McGibben
Michael K. McGue
Matthew E. McIntyre
Daniel T. McNeil
Melvin P. Meeks
Anthony W. Melendrez, Jr.
Gilbert T. Mendez
Henry Mendoza
Jarod M. Middleton
Stephen J. Milina
Timothy I. Miller
Mike Montuy
David Moseley
Patrick D. Mulcahy
Fernando Muñoz
Jeffrey R. Mushock
Benjamin I. Naranjo
Alexander Navy
Steven P. Nelson
Raymond J. Nibbi
Charles S. O'Connor
Jeffery S. Olivetti
David Olmos
Joseph E. Oppelt, Jr.
Anthony Orozco
Ralph Padilla
Matthew D. Paiss
George E. Palma
Michael P. Patterson
Tim H. Pedemonte
Manuel M. Pereira
Jeffrey B. Perez
Randy B. Perez
Eric C. Peters
Edward L. Powell
Michael J. Ramos
Anthony Rangel
Dawud A. Rauf
Thomas M. Read
Philip Reggiardo
Daniel R. Reinmuth
Christopher R. Remer
Charles H. Rice
Jeffrey P. Riley
Hyung Rae Ro
Mark D. Roberts
Clemente Rocha
John R. Rohrabaugh
Peter L. Roman
Arthur M. Rosingana
Scott Rosingana

Richard C. Ruggles
Shawn San Miguel
Jesus Sanchez
Michael C. Sanchez
Robert J. Santos
Edward B. Saunders
Douglas R. Schmidt
Jim Shea
Craig D. Shelton
Adelino R. Silva
Jeffrey A. Silva
Gilbert R. Siqueiros
James C. Smith
Gordon R. Snyder
Lloyd B. Soliven
Michael Sperrer
David K. Spurr
Joe R. Staley III
Barry Stallard
George M. Stasi
Dwight S. Stevens
Arlen J. Summers
Shawn Tacklind
Michael A. Tallerico
Cruz Tapia, Jr.
Victor M. Tapia
Sandra Teeples
Kimberly A. Throndson
James Q. Tom
Peter R. Torres
Gregory Toscano
Scott Trotter
Eric Ulrich
Jeffrey A. Una'Dia
Victor Velasquez
Joseph J. Vitales
Martin S. Walker
Richard M. Wardall
Thomas L. Warren
Jeffrey L. Welch
Tim K. West
Dean W. Whipple
Randall B. Wiens
Reginald O. Williams
Scott E. Wilson
John S. Wise
Keith Woeste
David J. Wohnoutka
April L. Zachary
Eleazar Zamora
Gary R. Zobrosky

FIRE FIGHTERS
Robert D. Adams
Wallace E. Adams

Luis R. Alanis
Jason Alaniz
Donald Alexander
Alfonso Alvarez
Doug Amaro
Stacey Andrews
James E. Aparicio
Todd L. Ashbaugh
Karren M. Augustine
Ernest Austin
Robert Bacon, Jr.
Michael F. Baldwin
Mark Barbour
David R. Barnett
Anthony Beck
Scott Bell
Arthur Belton
Todd Belton
David Betancourt
Steven J. Bevington
Craig Black
David Blackwell
Holger Blech
Jason Blinn
Stephen Bogue
Harold Boscovich
Gillian Boxx
Derrick Bradley
Paulo M. Brito
Steven E. Brown
Henry L. Brunson
Richard Caginia
Herb Campbell
Scott Campbell
Robert W. Carabal
Jeffrey Cardoza
Adolph Carranza
Fred Carrasco
Tony Carrillo
Raul J. Castro
Carlos Chaboya
Jesse Chacon
Luis F. Chacon
Gonzalo Chayrez
Lawrence R. Chua
Jayson A. Clements
John B. Cloutier
Marco Conde
Robert Cone
Neil Connelly
Thomas S. Connelly
Brandon Core
Nick U. Corona
Pedro Corona
Scott M. Coscarelli

David A. Cox
Richard A. Crawford
Marcos Cruz
Guillermo Culajay
Robert Culbertson
Stephen A. Cunningham
Ronald Curry
Kristine D'Amico
Peter Davis
Daniel De Long
Bryan D. De Mare
Michael R. Del Bando
Frank G. Diaz
Tom G. Diaz
Angel Dizon, Jr.
Bien Doan
Maxillian Duenas
Vincent Dupree
Edward S. Dziuba
David E. Embree
Brian D. Endicott
Carl J. England
David Ennes
Kevin L. Erbe
Hector M. Escobar
Gregory Estrada
Roberta J. Farrow
Joe Favorito
Forest D. Fernandez
Saul Flores
Kenneth Folsom
Louis Fong
Steven A. Forman
Rocco T. Francisco
Peter C. Franco
Aaron Freyler
Atanacio Garcia
Bret Gervasoni
Cheryl E. Goldsmith
Carlos Gomez
Michael X. Gomez
Alan F. Gonzales
Amalio Gonzalez
Paul A. Gonzalez
William H. Griffith
George Guerrero
Walter R. Guerrero
Salvador Gutierrez
Jesse Guzman
Shad Hall
Timothy R. Hall
Stacey A. Hansen
Sidney R. Harger
Chris T. Harmount
Leslie S. Harms

Mark D. Hathaway
Marc Haynes
Aaron M. Herman
Kenneth R. Hernandez
Virgilio Hernandez
Robert Herrera
Scott Herrero
Thanh Ho
John S. Hopper
Sean Hugger
Felipe Ibarra
Alfred Ignacio
Michael Igno
Fernando Jimenez
Santos A. Jimenez
Craig L. Johnson
Brendan B. Kasten
Matthew Kelly
Jamie G. Kerin
Bart E. Kernan, Jr.
Kelly H. Kersten
Mitchell C. Kim
Anthony R. King
Jason A. Krassow
Eric Kwan
Edward Lake
David Lang
Eric Larson
Alex A. Lee
Robert M. Leonard
Timothy P. Leong
Timothy Lewis
Michael Lillie
Daniel Lizardo
Vivian Lo
Nestor H. Lopez
José A. Loquiao
William Sean Lovens
Jeffery S. Lowrimore
Brett MacDonell
David N. Malandrino
Jeremy Mann
Diane L. Manners
Stephen Marsh
Paul T. Marshall
Cesar A. Martinez
John P. Martinez
José M. Martinez
Tyler R. Matcham
Mitchell Matlow
Raul C. Mayorga
Clifford E. McClanahan
Brad J. McGibben
Doug McLeod
Robert F. McQuaide

Louis P. Medrano
James Mendoza
Ruben A. Millan
Charles Tim Miller
Mario Minoia
Julian Molloy
Martin Mora
Gilbert M. Morales
Howard R. Morton
Christopher Murphy
Michael Murray
William C. Murray
Michael Nelson
Scott Nelson
Peter Nguyen
Steven Nguyen
Henry S. Noon III
Lawrence B. Noon
Patrick K. Noon
Laura K. Nores
Alonso G. Ochoa
Anthony J. Ojeda
Brian O'Regan
Joshua Padron
Mario Pagcaliuagan
Brian Palodichuk
David Parker
Derek Parmer

Sandra I. Pearson
Alcibiades Peña, Jr.
Tina D. Perez
Christopher Peuler
Chris Pickup
Victor Polverino
Alex R. Pons
Christopher Pratt
Brent A. Primrose
Brandon Ragan
Robert Ragsac
Louis Ramirez
Richard J. Regan
Thomas Reid
Adrian R. Reyes
Jeffery S. Rishel
Nelson Rodriguez
Richard B. Rosenquist
Francis Ryan
Christopher Salcido
Larry J. Samarron
Hector R. Sandoval
Jesse Savage, Jr.
James W. Schulte
David Scocca
Kirk A. Seal
Jeff A. Seaton
Evan Seligman

Eduardo J. Silva
Brian S. Smith
Obery Smith
Roger B. Smith
Greig Sniffen
Jarrod T. Sniffen
Cuong Son
Dale Souza
Paul W. Stamm
Dale Stephens
Jason A. Suarez
Joan M. Sutton
Michael T. Tapia
Cesar Tarango
Tremaine A. Thierry
Fraser C. Thom
Mark A. Thoman
David S. Thomas
Glen S. Thompson
Elizabeth A. Toffey
Benjamin Tolentino
Jeffery S. Tomlinson
Donald Torres
Scott Trabert
Robert Tran
Christian Truong
Gregory J. Tuyor
John A. Ureta

Ernest Valenti
Richard J. Valenzuela
Michael Van Dalen
Raymond Van de Star
Michael Van Elgort
Joseph J. Vierra
Asha Wagner
Scott Walker
Darren Wallace
Jon Walsh
William B. Wargo
Eddie L. Warner
Joshua Warren
Jonathan Watkins
Brian R. Weeden
Darryl A. Weeden
Erik C. Westcott
Dennis P. Wheeler
Andrew L. Whyte
James Williams, Jr.
Ronald E. Wohnoutka
Bryan J. Wong
Stan Wong
David Yee
Joe Ysselstein
Steven C. Zogg

Retired Fire Fighters

(Up to June 2002)

NAME	RETIRED	NAME	RETIRED	NAME	RETIRED
William H. Adams	12-26-1998	Walter J. Bugna	3-1-2001	Marco Cuffaro	6-10-1975
William U. Adams	7-5-1996	Rocky L. Burcham	4-6-2000	Gayle L. Cummins	12-4-1985
Donald V. Ahern	2-5-1998	Bobby G. Burdine	10-3-1996	Michael R. Curcio	8-1-1996
James D. Allen	7-9-1991	John T. Burleson	3-2-2002	Robert W. Currall	12-3-1993
Joe L. Altamirano	4-4-1998	Michael L. Burtch	4-9-1995	Edward J. Cutter	9-3-1998
John M. Alviso	4-6-1995	Paul J. Byfield	6-3-1987	Charles Cypert	3-1-1993
Oliver J. Anastacio	8-8-1982	Dudley C. Bynoe	7-12-1999	Dale D. Davis	9-1-1970
Algie Anderson	11-30-1983	James Caines	4-3-1991	Tom Davis	2-5-1998
Dennis G. Anderson	12-16-1985	Robert A. Caltabiano	6-6-1982	Howard De Camp	7-6-1977
Ernest Anderson	1-8-1992	Lawrence A. Campbell	2-1-1963	Donald J. De Dobbeleer	7-7-1994
Steven S. Anderson	9-5-1996	Joseph Cancilla	7-12-1981	Joseph S. De Lise	3-30-1980
Merril K. Angell	11-6-1984	Allan Canepa	9-2-1987	Bruce B. De Mers	8-3-1995
John D. Arnaz	12-7-1995	Walter M. Capp	3-5-1986	Robert D. Delgado	3-3-1993
Kay B. Ashby	6-7-1989	Forest Carbaugh	4-4-1998	Ronald A. Delgado	1-9-1993
Phillip Ayers	3-22-1997	John R. Carlyon	3-9-1996	Eugene D. Della Maggiore	8-3-2000
David A. Baca	9-5-1996	John N. Carr	1-7-1993	Lee E. Devens	4-17-1977
Robert L. Bacon	8-1-1996	Donald E. Carraher	9-2-1999	Francis M. Devitt	2-1-1975
Edward C. Barber	2-28-1998	Melvin Carriere	6-1-1995	Arlen C. Di Bartolo	9-4-1997
Milo K. Bardwell	8-1-2000	Richard Carroll	6-4-1985	John A. Diquisto	10-29-1988
Herbert R. Bartolini	4-1-1968	Douglas W. Carter	2-19-2000	Ralph H. Donnelly	1-15-1994
William S. Bartosiewicz	5-4-2000	Miguel R. Castro	8-1-1990	James W. Donohue	3-4-1973
William R. Bauer	9-3-1998	Sebastian J. Catania	10-1-1986	Robert L. Dorman	3-6-1999
Joseph Baxter	2-7-1991	Royce R. Chambers	3-6-1984	Donald R. Dorr	5-13-1980
Donald A. Bell	1-6-1988	Wayne A. Chapp	3-4-2000	Patrick B. Doyle	10-6-1981
Lloyd L. Benson	6-5-1986	John T. Charcho	1-5-2002	Roger Drake	6-5-1997
Thomas A. Bergstrom	7-15-1995	Steve M. Chaviel	1-2-1991	Woodward H. Drake	7-7-2001
C. D. Bernardo	8-1-1972	James A. Choyce	3-1-1974	Arthur R. Dundon	11-3-1994
Douglas L. Bernhard	7-11-1999	James K. Christensen	8-5-2000	Donald A. Dye	7-10-1983
William M. Berry	9-4-1991	Donald B. Christianson	7-18-1995	James E. Earnest	9-3-1992
James D. Bese	8-1-1996	James P. Ciraulo	5-26-2001	John W. Earnest	5-21-1996
Richard A. Bibby	12-1-1971	Salvador J. Ciraulo	3-30-1980	Robert W. Edwards	4-1-1987
William E. Black	12-25-1996	Joseph H. Clark	8-3-1988	James C. Elder	7-7-1992
Donald G. Blake	10-9-1993	Vincent H. Clet	11-6-1984	Jerry T. Ellis	4-6-1995
Theodore M. Bohn, Jr.	1-6-1981	Ronald E. Cleveland	9-5-1996	Arthur S. Emery	2-1-1993
Hilbert Bolton	7-12-1977	Ethan M. Coburn	5-6-1987	Mike M. Espinoza	8-4-1994
Benjamin F. Boozel	5-7-1985	Jimmie C. Coburn	6-15-1974	Carl L. Evans	8-1-1971
Henry H. Borch	1-13-1981	Robert J. Cocilova	11-5-1998	John S. Evans	5-4-1995
Daniel T. Bourbon	7-3-1993	Vernon S. Cole	6-13-1976	Merlin C. Evans	11-1-1985
Lanny G. Bowden	1-8-1992	Lee R. Collins	8-2-2001	Harold H. Evans I	8-14-1979
Jerry Boyer	1-7-1993	Terry J. Coman	6-9-2002	Harold H. Evans II	7-7-1994
George H. Bradford	8-7-1982	Dan R. Conrow	1-5-1974	Lawrence Faler	6-17-1989
George R. Bradford	1-10-1998	Francis E. Conyers	9-13-1980	Lawrence R. Favorite	6-12-1974
Duane R. Braun	7-7-1992	Sam D. Coomer	2-9-1971	George W. Federoff	9-2-1993
Richard L. Brazell	11-7-1990	Michael Cormany	8-20-1990	John Felde	1-7-1993
La Vern F. Brazil	8-2-1983	Charles Cosce	3-2-1995	Gary L. Flair	10-12-1971
William A. Brittell	3-17-2001	Edward M. Cottle	3-30-1980	James C. Foley	9-12-1992
Robert H. Britton	7-7-1992	Randall L. Courts	6-3-1999	Barry A. Ford	4-7-1994
Philip Broussard	11-1-2001	James L. Crawford	1-2-1974	Charles L. Ford	8-6-1986
Gerald Bryant	8-1-1990	Robert J. Crowder	1-8-1986	Robert E. Francis	6-3-1999

NAME	RETIRED	NAME	RETIRED	NAME	RETIRED
Rocco E. Francisco	8-1-1996	Kenneth E. Heredia	2-4-1999	Theodore A. Lopez	8-7-1991
Samuel M. Francisco	2-4-1999	Milton R. Herold	1-4-1989	William C. Lowe	7-15-1971
Bill D. Franks	8-9-1997	Thomas J. Higgins	3-1-1972	George Lucchesi	3-30-1980
Charles W. Frates	11-2-1982	Michael D. Hoffman	1-8-1992	Arthur A. Mac Lean	11-27-1957
James E. Friday	9-3-1985	H. S. Holmberg	5-1-1999	Kevin G. MacPhee	7-7-1992
Harold S. Funk	1-14-1979	Danny R. Holmes	5-14-1978	Dennis M. Madigan	9-19-1998
George J. Gaillard	1-25-1997	Mark A. Holmes	9-2-1987	Keith R. Malech	10-7-1987
Timothy J. Gallagher	8-5-1999	Thomas D. Hooks	5-1-1991	Merrill J. Malvini	2-5-1986
Arthur Garcia	6-30-1997	Earl E. Houlihan	11-11-1971	William G. Mancus	9-2-1999
Richard R. Garcia	8-8-1998	Gerald A. Hubbard	2-5-1986	Darryl D. Manson	3-7-1996
Roy T. Garcia	9-4-1997	Jeffrey B. Hunter	8-3-1995	Manuel G. Maral	3-1-1972
Samuel M. Garcia	8-7-1991	Jack M. Hutchison	3-7-1996	Leonard G. Marks	10-1-1973
George Gardiner	8-2-1988	Nicholas Hyland	3-1-1993	Leonard H. Marsh	3-18-1979
William Garringer	3-31-2001	Keith L. Ison	3-2-2000	Gregory A. Martell	1-9-1999
William L. Garroutte	4-4-1996	Edward J. Iverson	10-7-1999	Kenneth J. Martin	8-2-1989
Harry K. Gattey	2-4-1999	George A. Jacobson	6-1-1975	Andrew Martinez	2-4-1995
John M. Geimer	1-5-1995	Vincent A. Jangrus	1-13-1997	Jerry L. Mathis	4-6-1988
Stanley R. Gentile	12-5-1990	Richard M. Jennings	7-12-2001	Willard L. Mathis	7-1-1996
Timothy A. Gentile	2-5-1998	Donald A. Johnson	8-6-1998	Barry L. Matteson	1-5-1995
Edward D. George	5-4-2000	Gerald Johnson	7-2-1997	Nick S. Mayer	9-9-1984
Fred W. Gerbino	4-1-1987	Michael A. Johnson	4-8-1995	William K. Mayes	4-8-2000
John K. Gerhard	3-4-1978	Thorfinnur Johnson	10-29-1989	Tracy J. McDermott	7-3-1993
Eugene J. Germano	1-12-1980	Michael T. Jonasson	4-1-2002	Arthur T. McDonald	4-4-1996
James A. Giafaglione	2-9-2000	Robert A. Jones	7-12-1977	Gerald J. McDonald	3-7-1990
Frederick O. Gibbs	2-1-2001	Franklin D. Jost	4-29-1979	Robert E. McMurtry	11-4-1998
George Gilbert	3-15-1973	John J. Jurado	2-19-1980	William J. McQuaide	1-4-2001
Paul F. Giles	5-6-1995	Jack W. Kalp	9-5-1996	Irvin G. McVea	7-7-1981
Thomas W. Giles	9-7-2000	Donald W. Kelley	3-2-1995	Robert W. Meagher	1-1-1981
Michael Gilligan	1-7-1993	James D. Kelly	6-4-1986	Timothy P. Mealiffe	7-10-1999
Freeman A. Gingerich	4-6-1988	Orville J. Keyser	9-19-1976	Ernest Medeiros	11-5-1992
Charles J. Gluck	3-17-2001	Carl E. Kiepen	1-7-1999	Eduardo E. Medina	3-18-2000
Roland C. Goff	3-7-1996	Richard R. Kincaid	3-27-1975	Melvin H. Meeks	7-7-2001
Carmelo Gonzales	8-1-1990	James R. King	4-1-1979	Les L. Mehrkens	9-7-1988
Richard W. Gonzales	2-2-1995	Ronald E. King	8-5-1999	Terry V. Meinzer	9-4-1997
Luke H. Goodrich	2-26-1994	Keith M. Kjeldsen	7-2-2001	Robert D. Meyer	9-7-1995
Gerald Gradia	3-1-2001	Dean J. Knapp	10-10-1994	William J. Meyers	1-7-1993
Loren B. Gray	4-1-1973	John F. Knapp	7-15-1971	Richard M. Milat	9-3-1992
Thomas Gray	3-2-1991	Emmett Knutzen	11-2-1988	David P. Miller	7-2-1972
Denny R. Greer	10-14-1979	Donald R. Kouns	1-13-1997	Robert B. Miller	11-6-1991
Don R. Greer	9-3-1985	James A. La Mar	8-2-1989	Robert I. Minford	2-3-1988
Robert C. Gremminger	11-14-1996	Thomas J. Laman	4-4-1996	Michael J. Moffett	3-2-2000
Gregary P. Grenfell	5-30-1998	Melvin L. Lamb	12-13-1997	Alfred Montez	7-21-1991
Bill Grewohl	3-11-2001	William J. Lamb	9-15-1972	Darroll L. Morehouse	1-15-1994
Domenick Grossi	8-21-1999	Gaylord R. Lane	8-28-1983	David D. Moseley	8-3-1995
Edward E. Gurley	5-6-1987	Ronald K. Lane	9-7-1995	Paul J. Mulholand	2-2-1995
Oscar L. Guzman	8-2-2001	Marcel Lassalle	1-7-1990	Dennis D. Murray	3-2-1995
William P. Hackett	11-6-1991	Ronald B. Le Beau	12-16-1996	William C. Murray	3-10-1985
Donald R. Hague	1-8-1992	William L. Leavy	4-5-1997	William J. Murtha	4-1-1976
Royal P. Hamilton	7-3-1993	Donald W. Lee	10-2-1996	Richard K. Nakamura	2-22-1997
Thomas C. Hamilton	1-13-1997	Loren M. Lemmons	6-1-1988	Richard J. Neibaur	7-8-1978
Jerry L. Harrell	7-9-1998	Sean R. Leslie	3-1-1972	Murray E. Nelson	9-2-1977
Robert J. Harris	7-7-1992	Stephen R. Lima	1-4-2001	Richard L. Nelson	3-7-1996
Edward E. Hart	3-13-1993	Keith J. Livermore	6-1-1996	Robert P. Nelson	3-21-1976
George J. Hart	12-28-1996	John E. Llorca	11-17-1986	William R. Nelson	7-12-1997
Leonard J. Hartman	9-2-1987	Greg K. Lockwood	2-2-1995	Guy D. Newgren	6-28-1999
Allen W. Heath	7-25-1998	George Long	3-23-1985	Don M. Newman	9-14-1980
Clyde L. Henry	3-3-1994	Gary R. Longnecker	4-4-1996	Terry Newman	1-6-1988

NAME	RETIRED	NAME	RETIRED	NAME	RETIRED
Jack N. Newton	2-4-1987	Frank J. Ricceri	4-1-1976	Earl H. Sutherland	1-7-1993
Steve F. Newton	3-11-1999	Phillip K. Rice	2-5-1989	Randall R. Sutton	11-6-1991
Arnim A. Nicolson	1-1-1999	Harold Richardson	6-22-1991	Francis E. Swanson	4-6-1986
Richard J. Nolan	12-25-1996	Thomas F. Richardson	2-6-1999	Frank E. Tabbah	2-6-1997
Alec Noseworthy	2-15-1979	Mills Ridgway	7-9-1989	Douglas F. Talbot	10-3-2001
Joseph M. Nufer	1-2-1974	John R. Riolo	6-3-1987	Joseph L. Taormina	6-18-1998
Jack Olivetti	2-28-1993	Wayne H. Rist	3-29-1980	John L. Taylor	4-1-1993
Sylvia Olivetti	5-4-1995	Kenneth E. Ritchie	7-7-1994	Jesse L. Teese	1-27-1997
William F. O'Neill	6-3-1987	George E. Rizzo	1-4-2001	M. Earl Thompson	8-12-1985
Joseph J. Onzo	4-13-1980	Ronald J. Rizzo	3-4-1993	Irineo Tiopan	4-17-1999
Mike Oropeza	4-4-1996	Robert A. Robertson	6-13-1978	Richard Joseph Toledo	2-2-1995
Dale M. O'Rourke	1-27-1996	Orlando W. Rodrigues	2-3-1988	Corneal S. Tollenaar	4-1-1972
Clifford C. Ostermeier	5-20-1969	Luis R. Rodriguez	8-2-1989	Ronald J. Tomasello	8-12-2000
Ivan J. Oswald	7-7-1992	Allan B. Rogers	1-20-2001	Jerry A. Toney	11-18-1984
Leslie B. Owen	2-1-1983	Ellsworth J. Ryan	4-10-1982	Donald L. Torguson	1-2-1974
Blaine Owens	8-3-2000	Terrence P. Ryan	3-6-1997	Larry D. Torkelson	8-5-1999
Jan Ozga	5-9-1978	Robert J. Ryder	8-4-2001	Stewart Townend	4-3-1984
Emerson L. Pachaud	7-7-1992	Larry M. Salo	12-18-1994	James True	3-2-2000
Joseph Paradiso	7-5-1980	John Salois	3-7-1996	Frank J. Tuma	4-1-1973
Gary I. Parks	9-2-1999	Lawrence L. Samarron	3-5-1985	Gordon E. Turnage	3-8-1968
Joseph Penaflor	9-7-1988	Joseph X. Sanchez	4-1-1973	Ronald Turney	12-16-1996
Richard A. Pence	4-15-2000	Earl Santos	7-14-2001	Donald I. Tyson	12-4-1985
Thomas W. Pennington	12-25-1995	Richard P. Santos	1-4-2001	David Van Etten	3-18-1979
Donald Perkins	2-3-1994	John G. Schaar	1-5-1982	Gerald R. Van Horn	11-9-2000
Robert H. Perkins	8-3-1988	Edward T. Schneickert, Jr.	4-2-1985	John W. Van Ness	8-7-1997
Albert L. Persiani	8-5-1992	Gary L. Schneickert	7-3-1993	Robert Vermillion	8-5-1992
David V. Peters	1-5-1995	Warren F. Schuller	7-1-1995	Wilson R. Vickers	3-5-1986
Gunner Petersen	8-1-1972	Thomas G. Schultz	1-25-1997	Martin Vierra	10-5-1988
Leland A. Petersen	10-3-1996	John N. Scott	4-11-1982	Lawrence Volpe	8-5-1987
John M. Pieper	4-4-1996	Thomas P. Scully	4-6-2000	Matthew Vujevich	2-15-1993
Clifford R. Pierce	5-2-1998	Sam H. Seibert	3-28-1976	Gordon M. Wallace	6-8-1980
John R. Pierce	3-8-1987	William J. Selzer	1-4-1996	Robert H. Walls	5-1-1990
Robert W. Pipkins	8-4-1979	Ronald C. Sessions	9-11-1993	James M. Walters	1-9-1999
Donald P. Pirnik	12-28-1996	Jeff Shackelford	4-3-1984	J. C. Walton	4-1-1973
Maurice A. Pisciotta	5-2-1996	Ronald D. Shannon	7-7-1981	Donald A. Warning	3-14-1978
Stephen A. Pizzo	1-15-1998	George J. Silveria	11-7-1996	Loren R. Warning	8-1-1979
Robert R. Place	8-1-1971	Michael E. Simms	8-6-1998	Richard D. Wattenbarger	11-6-1991
Stephen E. Poli	5-6-1999	Ernest R. Sinclair	3-22-1988	Harvey Webb	11-6-1991
Charles W. Porter	3-4-1999	Glenn V. Sinnott	4-1-1975	Robert L. Webb	5-7-1985
Frank J. Portera	11-4-1993	John A. Skeen	3-7-1996	Winsford R. Wheatley	12-3-1986
Albert W. Potter	9-5-1996	Stephen F. Slinkey	6-23-1995	Michael A. Wheaton	5-17-2000
Douglas C. Potter	2-14-2000	Kerry N. Smith	2-1-1999	Henry A. Wheeler	1-29-1984
Ronald R. Powers	3-2-1988	Edward E. Solano	8-6-1998	George M. Wiens	4-13-1980
Tommy E. Pugh	6-4-1986	Theodore S. Sorensen	1-15-1998	Roger D. Wilkins	1-7-1999
James J. Rafferty	1-13-1997	Steven A. Souza	4-6-2000	Forrest Willcox	4-1-1993
Thomas G. Ramar	9-1-1994	Benjamin W. Spaulding	9-11-1983	David Williams	12-4-1991
Jesus Ramirez	8-1-1996	Michael T. Spinelli	4-7-1994	Jerry Williams	3-8-1997
Robert Ramirez	8-3-1995	Jack Spinler	3-5-1985	Ronald L. Willis	1-15-1974
Donald L. Ramos	3-5-1995	Glenn M. Spitzer	3-24-1996	Eric E. Wilson	12-29-1996
David P. Rauen	1-6-2001	William B. Staples	8-5-2000	Roger Wilson	4-6-1986
Charles L. Rebhan	3-3-1994	Edward T. Steele	4-7-1985	Thomas T. Winters	4-5-2001
Mauri K. Reeder	6-1-1995	Eugene F. Stenzel	8-1-1970	David J. Wood	5-16-1998
Patrick S. Reek	2-11-1995	Richard M. Struthers	1-1-1981	Phillip J. Wunderlich	3-4-1993
Robert R. Reek	9-6-1997	Lejames Suess	1-8-1992	Bob Yelton	5-4-1988
Robert E. Reid	1-7-1993	Ronald E. Sulpizio	7-7-2001	James W. Zubillaga	5-4-2000
James S. Rhodes	4-16-1995	Lawrence J. Summers	2-1-2001	Harry Zwart	4-2-2000

In Memoriam

(From 1972 to June 2002. See pages 222–224 for San José Fire Fighters who were lost before 1972)

Fire Engineer William Anger
Engine Co. No. 8
Killed February 21, 1981

The crew of Engine 8 had just administered first aid to a man trapped in an automobile at about 2:30 am. Engine 8 was returning to the firehouse at 17th and Santa Clara with Fire Engineer William Anger at the wheel. As they crossed the intersection at 13th Street and Julian Street (five blocks from the station) a car, estimated by police as traveling at about 70 miles per hour, ran a blinking red light and smashed into the side of Engine 8.

The tremendous impact caused the 15 ton engine to spin around and slam into a light pole. Fire Engineer William Anger was thrown from the engine and killed instantly. The other three members of the crew sustained moderate to serious injuries, two fire fighters were pinned against the light pole and the tailboard of Engine 8 and the captain suffered injuries inside the cab. Although injured, physically and emotionally distraught the fire fighters from Engine 8 valiantly extricated themselves and performed medical treatment on Fire Engineer William Anger and the occupants of the other vehicle.

Captain Robert Sparks
Engine Co. No. 28
Died March 17, 1981

Captain Robert Sparks was a 25-year veteran with the San José Fire Department. Halfway through the shift on Engine 28, Captain Sparks suffered a severe heart attack. Members of his company performed cardiopulmonary resuscitation and transported him to the hospital. Despite the crew's gallant efforts he passed away.

Since this book is about the San José Fire Department, local law enforcement officers and other public servants who were lost in the line of duty have not been listed. Their ultimate sacrifice for the community, does not go unrecognized. Our thoughts and our hearts go out to their families and friends.

The tragic events of September 11, 2001 will forever be remembered.
The fire fighters, law enforcement officers, emergency assistance personnel, of New York,
military personnel at the Pentagon, airline personnel and all innocent victims
that were tragically and senselessly killed on September 11, 2001
will never be forgotten.

Guardians of the Garden City

Guardians of the Garden City

The History of The San Jose Fire Department

by
R. L. Nailen

San Jose, California
1972

Dedicated
to the Memory of

Captain Peter J. Segard
Engine Co. No. 6

1888-1963

whose friendship and whose reminiscences
inspired this work

Table of Contents

*

Left page—Purity Stores, Inc. Market fire, 1370 Auzerais Street, December 7, 1969. An aerial ladder truck pours water on the fire, which started shortly before the store opened.

The men of Station Five: Dale O'Rourke, Capt. Leo Baziuk, Faro Krinkie, William Lannon and an unidentified firefighter, all of Hose Five and Engine Five battle the blaze at the Garden City Transportation Company, October 30, 1970.

Preface

"The history of the fire department is an important part of the history of San Jose and it is to be hoped someone qualified will in the near future write it up. . ."

John Cunan, foreman of San Jose's Empire Engine Company No. 1, wrote those words in the summer of 1882. His hope was never realized. Today, much of what he knew as local fire department history has forever vanished beyond the reach of "someone qualified." So has much that's happened since then.

This book has been written in a similar hope of providing at least a foundation on which a historian might build. Many gaps remain unfilled; the full stories of the Willow Glen, East San Jose, and West San Jose volunteer firemen could not be included. Much of San Jose's own departmental history remains buried in newspaper files and old Council minutes, or has been lost with the disappearance of Police & Fire Commission records. But this is a beginning.

My heartfelt thanks go to those who contributed so many leads to names, dates, and places otherwise forgotten. In particular; to retired Battalion Chief Larry Campbell, for years the department's unofficial historian, and possessor of the largest collection of pertinent material that I know of; Fire Prevention Bureau Chief John Gerhard, who opened the department's records for inspection; retired Assistant Chief John Knapp and Captain Ray Moody, whose photo collections were invaluable; former City Manager A. P. Hamann who furnished a manuscript copy of a brief history of the fire department's early years; Bill Horne of Mr. Hamann's staff who located files of old annual reports, and the only existing Commission minutes, among the boxes in a San Pedro Street warehouse; City Historian Clyde Arbuckle, whose files hold some rare mementos of the early days; retired fire officers John and Ed Powers, the late Charles Plummer, and Ralph Jennings; long-time commercial photographer John C. Gordon, whole priceless boxes of half a century's negatives and glass plates were a researcher's gold mine; to Judge Marshall Hall, the late Jay McCabe, and Lewis Sullivan; to the late Mercury Editor Oscar Liden, and the reference staff of the San Jose City Library; to Capt. R. M. Gossett of the Atlanta, Georgia, Fire Department for valuable advice on a similar historical project.

If readers become more conscious of the richness of local history, and come to the realization that this history is still being made **now** and must be preserved **now** if it is to be available to future generations, then this work will have served its purpose.

R. L. NAILEN
Milwaukee, Wisconsin
December, 1970

San Jose's County Courthouse still stands today. Original engraving as it appeared on 1871 Exempt Firemen's Certificate.

"The Public Spirit Of Our Citizens . ." 1854-1876

When California was admitted to the Union during the Gold Rush in 1849, the Pueblo de San Jose de Guadalupe was a settlement already generations old. Sustained by a modest commerce in grain and hides, unimpressed by the ravings of madmen like James Lick who claimed fruit trees could prosper in the Santa Clara Valley, the town consisted of little more than a few blocks of adobe structures surrounding the central plaza common to Spanish communities.

Nevertheless, it was the Pueblo de San Jose which was chosen to be the new state's first capital. Along what is now Market Street at the plaza's eastern edge, the California legislature chose a small two-story adobe, originally intended to be a hotel, to serve as the Capitol or "State House." In the far corner of today's Santa Clara County Fair Grounds, the determined visitor will find a somewhat down-at-heel replica of San Jose's State House of 1850. Genial and dedicated City Historian Clyde Arbuckle and his staff of seven hungry cats strove to preserve from the vermin and the elements a large collection of mementos from the San Jose of yesterday, there in the State House Museum (now closed to the public).

"The Legislature of a Thousand Drinks," that first session was called, for the cheerless prospects of "The Valley of Heart's Delight," as the legislature convened on Saturday, December 15, 1849, must have raised some mighty thirsts among those present. Beyond the huddle of pueblo shacks, the plain stretched unbroken to the distant foothills, while beneath leaden skies a procession of horses and wagons splashed through knee-deep mud to bring the politicians to their legislative tasks.

Before leaving town for good, the lawmakers granted a Charter establishing the City of San Jose on March 27, 1850—formally ending its pueblo days. On April 13, a Mayor (replacing the Spanish "alcalde") and Common Council (formerly the "ayuntamiento" or "Junta") met for the first time. Three months later this group adopted an ordinance providing for "fire limits."

People Who Live in Grass Houses . . .

Fire protection had been largely ignored before the establishment of the California Republic in 1846. Spanish villages were small, mostly adobe, and it was only after the arrival of "Americano" settlers that the transplanted tradition of bucket brigades and fire wardens began to take root. In June 1847, the Alcalde of San Jose and his Junta enacted the Pueblo's first fire regulation. It provided that "no house or edifice shall hereafter be erected with a cover of straw, grass, or flags, and all houses covered with said materials shall not be repaired after this date with aforesaid materials." Also banned were haystacks not "enclosed or guarded."

The ordinance of 1850 reconfirmed these restrictions, within about a quarter of a square mile in the downtown area. Limits of the "fire hazard district" were the Acequia, or ditch, about where San Pedro Street is today, Second Street on the east, St. James Street on the north, and San Carlos Street on on the south.

Added to the list of forbidden structural materials were canvas, willows, and cotton cloth. Yankee ingenuity was still finding old sailcloth handier than timber; in the absence of lumbermen and sawmills, the magnificent redwood groves in the nearby Santa Cruz Mountains were as yet untouched. Penalty for violation of this "building code" was fixed at "not less than twenty-five nor more than two hundred dollars."

Not fully realizing their remote situation, enthusiastic San Joseans went a step further on November 4 of that year and organized "Fire Engine Company No. 1." Shortly, however, some spoilsport pointed out that nowhere in the city, or in the entire County for that matter, was there a fire engine! Nor was any to be had anywhere on the Pacific Coast, as was made plain after the company applied to the Mayor and Council for the purchase of apparatus. No matter—there was no money to buy an engine anyway.

More suitably re-named "Eureka Fire Co. No. 1," the group gathered buckets together and went to work with a will. As one account put it, "The inflammable nature of the materials with which the buildings were constructed rendered it almost an impossibility to extinguish a fire, though this same frailty of construction enabled the firemen to destroy connections and prevent the spread of the fire." Perhaps this is where firemen got their undeserved reputation as house-wreckers.

The town fathers hopefully expected private enterprise to solve the fire apparatus shortage. In 1851, Mayor White put it this way: "I would respectfully urge that a fire department be immediately organized, and, if necessary, that an engine and other apparatus be procured, but there is reason to believe that the public spirit of our citizens will render any outlay by the City in this matter unnecessary."

His optimism was short-lived. Two years later, shortly before the dawn of April 29, 1853, fire proved itself no respecter of place or person by destroying the State House itself, adobe or not. This was too much. The following December 30, the City appropriated $2000 "for the purchase of a fire engine, with hooks and ladders, the president of the council being authorized to draw warrants and orders in such sums as he should deem advisable and pay the same over to the committee of citizens that should be selected by the people."

At the same time, the Council partitioned the City into four fire "wards," appointing a fire watchman or "warden" for each. Eventually developing into local political units which figured largely in civic affairs until the "reform" of 1916, the wards divided San Jose into quarters: First and Second Wards north of Santa Clara Street and west and east of First Street respectively; Third and Fourth Wards south of Santa Clara Street, east and west of First.

On January 6, 1854, the newly organized Hook and Ladder Company No. 1 notified the City Council of its existence as "a committee of citizens" and requested the purchase of apparatus. The Council appointed a group to handle this matter, as well as "to secure the

lease of a suitable lot on which to erect a building for the accommodation of the company."

Old 41 Comes to Town

Three weeks later, on January 27, the San Jose Fire Department was officially established by City Ordinance No. 239, at which time the Hook and Ladder Co. No. 1 was approved. The firehouse committee reported back that Frank Lightston (himself a member of the company) had agreed to lease his property on Lightston Street to the City for the nominal sum of 25c a year, if the City would show its good faith by erecting a suitable firehouse building on the site within one year. A grateful Council accepted the offer, and the two-story, 60 x 34 foot structure built there stood for years as one of the community's principal landmarks.

By the middle of 1854 San Jose's new department was ready for something better than tearing down burning buildings to prevent the spread of flames. On June 26, a Council committee was delegated to see if a hand pump fire engine might be purchased in San Francisco for a new Empire Engine Company Number 1, organized five days earlier, and admitted to the department in July. The committee advised that an engine was available for $1800.

Hose and water supplies were also on the committee's agenda. Hose was to be had for $1.50 per foot. As for water, the group recommended the digging of four cisterns, much the same as those used (even today) in San

Francisco. There were of course no water mains or hydrants then. One cistern was suggested at Market and Santa Clara Streets, another at First and Santa Clara, the third in front of the Mariposa Store (on Market Street just north of St. Joseph's Church), and the fourth near Jones' Store on First Street about where Woolworth's is today.

No difficulty was expected in keeping the cisterns filled. Fountain Alley, or Street as it was then called, got its name from an artesian well located where the entrance to Blum's was later situated. Abundant fresh water, just beneath the surface, plagued the early residents with downtown floods; once dug, the artesian wells proved difficult or impossible to cap. The cisterns, added to from time to time, served the City for over twenty years. In 1874, there were six of them, located in Market Street at San Fernando, Santa Clara, and San Augustine Streets, in First Street at Santa Clara and San Fernando, and at Second and San Antonio.

All the committee's recommendations were adopted. A total of $2546.25 was spent for the engine and hose, of which the citizens in their "public spirit" contributed $1355.

Townspeople also passed the hat for $404 which was used to buy a fire alarm bell.

Empire Engine Company's roster of volunteers read like a who's who of pioneer civic leaders—attorney Charles E. Allen, Foreman of the company; insurance man D. J. Porter, his First Assistant; James A. Clayton, realtor and auctioneer; and 48 other "charter members." The first engine was already a veteran of firefighting service, adding to the company's lustrous reputation.

It had been "Old 41" of the New York Volunteer Fire Department as far back as 1820, quartered at Delancey and Attorney Streets on Manhattan's lower East Side. One-time runners with the machine in New York were two of San Jose's prominent new citizens; architect Levi Goodrich, who later designed the Court House of 1868, and Abe Beatty, first proprietor of the Mansion House Hotel.

During the hasty organization of a fire department for the booming village of San Francisco, Old 41 was shipped around the Horn to the Golden Gate in 1850. For the next several years it served with the San Francisco fire company (Engine 1) led by Senator David Broderick (later a victim of the notori-

ous Broderick-Terry duel). Broderick himself had also been a New York fireman, running with Engine 34.

The apparatus of Hook and Ladder No. 1 was a little less specialized, and was built here in town by D. J. Porter and H. J. Haskell, assisted with the woodwork by pioneer carriage builder C. S. Crydenwise.

On New Year's Day of 1855, after Hook and Ladder volunteer James Gourley (a veteran New York fireman, born in Ireland) had applied the last coat of paint to the Lightston Street quarters, the men and equipment of both companies foregathered there for a grand parade. Wending its way through the downtown streets, the procession paused for prayer at the Methodist Church South at Second and San Fernando Streets. Miss Mary Crane presented the men of Empire 1 with a beautiful silk banner in behalf of the ladies of San Jose.

The department then paraded to the newly erected brick City Hall on North Market Street. Here, "they partook of a bountiful collation, and passed several hours in speechmaking." This was great stuff; firemen forthwith made it an annual affair, making sure of good weather for the occasion by shifting the date to the Fourth of July.

The Age of Steam Begins

In 1855, a "board of delegates" was formed to govern the Fire Department, with consent of the Council, made up of members from each company. To command the fire forces in action, the post of Chief Engineer was created. The need for these and other steps toward improved fire protection in the growing city was emphasized by San Jose's second serious fire, May 31, 1855. The scene was a congested, flimsily constructed shacktown along a narrow alley south of El Dorado (now Post) Street and east of Market. Several tenements and a group of stores were destroyed. Afterwards, the half-burned remains of a man were found in the ruins.

Spurred on by the tragedy, James Gourley bought a $400 second hand engine on his own, during an 1856 visit to New York. He offered to sell it to San Jose, to which the Council assented, if the citizens would organize another fire company to operate it. Gourley beat the bushes for volunteers, and soon had the men in hand. Named Torrent Engine No. 2, the new company went into service May 12, 1856.

The Fire Department then settled down to become a local institution. Many of the men were members of more than one fire company, apparently working at a fire with whichever of their outfits needed help the most. Typical of these were Levi Goodrich, J. Q. Pearl, and J. O. McKee. Always ready to turn out for picnics or parades, as well as fires, the volunteers became a nucleus for civic pride and social contact comparable to the service clubs or the chamber of commerce of today.

To celebrate the laying of the Atlantic Cable, in 1858, the entire department—which then meant about every able-bodied man in town—enjoyed a Bay cruise to San Francisco and back on Sept. 29, at the expense of Mayor Samuel J. Hensley. A member of Empire 1, and the president of the California Steam Navigation Company, Hensley had one of his firm's floating palaces pick the boys up at the thriving port of Alviso.

In 1859, after firemen saved his First Street home, Judge W. T. Wallace gave the department $1000. This was used to set up a fund for sick and disabled firemen, later evolving into the Firemen's Charitable Association (incorporated in 1865) with regular dues and benefits. Thousands of dollars were paid out over the years until the volunteer force disbanded, when the small remainder in the fund was divided among the men.

As the population grew, demand increased for a water supply system capable of supporting industrial and business establishments, as well as for improved fire protection. In the spring of 1864, foundryman Donald McKenzie applied to the city government for a franchise to provide citizens with artesian well water for both general and fire department use. This was the beginning of the vast San Jose Water Works system of today, which stores 2½ billion gallons to back up its far-flung distribution system. Within a couple of years water mains were being laid, pressurized by a couple of 10,000 gallon elevated wooden tanks erected fifty feet up on frame scaffolding just east of the Plaza, behind the McKenzie Foundry where the Montgomery Hotel stood in modern times. By March 1867 the cast iron cement-lined pipes reached north along First Street almost to Santa Clara Street.

The previous October, the boys of Torrent Company picked up a $2500 hand pumper from San Francisco (which was converting to

Empire Company's Silsby passes the San Jose Safe Deposit Bank Building

steamers) at the bargain price of $1500. When she arrived for the 11 a.m. parade, the Mayor, Council, and a delegation of Santa Clara firemen were on hand for refreshments and speeches. Tested in the afternoon at First and Santa Clara Streets "to the gratification of an admiring crowd," the new engine "will prove a squelcher when wanted" in the opinion of Mercury Editor J. J. Owen.

But the age of steam was at hand. During the heyday of the steamer, spanning half a century of local history, San Jose owned a total of seven machines of five different makes. The first was a Silsby, costing $6215.20, which arrived at the railroad station June 6, 1867. Travis's band led the firemen of Empire Company in procession to the depot about 10 a.m. There followed a parade downtown, the new engine being garlanded with wreaths and bouquets of flowers. After a picnic in Live Oak Park, the engine was tested and

could throw a one-inch stream 216 feet under 60 pounds steam pressure.

Empire's old hand tub, which today would be a priceless historical relic, wound up during the '80's at the County Almshouse, then disappeared—probably junked.

Arrival of the Silsby steamer naturally caused the old engine used by the rival Torrent Company to present "a very insignificant appearance," and the boys cast about for something better. The indefatigable Gourley again came to the rescue. In San Francisco, he located a handsome Hunneman end-stroke engine which was available for $1700 cash. Not one to buy a pig in a poke, Gourley spent some time testing the machine to be sure of its value, then reported back in satisfaction.

The hitch was that San Jose, strapped by the huge outlay for Empire's steamer, had only about $1200 available for fire purposes. It was agreed, therefore, that the purchase

End-stroke Hunneman hand engine identical to the model purchased for San Jose's Torrent Engine Co. in 1866.

would be made only if the balance needed could be raised by subscription. Members of Torrent Company gathered solemnly together and with much head-shaking they concluded such a sum was impossible for them to raise.

Gazing around him at the circle of down-cast faces, James Gourley threw down the gauntlet. Tossing $50 on the table, he cried, "Tis the last dollar I have, but it shall go for the new engine!" He dared the others to do as well. Immediately the coins began pouring on the table and in less than twenty minutes the required amount was raised. The Hunneman was bought, serving first Torrent, later Franklin Company, until 1880 when it was sold to the town of Turlock. It, too, has apparently long since been junked.

Gourley's active firefighting days were drawing to a close. He became the Fire Department's hydrant inspector, in which capacity he served until his death in October 1892 at the age of 76. Buried alongside him in Oak Hill Cemetery are several other firemen or "ex-firemen" who died in the '80's or '90's, including George Dash, first paid driver of the Empire hose cart. Only a hundred yards from busy Monterey Highway, in the cemetery's southeast corner, this forgotten little

area was once known as the "Firemen's Plot," owned by the Firemen's Association (perhaps the same Firemen's Charitable Association which began in the early 1860's). Officially, the shaded, grassy corner is now designated simply Block 10, Section A, Tiers 1 and 2. Many of the graves are unmarked. The last one to be filled in the plot, a third of which remains empty to this day, was taken in 1928 by Lieut. Theodore G. "Teddy" Haub who died at the age of 57.

Heyday of the Volunteers

San Jose assumed its true importance as a seat of County government in 1868 with the completion of the imposing Court House. Architect Goodrich was praised for his work, which has endured (except for changes made after the fire of 1931) for almost a century now. At the time, the Court House was the county's largest building, dominating the downtown landscape.

As the years passed, San Jose grew rapidly. The opening of the transcontinental railroad spurred a rise in commerce and immigration. The Fire Department underwent a host of changes. In 1869, the purely volunteer prestige of all its officers and men was enhanced by a little more tangible compensation.

6

A proposal to pay a salary to the Chief Engineer had failed in 1866, being contrary to the City Charter. But three years later, the State Legislature passed an act incorporating the department, and providing that all its members having five years of service should henceforth be exempt from jury duty, military service, or the payment of poll-taxes. This was the origin of the term "exempt firemen," by which many of the old-timers were known in later years. In the San Jose Historic Museum today, and in a few private hands, may be seen some of the handsomely engraved "Exempt Certificates" issued to San Jose's volunteer firemen.

Some were almost billboard size. More typical is the modest 8 x 10 inch document issued in March of 1866, anticipating the legislature's action, to George Donner II—a survivor of the famous Donner party tragedy. "Elected" to the Fire Department, Empire 1, in January 1865, Donner was "entitled to all the privileges granted by State and Municipal enactments" over the signatures of Chief Engineer D. A. Leddy (wholesale butcher by trade, as was his brother and fellow-fireman James) and Fire Department "President" C. P. Crittenden.

It was also in 1869 that the City was forced to end the overcrowding of its original Lightston Street firehouse, bursting at the seams with the equipment of three fire companies. In January, the Council bought a 20-foot frontage at 375 Second Street (later site of the Jose Theater) and erected a two-story brick building as quarters for Empire 1—which now had a hose cart to go with its steamer.

Across the way, a rented store served as the new location for Hook and Ladder 1. Torrent Engine 2 was removed to the City Hall on North Market Street, where it remained for the next 82 years; a longer time in one spot than any other San Jose fire company.

Apparently the Hook and Ladder boys were a cosmopolitan bunch, not favoring any special national origin. Not so with the fiercely competitive engine companies. Some 50 years later, Henry Humburg, son of Torrent Foreman Valentine Humburg and older brother of long-time San Jose Fire Captain John Humburg, vividly recalled his boyhood days. "Torrent was called the German Company," he said, "while Empire was the Irish Company. Many times my father came home

drenched because the rival companies would soak each other after the fire was out." Valentine Humburg, W. D. "Bill" Brown (later Chief of both police and fire departments) and Dan Haskell led the department's parades in full dress regalia, consisting of plumed hats, large white buckskin aprons and gauntlets, and of course the inevitable fire engine-red shirts. Each man carried a heavy steel axe. The 49 men of Torrent Company got their first hats in 1871; included were miniature helmets for young John and Henry Humburg, plus belts emblazoned with the name "Torrent." All this equipment was purchased by the volunteers themselves.

Other public-spirited citizens began to form new units, to join the fun. The first (and shortest-lived) of these was Washington Hose Company, organized in November 1870 and admitted to the Fire Department in December.

Unfortunately, the boys of Washington Hose were financially embarrassed. They appealed for City help, but the Council turned a deaf ear. As a result, the company was never provided with suitable apparatus, hose, or even quarters, though for a time they were housed in a store at First and St. John Streets where the Elks Building later stood. Such a situation dampened the volunteers' enthusiasm to the extent that, within a few years, Washington Hose quietly disbanded.

Next to organize were the men of San Jose's southern fringe. The Franklin Hose Company set up shop December 5, 1871, meeting in the vicinity of First and Reed Streets.

Horsepower and Paid Men

Meanwhile, the tough Irishmen of Empire Engine were forced to admit they had had enough of wrestling their two ton steam engine to fires by hand, becoming so exhausted in the process they might as well have stayed home. Taking their pride in their hands, they went before the City Council to request permission to acquire a driver and a team of horses to do the work. On March 20, 1871, the Council gave its approval, marking the beginning of 44 years of dependence by the Fire Department on its faithful horses.

During 1874, purchase of a $5000 Clapp & Jones steamer for Torrent No. 2 allowed the change of Franklin Hose to Franklin Engine Company No. 3—using the Hunneman hand engine handed down by Torrent.

Torrent Engine Co. No. 2 and Chemical Engine Co. No. 1. North Market, between Santa Clara and St. John Streets (the 1855 City Hall).

Throughout these early years there were few serious fires. One of them came on April 23, 1875, when St. Joseph's Church burned. The department's newly acquired horses, in the interests of economy, were mostly busy hauling gravel out at Coyote Creek. While firemen began a mad scramble to get their equipment to the scene, local drayman Pat McGuire went into action. Seeing the church afire from a distance, Pat and a crew of brother Hibernians piled onto his wagon and started down Market Street at a gallop, yelling "fire!" at everybody as they clattered along. They saved many of the church furnishings, with Pat personally rescuing the statue of his patron saint.

Six weeks later, to protect the city's northeastern suburbs, the Eureka Hose Company was admitted to volunteer ranks. A firehouse was completed in 1876, on North 8th Street near Julian. Eureka Hose, much later becoming Chemical Company No. 2, remained on this site for 73 years.

Little by little the growth in the department, and in the city itself, was diluting the volunteers' exclusive social structure. Nevertheless, the old-timers fought hard to retain what was left when citizens began in 1876 to agitate for a paid fire department.

At the time, nobody seemed to have in mind the abolition of the volunteer organization. The intent was simply to build a paid department around the nucleus of the available apparatus and firehouses (mostly city-owned). Volunteers were to have the option of disbanding, or starting over again with new apparatus and quarters of their own.

Naturally, the boys considered this as savoring of ingratitude. They had given long years of hard service with no compensation, and they objected to being summarily dismissed. The fire fighting equipment which the city proposed to take out of their capable hands represented many hundreds of dollars of their own money, which they had contributed for the general good; even though the city undoubtedly held legal title, the volunteers thought they deserved consideration.

Progress, however, was not to be denied. Free of debt, its property values greatly increased, and, it was felt, financially able to assume the burden, San Jose proceeded in October, 1876, to establish a paid Fire Department. Consisting of a Chief and 29 men, the new organization took over at the end of the month.

Now powerless to defend their position, the volunteers chose to disband. Just before midnight of October 31, they paraded sadly through the darkened downtown streets, for the last time. As the final stroke of twelve sounded, they left their apparatus in front of the City Hall, and went home.

———

The door remained open for other volunteer fire companies to form on their own initiative, and some did. But, in general, this was the end of the Volunteer Fire Department of San Jose, "as intelligent, well-disciplined and public-spirited body of men as was ever organized in any city in the United States." For many of the individual volunteers, it was not the end. The first paid Chief, for instance — J. Chris Gerdes — had been a volunteer; the old department was the only local source of experienced manpower.

Of course, the little 30-man paid force, professionals or not, could not handle the work that several hundred trained volunteers could. The institution of the paid volunteer or "extraman" was created to fill the gap. A civilian with his own full-time employment, the extraman was assigned to respond to fires with a particular company whenever the alarm sounded, for which he was paid a nominal monthly salary. Several of these men were detailed to each fire company, serving a vital purpose for many years.

Throughout another generation, San Jose's community leadership remained in the hands of men from the ranks of former volunteers —men like Henry Lux, John Balbach, John Stock, and Judge F. E. Spencer. In this atmosphere, the members of the paid department, like the volunteers before them, continued to enjoy a place of community importance.

The Franklin House of 1889 on South First Street, as it looked before the 1906 earthquake shook it apart.

9

Professional Status;
Volunteer Pride
1876-1898

Of all the periods into which this history has been divided, surely this one is based on the most fascinating source material, for we see these first years of the professional Fire Department mostly through the pages of the daily journal of Empire Engine Company No. 1. Much of this record was kept by John F. Cunan, Foreman of the company for many years, who thus did much to realize his own hope that early department history would be preserved for the San Jose of the future.

All the newspaper files in San Jose covering these years are in poor shape, and hard to get at besides. No other individual fire company journals seem to have survived. Even if they had, it would be hard to imagine another written with such a mixture of pride, honest Victorian sentimentalism, and high good humor.

"Always in the Lead"

Although the volunteer firemen had disbanded and turned over their equipment to the city, the fire companies retained their historic names, such as Empire and Torrent. It was 30 years before the various engine and hose companies were commonly spoken of by number instead of by name—about the length of time it took for the volunteers to become elderly men, displaced from public life by a new generation.

Many of the professional firemen were drawn from volunteer ranks, as has been said. It was also still possible for volunteer or auxiliary companies to organize even after October 1876. Alert Hose Company, the longest-lived of any such group, was formed in November 1876. Three years later, Alert purchased a $900 hose cart from the Stockton Fire Department. The company had its first quarters in the "City Stables," 252 Santa Clara at the corner of Lightston Street. (There was no "West" or "East" Santa Clara Street until the early '80's; the east-west streets were numbered block by block start-

ing west of San Pedro Street and continuing eastward; the north-south streets being similarly numbered from Julian Street southward. Thus what is now the 100 block of South First Street was then simply the 400 block of First Street).

In January of 1879, Protection Hose Co. came into existence. This group inherited the reel used by the short-lived Washington Hose at one time, locating on South 8th Street near the corner of San Salvador where the city owned property that had been part of a school site.

No sooner was this new company organized than the territory it shared with Empire Engine was the locale of San Jose's largest fire to date. This was the burning of the four-year-old San Jose Normal School in Washington Square.

Today grown into the educational metropolis of San Jose State College, its eastward expansion having now swallowed up the former site of Protection Hose, the school first came to San Jose only after a hard fight with various other cities contending vigorously for the honor. This was before the day when almost every urban area in California had its own institution of higher learning. Final loser to the Garden City was Napa, following a close 48-37 vote in the State Legislature.

In the early morning of February 10, 1880, a passerby spotted flames pouring from an upstairs window of the school. Box 41 was struck at 2:10 a.m., summoning firemen to a losing fight. The huge wooden structure was doomed. Smoke and the glare of flames blanketed the city for blocks around, with embers raining down among nearby homes to cause widespread damage.

Only the relatively isolated location of the school in its parklike square prevented a major conflagration. The morning sun rose over half a million dollars worth of charred ruins—insured for only a tenth that amount. Firemen were recalled to the grounds next day to put out a smouldering coal pile. The Fire Department had, of course, been totally inadequate to handle such a blaze in a structure "built to burn." Sprinklers, fire detection systems, fire-resistant construction — these were all far in the future.

One outgrowth of the Normal School's destruction was the recognition by San Joseans that their Fire Department could not be neglected because it was now a professional organization. Steps were taken to provide a third steamer.

Another result of this fire was a move to relocate the school elsewhere. It failed, permitting the growth of the State College of today. Ironically, the modern campus became for a time a minor thorn in the side of the modern Fire Department. Not only are the aging, crowded student boarding houses fringing the school a prolific breeding ground for dangerous fires; the department also has had to contend with arson on the part of playful students. The only recorded incident of deliberate obstruction of firemen in the performance of their duties, through theft of fire apparatus tools and equipment at a fire scene, has involved "prankish" college students—fortunately a small minority.

The Normal School blaze was one of 13 alarms answered by Empire Engine 1 in February of 1880. Another San Jose institution which has survived several fires to serve the city of today was damaged that same month. This was the First Baptist Church, then called the Baptist Tabernacle, at the corner of Second and San Antonio Streets. The first of a series of blazes, set by someone bent on destroying the church, came at noon on February 6, to cause only slight damage.

On May 22, 1880, the new steamer was accepted by the city and placed in service with the department's premiere company — Empire 1. The ancient Silsby was shunted over to Franklin 3, where it displaced San Jose's last hand engine. Empire's new pride and joy was an Amoskeag, modestly described in the company record as a "second class" machine. She was in fact rated slightly below the Underwriters' minimum rating of "fourth size" or 500 GPM. The Empire machine would pump "400 GPM at a fair rate of speed," being a crane-neck nickel-plated engine with two 6½ inch diameter steam cylinders, driving double acting vertical pumps of 4 inch diameter and 10 inch stroke. Valued at $4650, she weighed 3½ tons with three men aboard.

Water in the boiler was kept hot between alarms by a circulating gas-fired water heater installed by Engineer A. W. Hess. On an average, it took 4000 cubic feet of gas per month; three times that amount in winter, costing about a third of a cent per cubic foot—one of the company's big expense items.

A feature taken for granted on today's pumpers, but not yet standard in the '80's, was a relief valve adequate to prevent damage when a hose line was abruptly shut off. This made the use of shutoff nozzles impossible. The Alert Hose boys had no pumper, but used only hydrant streams, so they were able to use shutoff nozzles. At a fire in May of '82, Empire made the mistake of pumping into an Alert line; when the nozzle was closed, the hose immediately burst!

Running with the Empire steamer was a locally-built hose reel, carrying 800 feet of "carbolized" hose equipped with the "latest improved coupling." Typical of the times, Empire Company could be out the doors with both rigs inside 13 seconds after the alarm sounded; within 6 minutes, they could be hooked up, throwing water on a fire through two hose lines.

The fires confronting these early companies didn't involve the dangerous industrial chemicals, radiation hazard, or other exotic dangers faced by today's firefighters. However, there were some special nuisances that modern firemen are spared—at least in San Jose. In November of 1880, near First and San Salvador Streets, the boys were called out to extinguish a blaze in a large manure pile behind a barn. On another occasion, Empire was summoned to 10th and San Fernando where a back yard blaze damaged a privy. This time, it was recorded that "the Nagle brandy was sent around to the Boys after the fire and it came in good after getting a good wetting . ." (from the hose streams, we hope!)

Empire Fire House at 76 South Second Street — about 1880.

In a similar vein, on July 7, 1881, came what was perhaps San Jose's first dump fire —"in the dump where the city wagons dump the rubbish collected from the streets." In an age of universal horse and mule transport, the principal ingredient of this "rubbish" is easily surmised.

As if things weren't tough enough when the luckless smoke-eaters arrived at fires of this kind, the year 1881 brought a unique obstacle to their even getting there. San Jose's famous "electric tower" was built that year, straddling the busy intersection of Market and Santa Clara Streets. There was a theory in those early days of electrical science that the best way to light a town's streets after dark was with a single high intensity lamp, placed high above. San Jose was to learn by experience that the game wasn't worth the candle. The thing cost too much ($6000), it proved a fertile source of litigation between various electric companies—and firemen dashing out of the Market Street

Rebuilt after the 1880 fire, San Jose's imposing Victorian Normal School towers above Washington Square treetops. This structure would be lost in one corner of today's sprawling campus.

firehouse in any one of three directions had to thread their galloping teams through the tower's spidery supports. The tower blew down in 1915, which was just as well.

Firefighters, then as now, were equal to all emergencies. The Empire Foreman was usually able to record that his company had turned out in good order; "all the members . . . were on hand and worked like beavers." Those men were from various walks of life. John Cunan had been a landscape gardener; extraman Mike Zimmer, one of the first paid men of '76, was a butcher at the Central Market across Second Street from the engine

house. Other members of Empire Company in the early '80's were engine driver M. Cunan, John's brother; Engineer A. W. Hess; hose cart driver C. Desimone; extraman W. Macey, Hugh Young, Dan Gallagher, and Simon Camp. They were a proud group—after summing up his company's service at 36 of the 66 alarms they answered in 1881, Foreman Cunan wrote, "The reputation gained by Empire No. 1 during the twelve [sic] years she was a volunteer company has been sustained since . . . and I hope that during the year 1882 and the years to come Empire will always be found in the lead."

"We'll Put It Out
If We Can Find It . . ."

Interspersed among the manure pile fires was an occasional larger blaze. At 1:45 a.m. on Tuesday, July 5, 1881, the department turned out in the vain attempt to save the Opera House on the north side of Santa Clara Street between 2nd and 3rd. Almost half a block of small officeholders and shopkeepers along Santa Clara Street were wiped out in the two hour blaze, with a loss exceeding $50,000. Next day a re-kindle called firemen back to the scene.

Although undoubtedly the boys did "work like beavers," their failure to stop the flames inspired some critical comment in the local press. Wrote one editor several days later, "This fire has clearly demonstrated the fact that our fire department should receive more attention and a general overhauling. There is considerable incapacity somewhere . . . ."

Certainly there was one glaring area of incapacity about which the firemen could do little but gripe — namely, the alarm system. There were about nine alarm boxes or stations in the city as early as 1872, but of a poor sort. The Council had contracted for an alarm system, including a $1000 electric fire bell striker, in 1877, but they had gotten little satisfaction out of it. The boxes themselves, few enough in number, were located in private homes, their use being too important to trust to the average passerby on the street. But that didn't prevent false alarms. One day in the Second Ward, a boy dashed up to a house calling for the box key. On receiving it, he went at once to Box 14 at 5th and Washington, and turned in an alarm. There was, however, no fire.

Worse yet, the alarm wiring was operated (and the boxes rented out) by the American District Telegraph Company (ADT), today a responsible and most useful protective service, but then apparently none too reliable in San Jose. During May and June of 1881, there were at least five instances of false alarms caused by crossed wires in the ADT office. Next year it got much worse.

The operation of the boxes themselves left a lot to be desired. These quaint devices were fitted with a dial arrangement on the front, used not only for turning in fire alarms but for such other unrelated purposes as summoning cabs! It all depended on where you set the dial; a slip of the finger and along came the firemen. Or the ADT operator could get balled up. For example, in July 1881 appears this entry in the Empire log: "This alarm came from a house on San Augustine Street—they turned in for a Hack and operator turned in fire." Then there was the time when "occupants of the house say they turned in for Police but the operator in the Central office says it came in fire twice."

Empire Foreman John Cunan was beside himself with fury at the whole system. His pen fairly sputtered as he recorded a false alarm from Box 12: "the parties who rent that box declare that no alarm was turned in . . . My impression is that the women who rent that box being 'Fast Women' turned in the alarm just to have some fun . . . this thing should be stopped this is not the first time this has happened."

By Council resolution of March 20, 1882, Chief W. D. Brown was asked to submit quarterly reports on Fire Department operations, and in his first one at the end of that month he took pains to point out the "defective" condition of the alarm system, as well as the need for reconstruction of the firehouse stables. Brown "respectfully call[ed] the attention of your hon. body" to the fact that "The only boxes are in private houses and the people and firemen do not know who have the boxes and who have none, thus affording the fire a chance to get a big start before an alarm is sounded."

The vagaries of the telegraph circuits themselves are highlighted by several more of Cunan's wrathful comments. Regarding the incident of March 9, 1882: "The alarm of fire this evening was caused by the burning of a chimney in a house on the corner of Seventh and Julian Streets. The fire alarm telegraph struck different numbers in different engine houses. It struck 25, 27, 24, 28, 35. Empire Engine got it nearly right and went to the fire. Torrent No. 2 went toward the depot and the Hook and Ladder toward Gilroy."

On July 14, three rounds of the box came in 35-38-38. Empire took off for Box 35 at the Franklin Engine House; the Franklin boys galloped downtown toward Box 38, meeting Empire halfway. Raged Cunan, "So many false alarms since the American district alarm system was adopted that it is a wonder that [the] Fire department is not demoralized."

On the afternoon of June 2, after six out of seven alarms during May turned out to be false, an alarm from Box 43 was checked out by the Chief and Councilmen and proved to be false also. As a result, the ADT firm was fined $25 for carelessness. This happened again in September, to ADT Manager Bailey, who claimed to have received a fire report from "somebody" and then sent it out via telegraph. Unable to substantiate the call when the alarm proved false, he was stuck with a fine. Commented Foreman Cunan with satisfaction, "Sock the fine on every time.... and I warrant we won't have many .. " Shortly thereafter, Bailey sold out the office to new owners who were able to do only slightly better. Litigation ensued which continued for years.

By July 1883 the city was forced to attempt complete cancellation of the ADT service. Only the absorption of the entire system was eventually able to insure reliable operation.

It's worth noting what it cost to run a fire company in those days. For January, 1882, Empire's total operating expenses came to $288.30, including $225 for salaries and $46.40 for gas to keep the steamer hot. Also of interest is the inventory of company equipment —including some items not usually found in today's metropolitan firehouses. Empire had on hand a half dozen spittoons, valued at $6 altogether; one $14 ton of coal; a pair of "blunderbusses" at $30 (it is not recorded that these were ever officially discharged); two whips totalling $5; Engineer Hess's "patent indicator and unhitching apparatus" and related appurtenances at $70; plus the engine, a $300 hose cart and 750 feet of carbolized rubber hose at $937.50. Total value of the company's furnishings was $7468.35. Over and above this was the value of land and buildings occupied by the company. The lot, prime downtown property, mind you, was worth $1000, the building $8000.

A Glorious Fourth, and Some New Rules

Whoever it was that had it in for the Baptist Tabernacle got down to business at the end of that January. In the small hours of the 30th, a second fire in the church caused minor damage to a corner buttress. Hear the story of the discovery of this blaze, as told by John Cunan: "At this hour a milkman while driving past the Baptist Church . . . discovered smoke issuing from the northwest corner. He at once stopped his horse and endeavored to put out the fire with milk from his cans but from the fact that he was an honest milkman and had put but very little water in his milk that morning his efforts were without avail and his design fruitless." He then took off for Empire engine house to give the alarm. Alas, such prose is gone forever from fire company reports!

On February 25, Box 38 was turned in late in the evening for the third, and last, fire in the same building. This time she was a goner. After resting up from Empire's eight hours of service at this fire, Cunan pulled out all the stops to declare: "Never in the history of the San Jose Fire Department did they do as good work as at this fire." Chief Brown's men concentrated on saving the many exposed residences nearby, but the church was an $18,000 loss (insured for only $10,000). It was quite a blow to the congregation, just beginning to prosper at this location—a site which the First Baptist Church has since left for greener suburban pastures.

The church custodian, one Mr. Hitchcock, sleeping in an upstairs room, barely escaped with his life. Met by a sheet of flames as he tried to escape via the gallery, he was able to locate another way out just in time.

Driver M. Cunan of Empire missed out on this one. At a minor fire earlier in the week, he had become tangled in his reins when one of the horses reared at an accidental sounding of the engine whistle. Thrown down and trampled, Cunan was bedridden for some time. Less than a year later he was thrown again, when, en route to a fire, the engine lurched as its wheels caught in the streetcar track. In 1883 the poor man got it again—kicked by one of the horses, he was laid up for two weeks.

Such injuries were common enough. San Jose, however, was lucky throughout those early years, and continues to be lucky today, in that throughout a long history of spectacular and costly blazes there has been small loss of life.

Nonetheless the men of Empire began to harden themselves to some grisly spectacles as part of the romance of firefighting. One of the first came after 1 a.m. on April 30, 1882, when the watchman at Dougherty's lumber mill reported fire in the small home of laborer John Brett, on South 4th Street near San Carlos. Flames roared skyward from the frame structure as firemen clattered onto the scene—to be greeted by neighbors screaming that the Bretts were still inside. Empire Foreman Cunan, knowing the family and the layout of the home, dashed inside under cover of hose streams, through blinding smoke and steam, to find John Brett's roasted corpse within a few feet of the back door. Later, he located Mrs. Brett at the foot of her bed, both legs and arms burned away. As Cunan solemnly recorded in his journal later that day, "it was a sad and ghastly sight to behold."

Firemen's attentions turned to lighter matters on Independence Day. This year there were some special added attractions to the annual parade. For one thing, "The Glorious Fourth of July came and went and not a Single Fire nor a False Alarm." Cheered by an enthusiastic crowd, the men of Empire and others staged a memorable celebration. At the conclusion of patriotic observances at the California Theater, reported the local Times, "The Mayor and Common Council officers headed by the Fifth Infantry Band repaired to the Hall of Empire Engine House where the boys had spread an elegant dinner for their friends..." The Hon. A. Pfister (grocer and hardware merchant from up the street) spoke from the head of the table, saying he was "61 years old but it made him feel young again to be among the fire boys."

Wrote Cunan, "Here and there in this assemblage ·is seen with grizzled beard and scanty foretop one of those old time boys who assisted to organize the first engine company of San Jose..." One such was D. J. Porter, the First Assistant Chief of 1854, who stood up to reminisce over the first July 4th ever celebrated in San Jose, 28 years earlier. With songs, speeches, and toasts, the hours of nostalgia were whiled away, following which

"the guests dispersed to their respective homes well pleased with the firemen."

Such gatherings were seldom, if ever, to occur again. The oldtimers were disappearing. One of them, James Leddy, died in October of '82, his passing being the only event of concern to the fire service that month. For the first time in history of the department—and probably the last—an entire month passed (40 days, in fact) without a single fire alarm! A little bit of this was fine, but after four weeks Cunan was grumbling, "It knocks the men all out of time—it will take two or three fires to get the men all in good working order again."

His standards were high. Stopping by the engine house one September evening in 1882, a Herald reporter was invited to go out with the company for a drill. He was able to carry back, somewhat breathlessly, the news that Empire Engine had cleared the house in 13 seconds, gotten to the Market and San Fernando Street cistern in 1¼ minutes, and within 6 minutes after lighting the boilers she had two 150 foot streams of water playing from 400 foot hose lines. It was the fastest time to date.

To help keep the men and the equipment in such fighting trim, on December 11, 1882, the Mayor and Common Council adopted the first published rules for the government of the Fire Department. Besides prescribing drills for all men at least once a month (Rule XI), these regulations delegated the cleaning of hose to fire company members "in rotation," forbade non-members riding on apparatus (a rule not scrupulously observed), and required hose cart drivers to remain within three blocks of their firehouses when exercising the horses. Members in good standing were of course permitted to ride the rigs, providing, however, that the first three extramen to arrive at an engine company's quarters were given priority to ride the hose cart.

Rule I blew the whistle on absentees: "The Foreman of each company shall muster his men in their respective quarters and call the roll after each alarm of fire or drill. All members absent without an excuse from the Foreman, except in case of sickness, shall be marked in a Roll Book... Foreman... shall immediately report to the Chief Engineer the names of all absentees."

Apparently this wasn't rigorously enforced either. Barney Medane had joined Empire Company in October 1882, and failed to appear at his first fire on November 7. Warned Cunan in his journal, " . . . it don't speak very well for a new member to miss the First Fire I hope it won't Happen Again." But it did. Medane missed three out of four fires for the better part of two years before disappearing from Empire annals.

Rule II squelched any would-be Tom Sawyers in the ranks: "The Engineers shall clean their own engines; they are strictly forbidden to permit any person not a member of the San Jose Paid Fire Department to clean or help clean . . . " without the Chief's permission.

Not only were non-members—the former volunteers, in other words—booted off the rigs, and deprived of engine-cleaning privileges; Rule IV also prohibited their remaining in or about the firehouses "longer than what constitutes a respectable time for visit or pleasure . . " or after 10:30 p.m. without the Chief's sanction.

Snow Balls and Kid Gloves

Even at that, life was still fairly simple; firemen remained an unsophisticated bunch. An example was the doings during the noon hour on the last day of the year 1882. At half past twelve Box 9 rang in for a chimney fire on West Santa Clara Street. Near Pleasant Street, we're told, the boys "met with rather an unexpected reception in the way of a Snow Balling." Well might the writer use capital letters; only thrice in a hundred years has snow fallen to that extent in San Jose.

Continues the account: "It is the first time in the history of San Jose of Snow Enough falling and Remaining on the ground to admit of snow balling." The townspeople were "crazy with delight . . everybody took a Hand in the fun and as soon as the fire boys hove in sight . . . commenced the sport . . . The poor firemen had to run the distance of seven blocks with men and boys on both sides of the street pelting them with Snow Balls . . . and all the firemen could do was to dodge the balls as best they could and grin and bear it . . "

When the smoke-eaters arrived at the fire, putting it out was but the work of a moment, after which "they all took a hand . . . and came out victorious and routed the Enemy from the field . . it was a grand sight and not soon forgotten by the citizens of San Jose."

John Cunan was really warming to his narrative task. Commenting on the February 6,

1883, death of a Mrs. Young in her burning San Fernando Street home, while her husband lay drunk in another room, Cunan wrote: "on the night previous . . . [Young] was picked up in the street in a drunken stupor and assisted to his home by some friends. Subsequent events have demonstrated that it would have been better to let him stay and freeze if such a thing were possible."

In the chilly pre-dawn hours of March 8, 1883, Box 9 at the City Hall sounded for a $32,000 conflagration which swept three buildings on San Pedro Street north of San Augustine. Fire broke out in the Bennett-Patterson furniture factory, spreading rapidly to the box factories of Albert Lake and John Britton which flanked it on either side. All three were involved when firemen arrived.

Five weeks later came another Chinatown blaze, latest in a series which would eventually wipe out the squalid, rickety little settlement huddled along Market Street at San Fernando. Cunan thought little of the Oriental way of life in San Jose. Said he, "From the way in which the Chinese Houses are built . . . I will say that if a fire ever gets a good start it will make very lively work for the Chinese and I doubt not some Roasted Chinamen will be Found in the Ruins. I never saw . . . dirt and filth in so small a space in my life . . . it is a disgrace to the City of San Jose."

He did admit, though, that the Chinese had organized their own fire brigade, equipped with ladders and buckets, "and Every man is expected to take hold and do his Best in case of fire thus they have a fire department of their own and they are always on the watch for fire." The "human wave" tactic was employed even then, as the Chinamen flocked to a fire by the hundred.

John Cunan's journalistic activity, as well as his firemanship, caught Chief Brown's approving eye. In the annual report of March 31, 1883, Brown complimented the Empire Foreman "for the interest he has taken in his company and in keeping a correct account of the expenditures and workings of his company . . . " Some of the other foremen tended to be careless accountants, and "have shown great disregard and indifference as to how their respective companies were running."

For the fiscal year then ending, Brown recorded a total of 59 alarms (about two days' worth for the modern department).

Engine No. 1 from Empire Station.

Alert and Protection Hose Companies were still volunteer, with very small expenses; total Fire Department operating cost for the year was $15,882.19—only two days' expenditure for today's department! The apparatus was valued at $15,185 (two steamers, one hook and ladder, six hose carts and carriages). Real estate and improvements totalled $18,900. Altogether, the Fire Department's property was worth a little over $46,000.

There were some deficiencies. Hydrants, totalling 108 throughout the city, were too thinly scattered in the Bassett-San Pedro Street area. Empire Engine needed a new set of rear wheels. On the other hand, Chief Brown could boast of some improvements.

Stables in the Empire house were remodelled that spring, for $1000, so that the horses in their stalls faced toward the engine rather than away from it. To prevent collapse

of suction hose when engines were drawing water from the low pressure mains we had then, some new style suctions with metal reinforcement had been purchased. Empire reported that these worked well in May of '83 when a second fire in Brohaska's Opera House caused minor damage to it and two adjoining buildings.

Another deficiency, in a way, was the firemen's tendency to cling to volunteer ideals regarding working clothes. The resplendent uniforms made for a grand *esprit.* but they had their disadvantages on the job. A false alarm one rainy afternoon in May of 1883 wrung these anguished comments from the Empire Foreman: " . . . went home disgusted at being called out and laying out all their hose in the Mud and Rain it is tough to be called out in Such Weather even for a fire . . . it makes me too full for utterance to think of the fine clothes we had on of the shining boots and kid gloves and then to have to go and Reel Hose in the Rain and Mud But Such is life we will have to bear it with Christian Patience and Fortitude and Wait for our Reward in the Sweet Bye and Bye."

He added an acid postscript: "Dan Gallagher . . . of Empire No. 1 was conspicuous by his absence. I suppose he did not have his good clothes on and did not like to show up on that account he was reported to the Chief Engineer all the same."

The luckless Gallagher was soon forgiven. He was married later in the month, along with John Horn of the Torrent Company. For this occasion, Cunan's Irish blarney emerged in all its glory. Congratulating the lucky men, he expressed the "hope that no **Fires** of discord not even a **False Alarm** may ever disturb the even tenor of their Matrimonial life. But if any should occur May the **Engine** of Peace manned by Angels of love Shower the gentle drops of Reconciliation until the embers of Strife are entirely and forever Extinguished."

Torrent Skulduggery

Although San Jose's water supply was much poorer then than it is today, there was much more surface water in the city then. Besides the artesian wells, the creeks were flowing. A stream of particular contrast to the dusty slough of today was the Guadalupe.

In the early days, the full-flowing stream widened into a large pond between San Augustine and Julian Streets. Judge Marshall Hall, whose grandfather's home, where he was born, stood near the river on Autumn Street, recalls that there was once a neighborhood scheme afoot to turn the area into an aquatic pleasure resort! Further south, there were "swimming baths" operating near where the San Jose Water Works plant now stands.

Here was a power source that could operate a flour mill. In 1844, the Orange Mill had been built on River Street near San Fernando, adjacent to the Guadalupe. Known as the Sunol Mill then, it was the first flour mill in the Santa Clara Valley, with an initial capacity of 75 "fanagas" or bushels of wheat daily. Ten years later the mill was remodelled, converted to steam operation, and enlarged, at a cost of $60,000.

But all that was over by 1883. Used only as a wine and vinegar warehouse, the landmark caught fire on the night of June 16. The huge structure was a total loss—burning from top to bottom by the time Empire Engine arrived.

The 3:55 a.m. alarm was turned in from City Hall, and yet before the fire bell sounded to summon the rest of the department, Torrent Engine was there and had a line out. The Empire boys were wild about that. Cunan bitterly attacked the ADT alarm operators who were so slow in sounding the bell. "We'd be better off back ringing the bell by hand," he stormed, "instead of paying ADT a hundred dollars a month to do the job."

Soon, however, it appeared that more was involved than sluggishness in the alarm office. Rumor had it that Torrent used a pri-

vate "tipoff" wire which gave them the jump on other companies. The existence of such a wire was once common knowledge, but the City Council had ordered it removed when a lawsuit impended over the unreliable alarm system operation (the city then had 53 boxes in service).

On June 24, Chief Brown turned in a test alarm from the ADT office, insisting that it go out "on the square" with no advance tips to anybody. Torrent was not the first to arrive in response to the alarm. When the companies were sent back to quarters, Brown lingered in the office to await developments —which were not long in coming. An indignant Cunan reported, "When the Torrents got back to their House James Finley . . . went in to the Police Office and called the Central [ADT] Office on the telephone and wanted to know why in H_____ they did not set off the jigger and Chief Brown . . . heard every word. The Torrents have had that private wire in all the time although the Council ordered it out . . . they should be shown up to the police . . . "

The embarrassing episode failed to squelch the Torrent boys. Smarting from their exposure, they determined to have a little fun at the expense of Empire and the others. On July 26 at 5 a.m., they were routed out by a still alarm to handle a smoke scare at the Mercury office. Finding no fire to deal with, the Torrent crew returned to their City Hall quarters and proceeded to turn in a box alarm so they could time the response of the other companies! "They did it to us," vowed the men of Torrent, "so now we'll try it on them." Cunan contended himself with this icy rejoinder: "I hope the time made by Empire Engine Co. was satisfactory, and I also hope that any company doing such a mean trick again will be hauled over the coals by the Chief. There should be no 'Funny Business' allowed in the Paid fire department . . . "

The Mercury office had a bad reputation for nuisance fires anyway. As far as the firemen of the '80's were concerned, there was only one thing worse than a false alarm—and that was a bona fide fire which was out before the firemen could get there. John Cunan complained one evening, after a futile chase to the Mercury building, "This is the second or third time the department has been called out by an explosion of coal oil lamps in the Mercury Office and I think it is about time

that office would commence to buy better coal oil or use the electric light, or better still use gas."

The boys were not so disappointed when called to 5th and Julian Streets late in the evening of August 15. One building of the San Jose Fruit Packing Company, known as the "Jelly Room," was destroyed by fire. While other firemen assisted in stopping the blaze, the good work was credited (by Cunan) to "especially Empire Engine as the first two streams of water . . . came from that Engine and in fact it was them two streams that saved the building." Modest, though ungrammatical. Satisfied plant owners presented Chief Brown with a $100 check, later divided among the fire companies.

A New Regime

At this point we take our leave of Cunan's flowing prose, though Empire's journal continues to be our guide. The fluent Irishman was soon to leave the company. Bigger news than that was the comic opera antics resulting from the City Council's October 1883 decision to "elect" men to "fill" fire department positions which they thought needed new blood.

Chosen in the first election on December 3 were James Brady as Chief Engineer, W. W. Gillespie as Engineer of Empire Engine, and Thomas Fleming as Hook and Ladder Foreman. Councilmen passed an ordinance confirming the election — only to have Mayor Martin veto it. Former Engineer Hess of Empire, as well as the other two incumbents, retained a precarious hold on his job, but the three could collect no salary because the newly elected replacements also claimed the money.

This happy situation continued until April 1884, when a new Mayor (Settle) and Council took office and issued an ultimatum directing Brady, Gillespie, and Fleming to take over their duties—which Brown and his colleagues indignantly refused to honor. Mayor Settle then called personally on all the Foremen; went to Brown to beg his co-operation to avoid trouble; and triumphantly told him the Council had decided to elect Brown Chief of Police!

His honor upheld, Brown acquiesced to the change on April 22. Empire Engine responded valiantly when ordered out for drill by the new Chief—even though both Gillespie and Hess showed up to run the machine. The engine house area filled with a curious crowd, expecting to see a row, but good will prevailed. After sharing operation of the steamer, Hess went home, and the two men parted friends. Gillespie only kept the job six months before resigning.

Politics on a national scale also occupied a place of prominence in the San Jose of 1884. On a warm summer evening in July, valley Democrats paraded down Santa Clara Street in a grand Torchlight Procession—firing sky-rockets as they went—to open a successful campaign to elect Grover Cleveland. Some of the pyrotechnics set fire to flags flying from the St. Francis Block near Second Street; Empire Engine made short work of the blaze.

Traditionally, there had been but one means of extinguishment for even such small fires as this. The boys simply unlimbered a 2½-inch hose line and flooded the flames. A new wrinkle appeared in 1885. Responding to a minor fire only a few doors from the engine house, in the old What Cheer House at 2nd and San Fernando, the Empire crew got their line out but before they could go to work, the fire was over. An enterprising local businessman— James Hart, better known as the "Coffee King"—had thrown in a pair of "Harden Hand Grenades," an early type of chemical fire extinguishing bombs. Said the Empire Foreman in wonderment, "They done the business." Hart had just been made local Harden agent; his grenades enjoyed a vogue for some time. Often during 1885 they did good service in handling small blazes.

But the firemen were shook up. The boys had to stop and consider uneasily whether they were most interested in getting the fire out, or in showing off their own virtuosity. Only half in jest, the men of Empire went home muttering that "they will duck the King if he insists on Robbing them of the Honors of **first water.**"

Old-timer Tim Sullivan hands down the story that 1885 was also one of the last years of glory for another branch of the local fire service. Alert Hose Company, still volunteer, its high-wheeled hose cart still drawn to fires by a dozen pairs of brawny arms, went to a state firemen's convention that year and set a national speed record. Its crew, says Sullivan hustled the cart 300 yards to a hydrant and had their line in operation within 39 seconds. This was real sprinting. Perhaps they were helped along by the new $500 cart purchased that year.

Veteran of many races with such old "musheens," James V. Tisdall, one of the last volunteer Chief Engineers and also San Jose's first Chief of Police (1874), was buried on April 19. The Fire Department adopted a resolution to attend en masse the funeral of "our late brother," copies of the resolution to be "spread on the Books of the San Jose Fire Department." Regrettably, those "Books" have not survived.

In June 1885, the last of the volunteer hose companies petitioned the City Council for admission to the department's unpaid ranks. Known as Relief Hose Number 5 (the 5 was soon dropped), and set up to replace the defunct Protection Hose—which had disbanded in 1883—the new company took over the 8th and San Salvador Street site and operated there for 3½ years before being granted further "admission" into the professional ranks as a paid outfit. The company remained in this vicinity, later becoming Chemical 3, for sixty years. In 1889 and again in '91, the Council's Fire & Water Committee recommended removal of the Relief Hose House to Park and River Streets, but this was never done. When Relief Hose finally moved a couple of doors up 8th Street in 1898 to make way for a short-lived kindergarten school project on the corner, its old house was simply sold—for $30.

The Chinese Must Go!

Looked at a little more objectively than through the disgusted gaze of John Cunan, San Jose's Chinatown of the 1880's was a fascinating place. This was no slicked-up tourist trap of the modern sort, but a jam-packed, ramshackle segment of the Mysterious East itself — set down in the midst of a Spanish pueblo, crowded in on every side by the enterprising Scottish and German merchants. Its closely-built rabbit warrens defied conventional street numbering systems, being identified simply as "No. 2 (wood), Chinatown," or "No. 8, (brick) Chinatown."

The San Jose Civic Art Gallery is now located at Market and San Fernando Streets. Before the building was built there existed a north-south alley about 25 yards east that was known as Ah Toy Alley, leading back into the shadows teeming with pig-tailed Celestials.

Needless to say, the substantial citizens of the day considered all this a loathsome slum crying out for urban renewal. This was the era of the Exclusion Laws. The railroads were built, coolie labor was getting in the way of white prosperity, and in California the cry was raised: "The Chinese Must Go!"

It was thus a happy coincidence, one Wednesday afternoon in May 1887, that fire mysteriously erupted from a vacant store along Chinatown's Ah Toy Alley. By nightfall, after struggling for hours with "poor hose" and "low water pressure," firemen had been able to save only the real estate and the brick walls.

There was still the maze of shanties known as Wood Chinatown, straggling along Market

Chinatown in the 1880's on South Market Street between San Fernando and San Antonio Streets.

1887 Chinatown on Market Street between San Fernando and
San Antonio. These tinder dry shacks created a fire storm.

The Ruins of Chinatown after the fire.

Street south to San Antonio. Late on July 30 fire cleaned out this section also.

That left the Chinese community free to seek new quarters conveniently far from the center of town. They "chose" what became known as Heinlenville, around North 5th Steet between Jackson and Taylor, which soon grew into one of the largest Oriental settlements on the Coast. Faded and shrunken now, with its most colorful and historic buildings bulldozed away in the name of progress, it is still the hub of San Jose's Oriental community.

As far as firemen were concerned, the move meant no decrease in Chinatown's combustibility—the department just had to travel farther to fight the fires. From 1897 to 1899, for instance, there were at least five major blazes there, at which Empire Engine was on the job as much as 13½ consecutive hours.

Not that Caucasian residents were immune. After the fire of '83, Albert Lake had rebuilt his San Pedro Street box factory. Hallowe'en night of 1887 was enlivened by its burning down for the second time. Box 2 was transmitted at 9:30 p.m.; this was before the two tap signal was reserved for "fire out" and box numbers below 4 were abolished.

San Jose's German settlers had their turn early Sunday morning, May 6, 1888, when Germania Hall was destroyed. Formerly the "San Jose Turn Verein Hall," it stood on South 2nd Street near San Fernando. Proximity to Empire Engine House didn't help any, though, because at the time of the fire that engine was out of service for repairs.

"The Vile Work of an Incendiary," proclaimed the San Jose Daily Times, pointing out that the fire had appeared to start simultaneously both inside the building and out. Spreading rapidly from the stage through walls which had never known firestopping, the blaze was impossible to control. Of the German-American society's theatrical gear, library, musical instruments, and other paraphernalia, nothing was saved but a billiard table. Fortunately, the wind was light, and there was only a vacant lot to leeward.

Never bashful about criticizing firefighting operations, the Times editor complained of "a little lack of judgment on the part of the chief engineer in handling what streams he had at his disposal." Chief Brady had few enough. Not only was Empire out of service, but half an hour after the fire started, the Torrent

engine burst a boiler tube and was likewise put out of action. Torrent's old Clapp & Jones steamer had been breaking down for years; time and again during the '80's Empire was the "only company in service."

Such undependability had gone too far. In September, 1888, a new $4500 Silsby steamer arrived for Torrent No. 2, putting Empire's Amoskeag in the shade for a while—a discouraging development recorded without comment in the fine copperplate script of Foreman J. F. Dwyer of Empire Company. John Cunan, holder of Empire Company Badge No. 1, Assistant Chief during part of Chief Brady's tenure, and staunch chronicler of Empire's exploits, was gone. Many years later, his son Joseph would carry on the tradition by becoming Chief of the short-lived East San Jose Volunteers.

Into the Gay Nineties

That complaint of "poor hose" at the big Chinatown fire must have had some foundation. Firemen fighting the Lion Brewery fire on July 31, 1888, were reportedly "retarded in their work by the bursting of hose." The fire started late in the afternoon in a barn behind the home of blacksmith Thomas Carroll, on 3rd Street just below William. Flames soon involved the adjacent brewery on William Street, abandoned for over a year, and it was burned to the ground in an hour with a loss of $7000.

An alert Times reporter saw quite a sight while hastening to the scene soon after the alarm. But his description the next day was restrained: "As hose cart number 2 [probably Torrent's] was on its way to the fire, a man who gave his name afterwards to the police office as Jim Murphy persisted in seating himself on the hind box, thus causing the shafts to be unduly elevated, and ultimately the belly band was broke. He was urged to get off and persistently declined . . . " When profanity failed, the exasperated driver flicked his unwelcome passenger's hat off with the whip—"but he hung on." At last Mr. Murphy tumbled heavily to the ground as the lurching cart sped on its way, bruising his arm, but "being much in liquor," he felt no pain. In a triumph of understatement, the reporter closed by opining that the sodden Mr. Murphy "did not appear to belong here."

Chief Brady was replaced several months later. Rudolph Hoelbe, one-time assistant to Chief W. D. Brown, took over in January

1889. It was an eventful year for the department. In February, the City Council approved the removal of Alert Hose Company from its West Santa Clara Street stables to Rick Donavan's stables on San Fernando Street (not long afterwards, the company was disbanded).

Another change that year was the building of the Franklin House—new quarters for Franklin Engine No. 3, elegantly faced with the same Graystone Quarry sandstone later used to sheath the Post Office (later the main Public Library). Franklin now had a "new" steamer, having inherited the 1874 model cast off by Torrent Company. Building of the "new" City Hall in 1889 allowed Torrent to take full possession of the 1855 edifice on North Market Street.

Major fires were no more frequent than before, but for the next few years they were almost all in the downtown "high-value" district. George McKee's paint factory on San Fernando Street burned on March 24, 1889, followed in July by the $8000 destruction of Enright's Foundry on South 2nd. Box 37 summoned firemen to the Arguello Block at First and San Fernando in April 1890, where flames wiped out the Casino Saloon, Hearker & Spencer's general merchandise, and several other firms. Two months later a $4000 blaze gutted the American Bakery on West St. John Street, where the main Post Office later stood.

Early on a cold January morning in 1891, sleeping firemen in the Empire engine house were roused by shouts of "Fire!" Only a block away, flames and smoke poured from the windows of the Central Lodging House and Saloon on East San Fernando Street near First. Before dashing to the scene, the Empire men turned in the telegraph alarm from the engine house—but it failed to register. "Where are the others?" was the cry as they manned two lines against the spreading fire. A firefighter finally had to be sent to a nearby box to turn in another alarm, which brought some help.

The delay had fatal consequences. Searching the ruined buildings at dawn, firemen discovered a man's charred remains upstairs; about 8 a.m. a second corpse was found. Both buildings were total losses.

This disaster can be called the worst, but fortunately the last, serious failure of the alarm system. On May 1, 1891, a new Gamewell hookup went into service, the fruit of years of trial and tribulation with makeshift arrangements.

Next time you pass the tiny tree-shaded island of park dividing Market Street at San Carlos, take a look at a key part of that 1891 fire alarm system — the headquarters bell, silent now for more than fifty years. San Francisco's Globe Brass & Bell Foundry cast the big bell in July 1891 from 3000 pounds of bronze and silver. It was hung in the old tower at Torrent Engine's Market Street quarters, somewhat relocated when that building was replaced in 1908, and was finally taken down in March 1937 after its 80-foot belfry had become a termite-ridden hazard. Only by a narrow margin did it escape being sold for scrap.

Less than two months after the Central House tragedy, fire struck at 3rd and Santa Clara Streets, on the ground floor of the Odd Fellows Building. This was Ford & Nolting's grocery store. With a casual abandon that would give the shivers to any Fire Marshal today, the proprietors had fitted out a back room for the storage of coal oil and the new "gasoline." Not surprisingly, it was in this room that the fire started, about 3 p.m. on March 14. Flames shot from windows on the 3rd Street side, lapping into the hall upstairs and burning off most of the roof. The loss totalled several thousand dollars.

There was some delay in response to this fire, but not through faulty telegraph signals. Even at this late date, the fire horses were still used for other municipal purposes during the day when the need arose—as it had a way of doing when streets were being surfaced or there was garbage to be collected. When Ford & Nolting's burned, only Torrent Engine had its horses in quarters. All the other company teams were out hauling dirt and gravel "at a distance from their houses."

The boys had a chance to do better on July 6. At the same downtown corner, across 3rd Street where the YMCA was later erected, a conflagration erupted late at night when the horses were all at hand. Everybody arrived promptly (except Franklin Engine—its driver, Jim Kell, fell down the pole hole and was badly hurt). Nevertheless, an entire row of buildings went up in smoke; a stove shop, Appleton's Furniture, a laundry, notion shop, and residence, for a loss of $25,000.

About this time, somebody in San Jose either developed a love for fires or a hatred for horses. He began keeping firemen on the jump during the spring of 1892. After two

Smile, You're on Candid Camera—Haybarn at 11th and St. James burns, 1910.

unsuccessful arson attempts on a Mr. Moorehead's property at what is now Santa Clara and Montgomery Streets (then just outside the city limits), his third try succeeded admirably. Destroyed after midnight April 22 were two barns with 75 tons of hay, four horses, a wood and coal yard, and two houses. Further west, on Sunol Street, a barn and seven horses were destroyed in a $4000 night fire in May. John Devine lost his barn and team, with 50 tons of hay, about midnight on May 12, on East (now Montgomery) Street near Park Ave.

In the Fall, another series of barn blazes— all of them between 11 p.m. and dawn—resulted in $10,000 loss. October 13, 8th Street near St. John: a barn, four horses, a calf, 200 tons of hay; October 29, northeast corner 4th and Santa Clara: "Horse's Home" livery stable destroyed with two horses, two stages, five buggies, and several other vehicles. Before that one was even out, bystanders spot-

ted a glow in the sky which sent firemen galloping to Frank Brown's barns on North 7th Street near St. James. The department's hose carts were now half empty, and while firemen frantically tried to piece together enough hose to reach the fire, the barns were destroyed—with 25 tons of hay, two horses, and a goat.

Some tons of hay had been saved at the "Horse's Home" blaze. On the night of October 30, the incendiary struck again to wipe out this remainder. March 9th and 10th, 1893, brought more barn fires, one on North First Street, the other immediately afterward at 7th and Martha. Burned down were two barns, with five horses, a phaeton, and some hay. The luckless Enterprise Bakery at First and Willow lost its barn and four horses—and repeated the process within two months. So it went for almost two years, with no record that the alleged arsonist was ever brought to justice.

Besides arson and spontaneous combustion in hay barns, there wasn't a great variety of fire causes in those days. Reading through the old records one finds a monotonous repetition: "lamp explosion," "overturned oil stove," "lighted candle," "dropped lamp." But new headaches were beginning to appear; gasoline in the grocery store, or the newfangled electric lights in homes and offices. "Defective wiring" would become universal. T. W. Hobson's clothing store on West Santa Clara Street was damaged February 4, 1892, by a "fire which broke out during the night caused by spark from electric light."

But the worst fire the Garden City has ever experienced, a conflagration which was to devastate a square block complete with firehouse, was caused not by something new but by a deadly combination of old familiar hazards: Chinese fireworks, and a cigarette.

Engine 1's home on North Third Street, mid-1893. Hose Cart Driver is Jack Kent. Standing in front of the steamer, from left: John Gilleran, Jim Glynn, Arthur Brownell, ... Chappell, Engineer Jack Hamblen, and Joe Wampach (who became Foreman in January 1894).

1892
Fireworks On A Grand Scale San Jose's Worst Fire

It had been a busy Spring for San Jose firemen. Two months of burning barns, then in the small hours of May 15 poor Albert Lake's box factory burned again for the third time. This did not put an end to Lake's twenty years of making boxes of "Mahogany, Spanish Cedar, and other Fancy Woods." But it did result in the Fire Department's seeing to it that his establishment was equipped with its own fire alarm box—No. 51. Besides those at the fire stations themselves, it was one of only two building alarm boxes in the city (the other being at the Notre Dame Convent).

Worth $20,000 but only insured for $6000, Lake's corrugated iron structure was a total loss. Firemen of Empire Engine worked at the scene for almost 11 hours.

As the Fourth of July approached, enterprising Jake Faubel, a shooting gallery proprietor on the north side of San Fernando Street between 1st and 2nd, rented out part of his place to a Chinese fireworks merchant. At the dinner hour late Saturday July 2nd, an unidentified boy flipped a cigarette butt into the fireworks display — which erupted with most satisfying pyrotechnics.

Within minutes Faubel's building was a mass of smoke and flame. The alarm was given at once. But a rising west wind spread the blaze from building to building, beginning with a row of shacks behind the San Fernando Street premises, where boxes and other trash were piled in profusion. Curious crowds gathering in the downtown area soon saw that a conflagration was in the making.

Across San Fernando Street to the south, intense heat blistered walls and roofs. Firemen succeeded here in a desperate battle to keep the fire from extending in that direction, but even as they were winning here, the fire to the north attacked the rear of the Lick House Block facing on First Street (site of today's Security Building). Frantic groups of volunteers shuttled in and out of the adjacent First Street business houses, removing what goods they could before smoke and heat drove them away.

On the west side of 2nd Street, Martin and Downer's magnificent $50,000 California Theater, only recently renovated, roared into flame as the wind suddenly veered to the northeast. Nothing was left standing but the front wall; there was no insurance. Spreading towards Santa Clara Street, fire destroyed half a block of stores and saloons before being stopped largely by a vacant lot and another shift in the wind.

Firemen were now split into two isolated groups, one on First Street and the other on 2nd, because heat along San Fernando made passage all but impossible. Only one avenue of communication was open, through the corridors of the Letitia Building which escaped the flames.

Also hampering the struggling firefighters at every turn were crowds estimated to contain most of the city's population plus many from the suburbs. While many did yeoman work in saving goods from threatened stores, others turned to looting in the general confusion. Police eventually had to rope off the entire area. At one time, firemen manning a line on the Letitia roof were surrounded by spectators.

Salvation of that building was aided by one measure seldom employed in today's firefighting. Finding enough water somewhere, somehow, bystanders used a truck-load of flour contributed by Charles Bernhardt to make up a ton or so of paste. Plastering this goop over the outside of the building, where the heat was the greatest, "had a salutary tendency," according to the San Jose Mercury. One of the lodgers in the Letitia had returned to the building after once leaving, thinking he had been prematurely alarmed, but (reported the Mercury) "he changed his mind again when he saw the building being frescoed with Bernhardt paste, and again vacated."

Another downtown resident, packing his underwear on the upstairs porch of the Richmond Building on 2nd Street, panicked at the outbreak of fire in a small rear shed. Shouting to a passerby to "put out the fire!" which little less than a three inch hose could have accomplished, he poured down a volley of oaths when that gentleman refused and went on his way.

Others wasted no time in profane exhortation. One young lady nearly broke her neck by taking the stairs four at a time on her way out. Her only injuries: a barked shin, and the loss of an uninsured bottle of "Laird's Bloom of Youth."

The fire hose was still "of very poor material"; a number of lengths burst, and there was none to spare. To add insult to this injury, the fire jumped 2nd Street less than an hour after the first alarm, to attack the Empire engine house itself. The steamer was hooked up to a hydrant in front of the building, but its hose lines were in use elsewhere and could not be moved in time. Driven away by heat, the crew were forced over to Santa Clara Street as flames roared down the east side of 2nd. One by one the WCTU restaurant, Brosius' bookbindery, a print shop, barber shop, plumbers, and laundry went up, and finally the imposing brick building of the Methodist Episcopal Church South on the corner of 2nd and San Fernando.

Second Street was now impassable, rolling flames and smoke boiling up from both sides. No more hose was available at the moment, so a bucket brigade was formed to wet down the smoking front of the Masonic Hall on the southwest corner of Second and San Fernando. Other volunteers rescued many of the Methodist Church's furnishings and piled them on the vacant ground at the southeast corner (where the What Cheer House had been torn down), only to have them ignited by radiant heat and destroyed.

The church's great steeple crashed into the street about 8 p.m.—not a single hose stream had been available to play on the burning structure. Firemen were reforming their lines to the east, where fire was extending rapidly towards Third Street. A row of cottages on San Fernando ignited, followed by the 2-story brick Belloli Building at the corner of Third. Houses and sheds along the west side of Third

blazed up. Two small streams were able to check further spread towards Santa Clara Street, a last-ditch stand being made in the iron works of Kuchenbeiser & Sons.

Darkness had now fallen, but all of downtown San Jose was lit up by the glare of flames rolling along "like a prairie fire." After Belloli's blazing walls collapsed into Third Street about 9 p.m., fire jumped the street into the A & C Ham Company's pork packing house, from which supplies of brine had been taken to wet down the walls of the nearby McKee paint factory. Showers of sparks rose into the night sky to rain down on lumber yards to the south and east.

The yards were saved this time, with the help of a hose line supplied by the private water system at the Dougherty planing mill, and the packing house was the last building to be involved. Some of the mob of spectators gathered at Third and San Fernando had narrow escapes as the front wall went down with a crash; several were struck with flying bricks.

Many others elsewhere suffered minor injuries. Miraculously, no lives were lost. During the successful struggle to save the McKee paint factory, employee Joseph Faull jumped from the roof and was borne away unconscious. Volunteer firefighter Abe Jones fell 20 feet from a ladder. Three regular firemen were hurt too, but the worst disaster to the department was the loss of Empire engine house to the flames—the first and only time a San Jose fire station has been destroyed by fire. Fortunately, someone saved the Empire company journal! The Hook and Ladder company had moved from its Second Street home to a new building on San Pedro Street behind the City Hall; otherwise its quarters would have been burned too.

Throughout the night, two blocks of smoldering ruins shot a fitful glare into the sky. Merchants who had begun hasty evacuation from the west side of First Street began to return. Next morning, most of the losses could be added up. More than 40 residences, factories, and business establishments had been wiped out with a total loss of $480,000, less than half of which was covered by insurance—including Faubel's $300 shooting gallery. Empire Engine put in 26 hours' service.

Activity on the West Side

After the embers of San Jose's greatest fire had cooled, one of the first orders of business was to find a new home for Empire

Engine 1. The best that could be done was to take over an old hotel on North Third Street near St. John, next door to the building where the Turn Verein group had moved after their fire of 1888. On February 15, 1893, after it had been made over to house Empire's horses and apparatus, the new "firehouse" went into service. The steamer itself needed some repairs, including a new boiler, having been damaged in the conflagration.

Chief Hoelbe stepped down in January, to be replaced by J. F. Dwyer. Once a member of Alert Hose, Dwyer had become an extra-man with Empire Company in 1887 after Alert disbanded, rising to the rank of Foreman within a year. After serving as Chief Engineer until Henry Ford replaced him in 1897, Dwyer was apparently the only man ever to leave that post to return to the ranks as a fireman.

Like many Chiefs before and since, Dwyer had to wrestle with the perennial problem of service to areas outside city limits. The suburb then most often in need of such service was a collection of stores and factories that had grown up on San Jose's far west side, especially after the coming of the narrow gauge South Pacific Coast railway, which was completed from Oakland through San Jose to Santa Cruz by 1880. Today, its route is followed by the Southern Pacific main line through west San Jose, and the SP passenger station stands where the old narrow gauge depot was once located. A landmark of this community was the Alameda Flour Mills, operated by Crandall & Son, in whose honor the area was known as Crandallville.

One of Crandallville's first serious fires occurred Tuesday night, June 29, 1893. Starting in (of all places) the bath room at the rear of Posky's barber shop on The Alameda, it raged through a house, Whitcher's wire fence factory, and the Excelsior Wood Yard. Several railroad cars were damaged. Although the fire was two blocks outside the city limits, its threatening size induced Chief Dwyer to send one steamer (Empire) out to bring things under control — which took three hours.

Empire Engine, along with the rest of the department, breathed a sigh of relief as the month of July, with its fireworks, brought no repetition of the disaster of 1892. They did have an anxious moment in mid-August, again on San Jose's west side. Late one Saturday evening, a passerby saw flames break-

ing through the roof of Frank McKiernan's hay, wood, and coal warehouse at Vine and Santa Clara Streets. Although the building couldn't be saved, firemen manning four hose lines prevented the fire's spread to an adjacent smithy, a woodyard, and a bakery. Supposedly tramps set the warehouse afire; McKiernan claimed that drunken hoboes had been arrested on his property several times. "They hang around in the vicinity and drink sour wine." (Have things changed so much in 70 years?)

A much less threatening fire, but nonetheless an historic one, turned out the men of Empire shortly before midnight on October 4, 1893. Upon arrival at the "Empire Street School" (Grant School), they extinguished flames attacking what they described as a "dwelling on wheels" parked nearby, the home of a Mr. Connelly. So far as we know, this was San Jose's first fire involving a trailer house or "mobile home"—the first of many to come.

The year 1894 brought a solution to the problem of dealing quickly with the small fires which constituted the majority of the 6 or 7 alarms per average month, without the labor of laying out large hose lines, or the resulting heavy water damage. Following the nationwide trend of the '90's, San Jose acquired its first horse-drawn chemical fire engine. Fitted with a pair of 80-gallon soda-acid tanks mounted fore-and-aft between the front and rear axles, Chemical 1 was one of the largest such rigs ever built, and the biggest ever used in this city. Rebuilt onto a succession of chassis after the department was motorized, it served for over forty years.

Another historic event was the longest out-of-town trip ever taken by San Jose firefighters on a mutual aid call. On April 16, 1894, fire in downtown Santa Cruz, 30 miles away, mushroomed into a conflagration which threatened to destroy the city's entire business section. San Jose responded to an appeal for aid, dispatching Franklin Engine 3 and Relief Hose Company to the Southern Pacific station where the apparatus was loaded on flatcars and rushed over the mountains to Santa Cruz. The two companies were instrumental in saving the Surf City. Next day, the Santa Cruz press carried accounts of "the trip of the San Jose firemen for the relief of this city."

Fortunately for Santa Cruz, the railroad was still in operation at that time. In July, a general railroad strike was called—a bitter struggle ended only by intervention of Federal troops. In San Jose on July 6, banner headlines proclaimed "Mob Rule," "A Human Blockade," "Men Lie on the Track for over Two Hours," "Train Stopped by a Child." Strikers allegedly derailed cars and spiked switches to tie up Southern Pacific operations.

In Chicago, fires had been set in the rail yards where 22 persons were killed during early July rioting. But the only major blazes here occurred after the strike was over. First was Fleiger's pottery works, on Autumn Street north of the railroad tracks (where the street no longer crosses). Insured for $28,500, the plant was a total loss after fire broke out at 2:30 a.m. on August 8. The second, a week later, was again in Crandallville. For the second time in ten years, two saloons were destroyed on The Alameda at the corner of St. Mary Street (now South Autumn).

The third was a big one. At 429-431 West Santa Clara opposite the foot of Delmas Ave. stood the Red Star Laundry, with Peter Baltz's two-story frame business block adjoining it on the east. The laundry had just closed for the weekend, at noon Saturday Sept. 22, and senior partner J. B. Leaman had gone to his nearby home after finding nothing amiss on the premises. Two hours later fire was discovered inside the laundry. By the time firemen got three hose lines into action the entire plant was burning, and in another quarter hour its front wall collapsed into the street. Leaman ran to the scene, to watch helplessly as flames wiped out his work of four years in a matter of minutes.

Radiant heat soon touched off the Baltz building, and the San Jose nursery to the west, both of which were gutted. The nearby Alameda Lumber Company ignited briefly. Destroyed in the Baltz building were three stores, a saloon, a lodging house, and a cigar factory. The total loss was almost $30,000.

"The Heathen Chinee is Peculiar . . . "

Lumber yards or mills figured in many of San Jose's large fires in those days—it was still true in the 1950's. Seventy-five years ago, there was a concentration of such places along Fourth Street, where at least four major yards extended along the three blocks from St. John Street to San Antonio and west to Third.

Largest was the Santa Clara Valley Mill & Lumber Company, with offices on San Fernando Street about where the California Book Co. stands today, and buildings and yards straddling that street. (Part of the old mill was incorporated into Brehm Bros. garage which opened in 1925 on the northwest corner of Fourth and San Fernando, and was razed in 1966 for a parking lot.)

It was this expanse of combustibles that had been saved with such difficulty from the conflagration of 1892. Unfortunately the mill was shut down for the night, with only a watchman in attendance, when at 12:15 a.m. on September 9, 1895, a small fire was discovered in Dr. C. K. Fleming's nearby barn behind a group of Third Street homes called the Reinhardt Flats.

Leaping from one building to the next, the spreading blaze ungulfed three of the four houses and then swept into the lumber company property. The watchman tried vainly to get his plant fire apparatus into action, but the fire was too fast for him and he had to run for his life. Firemen were confronted with a sea of flames, which raged out of control for two hours. Assistant Chief John Moore directed the department's operations until the following evening, Chief Dwyer being out of town. Lumber company properties across Third Street to the west were saved, as well as some of the buildings on the northwest corner of Fourth and San Fernando, but the loss still reached $100,000.

A huge crowd gathered, including a number of "visiting cyclists," here for bicycle events, who distinguished themselves in removing to safety the contents of exposed Third Street homes. Less honorable were the "salvage" efforts of looters who appeared in the crowded confusion at many large fires.

Most of the time they merely took advantage of a blaze after it broke out. But in 1895 came a pioneer effort in another direction— the setting of a fire to conceal theft already committed. It took place, appropriately, at the estate of former Judge F. E. Spencer, a charter member of Empire Engine Company in 1854, at 216 Autumn Street.

Living there with the Judge were his daughter and son-in-law, Dr. and Mrs. J. U. Hall. One evening in July, during Mr. Spencer's absence from the city, the Halls had gone out for a drive leaving their Chinese cook working in the kitchen. After their return at 8:30, Dr. Hall went to his upstairs room and found the door locked. It was hard to open, as if tampered with. He finally got in, lit the gas, remained for a few minutes, then turned off the gas and went downstairs. About 20 minutes later, while talking in the sitting room, the family heard peculiar noises overhead. Dr. Hall returned to his room to find the ceiling and wall ablaze as if fire were coming down from the attic.

Mrs. Hall had excitedly followed her husband upstairs when she learned their room was ablaze, bent on saving her jewelry. The bureau drawer containing her valuables was locked, and the key in its usual place, but when the drawer was opened a purse full of money was missing, as well as diamonds worth $1000.

Without further ado the family fled their home. The cook was immediately suspected, not having been seen since the Halls had returned home. After firemen arrived, someone spotted him among the throng of spectators on the spacious grounds of the house, but he disappeared before the sheriff and two deputies got there.

"The department responded promptly" to the fire alarm, but the attic and most of the upper story was destroyed. A confused mass of humanity milled about the darkened grounds, often breaking and trampling valuables that others had removed from the home. Fire loss on the uninsured property reached $5000.

This same cook, Jim, had acted suspiciously some weeks before. Awakened by the sounds of apparent prowlers, the family found him "pretending to be engaged in making a batch of bread in the kitchen." They thought this rather unusual, since it was 1 a.m. Jim explained it away, but it subsequently appeared he had even then been trying to make off with the valuables.

After the fire, officers searched for him in Heinlenville; shortly before midnight he was picked up across the street from the Spencer residence and jailed. No jewelry was found on him. He claimed to have left the house after finishing the dishes, returning when he heard the fire bell.

Says Superior Judge Marshall Hall, son of the Halls, "It is my understanding that they were never able to convict him or recover the loot. The next best accomplishment was to deport him to China. If my memory from childhood serves me correctly, there was a final postscript to the effect that he got into similar trouble in China and was beheaded."

The next several years were quiet except for a steady succession of blazes in the "new" Chinatown—which somehow managed to be old and decrepit as soon as it was built. There was one bad fire on the west side. Box 5 came in shortly after 10 p.m., Oct. 28, 1896, for the abandoned streetcar barns on West Santa Clara Street near Delmas Ave., being used as a blacksmith shop and hay storage. They burned to the ground. Two days later, the ruins blazed up again, bringing firemen back for four hours of mopping up.

With or without fires, the expense of running the Fire Department continued month by month, with major blazes serving to call attention to the need for still more expense. San Jose's fire protection was now a $20,000 annual business. New developments like the chemical engine, and the increasing need to regulate the construction and occupancy of buildings, were making the fire service too complex an operation for the Mayor and Common Council to administer along with the many other facets of city government.

To solve the problem, many larger cities had formed "commissions" to devote full time to governing their fire departments. In the spring of 1898, amid cries of "Cuba Libre" and "Remember the Maine!", San Joseans followed their lead by changing the City Charter to establish a Police & Fire Commission to take over public safety administration—to determine budget requirements, manpower allocations, equipment needs, etc. Few of San Jose's public agencies have been as important to the city's welfare, or as colorful in their contribution to its history. Fewer still are as thoroughly forgotten today.

Twenty dollars a month and all the beer you could drink . . . .

Bill Sullivan, Hook and Ladder Foreman.

Being a fireman before the turn of the century—anywhere, not just in San Jose—was a life of excitement, glamour, and adventure. It certainly wasn't just another job—not to the townspeople, in whose minds was the image of the intrepid rescuer rather than the loafing pinochle player; not to the small boys who had only a few down-to-earth heroes to worship; not to the men themselves, proud of their status, fully conscious of their prestige as defenders of community lives and property.

Furthermore, there was (paradoxically) in the little town of San Jose a community spirit not found in the big city that is San Jose today. There was more to this than a physical size small enough for a single downtown fire bell to bring out all the "call men." There was a common interest, a sense of belonging, that bound people together.

Such a spirit makes volunteer fire departments possible. That spirit doesn't decay just because fire protection problems outgrow the solutions a volunteer department can provide; yet without such a community spirit the biggest and best paid department will have a tough time coping with the apathy, misunderstanding, or downright hostility from the people it is trying to protect.

In San Jose, it was generations after the volunteers disbanded before the "volunteer spirit" disappeared completely. It has gone, now, leaving some conscientious firefighters concerned about the "public image" of their department submerged in an indifferent community. That this should happen at a time when the Fire Department's equipment, training, and professional standing are far above anything dreamed of 75 years ago, is ironic indeed.

Politics . . . From Mayor To Manager . . . 1898-1916

Probably no period in the San Jose Fire Department's history was so packed with turmoil as the years from 1898 through 1916. Those years saw two major reorganizations of the city government, with corresponding changes in the fire service. They saw a multitude of disastrous fires, including one in which there was greater loss of life than any other before or since. They saw new equipment, new firehouses, and expansions of the city itself which would not be repeated until the hectic years following World War II. Above all, this period witnessed the departure from active service forever of those faithful and devoted comrades-in-arms who had so long been the mainstay of every fire department—the fire horses.

William Osterman, first president of the 1898 Board of Fire & Police Commissioners.

The Commission Takes Over

The Board of Police and Fire Commissioners, reporting to the Mayor and Common Council, held full power over all operations of the San Jose Fire Department after the charter revision of 1898. During the next two decades its members were to include such civic leaders as Alex Hart, of department store fame; clothier J. S. Williams; realtor Victor Challen; and many others. For a while there was even a member with the intriguing name of James P. Sex. And somehow appropriate, too; as the Board became deeply enmeshed in town law enforcement it was increasingly involved in the problems of San Jose's "wide open" dens of iniquity.

But that's another story. On May 3, 1898, the newly organized five-man Board met for the first time. The Commissioners began by electing William Osterman President of the Board. Secretary was H. J. Martin; other members were E. P. Lion, W. H. Carmichael, A. McKenzie, and H. Drieshmeyer, Jr.

Next was the necessary re-appointment of all those Fire Department members who were to be retained in their jobs. Among them was young Henry Ford, who had been appointed Chief by the Council in 1897 after serving six years as Foreman of Eureka Hose. Other

routine matters included consideration of recent bids of around $16 a ton for supplying the Fire Department with ten tons of "egg size Welsh anthracite coal."

Then the headaches began. To wind up one of the last major squabbles over that perennial troublemaker, the fire alarm system, San Jose brought suit against S. E. Smith to recover $400 in legal fees the city had spent in the successful defense against Smith's earlier

Fire Chief Henry Ford, 1900.

The rambling Vendome Hotel on North First Street, where Fireman McDermott lost his life in 1898. Not a trace remains today of the elegant hostelry, torn down in the summer of 1930.

suit to restrain the Council from awarding an alarm system. The Commission had to oversee this unsavory mess.

In June and July of 1898, city ordinances were passed "making regulations concerning the erection, alteration, repairs, and use of buildings in the City of San Jose." Fire zones were thereby set up, which to this day are fertile ground for controversy—witness the recent arguments over revision of these zones to take in high value suburban property.

It was the Commission's job to enforce these regulations even to the extent of approving all permits for new or repaired buildings. Reports of the Board meetings include far more column-inches on building permits and inspections than about fire or police problems. Not only that; when the Commission was set up, electricity was still as much a novel and dangerous fire hazard as anything else. So the department of electricity, and the City Electrician, was placed under the Commission. Electrical inspectors' salaries were charged to the Fire Department budget. Building inspectors also reported to

the Commission. An ordinance was adopted by the Council "for the protection of property from electric wires and electric appliances," which drew a protest in 1900 from the Board of Fire Underwriters because it inadvertently failed to embody the former prohibition of tapping trolley wires for light and power.

One issue to come before the early Board is familiar to any fire official today. In 1904, Commissioners had to consider regulation of bicyclists who were "accustomed to follow in headlong flight the reels, trucks, and engines of the fire department to fires," keeping the drivers "in a state of nervous suspense." History does not record that then, as now, their efforts met with much success.

Meanwhile, there came the first of a series of fires throughout the city and its suburbs which were to test to the utmost the resources of the San Jose Fire Department. Late in the evening of September 27, 1898, a short circuit developed in the new-fangled electric lighting at the rambling, elegant Hotel Vendome ("Pride of the Section"). Smelling burning rubber in the second floor gallery, the night clerk sent a bellboy to investigate. En route, the boy was bowled over by night watchman Mat Dixon charging down the hallway shouting "Fire!"

Beginning in a fuse box, flames spread rapidly through the famed hostelry via the "flues" carrying wiring from floor to floor. Firemen might have gained the upper hand except for the alarm system; the clerk rang in three taps for a "still" alarm on the manual box, and the initial response was hardly adequate. Eventually a general alarm was sounded from Box 31 at First and Empire. The hotel's fifty guests were evacuated with much effort but no injuries—women and children in their nightclothes streamed out into the spacious grounds.

A large crowd gathered, for "The residents of this city were appalled . . . when a glaring red reflection on the cloudy sky and the sight of blazing roofs . . . told the story that the Hotel Vendome was in flames."

The usual "volunteers" from the San Pedro and Market Street saloons soon showed up, milling through the hotel's lower floors and tumbling heavy furniture down the stairwells to "save it" from the flames. Chief of Police Kidward caught one group of stalwarts about to tip an elegant upright piano over the balustrade. Two others were restrained from dumping a heavy bureau with plate glass mirror from a third floor window.

While these antics were in progress, the fire ate steadily into the upper floors, setting the stage for more tragic events. Around midnight, "a creaking noise was heard, and with an awful crash . . . the walls of the rear of the hotel . . . fell in, carrying the fourth, third, and second floors, which piled up in a confused mass on the dining room floor."

Eight firemen were caught in the collapse. Two of them escaped this time, only to die in action years later (Paul Furrier and George Welch). Extraman J. C. Nagle of Eureka Hose dug his way out of the rubble with badly scalded legs. But his companion Miles McDermott was not to be found. Next day, weary searchers finally located his body under twenty feet of debris.

Also a Eureka extraman, McDermott was a stonecutter by trade. The plight of his almost destitute family led to the formation in March 1901 of the Relief Funds of the San Jose Police and Fire Departments, two of the many organizations which over the years attempted to sustain the widows and children of those who gave their lives in service to the community.

Some of the conditions of employment in the Fire Department of those days ought to be noted here. Salaries fluctuated somewhat, especially (as will be seen later) for the higher officers. But during the Gay '90's the extra or call men received $15 monthly; later

In driver's seat is late Merle Gray, who was managing editor of San Jose Mercury Herald. Building in background was old Garden City Implement structure near present building at 284 So. Market Street. Fireman is Arthur McQuaide.

The Chief's buggy at Market Street, 1901, during Chief Ford's absence on sick leave. Note the old "knucklebuster" hydrant, common around San Jose until the late 1940's.

$20. These men formed the bulk of the department's manpower.

Normally they lived or worked near the firehouses. For example, Charlie Plummer was a call man for some time. Jay McCabe recalled that Plummer tended bar at Market and Santa Clara Streets. Said McCabe, "Many's the time I saw him run out with his bar apron flying and jump on the hose cart as it went by."

Call men drilled with their companies, and were selected in rotation for "nights to sleep in the house." Generally two men each night drew this duty in the downtown engine companies, supplementing the professional driver, engineer, and officer on duty.

Woe to the extraman who might be absent from his post without good reason. The case of one R. Bacigalupi, of Truck 1, was typical. At the Arcade fire in 1907, he toiled valiantly through the night until the small hours. There seemed nothing more for him to do by then, the situation being well in hand, so he went on along to his butcher shop to prepare for the next day's business. When his partner arrived to mind the store, he returned to the fire—to be curtly informed by his Captain "You have been replaced in the company." At a hearing before the Commission a month later, the luckless Bacigalupi was summarily dismissed from the department.

For the full-time force, typical salaries were: fireman $70 per month, Chemical Com-

pany captain $75, hose cart drivers the same, engineers $80, engine drivers $100. Offsetting their higher salaries, hose cart and engine drivers were obliged to furnish one and two horses respectively. Oddly enough, the Chief (who was furnished a buggy by the city but also had to supply his own animal) only received $50 monthly—perhaps his prerogative of being able to sleep at home rather than at the firehouse made him less deserving of other compensation.

As the century drew to a close, the smoke-eaters continued to earn their money. Early July 30, 1899, fire was discovered in the Castle Bros. warehouse on Ryland Street. The credit goes to Conductor Edwards of Southern Pacific Train No. 34 in the nearby yards, who became perhaps the only man in San Jose history to turn in a fire alarm by having it sounded on the locomotive whistle! The boys turned out of their Sunday morning bunks in good order, but too late—the warehouse and two adjacent freight cars on a rail siding were a total loss, $20,000 worth.

August was a hot month that year. Johnny Johnson lost his $200 barn complete with 321 tons of hay, on San Pedro Street between Fox and Ryland, on the morning of the 13th. It was the fifth big blaze in two months.

The San Jose Fire Department entered the 20th century with more than fifty men in service (including the extramen). No new companies had been added for some years, however, and the lack of modern equipment was now felt in several areas. In June 1901, a bond election was held to secure funds for municipal improvements; by December 15 a new Metropolitan steamer was placed in service with Empire Company.

Chief Brown Comes . . . And Goes

A change in command was also necessary by mid-1901. Chief Henry Ford, ill and out of action much of the time, was unable to sustain the burdens of his office. Casting about for an experienced replacement, the Commission came up with Dick Brown — a man destined to become San Jose's most popular fire chief, at the same time furnishing an outstanding example of some basic defects in the city's handling of its fire service.

Brown had served well in the Fire Department. But at the time of his appointment to its top command, he had not been a fireman for three years. Born and raised in San Jose, the son of W. D. Brown—Chief of both Police and Fire Departments in the '80's — Dick started his career as a bartender in the old Newland Hotel. At 23, he became an extra-man of Franklin Engine Company No. 3, and two years later was appointed Foreman. Soon afterwards, he quit to join the police force. A commanding figure, tall and heavily built (his father had been 6'7") Brown was pounding a beat when called upon to serve as Fire Chief.

Civil Service, of course, was far in the future. Knowing the upheavals which have disturbed the Fire Department in more modern times—the protested examinations, the wrangles over points on the eligibility list—one can well imagine the intrigues that must have revolved around appointments like Brown's. Charles Brodie, Ford's Assistant Chief since January 1, 1901, was passed over, as were all the officers and men of the Fire Department. Neither Brodie nor Acting Assistant Claude Everett were ever heard from again. So, good man that Brown was, and popular though he was with many, he would have his enemies.

About this same time, the Police and Fire Commission finally began to enforce the law requiring fire escapes on all buildings of three or more stories. Full compliance was expected by October 1. It was carefully pointed out that there would be "no favoritism" in the matter.

Richard Brown and Charles Brodie in 1900.

Another act of the Commission that year harked back to Miles McDermott's death at the Vendome fire. The Board organized the "Relief Fund Association of the San Jose Fire Department" to benefit families of disabled firefighters. An impressive souvenir booklet was published, of which a couple of copies have survived. Its pages carry fascinating pictures of the San Jose of that time, a few of which are reproduced elsewhere in this account. Accompanying the pages of saloon advertisements were blurbs for "The celebrated Old Joe's Steam Beer," produced by the Eagle Brewery, which reared its crenelated battlements where the Sainte Claire Hotel stands today. No all-digit phone dialing then; exchanges included Red, Black, Main, and (of all things) John. Fire alarm signals were simpler, too—3 taps or strokes of the bell meant a still alarm and also served as a noon signal. Two taps meant the fire was out. Three taps repeated three times was a call for the chemical wagon; two taps thrice repeated summoned the hook and ladder.

Companies, their locations, and equipment, were as follows: At Market Street headquarters, Torrent Engine 2, with steamer and hose reel; the Chief's buggy; and Chemical 1 with its two-horse hitch. On North Third

38

Street near St. John, Empire Engine 1, with steamer and hose reel. On San Pedro Street behind Headquarters, Hook & Ladder 1 with its Hayes aerial, on which the tillerman sat under the aerial ladder behind the rear wheels. Near Reed Street on South First was Franklin Engine 3, with steamer and hose reel. Covering the suburbs, we had Eureka Hose 1, North 8th, with its hose reel, and Relief Hose 2, South 8th, with a four-wheeled cart. In reserve were two engines and a hose cart. Scattered around town from Delmas and Santa Clara Streets to 14th and Jackson were 62 alarm boxes.

In the election year of 1902 a major political scandal rocked San Jose, and by the end of 1903 Chief Brown was in trouble. Formal charges against him were dismissed early the following year, but on September 12, 1904, he was again hailed before the Board. This time the accusations were:

1. Partiality and favoritism in treatment of men, in that he had failed to suspend Jos. O'Brien for drunkenness on July 4—though he had summarily fired Extra-man Jacob Walt (one-time Foreman of Franklin 3) for the same offense.

2. He was derelict in his duty.

The unfortunate O'Brien had missed the truck when an alarm called out his Hook and Ladder Company, later claiming to have been asleep and not heard the bell—though it was located directly overhead and weighed one and a half tons.

Actually, if Walt or O'Brien had been somewhat under the influence on occasion it would have been no surprise in those days of wide open and well patronized downtown saloons. And the boys were never above hoisting a few out behind the fire hall—as our illustrations will show. A 144-hour work week was enough to drive anyone to drink!

Firemen spoke on both sides at Brown's "trial"; Foreman Furrier of the truck company defended O'Brien, while George Hines and Bill Tennant spoke up for Brown. Tennant claimed O'Brien was not only drunk on duty but was still drunk later when reprimanded by the Chief.

All this did Brown no good. It was clear that he had done nothing more than warn the offending truckman, despite an earlier directive from Commissioner McCarthy that he "instantly suspend" any man found under the influence. This was enough for four of the five Commissioners, who had obviously been waiting their chance—they fired Brown out of hand. On the 15th of September, his

Cheers! More of the July 4, 1900, celebrants—Paul Furrier of Truck 1, Capt. Hogan of Chemical 1, and John Lavon.

George Hines, Fire Chief in 1904.

job went to a short, dapper little man with sweeping mustachioes: George Emory Hines, driver of O'Brien's company. Within a year, Hines died of a heart attack while visiting in Lodi. His funeral was the city's largest up to that time, with the entire Fire Department in his cortege. As Chief, he was replaced by George Tonkins.

It may have been that the "new" Commission (some offices having changed in the May election) was out to earn the praise re-elected Mayor Worswick had lavished on it in July. He spoke highly of the Board's having conquered the "lax business methods" of the former group.

East Side, West Side

Some other items of interest for 1904: the Jose Theater was built, on the site of the old Empire Engine house prior to 1892. The theater's interior appointments must have been unusual; it was inside the Jose that 18-year-old Carl Showalter, wearing roller skates for the first time in his life, set a world speed skating record of 2 minutes 26 seconds for a two mile heat in 1904. That year, San Jose's assessed valuation topped $16 million (1963 figure: over half a billion).

Franklin Engine had a mishap downtown; not the last of its kind, either. The company had been out on a run of some kind—apparently not a fire call—and were returning to quarters about 5 p.m. on a Sunday evening in June. Messrs. Walch and Doak of the Union Distilling Company happened to be aboard for the ride. On Market Street at San Fernando these passengers suddenly glanced up to see the San Fernando streetcar bearing down on them, the motorman frantically ringing his bell. "Whip up the horses!" they shouted to driver James J. Kell. But too late; they were struck fair and square, and over went the rig. Kell was knocked from his seat, but all escaped unhurt.

The East San Jose fire hall, on what is now S. 23rd Street. Equipment was limited, but there was no lack of enthusiastic volunteers. At left, the new Carnegie Library, now a branch of the San Jose Public library system.

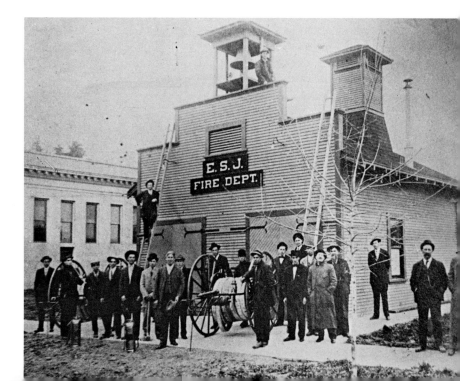

Burning of the Fredericksburg Brewery on Cinnabar Street, Sept. 1902. Minus most of its architectural trimmings, the brewery is still in use by Falstaff today.

Just outside the western city limits, the previous month, there was another serious fire which helped launch a 20-year campaign to annex those areas to the city. Buildings had burned in the old Agricultural Park Fair Grounds, where Barney Oldfield raced on "The Coast's fastest track"; another blaze caused heavy damage in September 1902 to the medieval Fredericksburg Brewery (begun in 1869) just off The Alameda. During this fire the great turreted tower of the malt house collapsed across Cinnabar Street. In May, 1904, it was the Notley Woodyard on Park Avenue at the narrow-gauge tracks.

Only force available to deal with this fire, as well as the others mentioned, was the forlorn reel of the Crandallville Hose Company.

This outfit, also known as the West San Jose Fire Company, or West End Hose Company (it had more names than rigs), was an on-again off-again volunteer group having a fire-hall near what is now the Southern Pacific passenger station. The present day Crandall Street—one block long—commemorates the little business and residential area which furnished its manpower.

They didn't make it to Notley's until after the office was ablaze, and could do little even then—having neither pumper nor hydrants at their disposal. One futile stream was produced from a pump at the nearby "electric light works," demolished in the early 1960's after long service as a P.G.&E. substation. Notley's coal bins flamed fitfully throughout the night.

Later that year the West San Jose boys undertook to remedy some of their deficiencies, requesting the Fire Commissioners' permission to purchase some old SJFD hose. Presumably, any hose they used would be subject to so little pressure that it wouldn't be necessary to get the very best grade. (Four years later, the group had a Chief, J. A. Meinan, and 27 members, and was trying to arrange for the sounding of fire alarms on factory whistles because the distant fire bell was too often mistaken for nearby narrow-gauge locomotives.)

In the Spring of 1905, San Jose's Chamber of Commerce was pushing hard for annexations of such outlying territory. The Chamber pointed with something less than pride to the city limits which hadn't changed in 25 years—think of it!—half the community's population now lay outside those limits. They hoped for April elections to bring in East San Jose (they were six years too early), the "Willows" (not for another 30 years), the open land north to Gish Road, and the area out along The Alameda (20 years away).

The campaign fell flat, and the city remained as it was. In the Fire Department, morale declined as equipment and stations decayed, and political upheavals continued. As yet, however, it was hard to point to loss of firefighting efficiency. At any rate the boys had plenty of practice.

A typical stunt to keep them on their toes was the test alarm, like that staged by the Commission late one evening in June 1905. Gathering secretly in front of the City Hall, members of the Board stationed themselves as "sentries, watch in hand . . . at the entrance of each street, watching for the first flash of the fire lanterns, which would signal the oncoming wagons." At a given signal, Commissioner Hambly pulled the box. "The chemical wagon got the start, and with but two turns to make the big black horses were drawn back on their haunches in front of the City Hall just one minute and 50 seconds from . . . the alarm." Torrent Engine 2 was next in two minutes flat; then Empire 1 in 2 minutes 25 seconds; then Franklin 3 in 3 minutes 20 seconds; Hook & Ladder 1, 2 minutes 15 seconds; Relief Hose, 3 minutes 15 seconds. Evidently Eureka Hose, with its new "combination" wagon, was spared the effort, being so far away.

Chemical 1's time was a new record. It's interesting to speculate on how rapidly to-day's equipment could make that run— the horse-drawn rigs beat the first chain-driven motorized equipment all hollow in tests before World War I.

August 1905 brought one of the first steps in department modernization. Empire and Torrent Engines each placed a four-wheeled hose wagon in service, superseding their two-wheeled carts. Such wagons were only now becoming popular, though San Jose had one as far back as 1874, and Relief Hose had the first one in the paid department well before the turn of the century.

For one thing, they could carry more hose. For another, they could carry much else besides. When long hours of pumping at a major fire exhausted a steamer's coal supply, the hose wagon was sent to bring more from the one-ton supply kept at each engine house.

Finally, as Charlie Plummer — Torrent's hose wagon driver — soon discovered, they were just the right size and shape to carry a mattress and set of springs slung underneath. Detailed at the larger fires to stand by for coal hauling and to care for the company's horses, Charlie slid his bed out from under the wagon and was able to "stand by" in comfort!

One of the first big blazes after Plummer's entry into the professional ranks began at 4:30 on the cold morning of November 10, 1905, apparently touched off by some sort of explosion in the engine room of the San Jose Rail Road carbarns at South First and Oak Streets. The engine room had been used as a

powerhouse until 1901, when the streetcar company shut it down and began to purchase its power. (The concrete foundations of the boilers could be seen for years afterward among the weeds just off Oak Street; the property later became a lumberyard and is now occupied by a Safeway supermarket.)

All power was off in the barns, where 26 streetcars had been put away for the night. As smoke poured from the boiler rooms, Watchman Louis Southwick ran to the phone to call the Otterson Street power house of the United Gas and Electric Company. Workers there closed the breakers in response to his desperate request for electric power so the cars could be removed to safety. But the circuits were shorted somewhere, and everything tripped out. Southwick then phoned for Franklin Engine. Fire began to sweep into the car barns as the first bell strokes boomed out Box 39. Chief Tonkins soon arrived and pulled the general alarm. Rhapsodized a Mercury reporter, "Sleepy firemen on the clanging, bounding hose wagon glanced at the great glare and buttoned their coats uneasily."

It was a quick burner. Not a car or a piece of machinery was salvaged as the barns were levelled to the ground; the loss totalled $136,000. Cause of the fire was never discovered, although a nearby resident reported seeing a man run from the building and disappear down Oak Street immediately before discovery of the fire.

During 1906, the continuing growth of San Jose's fringes across Coyote Creek resulted in the incorporation of East San Jose as an independent city. A fire department was soon organized there, with a little station on Adams Ave. (now South 23rd Street) behind the lot where the East San Jose Carnegie Library was built the following year. Chief of the volunteer department was Joseph Cunan, son of the Empire Foreman of the '80's.

Truck 1 on South Market Street about 1908. Building alongside was the old San Jose Auditorium, about opposite the rear of the UA Theater of today.

EARTHQUAKE!

On April 18, 1906, San Francisco's devastation by earthquake and fire overshadowed the smaller-scale damage to Peninsula communities, but San Jose took its share of the beating. It was many days before full newspaper accounts appeared locally. Even then, some of the most important happenings here were passed over lightly in the general confusion.

Luckily, San Jose's water supply remained intact, although fire alarm circuits were scrambled. However, Fire Department operations were in chaos from the outset. Hook & Ladder 1's quarters on San Pedro Street collapsed in a shower of bricks, putting the company out of service and killing Foreman Paul Furrier as he fled the building. A chimney fell at the former Eureka Hose house on North 8th, now re-named Chemical 2. The doors of Relief Hose Company's South 8th Street station jolted open and the horses dashed into the street in terror, a scene which was repeated at most other firehouses.

Reserve apparatus was hastily rounded up and stationed at strategic points. The former City Hall serving as quarters for Chemical 1 and Engine 2 lost most of its upper works; it was necessary to relocate the chemical wagon to Market and Devine Streets. Engine 2 moved temporarily to an empty barn, while its hose wagon took a position at Market and San Carlos.

Meantime fire was breaking out downtown. The three-story Market Building, 71-79 South Second Street, collapsed and caught fire at once. Next door to the North was the Lieber Building, next to burn. The new 5-story Dougherty Building followed, for a loss of $100,000; then the 3-story Louise Building at the corner of San Fernando—where the flames were finally halted. Total damage in the city ran into the millions, much of it from the spectacular destruction of this half-block.

This conflagration, plus the shaking-down of many buildings around the city where fire did not break out, completely obscured the small fire which cost more lives than any other in San Jose before or since. Even the address of this blaze was omitted from contemporary accounts. A Mercury extra of the 18th reported it to be the El Monte lodging

Quarters of Hook & Ladder 1 on San Pedro St., where Foreman Paul Furrier died in the 1906 earthquake.

house on Locust Street; a week later it was a "cottage" in the Second Ward ignited by an overturned lamp. At any rate, seven occupants in the building were burned to death.

Downtown there were some narrow escapes. Firemen Terry and Narvaez of Franklin Engine 3 were later commended by Chief Tonkins for thir rescue of a woman from the Dougherty Building.

At 6:30 p.m. on the day of the 'quake, the great fire bell sounded 11 taps repeated in quick succession: the militia call. San Jose was put under martial law. Residents were forbidden to light fires in any buildings with broken chimneys. Total "damage" to Fire Department buildings and equipment, including immediate repair needs as well as some deficiencies of long standing, was later set at $59,450; nearly a mile of hose was lost.

Once things were under control, so the story goes, at least one San Jose fireman volunteered for service in San Francisco where fire continued to spread. He was Frank Albert, reportedly a driver for Empire Engine, who drove his team to the city to see what he could do. Albert was stricken with typhoid, but recovered, living to the ripe old age of 72. He left the San Jose Fire Department in 1913 after 8 years' service—at the age of 23! During the following weeks "considerable credence" was given to rumors that the badly damaged Market-San Pedro Street firehouse

BLOCK ON FIRE—*Fire destroyed several buildings on the west side of South Second Street between San Fernando and Santa Clara Streets. This view is taken from the southeast corner of Second and San Fernando looking north.*

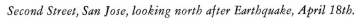

Second Street, San Jose, looking north after Earthquake, April 18th.

After the 'quake: April 20, 1906. Torrent Engine 2 and Chemical 1 pose outside the remains of the Market Street firehouse.

properties were to be sold. Proceeds from the sale would finance construction of a "large and up-to-date firehouse in the southern addition of the City Hall park" (in other words, about where the USO stood in more recent years). These reports, however, turned out to be 180 degrees off in direction and almost half a century off in time.

More immediate action was triggered by Chief Tonkins' "exhaustive report" of his department's actions during the disaster. In May 1906 the report reached the Police and Fire Commission, now headed by Chairman S. E. (Shirttail) Smith, well-known local haberdasher.

The Chief got right to the point: "I would respectfully recommend to the Commission that steps be taken as soon as possible to equip the fire department with more modern and powerful fire-fighting apparatus." San Jose then had a total force of 60 men, 17 horses, and 1½ miles of hose.

There were several immediate needs, besides the generally decrepit condition of the firehouses themselves—Chemical 2, over 30 years old ; Engine 1, a makeshift structure thrown together after the 1892 conflagration; Engine 2 and Hook & Ladder 1, wrecked by the 'quake. Chief Tonkins called for 4000 feet of new hose, one first size 1300 GPM steamer, one second size 700 GPM, and a "water battery" or monitor nozzle which could be attached to the aerial ladder for throwing water into upper floors.

Departmental Dry Rot

Meanwhile, the Commission also faced the problems of rebuilding the city. Hundreds of buildings had been damaged. Ruins of the Louise Building were a downtown eyesore for another two years. Each structure had to be inspected, and permits issued for repairs, or orders issued for condemnation. All this was under the jurisdiction of the Police and Fire

46

Commission. Groups of inspectors fanned out through the city for weeks, reporting their findings regularly to the Board.

On top of that, property owners were thrown into confusion over their legal rights to make repairs to currently sub-standard buildings which had existed before their sites were put within the "fire limits." The Commission had asked the Council to pass an ordinance permitting repairs to wooden structures inside the limits, announcing it in such a way that people took it as an accomplished fact—only to find the ordinance did not exist and their rebuilding operations were illegal.

While such matters were being thrashed out, Chief Tonkins had to make do with what he had until an election could be called to vote monies for the Fire Department. This was finally scheduled for June 25, 1907.

The weeks just prior to the election seem to have been taken up largely with disciplinary problems in the department. Araby Damonte, Hook and Ladder tillerman, was suspended in May for "conduct unbecoming a member of the department," and was hailed

before the Board for trial. Lack of Commission records for those years leaves us in the dark concerning his offense. Likewise we are not told why A. Fisher was suspended for "neglect of duty," or why the Board fired J. Williams.

But preserved for our enlightenment is the serious nature of the crime for which Engineer B. F. Conly was compelled to forfeit 60 days' pay. Some of the firehouse blankets had gotten dirty, and Conly took it upon himself to send them out to the Kelley Laundry for cleaning, not realizing the necessity of obtaining the required permission to do so. Chief Tonkins therefore preferred charges.

While this sort of thing occupied the back pages of the papers, the front pages were taken up with news stories and editorials exposing the pitiable condition of the Fire Department's stations and equipment as the outgrowth of community indifference. Voters were urged to approve issuance of bonds to correct the situation.

The North Third Street station drew especially heavy fire. Once a hotel, its main struc-

The San Jose of 65 years ago: looking north on Market Street from City Hall Plaza. In the distance is the electric tower, an ill-fated experiment in street lighting which blew down in 1915.

The same Third Street scene in 1908, with new apparatus and a new station. Hose wagon driver is unidentified; others are left to right: George Welch, George Perry, Engineer Frank Monroe, and Ed Waibel.

ture was of adobe. "An aged adobe shack," the press called it on June 11. Its front sheathed with "rotten boards," the entire building slowly "sinking into the earth," this was the home of "the one engine the city can count on." "Housed in this old adobe, it looks much as a diamond necklace would in a swine trough." The jewelry in question was the Metropolitan steamer Empire had placed in service six years earlier.

The other apparatus was of more venerable vintage. The Mayor pointed out that one other steamer in active service was 40 years old. Nothing had yet been done to provide a new home for the Hook and Ladder Company; available records do not state where it was

being housed. The damage to Market Street Headquarters had been "repaired" by removing the debris and using only the remaining lower story of the building.

The $95,000 bond issue was to cover a total of four new stations, including an entirely new company in the Fourth Ward—San Jose's near southwest side. There was $5000 for new hose; 100 hydrants; the "water battery"; and new steamers for Engines 1 and 2 plus a new ladder truck.

1907: The Long Hot Summer

The issue carried. And a good thing, too. If there were any voters doubtful of the need, they were provided with a number of clinchers during the remainder of 1907. The first one came on the foggy evening of June 7, only two days after the election.

About 7 p.m., a smoldering bale of cotton waste burst into flame in the rear of the Osen-Hunter Garage on the south side of West St. John Street between First and Market. Proprietor George Osen, pioneer automobile builder and noted cross-country cyclist of the '90's, proved himself no better than the average person in putting the fire out single-handed. By the time he was driven from the building, it was too late for firemen to save the structure.

Their efforts were hampered by continual gasoline explosions, and a mob of thousands who poured into the area. Some 40 of the bystanders did make themselves useful by helping wheel forty autos out of the blazing garage. Ten other cars were destroyed, being disassembled for repairs and impossible to move.

Firemen used six lines in subduing the flames. Open windows in the upper floors of an adjacent lodging house on First Street led to considerable water damage there, but the fire did not spread. The Chief and one of his men were knocked flat by one of the many explosions, but emerged none the worse for it. Five hours after the initial alarm, the "all-out" signal was given, and 56 firefighters made their weary way back to quarters. Total loss: $58,000.

The month of July was only two hours old when a blaze flared up in Chinatown. Box 61 was pulled as flames jumped from house to house over half a flimsily constructed block. At 4:10 a.m. came a special call for another engine; it was two more hours before the blaze was struck out. Cause of this fire was an overturned lamp in the house of the Wah Hing Tong, better known as the Chinese Wash House Owners Association.

Hose 1 in 1908, its new "water battery" polished to perfection. Driver is Charles Plummer.

Engine 1 at City Hall Plaza, about 1909. Driver is probably Tim Sullivan; just to right of unidentified mascot is Engineer McQuaide.

Loss was over $10,000, a good part of it in gold and silver coin which the Chinese, distrustful of banks, kept among their dwellings. San Joseans during the next few days enjoyed the rare sight of Chinese diligently raking over the ruins in search of treasure. The Secretary of the Wah Hing Tong recovered some $200 in melted coin.

Fire struck next at the corner of 6th and Santa Clara Streets, on the site later occupied by the Garden City Chevrolet showrooms. An imposing entertainment pavilion called the Princess Rink had been erected here the preceding Fall.

Claimed to be San Jose's largest building, the Princess seated 6000, treating them to the latest thing in automatic music-makers: a $3000 "orchestrion." Fortunately, there were only ten people in the building on the night of July 12, when the Princess caught fire. The cause remained unknown, although a vagrant tinner was caught by police after running from the rear of the building to take refuge under a nearby porch.

Rink Manager H. S. Bock heard "crackling" overhead as his staff prepared a movie for showing later in the evening. A boy sent to investigate found flames licking among the bunting-draped rafters, beneath the sheet-iron roof. Box 64 at the corner was pulled at once; but failed to function. Another box was later pulled two blocks away at 7th and San Fernando, but the delay was fatal.

When firemen arrived, the Princess was alight from end to end. Flames spread to J. D. Phelan's barn on South 6th; the San Fran-

cisco millionaire also owned the rink property itself, suffering a $16,000 dent in his fortune that night.

A crowd of 10,000 spectators hastily scattered when a hose stream got "out of control" momentarily to give some 500 of them a good soaking. One woman was knocked off her feet by the stream. Other ladies in attendance suffered damage to their frocks when one of the engines operating at the corner lifted its safety valve with a great burst of steam.

In August, the scene shifted back to territory more familiar to hard-pressed firefighters—Bassett Street. At 9 o'clock in the evening of August 3, a resident across the street from the California Fruit Exchange plant noticed sparks dropping from under the building's floor to the ground below. Box 23 was pulled, but the fire had too great a start. Flames, visible for miles, soared over the downtown area. Trees caught fire a hundred feet away. So did three houses across Bassett Street to the north. Firemen soaked each other's clothes as they dragged their lines in close enough to put water on the inferno.

Spectators in a vacant lot behind the packing house were scattered by the sudden spray from a hose stream, turned in their direction to stop an incipient grass fire. The water "struck in the center of a mass of people, scattering them in every direction . . . dresses were torn in the scramble."

While others might panic in the face of startling events, barber George Meisel set an example of coolness under fire—literally. His shop was located in a cluster of buildings where Hart's department store later stood. On the night of July 13, 1907, the chimney of the Royal Restaurant (24-26 South Market) touched off a roof fire that spread rapidly in concealed spaces above the ceiling of Miesel's establishment. A large crowd gathered as firemen worked to quell the flames. Through it all, Meisel calmly continued to ply his straight razor and shave his customers—who displayed plenty of courage themselves.

Haircuts, by the way, went up to 35c the following month; alarmed citizens threatened a return to the Chinese queue in retaliation. Other news items of the day: the "Sunset" automobile was rolling off a South First Street assembly line at the rate of 8 cars per month. An un-named motorist set a new San Francisco-Los Angeles speed record—just 7 minutes shy of 18 hours. San Jose was growing; Hanchett Park residences were going up, while inside the city limits General Naglee's old estate was being subdivided south of San Salvador Street.

By the time the long hot summer was over that year, San Jose firemen heard some long-awaited good news. Plans for a new Market Street headquarters station were accepted from Architects Wolfe and McKenzie on September 21. The Police and Fire Commissioners had brooded over the details for two weeks, then modestly announced that this building (to cost $27,000) would be "one of the finest fire houses in any city on the coast." Market Street frontage would be 80 feet, housing (left to right) Chemical 1, Truck 1, and Engine 2. Depth of the building would be 69.3 feet.

Upstairs — luxury appointments to dazzle the eye of the most sophisticated hoseman: a 24-man dormitory, reading room, and billiard room.

Architect Binder had his somewhat less luxurious plans accepted for new quarters to replace Engine 1's "adobe shack." Costing $16,000, its 40 x 45 foot structure was to have a steel frame with reinforced concrete walls. That's the way it was built, too, the first of a very few such firehouses ever built here, and the only one with a structural steel frame throughout—which gave the wreckers a job when the place was dismantled 48 years later.

To grace the interiors of these new stations, engines were purchased in the East. On order from Cincinnati's Ahrens Works was a First Size Continental, pulled by a three-horse hitch and weighing 8800 pounds unloaded. Pumping capacity was 900 gallons per minute (200 GPM better than the best of San Jose's older rigs). Featuring the latest design of electrically welded seamless boiler, this steamer was for service as Engine 1. Empire's old steamer, it was announced, would go to the new Fourth Ward engine company.

Exercising the horses: Mike Higgins takes his three-horse hitch for a turn around the old City Hall, almost 70 years ago, with the new Metropolitan steamer of what was then still known as Engine 2.

Here is the San Jose Fire Department's oldest piece of apparatus in active service: the 1908 "water battery" now mounted on today's Hose 3.

The other new engine ordered was an Extra First Size Metropolitan, by LaFrance—"bigger than any in San Francisco." With coal, water, and crew on board, this beauty weighed in at more than five tons. On its arrival at Market Street, the old apparatus there would go into reserve.

Those wonderful machines, of course, are gone now. What a pity one of them could not have been preserved in original form as a museum piece! But at least the department has kept in active service one other item of equipment purchased during 1907. This was described in September as "a recently invented device known as a water battery which throws a 2¼ inch stream 250 feet will arrive with the other fire engines and will be placed on the hose wagon in this section [at Market Street]." This was what Chief Tonkins had apparently planned to mount on the ladder truck.

In today's parlance, it was a monitor nozzle, or turret pipe, fixed to the bed of the hose wagon with several connections for hooking up hose lines. By means of elevating and traversing handwheels, the nozzle could be aimed over roofs, into upper windows, etc., to considerably extend the range and power of streams at large fires. Used for many years on a succession of hose wagons with Engines 1 and 2, it is now mounted on Hose 3 and has done good work at many a major blaze in modern days.

Unlike most newer monitors, this early model has a gooseneck type of joint requiring the operator to be fairly dextrous in simultaneous operation of both sets of handwheels to get the nozzle pointed in the right direction. Assistant Chief Cavallero reportedly had his troubles with the mechanism during the exciting hours of the Blum's fire in 1933, and wound up spraying water all over the area— "he had that nozzle pointed everywhere but in his ear," recalls one old-timer.

More New Stations

During the first week in October 1907, as financial panic gripped the country, the Commissioners approved George W. Page's plans for Franklin Engine 3's replacement station on South First Street. This one came to only $6000, even with inclusion of an unprecedented luxury: a kitchen. The lack of good restaurants in this outlying neighborhood was recognized as an inconvenience to firemen. It was customary for firemen on duty to be given "meal hours" during which they would repair to a nearby greasy spoon for their meals. Because this was difficult in Franklin's district, many of the men there had been cooking for themselves using makeshift facilities in the old house.

Also accepted were W. C. Phillips' plans for a new chemical house on South 8th Street, cost unspecified. Construction on this, and the Franklin house, was to begin within the week.

That week closed on a fiery note. Shortly before midnight on Saturday, October 5, fire was reported in the North First Street tomb-

Engine No. 1—The boiler on this steamer was made by the American Fire Engine Company. The Monitor (on hose wagon on the right of the picture) is still in use.

stone works of the Western Granite & Marble Company adjacent to the railroad tracks. The tall 15,000-square-foot structure, crammed with machinery and headstones, was a quick burner—along with an adjacent residence. Some furnishings were rescued, but the loss totalled $45,000. Suspicion focussed on stray locomotive sparks as the probable cause.

That explanation wouldn't do for the threatening downtown blaze the following Friday night, which gutted The Arcade, an elegant department store operated by a Mr. Stackhouse and the brothers Canelo — a 68-foot frontage at 83 through 91 South First, corner of San Fernando.

"Special Watchman" Rawler, patrolling the downtown area late in the evening, was trying the front door when he smelled something burning. Peering through the glass doors, he saw heavy smoke inside, at the northwest corner of the three story brick structure. As he watched, flames shot through the smoke. Almost simultaneously, some unidentified person turned in an alarm.

All three of the city's engines (including "the only one San Jose could count on") were soon working, eventually supplying 8 lines. Exposures were severe, including St. Joseph's Academy to the rear, which was damaged by water. All things considered, it was a real credit to the firefighters that the blaze was confined to The Arcade—the fire was far advanced before firemen were called.

A number of men were injured fighting the $20,000 Arcade fire. Fireman James Dwyer was knocked out by a falling beam. Chief Tonkins stepped on a nail and was out of action for several days. Assistant Chief John Cavallero fell unconscious, struck by a nozzle; Sam Terry of Franklin Engine cut his foot. The general alarm assignment took two hours to control the fire. The following evening, a hose wagon and the ladder company were called out against the threat of rekindle in the ruins.

Several days afterward, John Waibel complained to the Commission that he was running into unprecedented problems in removing the old Third Street engine house. He had gotten a $50 "award" to remove the building and clean up the premises for construction of the new house. Although the part-adobe construction of the old place was common knowledge, nobody had apparently realized that the main walls were adobe throughout instead of just on two sides. Demolition was proving tedious; the Commissioners extended their sympathy.

At the same meeting, there was a report from the committee of two (William McCarthy and Louis Henning) searching for a site for the new Fourth Ward station. Their recommendation was a lot on Spencer Ave., between Park and San Carlos, only a block from the Park and River Street location contemplated by the City Council in 1889.

Other business before the Board included setting "trial" dates for Extramen Bacigalupi and Wheeler, accused of "insubordination" at the Arcade fire (Wheeler left the State). Salaries of regular department engineers were reased to $100 monthly, and bids were received on a new Chief's auto. Osen-Hunter offered to take in trade the $750 machine "now in use," and would furnish the city an 18 HP Mitchell runabout for only $400 more. San Francisco's Maitland Co. offered a $1900 Clyde 1908 Model G.

The bids were rejected, for reasons unknown in the absence of any Commission minutes. But the Spencer Ave. firehouse site won approval on November 5. Also, Chief Tonkins reported a grand total of 10 box and 9 still alarms for the month of October. City Electrician John Guilbert advised completion of the task of removing all fire alarm apparatus from the old firehouses and transferring it to the "temporary" quarters used by the displaced companies while new stations were under construction. Some 2200 feet of new hose was purchased, and bids requested for 80 new hydrants.

Along with fire alarm circuits, downtown electric wiring in general came under review by the Commission that year. Throughout the country, urban areas had long since become a nightmare of wire and cable supported on tall poles, not only unsightly but hazardous. Burning buildings could not be laddered because of the interfering maze of curbside wiring.

It was first proposed in May that poles and wires go underground in San Jose. In November, the Commission adopted a resolution

Fire Chief George Tonkins

creating an underground wiring district. Included in the area were First Street from St. John south to San Antonio, Santa Clara Street from San Pedro to 4th, and several other neighboring bits of territory. As the resolution put it, the problem arose "because of the danger of buildings becoming ignited from such wires, cables and devices, and of firemen being prevented by such wires . . . from properly performing their duties . . . "

Contracts were let in December, 1907, for all the new stations. December 9: Market Street house, to Contractor J. C. Thorp on bid of $25,113; December 27, Z. O. Field got the Third Street job for $12,990, and Franklin (Station 3) went to Trace and Keith for $5350 (this job and the Chemical 3 contract had been held up pending resolution of high bids on Third Street). Early in January, the South 8th Street house — once Relief Hose, now Chemical 3 — went to Pawley and Son for $4289.

Last of the Steamers

Meanwhile, the new engines had been shipped West, arriving in San Jose on December 25, 1907—a memorable Christmas present for the department. Because engine drivers in those days had to provide their own horses, Ed Waibel at Third Street and Mike Higgins of Engine 2 were busy acquiring and breaking another horse at each location to fill out the three-horse span required by the heavy new apparatus.

The day before New Year's, city officials plus a large crowd of admiring bystanders gathered at the corner of First and San Salvador Streets to see the $6150 Continental put through her trial paces. Starting with a cold boiler, the steamer got up five pounds of steam in 100 seconds; 20 pounds in 2 minutes 55 seconds; 40 pounds in 3 minutes 55 seconds; and reached a hundred pounds in 6 minutes 10 seconds. After an hour's run in which she threw 1100 GPM a distance of 200 feet through two lines, at 220 psi., she was accepted for service.

A week later, the LaFrance Metropolitan (invoiced at $6325) was likewise tested, taking two minutes longer than the Continental to reach full steam pressure. Proud officials claimed that on the Pacific Coast there were only three equals to this new engine: one at Eureka and two in Los Angeles.

At the same time, they announced that a new hose wagon for Engine 2, especially designed to mount the "water battery," was being built in San Jose. February 24, a new 75 foot aerial truck from American LaFrance Fire Engine Co. was tested, and accepted on March 1 after repair of a couple of broken clutch dogs. Chief Tonkins himself paid a $28 freight bill on the $5172 rig; presumably the Commissioners reimbursed him.

Early in March 1908, the designs of Wm. Klinkert and Sons were accepted for the Spencer Ave. station. Bids were received in April, ranging between $4046 and $7597; later the low bidder discovered a clerical error and withdrew. The contract was awarded April 10 to Thomas Livingston for $6297.

Meanwhile construction proceeded at Third Street and on South First, as well as at Market Street where the cornerstone had been laid March 27. Contractors received payments of $8000 in April. On May 5, Chemical 3's completed quarters were accepted by the Commission.

Work was also going forward on overdue improvements to the alarm system. Seven new gongs, with meters and relays, were bought in April. The story of the weird and

wonderful development of that system over the years would make a book in itself, but unfortunately a great many of the details are lost to us. We do know that in 1908 the long-standing practice of leaving street alarm box keys in a "safe place" to discourage false alarms was still in vogue in San Jose. Normally the key was left with some trustworthy person living nearby; without it, the box could not be used. But in June, the obvious disadvantages of this arrangement were recognized. For $148.50, 54 glass-front "key guards" were bought from the Gamewell Co. for installation on existing boxes. New boxes to be ordered in future would already come so equipped.

Engine 3, as the Franklin Company was now officially known, also made some progress. While they didn't rate a new steamer, at least a brand-new $1420 Ahrens boiler was purchased to bring their old rig up to snuff. And on July 5, 1908, Franklin moved into a new building. This called for a celebration, an occasion to which the boys were more than equal.

Reported the San Jose Mercury next morning: "Yesterday afternoon and last evening members of Engine Company No. 3 entertained their friends at a 'housewarming' in celebration of their occupying the new firehouse . . . on South First Street." Chief

Tonkins and his wife were present for the program, featuring a choice selection of readings and musical numbers by members of the department. In those unsophisticated days before "canned" entertainment, such performances were popular fare. The numbers included:

"Fireman's Dream", violin solo,
                    L. "Lundfus" (Lunsford?)
"The Happy Engineer", German solo,
                    H. Drexler
"The Fast Horses", Irish dance,
                    J. Kell
"How to Run the Company"
                    Capt. "Teney" (Terry?)
"The Terrible Swell", short story,
                    Odie Plenton
"Coming Down Stairs, Won't Do It Again",
    song,   C. Rothe
"The Midnight Alarm", mandolin-guitar duet,
                    Ed Tobacties, Theo. Haub

As a grand finale, the boys staged a "pole drill" which was won by C. Rothe coming down the pole headfirst at high speed. Capt. Terry then presided over a banquet before the party broke up.

Not long after this, for more select audiences, the boys of Engine 3 devised further entertainments. Says Ralph Jennings, "The place was shaky—several fellows would get off in the next room, start rocking the floor, then holler 'Earthquake!' and run like hell!" This produced interesting reactions from unwary visitors with vivid memories of 1906.

Slaughter at City Hall

All was not yet rosy, however, in the San Jose Fire Department. Only three days after the Franklin House festivities, the leadership of the department from the Commission down was thrown into chaos by political upheaval only too common for the times. The newly elected administration of Mayor Davison, with a fresh Council, had gone into office, bringing the immediate resignations of both Fire Chief Tonkins and Police Chief Carroll. The entire membership of the Board of Police and Fire Commissioners was removed; three men resigned, and Mayor Davison promptly suspended the other two (Henning and Hambly).

It was at this time that Dick Brown, Fire Chief five years before, was returned to his former office. He had spent the interven-

Chief Richard Brown, whose years as the city's most popular Fire Chief ended with his tragic death in 1910.

ing years running a saloon of his own on The Alameda, then tending bar elsewhere.

In spite of his own honesty and popularity, the political axe continued to fall heavily among his men. A Mercury headline of July 23, 1908, proclaimed "Slaughter" in both police and fire departments, as wholesale demotions, transfers, and resignations took place. John Cavallero was reduced from Assistant Chief to Extraman, and (understandably) quit within a week—replaced by Joe McDonald, who himself didn't last long. Years later, it was left to Cavallero's nephew Dominic to carry on the tradition by serving as Assistant Chief for 20 years.

Araby Damonte was reduced from Tillerman on the Hook and Ladder to Extraman, and his place taken by former Extraman Walter Page—the initial step up the long ladder to the post of Second Assistant Chief which Page reached by the time of his death almost 35 years later. Frank Boronda was bumped from Captain to Extraman, Chemical 1, then resigned; William Tennant was busted from Fireman to Extraman; Charles Plummer from hose wagon Driver to Extraman.

Several men with years of good service, including D. P. Narvaez and John Humburg, were dismissed. Unwilling to submit without a fight, these few went to court in a valiant effort to save their jobs — an effort which succeeded after five years of what was said to be the bitterest legal battle ever fought in San Jose. Superior Court eventually upheld the rights of these firemen to their jobs and to more than $1000 each in back salary, in July 1913, after ruling that the charges under which they were fired were not properly filed until after the dismissals had been ordered.

Even the City Electrician, John Guilbert, was not immune. He was summarily fired in the Fall, for no stated reason; then evidently he was hired back, for he continued to report to the Commission in his official capacity.

About his time there was another major blaze on The Alameda, outside the city limits, which wiped out half a block of buildings. This resulted in a resurgence of fire protection activity in the western suburbs. Early in August, Crandallville property owners, 150 strong, "gathered at the hose house in the narrow gauge depot" to re-organize the West End Hose Company. No more of that second-grade castoff San Jose hose, either; "new and strong" hose would be needed. Besides Chief Meinan, a full staff included a Secretary, Treasurer, and Trustees F. Williams, I. N. Van Doren, lumberman S. H. Chase, and E. Cleaves (Cleaves Ave. perpetuates the name today). The volunteers held their first drill on the evening of August 11.

How successful they were in having fire alarms sounded on factory whistles generally is not known. But by October, some progress had been made; Chief Brown announced that alarm wires were run into the Temple Laundry and the Eagle Brewery, to activate whistles at those two locations — both, however, almost out of earshot of Crandallville.

On October 16, 1908, Commissioner Kidward finally made formal recognition of a long-standing anomaly in the numbering of the city's engine companies. Although Market Street was headquarters, located in the First Ward, and thus the logical location for the "first" among San Jose's steamers, the engine quartered there had always been known as No. 2. Historically, Engine 1, the old Empire Company, so numbered because it was founded first, had been located in the Second Ward.

Kidward's motion corrected this by renumbering the Market Street company to Engine 1, the Third Street company becoming No. 2.

The designations have remained unchanged since.

At the same Commission meeting, Chief Brown introduced a little disciplinary action of his own. Extraman Charles Plummer, a veteran of four years' service, was hailed before the Board and suspended on Brown's charge of "using vulgar and profane language within the hearing of members of his company, and with disrespect to a superior officer." Furthermore, "it is said that Mr. Plummer's offense consisted in expressing a somewhat profane and vitriolic opinion of Mayor Davison and present members of the Police and Fire Commission."

Charlie Plummer was never one to hold his tongue, then or later. Many were to learn this during the 18 years he was Chief of the department. In 1947, several years after Plummer's retirement and replacement by Lester O'Brien, City Councilman Al Ruffo (not always the most diplomatic of men himself) was quoted in the press as stating that San Jose had the "lousiest" fire department in the County prior to O'Brien's time. Soon afterward, it was Ruffo's painful duty to complain publicly that ex-Chief Plummer had phoned him threatening to "blow the lid off City Hall" if Ruffo didn't retract the canard against the fire force entrusted to Plummer's care for so many years. Both men soon forgot the whole thing.

Plummer's 1908 outburst was indicative of what the City Hall infighting was doing to department morale. Throughout the country, agitation was rising against the type of city government in which every newly-elected slate of officials meant indiscriminate hiring and firing with a mad scramble for position, only to be repeated when another election came around. Stable leadership, and the job security of individual employees (including firemen) demanded something better. Before many more years, this agitation would come to a head in San Jose.

Farewell to Chief Brown

While some firemen made the front pages, others continued a daily routine which was hazardous even without fires. Out exercising the horses one day, Teddy Haub tangled with an interurban electric car and came off second best; one of his unfortunate animals had to be destroyed. In November, 1908, Driver Smith and Engineer McQuaide took the new

Continental steamer out to exercise their team on North Third Street. As they moved along at a smart trot near St. James, the kingbolt suddenly snapped. The tongue became detached from the engine, causing the driver to lose control. Soon he was pulled from the seat and dragged. Untangling himself just in time, Smith saw the engine careen into the gutter and topple over as the horses, still dragging the loose tongue, galloped wildly on to the end of Third Street where a berry patch halted their flight.

The engine was righted "with considerable labor" but cost $500 to repair. Ahrens was billed for half this amount, the city claiming the tongue should have been furnished with safety chains.

It was an accident outside the city itself, however, that made the biggest news. A shocked community opened its morning newspapers on September 11, 1910, with the solemn tolling of the firebell as accompaniment, to see spread across the front pages the news of the untimely death of Chief Richard Brown.

Editorial tributes to him read in part "As a public official he was nearest the ideal"; " . . a most zealous and efficient officer"; "Quiet, genial, personally one of the most popular men in the city." Brown was only 36.

The preceding week, he had driven his official automobile to Stockton for the Coast Convention of Fire Chiefs. He then had the car shipped down to San Francisco by boat, whither he accompanied it for that city's Admission Day Parade on Friday, September 9. Next day, Brown began the drive home down the Peninsula together with local businessman Ivan Treadwell. As Treadwell attempted to light a cigarette near Tanforan, Brown lost control, and was thrown out and killed as the car flipped over on him.

The funeral was San Jose's largest and most impressive in years. Though no children survived him, Brown left a nephew, Ralph Jennings, who served many years as a fire officer. As a boy, Ralph remembers riding in the mile and a half long funeral procession on First Street, September 12. Its route led from the funeral home on North First to Third and Santa Clara, then east to St. Patrick's Church. From the church the cortege made its way to First and San Salvador, then on to Oak Hill Cemetery.

Brown's huge casket was drawn by two horses. A crowd of thousands lined the curb in silence as units of the San Jose Police and Fire Departments trundled slowly past, bearing crepe streamers on whips and harness. All fire stations were draped in black. Pallbearers included Assistant Chief Frank Whiteside; Captains John McGrath of Chemicals 1, Walter Page of the new "Engine 4" on Spencer Ave., John Gilleran of Engine 3; Lieut. George Welch of Engine 2; and Engineer Art McQuaide of Engine 1. Assistant Chief McCloskey of the San Francisco Fire Department brought a floral tribute from his men.

Almost at once popular sentiment arose to set up a memorial to the late Chief, and to raise funds to pay off the mortgage with which his widow was burdened. By September 21 collections reached $3000, a more than ample amount for both purposes. The resulting monument to Chief Brown's memory may be seen today, a six foot shaft surmounted by a firemen's helmet and chief's trumpet in stone, among the shade trees just off Curtner Ave. in Oak Hill's northeast corner.

To replace Dick Brown, the Commission decided to transfer Chief of Police Ed Haley (driver of the Empire hose wagon 25 years earlier) to the Fire Department. The feelings of First Assistant Chief McDonald, who had come up through Fire Department ranks, and Second Assistant Chief Whiteside, can well be imagined. However, (though many years elapsed before economy-minded officials talked seriously of combining the police and fire services) there was in those days a tendency to consider manpower interchangeable between the two departments — as witness Brown's own career. In many families both services were represented. John J. Murphy, late father of District Chief Gerald Murphy of the Fire Department, was a long-time police officer. In 1924 in a famous local gun battle he killed a man who had fatally wounded Detective Van Dyke Hubbard—himself a brother of Fireman Dean Hubbard. In later years, veteran firemen Gil Cardoza and James O'Day transferred to the police force.

The same week Chief Brown was killed, the Common Council adopted a tax rate for the following year: $1.14 per $100, of which 28½c was for Fire Department operations. In this age of a $3 million budget, it is interesting to note that the budget adopted for

San Jose Fire Department's first Chief's Car (in which Chief Brown was later killed) at Market Street in 1908. Above, left to right: Art McQuaide, Jack Layton, John McGrath, Ed Weibel (Waibel), Chief Brown at the wheel, Joe McDonald, Fred Hanks, Araby Damonte, Harry Smith, Frank Whiteside, Dan "King" Durkin, and Police Officer Chris Shannon.

the 1910-1911 fiscal year (including some capital expenditures at that) totalled exactly $59,313.37—about enough to pay the salaries for one engine company today.

Department finances were given a boost the next June 19 when San Jose's voters approved a $377,000 bond issue. San Francisco attorneys had to be consulted to clear legal questions associated with issuance of the bonds. Of this total, $60,000 was earmarked for more new firehouses and equipment—and for the purchase of the city's own fire horses. For at least four years, means had been sought for San Jose to own the animals instead of depending on each driver to furnish and maintain his own. Unfortunately, the administration's foresight left something to be desired; it was more than a generation after the last horse left the fire service before the bonds were paid off!

That summer of 1911, the San Jose-Santa Clara Street Railroad Company announced its readiness to abandon most of the old car shops at First and Oak Streets, which had been fully rebuilt after the fire of 1904, in favor of expanded quarters on The Alameda. (Half a century later, those new quarters in their turn were to be the scene of San Jose's most costly fire.) This new location then had no fire protection at all. Residents were already conscious of the need. A meeting of the Alameda Improvement Club at Hester School on December 12 resulted in appointment of a committee of three to "look into" this problem; one member was Professor M. R. Trace.

Another of San Jose's institutions, now vanished from the downtown scene, was burned out during the final weeks of 1911. Late diners in Chargin's Restaurant, in Fountain Alley, were taken aback when the cook appeared from the rear at 4 a.m. on December 12, with his hat and coat, announcing to all and sundry that he was going home inasmuch as the rear of the nearby O'Brien candy store (30 South First Street) was on fire! Upon investigating, astonished patrons discovered his story was true. Meanwhile, the night watchman at the First National Bank had telephoned the Market Street firehouse to advise that he had smelled smoke in the neighborhood for an hour.

As Assistant Chief Whiteside turned into First Street with a chemical company, flames burst from the two-story O'Brien Building. A general alarm was sounded at once. Streams were operated from the street as well as from Chargin's roof to the rear, while a pall of smoke rose over the downtown area from tons of candy and oil stored on the premises. Adjoining occupancies, including Bernauer's heavy stocks of imported furs next door, sustained thousands of dollars in smoke and water damage.

O'Brien lost $50,000 that night. But the candymaker—server in 1878 of the first ice cream soda west of Detroit — had been in business 40 years, the firm was to last almost another 40, and the fire meant only a brief pause in his operations. By 6 a.m. he had a sign up over temporary facilities at 120 South First, where he was busily turning out a fresh stock of candy.

The ruined building had been rebuilt following heavy damage by the 1906 earthquake. After O'Brien moved out for the last time, it housed a succession of firms and underwent many remodellings. This very structure, occupied by a restaurant, was again destroyed by a 2-alarm fire in May 1964; later operating as a night spot named Caesar's it was hit by a $25,000 blaze in December 1969.

Traffic Problems Worsen

Also near the end of 1911 came another blaze in the San Pedro-Bassett industrial area —destruction of the packing house of H. E. Losse and Company. Only noteworthy feature of this fire was a near-collision between one of the rigs hurrying to the scene and a streetcar stopped in the middle of an intersection. Cars were supposed to stop when the fire bell was heard, particularly when in the vicinity of firehouses, but nothing had been done to prevent their creating a serious obstruction by stopping in intersections.

Chief Haley mentioned this in an outraged complaint to the public on December 21 concerning the hazards besetting his men in responding to alarms. What set him off was a collision the previous afternoon between Assistant Chief Whiteside in the city's "Auto fire engine" and a delivery wagon.

Admittedly, Whiteside was whooping it up a bit, en route to an alarm from Box 125 at 12th and Santa Clara. Driving east on Santa Clara Street at 40 to 50 miles per hour in his Winton equipped with chemical tank, Whiteside was suddenly confronted by a delivery wagon of the Franklin Grocery Company. Its driver had pulled out from Third Street in

This was Chemical 2 before the original 1876 building was replaced in 1913. Left: the Winton "automobile fire apparatus" used by Asst. Chief Whiteside (note chemical tank). On the wagon: driver Peter Segard and Captain William Sterling.

spite of the auto's alarm bell and whistle. (Actually it was Chief Haley's car, but Haley loved horses and refused to drive the new-fangled contraption.)

The vehicles themselves never came together, but Whiteside was struck in the head by the horse's jaw as he spun past. The blow knocked him out. The auto's rear wheel struck the horse's forelegs, knocking it down, but the auto then careened out of control for a block, halting only when it crashed against a trolley pole near Fourth Street. Hundreds of startled spectators, witnessing the vehicle's mad flight, saw Whiteside thrown out as it piled up.

Though he was badly bruised and lacerated, suffering temporary amnesia, and the car itself had its chemical tank torn off, the whole thing didn't seem too serious. There were rumors, however, that Whiteside was never quite the same after the accident. It was not too many years before he left the department under a cloud to disappear from public life.

At any rate, Haley appealed to citizens to obey the law requiring all vehicles to pull over at the sound of the bell. Said he, "There are countless others who run to fires . . . which are constantly forcing the members of the Fire Department to take their lives in their hands." Only the day before Whiteside's accident, the Chief pointed out, a young man of prominence in the city "ran an automobile slowly along in front of a fire engine, zigzagging in front of it and refusing to allow driver Tennant to pass him." Haley was taking the matter up with the City Attorney, promising that he wouldn't prosecute if the youth's father would agree to deny his son further driving privileges.

Increased speed of the "auto fire engine" was a special problem—still unsolved. With a high degree of prophecy, Haley pointed out that the automobile had saved many times its cost, "but its use will be destroyed if the streets continue to be so congested that it cannot run to fires any faster than the other fire vehicles."

In spite of the difficulties, motor apparatus was on the way. Engine 4 was San Jose's last new company formed around horse-drawn equipment. In December 1911 the Commissioners called for bids to replace the boiler of her old steamer, and the work was done three months afterward. Perhaps the repairs were unsuccessful; at any rate within two years the company was officially re-named Chemical 5—the steamer was gone for good.

The Commission's composition was now as follows: President W. F. Kenville; Secretary, printer Henry Murgotten; J. F. Mecklem, clothier J. S. Williams — who died only recently at 94, the Commission's last surviving member—and realtor Victor Challen.

This group bought 2000 feet of new hose at the end of 1911, with prices ranging from 85c to $1.10 per foot. Shortly thereafter, the old hose was tested at 150 pounds pressure—little more than half the annual test pressure used today.

During 1911, the 5-year old City of East San Jose finally succumbed to the pressure to annex to its larger neighbor. Its fire department was of no particular use to San Jose, consisting only of a couple of hose reels, ladders, and local enthusiasm. Yet San Jose had to make good on its offer of fire protection to the annexed territory. Chief Haley came up with this scheme for covering the new suburb: All the territory north of Alum Rock Ave. would be protected by Chemical 2 on North 8th Street. Chemical 3 on South 8th would handle the area south of Alum Rock Ave. Because there might sometimes be fires requiring more powerful means of extinguishment, Haley decided that Engine 2 would also

respond from Third Street, going only as far as the Coyote Creek bridge, where "unless fire or smoke is observable [it] will await orders." How this novel idea would work on dark, foggy nights, and without benefit of radio communications, was not clarified.

Crandallville, as far west as White Street just beyond the Southern Pacific branch line depot, also joined San Jose in 1911, along with the Gardner District which was briefly known as the Fifth Ward.

In February 1912, Chief Haley requested that the Board consider reducing the size of the fire horses, so that all one horse wagons could be pulled by two smaller animals. He did not elaborate on the request, aimed perhaps at greater reliability in case of sickness or injury to one of the horses. But by October, the idea was of academic interest only. The Commission had read the handwriting on the wall. All bids for new horses received that Fall were rejected, although plans were already afoot to buy a new team for Engine 3 at prices ranging from $475 to $600.

Instead, contracts were let for two motorized chemical engines—the first motor-driven vehicles (except for automobiles) ever purchased for the San Jose Fire Department. There had been six bidders: Seagrave, LaFrance, and the local agencies of Harrison P. Smith, Webb Motor Fire Apparatus Company, Reliance, and Osen-McFarland. Osen-McFar-

land's bid of $5950 was accepted for a Pope-Hartford machine; Reliance landed a $5650 contract to deliver a Knox Combination (the Knox Automobile Company of Springfield, Mass., was one of the earliest builders in the field.)

When some of these primitive chain-driven trucks were put through the same time trials as their horse-drawn predecessors, they were left at the post. But in low operating cost, and in endurance, it was soon apparent that they were far superior to hay-burners.

New stations were needed again, now. In the first place, something better had to be done to take care of East San Jose. Secondly, Chemical 2's 40-year old house was in need of replacement. Finally, the shift of the Chinese colony to San Jose's north side, with the development of a business district in that area, called for additional fire protection there. In February 1913, a $2750 bid was accepted for construction of a new station at Second and Jackson, where the city had owned a "fire lot" for some time.

Shortly thereafter, the Knox rig arrived and passed its acceptance tests, winding up at Spencer Ave. as Chemical 5. In April, the Pope-Hartford came to town. At the same time, plans were approved for a new station at 17th and Santa Clara eventually to be known as Chemical 6; in May, replacement quarters for Chemical 2 went out for bidding. Both these latter stations went to F. J. Scherrebeck for $2720 and $3375 respectively (by way of comparison, San Jose had budgeted $70,000 for its latest planned station on the southwest side).

The Jackson Street house was designated Chemical 4; here the Pope-Hartford, with its twin 35-gallon chemical tanks, served for years. San Jose also needed a "house for the fire alarm station" then—a need not to be filled for almost half a century. The "Public Structures Committee" smiled wistfully on the idea, but only briefly.

Bill Tennant—Sea Lawyer and Water Saver

Though many firemen may have believed as Charlie Plummer did about the quality of the administration overseeing San Jose's fire service, few were diplomatic enough or popular enough to lay bare some of the problems without being completely squelched. Such a man was William F. Tennant.

Only known photo of Chemical 5, the Knox-Martin "combination" which was San Jose's first motorized apparatus. At left, Harry C. Dennis, who retired as a Captain in 1938. The picture was taken 40 to 50 years ago.

A lifelong bachelor who was able to risk his job as others could not, Tennant had been a fireman since the '90's. One oldtimer said of him, "Bill Tennant did more for firemen through laws and courts than any other man." His chief activity was to call attention whenever and wherever he could to any unfair treatment of the men, in such a way as to enlist wide public sympathy for himself and the fire service.

Time and again Tennant was transferred, or reduced in rank, for his "troublemaking" activities. Ironically, he outlasted all his superiors, ultimately retiring as Captain of Chemical 4 in May 1932. His obituary, not long afterwards, stated that Tennant had been acting Chief during one of Chief Henry Ford's attempts to regain health by a Hawaiian sojourn. Not only was his loyalty to his profession legendary—his thrift was too. Fellow firemen recall his washing firehouse cooking utensils in the toilet to save city water; it was even reported that he used axle grease to fry his eggs rather than spend money on lard!

Tillerman on the Hook and Ladder for a time, Tennant was driver of Engine 1 early in 1913. In the Spring, his agitations led the Police and Fire Commissioners to "arbitrarily" break him to Extraman — although at this time he had more years of service as a regular fireman than most other members of the department.

Rather than put up with the punishment, Tennant chose to advertise the Board's capricious disciplinary practices by taking his case to court. Needless to say, the June 1913 Superior Court decision upholding Tennant did not endear him to the Board, nor did the immediate demand by his attorney that the Commissioners pay over Tennant's May salary of $90.

By using this means of focussing public attention on the Board's actions, Tennant undoubtedly added weight to the growing movement towards removing control of the uniformed services from the Commission permanently. (To make things worse, it was about this time that the courts reinstated several firemen dismissed in 1908—another bitter pill for the Commission to swallow.)

They had their way with him eventually, of course, but not before arousing strong opposition from the local press. In July 1913, the San Jose Mercury's editor wrote acidly on

Captain W. F. Tennant, stormy petrel of pre-World War I days.

his front page, "Thus far the endeavors of the majority in the police commission to dismiss William F. Tennant, one of the oldest firemen in the employ of the city, have not been successful, and the latest move to get him out of the way is to have charges filed against him by Fire Chief Haley . . . " [that he let one of his horses fall on March 17 while going to an early morning fire] "but whether the offense has become more serious since the rainy season closed, or whether it was just noticed by the head of the department, is still a question." The man was simply a thorn in the administration's side.

John Wentzel, veteran of Engine Co. 3.

He was finally suspended on August 18, on charges of incompetence brought by Chief Haley—who had to reach pretty far afield. En route to a minor Bassett Street fire, the complaint was, Market Street crews "had some difficulty in getting out of the building." One team was crowded upon the sidewalk as Tennant and Jack Wentzel (driving Hook and Ladder 1) somehow got tangled up under the electric tower at Market and Santa Clara. The Chief accused Tennant of being "slow" and "careless"; there were no injuries or damage.

Tennant was out for 30 days, and warfare began within the Commission over the issue. "The public is . . . outraged," stormed the Mercury. Tennant's suspension was on "trumped up charges," sputtered the editor: it was "politics run mad," with "no consideration for men of merit." Reviewing the weeks of controversy, the Mercury explained that "a few weeks ago, Tennant had been reduced in rank and the position given to a friend of the administration who, it will be remembered, while hastening to a fire, lost control of his machine, which toppled over and was damaged." (The nameless replacement was then himself dismissed.)

Mayor Monahan kept the pot boiling by tearing into the Commissioners for their laxness in law enforcement. On July 5, the Mayor —"by virtue of the authority vested in me . . . by . . . Sect. 4 Article 6 of the Charter"—suspended Commissioners Alex Hart, J. S. Williams, and Victor Challen, as well as Chief of Police George Kidder, on the grounds of "wilful neglect and misconduct, to wit—failure to suppress lotteries, liquor sales, and gambling." Having served their purpose of stirring up the community, the charges were promptly dismissed.

The Worst Fires Since 1906

Just to make sure the Fire Department remained in the public notice, August 19, 1913, brought the most serious fire in years —the burning of the S. H. Chase Lumber Company property at 463 West Santa Clara Street (a site the firm vacated only in recent years, to be succeeded by the Starlite Restaurant).

It was a working day, and a hot one to begin with. Shortly before lunchtime, smoke was seen curling up through the floor boards inside the sprawling two-story mill. Box 65 was struck at 11:51 a.m. as the 35 employees rushed to safety. Twelve of them upstairs heard the plant engineer, Jim Kitchen, sound the alarm but thought it was the noon whistle and almost didn't get out. Some had to jump for it. As flames roared through the plant, Kitchen tried vainly to reach his pumps to start water flowing through the manually operated sprinkler system.

All downtown fire companies turned out, aided by the new "automobile combination" hose-chemical rigs from Spencer Ave. and

Jackson Streets. Cooled by hose spray, firemen ran a gauntlet of fallen high voltage lines hissing and crackling along Montgomery Street, to reach positions from which they could attack the towering blaze. Eventually all electric power on the west side was turned off, causing a grand tie-up of streetcar traffic.

Paint was scorched on the gas storage tank near the corner of San Augustine and Montgomery. Flames leaped across Montgomery Street to the west, damaging the Stafford & Bard smithy, Sheldon's Carriage Shop, and razing homes at 29, 33, and 37 North Montgomery. Nearby on Santa Clara Street, a bicycle shop at 447 and a branch Post Office station at 445 were heavily damaged as a stiff north wind created an inferno inside the Chase buildings.

Several firefighters were hurt. George Welch of Engine 2 was knocked out by a hose stream; Captain Herman Hobson of Engine 1 was singed, as was his engineer Art McQuaide and Fireman Fred Hambly "who stood by when the flames were so intense that they scorched the paint from the engine" (its steam gauge glass was cracked by heat). Loraine Horn, manning a line on the second floor, let it get away from him and was knocked through a window to the ground, unconscious.

Not until 7 p.m. next day was the fire declared out. Sandwiches and coffee for the hard-pressed firemen were ordered out from a downtown delicatessen by Mayor Monahan. For part of the time, Santa Clara firemen stood ready to move into San Jose if needed. Total loss was about $90,000, only a third of it covered by insurance. All Chase's lumber stocks were lost, plus the "reserve" mill which was idle at the time although the main plant had been running full blast. Cause of the fire was said to be an overheated band saw bearing.

Firemen McQuaide and Hambly were commended for their steadfastness by Fire Commissioner J. F. Mecklem. Chief Haley was moved to also publicly thank bystanders who had helped: "I wish to extend my sincere thanks for the kind assistance lent by the young men of San Jose in fighting the flames . . . the task was a big one for the department, and their aid in the time of need was invaluable."

Some of the fire engine chasers were of value, after all. San Jose has never been noted

Somewhat the worst for wear after a minor fire of its own, but still standing in October 1963: Chemical 2's house at 255 N. 8th.

for its active fire fans or "buffs" as have many of the larger Eastern cities, or even San Francisco. But there were a few: several members of the Doerr family, for instance, or Superior Judge Marshall Hall, made an honorary fireman in January 1964 in honor of his years of support to the department (however, not the city's first honorary fireman; Councilman Fred Doerr was designated honorary Battalion Chief years ago, and Willow Glen Volunteer Fire Chief Steve Mascovich got the same reward after Willow Glen joined San Jose in 1936.)

But long-time honors for fire buffing are due to one of San Jose's grand old men—the late Jay McCabe, who began his fire-chasing in 1897. Though he eventually passed it off as a gag, perhaps unsuited to his mature years, it is recorded that McCabe appeared before the City Council in November 1913 to request "official permission to pass within fire lines established by ordinance." His request was referred to the Police and Fire Commission, in the absence of whose minutes we can only guess at the result.

He did well enough without official sanction. The McCabe home on South 14th Street was back to back with the 13th Street residence of fellow-buff Louis King—who at one time was a member of the Commission and had an alarm bell in his house. Recalls McCabe, "I'd hear King's gong and be gone before he was! There were four of us in those days: me and King, Henry Doerr, and Jack Shea; we got to most of the fires." The late Mr. Shea was later described in the Mercury as a "champion for many years of fire department improvements . . . who served as a special deputy sheriff and arson investigator."

Two months to the day following the Chase conflagration, and only three blocks away, fire was discovered at 9:45 p.m. in the Haven & Company packing house on Cinnabar Street near Montgomery. Southern Pacific railroad workers were first on the scene, dragging in half a dozen hose lines from the nearby roundhouse to protect several exposed buildings. A box alarm was pulled at 10 p.m., followed quickly by a general alarm. By now the Haven plant was a goner; fire had jumped the street to the Castle Bros. packing house. Windows half a block away were cracked by radiant heat. A crowd of hundreds gathered to watch San Jose firemen and SP crews make a desperate and successful stand to save the threatened buildings of J. K. Ormsby and Company (the only area structures which were brick and iron rather than wood), thus preserving them for total destruction by another blaze in 1924. All that was saved from the first structures involved was Castle Bros. books and records, lugged to safety by volunteers. Total loss to the two firms was estimated at $150,000.

At the height of the action, Engine 3, Truck 1, and Chemicals 3 and 4 were recalled from the fire to a second outbreak which destroyed a boarding house at 121 East St. James.

Rising over the mountains to the southwest during that week, as a fitting backdrop to the local scene, was a mushroom cloud of smoke from a huge forest fire in the Zayante area,

J. F. Dwyer, one-time Chief of the San Jose Fire Department, who later served as a member of Engine Co. 3; taken about 1912.

Captain Louis Bein, Truck 1, about 1912.

threatening Mt. Hermon. Hundreds were on the fire lines.

On October 21, exhausted San Jose firemen went into action again—this time downtown. At 40 South First Street, in the old 3-story stone-fronted building (dated 1889) where Herold's Shoes is located now, the leading dry goods firm of Stull and Sonniksen had just brought in 20 truckloads of new stock. The clerks had left for the evening. As he was closing up the store, a stock boy smelled smoke. Box 35 was pulled at 5:58 p.m. When firemen arrived, the basement was already filled with smoke, and fire was shooting from ground floor windows.

Firefighters took severe punishment during the two hours the flames were uncontrolled. Many were overcome by heavy smoke from tons of burning clothing and home furnishings, among them Chief Haley, Captains Hobson, Siebuhr, Stewart, Costello, and "Lieutenants" Welch and Narvaez (actually the official rank of Lieutenant seems not to have existed at this time). Fireman Damonte was for a time believed dead, but finally came around. While working with a crew opening up the floor to get at the basement, Walter Page had his hand laid open by an axe. Among those first into the building were Assistant Chief Whiteside and Fire Commissioner McCarthy. Both fought their way in through blinding smoke and then collapsed, reviving enough to crawl back out along a hose line.

Two lines were finally gotten into the basement from the rear, drowning the blaze in water up to a man's neck. It later took two days to pump out the flood. The firm survived the $48,000 loss, only to go under in the depression of 1930.

Adding to the firemen's problems, for perhaps the first time in downtown San Jose, was the mass of autos driven into the area by sightseers. Eight motorists were arrested on the spot for driving over hose lines. One hose was broken. Next day, all the miscreants received a $5 fine in city police court, as well as a thorough editorial lambasting in the Mercury.

Working Conditions

William "Coffee Bill" McCarthy was one of the more colorful characters to grace the Police and Fire Commission. Proprietor of a coffee and spice house on West Santa Clara Street "between the bridges," he was described by one contemporary as "a typical small town ward-heeler politician." Perhaps it takes a little more than that to help lead the way into a burning building. At any rate, the Fourth Ward was McCarthy's pet. It was he who spearheaded the drive to locate an engine company there. It was he who helped select the Spencer Ave. site which that company occupied for more than 40 years. And it was he whose name bridged those four decades via the stylized initials "WM" which formed the front door window frames at the firehouse. Jay McCabe relates that, appropriately, one of "Coffee Bill's" daughters later married a man named Bean.

Some other happenings of these last pre-World War years show the extent to which the firemen's working conditions were still far from ideal. There has been much progress. Consider: Fireman G. H. Perry was hurt in 1913 while going home to dinner (most of the firehouses still had no kitchens and were on the "meal hours" system). His leg was broken when his horse fell on him. There was no compensation; at the end of November the State industrial accident committee advised San Jose that the city was not liable.

Or consider the matter of provision for pensions, or widows and orphans. Funds the Commission had set up in 1901 were either depleted or abandoned by 1913, so in October the Commissioners made another abortive attempt to provide something of the sort. A "Relief Pension Fund" for firemen was launched, with the interesting twist (adopted in 1914) that all fines collected from disciplined members of the department would swell this kitty. For the long-term welfare of themselves and their families, firemen were thus encouraged to get into trouble. Fortunately the system was short-lived.

Even the most minor fringe benefits of the fire service had to be jealously guarded. When the local streetcar company had gotten its franchise to operate in San Jose, one of its terms was an exemption of uniformed firemen from full fare payment. In December 1913, some of the permanent firemen reached the City Council with complaints that they were being charged anyway. Street railway manager Frank Chapin assured the Council the oversight would be remedied.

A good reason for the boys to watch their nickels was that they were far from being overpaid. In February 1914 some thirty permanent members of the department petitioned for a wage increase, claiming San Jose's salary levels to be below those for comparable cities elsewhere. At the time, common day laborers were being paid only 20% to 30% less than firemen—and they weren't asked to put in a 24 hour day, or to risk their lives into the bargain. Taxes were high; the new Federal income tax was expected to hit almost half a million American wage earners in 1914.

Whether the petitioners had any luck we don't know, but it's doubtful. In less than two more years, the Commission would be squabbling over proposals to close fire stations and lay off both regular and call firemen because of lack of enough money to run the department.

The First Motorized Pumper

Early in 1914, the city decided to motorize more of the department. There was far too much money tied up in the relatively new downtown steamers and aerial truck to con-

sider replacing them entirely with new rigs. As a reasonable compromise, one of the most weird and wonderful contraptions ever used in any fire department was ordered for San Jose. This was a Knox-Martin tricycle tractor to replace the horse as Truck 1's pulling power. It arrived in the Fall, was accepted in mid-September, and the first payment of $1200 authorized. Just to see what it could do, one complete motorized pumper was also ordered.

This experiment was the first of several concessions to modern times. New firemen applying for jobs (to fill the ever-present vacancies) were now required to furnish a health certificate at their own expense. To help insure maintenance of this health, the Chief was instructed that all his men were to have helmets; any man entering the departmen without one after October 1 was to be fined 50c (thus giving a tremendous boost to the Relief Pension Fund). Furthermore, a 25 mile per hour speed limit was ordered for all motor fire apparatus.

The Commission did well to take care of all these innovations, for during much of 1914 there was no quorum (and hence no business

Knox Martin tractor and steam pumper currently being restored for display by the San Jose Fire Department.

transacted) at three out of four Board meetings. The cause was partly the suspension of two Board members for one of the periodic malfeasances alleged by one faction or another within the Commission.

A big item disposed of was the complete "reorganization" of the Fire Department to take effect September 1, 1914, pursuant to Section 7, Article X of the City Charter, which gave the Commission power to determine the number and placement of each category of department member. This was the new table of organization:

> Chemicals 1, 4, 5: 1 Captain, 1 Driver, 1 Hoseman.
>
> Chemicals 2, 3: 1 Captain, 1 Driver, 2 call men.
>
> Engines 1, 2, 3: 1 Engineer, 1 Driver.
>
> Hose 1, 2: 1 Captain, 1 Driver, 1 Hoseman, 3 call men.
>
> Hose 3: 1 Captain, 1 Driver, 3 call men.
>
> Truck 1: 1 Captain, 1 Driver, 1 Tillerman, 3 call men.

What was then being called the "East San Jose Hose" (sometimes Hose 4, eventually Chemical 6) was to have only a driver and 2 call men.

To administer and support this establishment, the department was to have 1 Chief (at $150 monthly), 1 Assistant Chief ($125), 1 hydrant inspector, 1 utility fireman, and 1 utility engineer.

Alarm signals got more complicated, too. Three taps called for Engine 1, Chemical 1, and Truck 1. Four taps called for Engine 2

The grand old man, Captain John J. Gilleran, one-time hack driver who spent half a century as a San Jose firefighter.

and Chemical 2; five taps, Engine 3, and Chemical 3; six taps, "Engine No. 4." Special calls included: two taps Chemical 3, four taps Truck 1, five taps Chemical 1, six taps Chemical 2.

On September 28, the short-handed Commissioners tackled the ticklish question of sending fire apparatus outside the city, and came up with the following rule (subsequently OK'd by the City Attorney): The Fire Chief was empowered to send such equipment as he might select, or to arrange for San Jose firemen to "cover in" for an outside community, but only "upon the request of the Mayor or some competent person's order, and with the understanding that a charge be made of fifty dollars per hour for each apparatus so sent, which charge shall be guaranteed by the person sending in the call."

Exceptions were made in the case of conflagration, "or in the case of any charitable or eleemosynary institution in the vicinity of this city." Real mutual aid was decades in the future, but here was a beginning of sorts.

After the horses were gone, Chemical 2 looked like this on its Federal chain-drive chassis.
The two-man company consisted of Captain William Sterling and Driver Frank Thorpe.

At this same meeting, engineer-mechanic Art McQuaide, who took care of apparatus maintenance and repair at the time, made his last report on work done "in the machine shop of the department," located in the old San Pedro Street truck house. It was "discontinued" the following month, and McQuaide lost his $25 monthly bonus covering his mechanic's services and the use of his tools. Perhaps the Commissioners mistakenly thought the advent of motorized apparatus would eliminate all need for a mechanic. Or perhaps McQuaide had no qualifications for working on the new gas buggies. It was going to be hard to find anyone among the department's engineers who were capable of doing automotive work. Examined and licensed for each class of steamer, members of the International Union of Steam Engineers, these men were specialists in a dying technology.

Fire prevention also got some attention, with the drafting of an ordinance for Council consideration providing for inspection of premises by the Fire Department—an innovation then, now common practice.

In other, closed "executive sessions" of the Board, Chief Haley was beginning to complain about peculiar actions of his Assistant, Frank Whiteside. Other subordinates were in trouble too. Ralph Padgett and Bill Mason, fairly new men, were both suspended in October; John McGrath was demoted from Captain of Chemical 1 to hose wagon driver. Loraine Horn was brought in for trial on unspecified charges, which were later "settled satisfactorily." Oddly enough, stormy petrel Bill Tennant actually drew a promotion—acting Captain of what was then called "Hose 4" in East San Jose. Evidently the earlier idea of having only a driver on duty there wasn't working out.

Another source of difficulty was the practice of regular firemen hiring temporary substitutes for them during meal hours or other absences on personal business. "We could take the day off," recalled Capt. Pete Segard, "but we couldn't go out of town." To make sure such absences didn't render firefighters unfit to remain on duty, the Commission passed this 1914 resolution: "Be it resolved: that no member of the Fire Department shall while on duty, visit, enter or remain in any saloon or other public drinking place."

Cliff "Cutie" Miramontes of Engine 1, 1912.

The Chief sometimes had no idea who the substitute was or what his qualifications as a fireman might be—most unprofessional. On October 15, 1914, it was decreed that: "No member of the fire department shall be permitted to employ any substitute unless the name of such substitute shall appear upon the department roll board." Furthermore, any persons seeking such employment were henceforth required to furnish the same health certificate as the regular men.

Personnel problems took a back seat during November to one of the historic firsts in the San Jose Fire Department: the arrival of the first motorized pumping engine. Appropriately, it was to remain in active service longer than any other engine acquired since—more than 30 years.

This was a 1914 Seagrave "Type Q" pumper, one of the earliest centrifugals and one of only a few units of its model. The bill for it, paid on November 30 shortly after its acceptance by the City, came to $9750. Assigned to Engine 1, it proved none too dependable in the hands of men still accustomed to curry comb and feed bag—in spite of the Chief's arrangement for an "instructor" for Engine 1's driver and engineer, who at the time were still two different individuals. In February

First motorized pumper purchased for San Jose was this 1914 model, one of a few special units built by Seagrave. Assigned to outlying engine companies most of the time, she is shown here at the Spencer Avenue "McCarthy House."

1915, Haley banished the contrary machine to Engine 3, where it remained throughout much of its career. In March, the Commission was forced to appeal to the local agent (Gorham Fire Apparatus Co. of San Francisco) to send its man "down here to see what can be done to said engine."

Somehow, enough was "done to said engine" to keep it going until 1938, when it was almost completely rebuilt at Oakland's Hall-Scott factory. But after that the old relic never steered well, and cost almost $900 in maintenance over the years remaining to it. When new equipment arrived following World War II, it went into reserve status. When last seen in mid-1953, the rusting hulk was just another eyesore among the weeds of the Corporation Yard on North 6th Street.

Early troubles, however, failed to deter Commissioners from following the motorization trend. Bids were called for on "four or less" ton-and-a-half trucks for converting chemical and hose wagons, said vehicles to have two electric headlights, one "oil tail light," double chain drive, four cylinders, front fenders, rear dual tires — in short, all the latest accessories — on terms of $50 down and $50 per month. The Board must have liked the deal proposed earlier by Osen-McFarland, who offered to rent the city a truck for $50 a month to try out "if it should be found available for fire purposes."

"No More the Faithful Animals . . ."

The closing months of 1914 brought to a sorry end the career of Frank Whiteside. He had been arrested on November 16 and hailed into traffic court. Misuse of his "official auto equipment" was the charge, which doubtless had the effect on Haley of waving a red flag in front of a bull. Traffic Officer Jackson testified that Whiteside, while "not on fire duty," had cut the corner of First and Santa Clara Streets. When collared, Whiteside protested so "vigorously" that it took two officers to bring him in. Argument continued loudly in the courtroom, ending in a formal charge to which Whiteside pleaded guilty. He promptly drew 30 days in county jail (suspended) plus six months' probation.

Called repeatedly to account before the Police and Fire Commission, Whiteside failed to appear—even after his salary was cut to $100 a month. Finally, on January 20, 1915, he resigned from the department — never having attempted to protect his name as one of the "very popular" members of the Fire Department. That name is not found again in the annals of San Jose. Herman Hobson was appointed to replace him as Assistant Chief.

The handwriting was on the wall for many other public figures of San Jose. Berkeley's Professor Reed, widely known advocate of municipal reform, was now working with the "Citizens' Charter Committee," which had failed to change the charter in 1912 but had not given up the fight. Reed's plan for City Manager government in San Jose was on the way to success in a matter of months, spelling the end for "ward bosses" and for the Police and Fire Commission.

Future years might bring little nostalgic regret for those departed worthies. But some of the most faithful members of the Fire Department were also to be forced out. For in January 1915 the Secretary of the Commission formally asked City Council permission to sell all the fire horses which the Commission might wish to dispose of.

Sell the fire horses? Unthinkable! Yet one by one, they were retired and disposed of— O. A. Harlan & Co. offered $100 "for the black horse known as Frank"; Ernest Andre bought "Reuben" for $75; "Jack" also went for $75. These were sad days; the fireman's love for his horses was legendary. Every American community had its own folklore built around the indispensable animals.

Years before his death, Chief Brown had explained the training and utilization of San Jose's fire horses. His remarks point up one of the most colorful aspects of fire depart-

Lieutenant George Welch, member of Engine Co. 2 for 33 years, who fell dead in 1929 while leading his company into action.

ment operations of half a century ago. Said he, "Those horses know their business just as well as the men, and take just as much interest in it." The animals cost (in 1904) $250 to $300 each—no small investment for the driver of a team, who in Brown's time had to provide and maintain his own horses. Said Brown, "That expense is considered in fixing [the drivers'] salaries, which are [again in 1904] $100 a month for the driver of a double team and $85 for a single team."

Horses were exercised daily. Each was kept bridled and bitted constantly, which some supposed would interfere with their feeding. Chief Brown explained, however, that the only effect was "to the extent of causing them to eat a little slower, which is all the better for them."

Different types of fire apparatus called for different weights of animals. For the chemical wagons, Brown said, "We have light, active stock; animals weighing from 1100 to 1200 pounds. For the hose carts we have about the same, as they have no great weight to draw and need to be early on the ground."

For the four- to five-ton engines, animals weighing about 1500 pounds were employed.

The horses were trained by local firehouse signal bells, being taught to pull on their halters at the sound of the gong. Continued Brown, "You see, the horses are hitched in their stalls by a halter with an electric connection, so that when an alarm is turned in the horse hearing it pulls back on the halter, which at once slips and releases him so that he can run to his position for hitching up."

Once responsive to the bell, the horses were then led into position and repeatedly hitched up until the entire process became firm habit. A trained team could be in harness, ready to go, within ten seconds from the first stroke of the alarm.

After the long, fast run to the fire, each sweating animal was unhitched and blanketed at once, except for the chemical engine teams —the usefulness of this apparatus depended upon its mobility.

Chief Brown expressed some definite opinions on the construction of rolling stock best suited to equine motive power. Rubber tires were coming into wide use; San Jose's Chemical 1 had them. Brown conceded their advantage in minimizing skidding on cobbled streets, having once seen the chemical wagon skid for an entire block on steel tires. On the other hand, rubber tired vehicles were harder for the horses to pull than those with the "ordinary steel tires." The horses' shoes themselves skidded, too, leading to their eventual replacement with rubber pads.

Ball bearing axles were coming in, too; "Improvements are being made all the time," as Brown put it. For example, "With the old-fashioned trucks, when the tillerman rode behind handling a projecting rudder, it was as much as a man's life was worth sometimes to swing around a corner . . . Now the tillerman sits on top of the truck over the hind wheels, where it is comparatively safe." Drivers were strapped in their seats for safety, though it was rare for a horse to fall.

Many were the anecdotes to be related of this horse or that. At the South 8th Street station, a big bay named "Rooster" got smart enough to turn in his own false alarms. Related the Chief, "We have on the houses local bells for turning in still alarms. One day the foreman of the company was temporarily at his home nearby, and other members . . . were somewhere around the vicinity, when suddenly a still alarm on the local bell brought them all to the fire house on the jump. But what they saw was old 'Rooster' with the rope of the alarm bell in his mouth jingling it for all it was worth!" He had gotten loose from his stall and went straight for the rope.

Retired horses of course found it difficult to break away forever. One who got "off his feed," being turned out to grass in a lot near Franklin Engine where he'd served for years, jumped the fence when the alarm sounded and fell in alongside the team as before. Another was sold to a San Francisco milkman. On the milk route one day, with the driver off making a delivery, along came a fire engine rattling down the street. The horse took off, wagon and all, to race the engine to the fire, scattering milk cans all along the route!

Now, in 1915, those days were coming to an end. In January, Commissioners accepted W. J. Benson's $9980 bid on four Federal motor trucks for the Fire Department; delivery in four months. At the same time Osen-McFarland offered a Mitchell truck for $1575, but this bid was rejected when the Mitchell turned out to have only single rear wheels instead of duals. The Commission later thought better of this, proposing to lease the Mitchell for $50 monthly.

As the trucks began to arrive, the old horse-drawn running gear was sold, while many of the hose beds, chemical tanks, etc., were rebuilt onto the Federal chassis. Henry Artana's firm (later San Jose's Reo agency) bought several of the superseded equipment; Chemical 1's running gear brought $85, with six others selling for a total of $200. Some of the conversions took considerable time. Chemical 2, for instance, lost its horses March 23, 1915, and was then out of service until mid-October except for a couple of days in July. Area residents were understandably anxious about their fire protection while the change-over was in process.

More Fires, Less Money

With so many new acquisitions, plus continuing repairs to old equipment (Engine 1 needed firebox work that year), the Commission encountered financial problems. There certainly wasn't much return for the sale of outmoded rigs. Even the horses were bringing in only a third of their original cost. San Jose's old Hook and Ladder, replaced in 1908, was vainly offered for sale to ten nearby cities in hopes of raising a little something extra. Artana finally bought it for $100.

The novel kitchen in Engine 3's new house was already giving trouble, and money was needed to "put it in working order." Lou Lunsford of Engine 3 was drawing $90 monthly instead of $85, in consideration of his acting as "engineer" on the new Seagrave for four days per month. After the departure of Whiteside, the Assistant Chief's salary had been raised back to $125 as of March 1, 1915, along with a boost to $175 for the Chief. Within two months it was necessary to cut back both salaries by $25.

More sales followed. White & Lipe Machine Co. offered $150 for two old steamers. The East San Jose hose house was sold for $20. Also, the Winton 6 (Whiteside's official car) could be spared—it needed repairs anyway.

Engineer Lou Lunsford of Engine 3, father of Civil Defense Director and Battalion Chief Russ Lunsford.

This handsome Irishman is John J. Powers, who retired in 1954 as Captain of Engine 2, after 42 years' service.

76

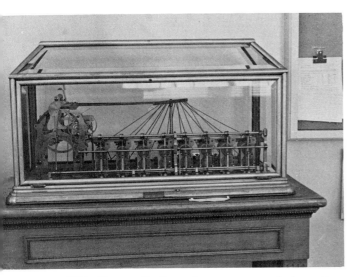

This Gamewell Alarm is now a part of the antique fire equipment on display at the Central Fire Station. It was used for a half century in the old City Hall.

But on April 22, 1915, the Commission went so far as to seriously consider a resolution (later tabled indefinitely) to radically slash the department's operating costs. On the grounds that "there is not sufficient funds or will not be to maintain the fire department," its terms called for closing Chemical 4's station, the apparatus to be stored at Chemical 2. Chemical 6 was to be closed, its rig stored at Chemical 3. Three regular firemen and five extramen were to be eliminated, effective May 1.

Ultimately at least one of these steps was necessary. Chemical 4 was closed for a time, reopening in late 1920. But somehow most of the crisis was averted.

As far as fires went, 1914 had been an easy year. There were 78 box alarms and 106 stills, with a total loss of $35,524 — only 79c per capita. San Jose now handles that many alarms in an average week! Business picked up in 1915. At 3 a.m. on May 29, in the modern Bean Spray plant at Terraine and Julian Streets, watchman J. R. Downs noticed flames reflected in the windows of Longfellow School across the street. He immediately telephoned an alarm, then turned on the outside water curtain sprinkler at the east side of the Bean plant. Fire had broken out in the Lorentz cooperage next door, filled with new barrels, and raged out of control for hours, causing $42,000 damage to the two plants. Two engine and four chemical companies responded.

On the afternoon of September 2, there was a real battle. For the only time in its history, the San Jose Fire Department was con-fronted with four simultaneous fires—two of them major. First, during the noon hour, came two alarms from Box 75 for fire in Johnson's hay, wood, and coal yard on San Pedro Street between Fox and Ryland—where a hay barn had burned in 1899. The whole department turned out, for this time Johnson's whole place was involved: three warehouses, five horses, 300 tons of hay, the offices, wood and coal storage. Flames spread quickly to the A. H. Averill Machinery Co. at Fox and San Pedro, to a house at 65 Fox Ave., then jumped down the block to a barn at 95 Fox (which was considered Fire No. 2).

Firemen were severely handicapped by poor water supply. With one engine pumping from each of the two hydrants in the vicinity, only feeble streams were forthcoming from the single 4-inch main. So they took turns—first one pumped to capacity with the other shut down, then vice versa. The water company was finally able to raise its pressure. Only by herculean efforts was the nearby Warren Dried Fruit plant saved, along with the 50-year-old Inderreiden Packing House at 200-206 Ryland Ave. Several neighborhood homes were scorched, but chemical crews kept them wetted down.

"Teddy" Haub, driver of Engine 3; passed away in 1928.

Johnson was seriously burned trying to save his horses. One poor animal he was leading to safety failed to follow as he crawled out, and a policeman had to drag Johnson from the smoke as he attempted to go in again.

Suddenly, someone shouted "Smoke downtown!" Dismayed firefighters looked up to see a black column rising to the southeast. Apparatus was en route from the fire scene to investigate when at 1:45 Box 26 was pulled. Flames were spreading rapidly in the Osen-McFarland garage on the northeast corner of First and St. James, in the closely built block which was San Jose's "automobile row."

Driving in for some gas, one Dick Keeble lit a match and his under-the-seat gas tank ignited. "One of the largest and best-known firms on the Coast," the two-story establishment was gutted. Eleven autos (including eight new Dodges just received that morning) were destroyed, 22 others saved. In a primitive salvage endeavor, one of the Fire Department's hose wagons backed up to the side door, volunteers hooked a rope from the wagon around the front wheels of several autos in the garage, and they were towed to safety.

Firewalls helped the hard-pressed firemen to save Letcher's Garage to the north, and the Christian Science Church on the east. This was Fire No. 3.

Unknown to the firemen battling flames on First Street, the burning garage had brought down electric lines around the corner, causing a short circuit which ignited Fire No. 4 in the Sainte Claire Club a block away. Fortunately, this blaze was minor, preserving the structure for a devastating fire almost 40 years later.

Total loss was estimated at $150,000. Careless smoking at Osen-McFarland was believed to be the cause there; what started Fire No. 1 was never determined. Next day, it was announced that 3000 feet of new hose was to be purchased "at once."

Captain H. F. Damonte of Engine 1 missed out on these festivities. He was then returning from a steaming summer in Chicago, where as part of a 60-day leave of absence granted by the Commission he had spent 24 days on active service with the Chicago Fire Department. His condensed report of what he saw and did there takes up several columns of fine print in the Mercury of Sept. 4, 1915. It was truly an experience. On arrival in the Windy City, Capt. Damonte reported to Fire Marshal O'Connor, who assigned him to Engine 98, 202 E. Chicago Ave., north of the Loop. There were 11 alarms the first day, "as many as San Jose has in two weeks." Merely for his Battalion Chief to cover his district on inspection trips required 65 miles of travel over a two-day period.

Every morning at 9 a.m., the company performed "house drill," practicing hitching up, lining out hose, etc. Marvelled Damonte, "Everything possible was done for me. I owe a debt of gratitude to every officer and man . . . for their kindness." He brought back voluminous details of the operation of coal wagons, training methods, Chicago's use of coal oil torches rather than "Greek fire" for lighting fires under the steamers' boilers, and the like.

One of the most memorable incidents of Damonte's Chicago duty was his accompanying the Battalion Chief called out on July 24, 1915, when the excursion steamship "Eastland" overturned in the Chicago River with a loss of 812 lives. Damonte worked alongside Chicago firemen in the tragic task of recovering bodies from the river.

Although Damonte was impressed enough to recommend that all San Jose fire captains be given the same opportunity to work out with a metropolitan department — such as San Francisco's—there is no record that this was ever done.

Shortly after Damonte's return, the Police and Fire Commission called for bids on two more tractors to motorize Engines 1 and 2. On October 26, W. J. Benson's bid was accepted. These machines were to have one "large electric headlight," dual rear wheels, a 4 cylinder engine, and the bidders were to make "allowance" for the six horses now used to pull the engines. In other words, the Commissioners, not doing so well in disposing of the animals which had so recently become city property, now saw a way to make suppliers of the superseding motor equipment take over the problem themselves.

Capt. Damonte's report on Chicago's coal wagons bore some fruit the following month. The Board directed Chief Haley to keep a "utility wagon" loaded with coal at the Market Street firehouse, ready for use.

Disciplinary problems occupied several executive sessions of the Commission — their details not appearing in the minutes of regular meetings. Capt. M. H. Narvaez of Chemical 3 was fined a month's pay ($90) for "unbecoming conduct"; many others were transferred or demoted.

Good Machines, But You Can't Love 'Em

Overshadowing such details was the drama caught by long-time newsman Wilson Albee who wrote these lines for the San Jose Mercury of December 2, 1915 (fittingly, a gloomy day of unsettled weather) : "No more will the faithful animals spring from their stalls at the first tap of the gong, aquiver, every muscle ready to strain in the harness until the last breath . . . " The tractors had arrived; Engine 1 said farewell to horses at the end of November, and Engine 2 was due to follow suit on December 3 or 4. Last to go was Chief Haley's own beloved horse.

His high praise for the animals sounded a plaintive note in the chorus of farewell: "You cannot drive them into a ditch and if you let them alone they will never strike a tree, a pole or any other obstruction with the apparatus . . . They may be slower than the motors, but there is nothing more certain than that they will get you to the fire." They were a third more intelligent than average horses, the Chief added.

Engine 1's three horses were especially missed. They included Blutcher, a big 8-year-old black, junior member of the team with four years' service; his teammates were Frank and Dick, 11 and 13 years of age respectively. Veteran driver Tim Sullivan took them out on their last run, later pointing sadly to the new rigs and exclaiming, "They're good machines, all right, but you can't love 'em and they can't love you. It's going to be mighty lonesome without Blutcher, Frank and Dick."

Sullivan hung on for a time, driving the Pope-Hartford—it was a long while before he quit trying to stop his machine by shouting "Whoa!" Eventually he left the department, in 1919, to take away with him a lifelong love for horses and horsemanship.

One of the last horses in the department was reportedly sold to a Mr. Nelson, proprietor of a wood yard near Reed Field. During the remainder of its long life, the animal was regularly exercised by pulling the Reed Field lawn mower.

And so the year 1915—and an era—passed into memory. The following year turned out to be equally historic. To start things off, Commissioner J. P. Sex came under fire in January for "neglect of duty," and was suspended until his resignation in February. Mayor Husted charged angrily that Sex had served as defense counsel for an accused arsonist!

At 2 a.m. on February 1, fire destroyed a barn in the rear of the Ravenna Paste Co. macaroni factory at 49-53 North San Pedro, causing $3000 damage plus loss of several horses, two wagons, and much hay. Barn fires were epidemic then, but this one furnished one of old-time fireman Peter Segard's more colorful reminiscences. In his words, "We drove 22 horses down San Augustine Street clear to the creek to keep them from running back into the fire. Then we had to try to get an engine into the Notre Dame Convent to protect their property.

"So after we left the horses we drove around to the convent gate and rang their bell. Nobody answered, so we went back to Market Street and called them on the phone." It wasn't that the firemen were too polite to try forcible entry; the good sisters of Notre Dame kept a pack of vicious dogs which were loosed inside the convent's six-foot wall at night to discourage trespassers.

"We told them who we were," Segard continued, "and that we had just rung their bell. 'Yes, we heard you,' they said. We told them we wanted to get an engine inside their wall to protect their buildings. But the good nuns evidently preferred the fire to the firemen. If they had any trouble, they said, they'd call us!"

The fire was contained, the convent buildings untouched — only to be torn down in 1926 when the property was sold. The last remaining structure, the Rosicrucian Press building, was demolished to make way for the northerly extension of Almaden Ave.

The following month, another early morning blaze was much more serious. This was the second, and so far the last, major fire at the "Normal School," now San Jose State College. It was discovered at 12:50 a.m. on

March 24 (cause unknown) and swept through several acres of buildings aptly known as "The Shacks" along the San Carlos Street edge of Washington Square. For some reason that portion of the campus continued to harbor such construction until recently. Two alarms were sounded; crowds of students swarmed into the area to do yeoman work in saving books and furniture.

Under "state policy," no insurance coverage was provided on the ramshackle structures which had been built in 1906 to house the educational plant during repair of extensive earthquake damage to permanent buildings. Among the tenants were the Manual Arts Department and a machine shop. The nearby gymnasium, its walls smoking, was saved, but many artistic creations and items of machinery were lost — a total of $20,000 worth.

Not far away were the mattress and upholstery shops of Robinson's Furniture Co., at 87 South 4th Street. At 9:45 a.m., on May 16, 1916, a still alarm and Box 56 were turned in for fire in the mattress shop. The hazardous operations carried on there can well be imagined. A "silk-floss mattress-picking machine" ignited when friction heat or static electricity touched off the highly flammable lint-like material—flames exploded through the interior of the corrugated iron and frame structures as employees ran hopelessly for a nearby fire extinguisher. When they returned, it was too late.

The Fire Department was hampered by the absence of Engine 3, Chemical 5, and Assistant Chief Hobson, at a chimney fire far out on Royal Ave. Before the age of radio, simultaneous fires crippled the department's capability and were fortunately rare.

After three hours' work with 7 hose lines, the $17,000 Robinson fire was controlled. In smoking ruins were the shops, two sheds, a warehouse filled with home furnishings, and two automobiles. Firemen were able to prevent ignition of a nearby planing mill.

This was not the last destructive blaze to visit Robinson's. Another firm that was to become an important repeat customer for the Fire Department was T. J. Gillespie's hardwood lumber mill at the corner of East (now Montgomery) Street and San Fernando.

Poor Gillespie was jinxed where fire was concerned. A lumberman for 42 years, he had once operated at 78 Orchard Street (now Almaden Ave.). When Frank McKiernan's properties at Vine and Santa Clara burned in 1893, Gillespie had barely escaped destruction. His own buildings had several minor blazes during the '90's. In 1901 he moved to an old 3-story cotton mill, where later stood the plant of the Patterson-Williams Co.

Here was a firetrap in an age of firetraps. Its four-inch thick oil-soaked floors, every interior surface coated with a mixture of lint and sawdust — all was made to order for a quick burner. Shortly after midnight on September 14, 1916, the inevitable happened. Herb Gillespie and a boy employee, sleeping on the second floor, were roused by crackling flames and choking smoke. An alarm was turned in at once. (Next day, Gillespie complained bitterly about the "20 minutes" it took firemen to reach his place—a criticism stoutly rebutted by Chief Haley.)

It didn't matter much. When firemen did arrive, in what Haley indignantly contended was "4 minutes at the outside," they were able to get only five streams on the fire from the single 4 inch main in the area.

The initial response to Box 452 included Engine 1, Truck 1, and Chemical 5; as Assistant Chief Hobson rounded Market Street into Santa Clara, he could see flames looming over the rooftops more than half a mile away. A second alarm followed; fire soon spread from the main building to an unoccupied grocery store, then to a lumber shed containing $10,000 worth of the best eucalyptus wood.

Gillespie was a shrewd character. Almost alone among California lumbermen, he had developed methods of processing the tough eucalyptus wood then so common in the Valley. It was good hardwood, but almost impossible to make anything out of. This was the basis of Gillespie's business, which fell victim to a $30,000 loss that night.

Peter Segard was engineer of No. 2, pumping at Autumn and San Fernando, just out of sight of the blazing mill. About an hour after the first alarm, he recalled later, "We could see that something had happened, but we didn't know what. Police wagons were rolling in and out of the area apparently being used as ambulances."

What had happened was the collapse of the front wall and porch roof of the grocery store, just as the men of Segard's company tried to enter. Caught in the collapse were Capt. Gaylord H. Perry and hose wagon driver George Arrighi, who escaped with bruises, and George Welch, who suffered a broken leg and head injuries. At least one policeman and a bystander were also hurt.

Police finally had to beat back part of the crowd of thousands with their clubs. To add to the excitement, failure of a nearby power line darkened much of the city for an hour.

There were many main electric lines near Gillespie's, for only a block away was a main P. G. & E. substation. During the controversy with the mill owner after the fire, Chief Haley said the mill was so great a fire hazard that the electric company had already relocated one of its main lines away from the adjoining street. He also pointed out that a fire hydrant right next to the building had been removed, because if the place did catch fire the hydrant would be unusable.

Gillespie angrily alleged that firemen made no efforts at salvage—probably true enough, with the limited manpower at hand. Besides, salvage work was not highly stressed in the fighting of industrial fires then. Unfortunately, the sprinkler system that might have saved the situation did not operate. Gillespie claimed the valve was closed by the "arsonist" who touched off his place.

A good deal of Gillespie's raw material was being destroyed that week. A huge forest fire was eating its way through the hills behind Los Altos, threatening the whole region between Big Basin and La Honda. Hundreds were on the lines, including large numbers of Stanford University students.

New Deal In City Government

Looming over these events was the windup of the years of controversy over the City Charter and the form of San Jose's government. After a long and heated campaign, a reform was finally approved by the voters, going into effect in the middle of 1916. The new charter was modelled on that of Galveston, Texas, where nationwide attention had been drawn to the corruption of that city's administration and to the noteworthy nature of the curative measures. New York editor S. S. McClure was quoted as saying that the charter proposed for San Jose was an improvement over Galveston's.

A key feature was the "business manager," divorced from the pressures of local politics, who would take over most of the administrative staff functions. "It will be business in place of politics," exulted the San Jose Mercury—perhaps a bit prematurely in view of the political furors that have swirled about at least two local City Managers in ensuing decades. Even then, there was already internal warfare among the new charter proponents: should the manager be subject to recall or to a vote of the people? (still a loud argument in San Jose's more recent years).

Another feature was the elimination of the pulling and hauling between various city districts or "wards," with a Council composed of one member elected from each ward plus one "at large." From 1916 on, all Councilmen would be elected at large, able to take a city-wide view of municipal problems.

A major drawback to the old ways, one which directly affected Fire Department operations, was that the Mayor (who appointed the Police and Fire Commissioners) could be voted out of office, but his appointed Commissioners remained in the saddle until their terms expired; "they can outrage the voters by their acts but they cannot be reached." This worked both ways, for the new Mayor was also free to harass Commissioners "left over" from a previous administration — as Monahan had done in 1913.

An even worse defect, which the new charter would partially remedy, was the lack of a Civil Service—the lack of any real job security for firemen or police officers, the lack of promotional standards, the lack of any appeal from the Commission's arbitrary hiring and firing procedures.

All this was changed when, on June 29, 1916, the Police and Fire Commission of San Jose closed its books for the last time.

The Snows of Yesteryear . . .

Thus ended San Jose's colorful years of fire horses and steamers, in which were laid the foundations of today's fire service. Who or what has survived from those days before World War I? As of 1964, Louis Siebuhr, once Captain of Engine 1, whose 43-year career began in 1903, lived on at his North 9th Street home, with little to say about "the old days." John Powers, who retired in 1955 as Captain of Engine 2 after 43 years' service, has only scattered recollections of those times. A handful of others could be found, mostly too ill or feeble to reminisce much—such as Jack Wentzel, or ex-Commissioner J. S. Williams. Charles Plummer was still with us, willing to recall his youth by the hour, though his memory was fading. During the years since 1964, most of these survivors have passed away.

The real pity of it isn't that so few men survive. The passage of half a century brings its inevitable result. But nothing much else is left either. We do have the fire bell, in the former City Hall Plaza. Gone, however, is the handsome little station on Spencer Ave., the "McCarthy House," with "Coffee Bill's" initials wrought in the big front doors. Gone are all the Federal chain-drives, the Knox and Pope-Hartford chemicals, the hose reels and wagons, the Hayes aerial and its "new" replacement of 1908, the steamers and their tractors (although the dingy remains of one survived for years in Levin's Machinery & Salvage yard—widely supposed to be one of San Jose's rigs, it is actually from the San Francisco Fire Department). Though counterparts of the old rigs remain in almost every surrounding community, none are left in San Jose. Since 1964, the Fire Department Shop has done some beautiful work in restoring old rigs for possible museum use — but little or none of that apparatus ever saw service in San Jose.

Even photographs of much of the vanished apparatus, or of the great fires of 50 years ago, are not to be found today—not in the Fire Department's annals, the libraries, or the State House Museum. The few pictures in these pages are in large measure the last surviving copies from negatives that have been destroyed, or lost for years.

Today's museum pieces that might attract state-wide or even national attention were sold or junked for a pittance. Nor have those more recently obsoleted fared much better (such as the little Mack-Hedberg 1938 squad wagon—one of the city's handsomest equipments).

Yesterday's San Jose Fire Department is gone for good, but it is the hope of many that some means may be found today to preserve something of today's department for tomorrow's generations.

Two Platoons And
A Growing City
1916-1932

Many of the questions "settled" by the 1916 charter changes were never settled at all. Even today, thoughtful citizens debate the wisdom of the latest practices regarding a "vote of confidence" for the City Manager. In mid-1964, others debated a proposal to enhance the Mayor's figurehead status by giving him more power.

But there is no doubt about one thing. The hiring of police officers or saloon keepers to head the Fire Department was at an end. Establishment of a stable Civil Service, whatever its shortcomings have been, was a great stride forward.

Last Call for the Call Men

The new regime had its problems even in the beginning. It was not without its enemies, who made the most of City Manager Reed's unexplained firing of Police Chief Fuller and City Engineer Maggini in November. The following month, some newly appointed firemen refused to accept their jobs — perhaps expecting the same old treatment. But others took their places, fortunately.

There were vacancies to fill in the Fire Department. The 36 regular men needed to be increased to 46, said the Underwriters. As for the extramen, neither Underwriters nor Manager Reed thought much of them. In 1904, there had been 26; by 1914, only 19 positions remained, and at the end of 1916 only 15 places were filled. Intensive recruit-

ing, however, would have to wait. Events in Europe, as 1917 began, foreshadowed other uses for manpower.

Just two days before U. S. entry into World War I drove all else from the front pages, fire destroyed one of the city's downtown landmarks of a more peaceful age.

San Jose had been a great theater town. During the '80's and '90's, citizens weren't debating the need for a civic theater to bring in the great of the entertainment world. Performances came to San Jose then, with or without benefit of the latest in stages or acoustical hall, because of the demand of large and appreciative audiences. We had the Chicago Symphony; the Mormon Tabernacle Choir sang on the Court House steps.

After the California Theater vanished in the great fire of 1892, its place was taken by a 2-story wooden exhibit hall at San Fernando and San Pedro Streets, erected six years earlier by San Jose's Horticultural Association. Oliver Morosco, one of the great showmen of all time, and an experienced and successful theater manager though still in his teens, directed its remodeling into the Garden Theater.

For the next quarter century the nation's greatest stars trod its boards. Evangelist Dwight L. Moody preached there. Madame Modjeska played "Camille" at the old Garden; Julia Marlowe appeared in "Twelfth

Night"; everything from Uncle Tom's Cabin to grand opera. Inspired political meetings were held there; statesmen such as Speaker of the House Thomas Reed addressed the crowded gallery.

Ironically, the Garden's theatrical life, created by one fire, was ended by another. Flames which raced through the old building during the noon hour on April 4, 1917, were breaking through the roof when firemen arrived in response to two box alarms. Several streams were trained into the theater from the street; other lines were dragged down the west side of Market Street to protect half a block of exposed stores, garages, and homes. These were saved, but the theater was a $15,000 loss, including a ground floor sign shop and printing plant. Faulty wiring was supposedly the cause.

San Joseans mourned its passing. The Mercury reported that, at a late hour, saddened old-timers were still making their pilgrimage, on foot, in carriages, or by automobile, just to view the smoking ruins.

City Manager Reed was less impressed with the sentimental value of the property than with the good work of his Fire Department. Said his letter to Chief Haley, "It was one of the finest pieces of fire fighting work ever done in this community . . ."

This was the last major fire for San Jose's paid volunteers, the extramen. That summer, with the newspapers full of draft calls, exposure of slackers, and the like, the City Manager quietly gave the death blow to the extraman system. On Monday, August 6, he announced that the last two call men had been dropped from the department the preceding Saturday. Claiming that their main utility had been for night alarms—where the necessary trained manpower was coming from during daylight hours, he didn't say— Reed added: "Under the old system . . . the efficiency of the department was greatly hindered, as no special dependence could be placed on employees of this sort . . ." Miles McDermott must have turned in his grave.

They were offered the option of applying for "reinstatement" as full-time firemen; a number of them did so. So ended the service of the "call men." For the first time in 40 years, the great Market Street fire bell was silent.

Now that the entire fire force was a close-knit professional group, its members began actively promoting their own welfare. For a time during the '80's, there had been benefit balls to raise money towards the support of firemen's widows and orphans. The custom had died out, along with the "Firemen's Charitable Association" of volunteer days, and the "Relief Fund" set up by the defunct Commission.

On January 26. 1918, the Fire Department staged its "first" annual benefit ball of modern times. Planned by the half fraternal, half philanthropic Richard Brown Club, the informal Moose Hall dance to Bert Marquart's orchestra netted over $1000. Even though there was a military ball the same evening at the Hotel Vendome, enough blue uniforms were in town to lend color to both affairs. The "floor committee" in charge included Assistant Chief Cavallero; Captains Bill Sterling, M. H. Narvaez, Louis Siebuhr; Tim Sullivan; and Lieut. Ted Haub.

In later years, the annual Firemen's Ball was held jointly with the Police Department, and was only discontinued in recent times after the Firemen's Rodeo became a bigger drawing card.

During the rest of 1918, the professionals had their hands full enough to make them wish for the call men back again. On March 31, at the northeast corner of the railroad tracks (4th Street) and Lewis Street, a Southern Pacific switchman saw fire inside the Jaffe Cereal Company plant—formerly the Fig Prune Cereal Company. It was late at night, but he took no further notice because

84

he knew that coffee roasting machines in the plant were often operated at night. Unfortunately, he didn't know that this particular night the plant was shut down. There was no night watchman.

Half an hour later, when the switchman passed by again, the roof was afire. He ran for a nearby alarm box. Firemen responding to this and several other calls attacked the flames on all sides, but were only able to save the nearby buildings of the Pyle Cannery and Harlan Packing Company. The loss exceeded $35,000.

At the end of May, lumberman T. J. Gillespie's remaining plant on West San Fernando Street was destroyed for the third and last time by a 4 a.m. blaze. Here there was a watchman, to make valiant efforts with hand extinguishers and buckets, only to faint from over-exertion. The loss was small ($3500) because Gillespie's buildings had not been fully rebuilt from a $6000 fire on the night of December 10, 1917.

Less than a week later, a passerby discovered fire at 3:30 a.m. June 5, in the uninsured two-story carriage factory of Mike Brodel at 554 South First Street. A stiff northerly breeze carried embers for blocks. Destroyed along with the $17,000 Brodel building and its contents of autos and truck trailers were a 2-story rooming house, and three small stores, at 538 and 544 South First. Several chemical companies put out spot fires springing up in the surrounding neighborhood, and guarded the rear of threatened homes on 2nd Street.

The War's Over

Having prematurely "celebrated" America's declaration of war with a serious downtown fire, San Jose proceeded to honor the Armistice in exactly the same way—at 10:45 p.m. on November 7, 1918. It was the worst in years, and gutted the Harrison P. Smith Auto Company (San Jose's Reo-Overland agency) on the northeast corner of First and San Carlos Streets, where the J. J. Newberry store was later located.

Starting in the downstairs repair shops and feeding on the gasoline tanks of a hundred cars, plus large stocks of oil and paint, flames raged out of control for six hours. Only the brick firewalls kept fire out of adjoining stores. Firemen manning ten hose lines were forced by gasoline explosions to fight from the street. Captain Walter Page of Chemical 5

was thrown into a wall and knocked out when a hose burst.

This was the first major test of the department's new Chief. Sixty years of age, unable to reconcile himself to the loss of the fire horses, white-haired Ed Haley had resigned to take over management of a local dairy. History was made in the choice of his successor, Herman Hobson, Assistant Chief since 1915. For the first time in the paid Fire Department, the second in command was elevated to fill the vacant Chief's post. This precedent has been followed since, with one notable exception in 1944.

Haley disappeared from public life, but his declining years were far from inactive. Born in San Jose in 1858, he grew up helping his father on the family farm. Next he became a painter and decorator. Following several years as hose cart driver for Empire Engine, Haley was a police constable, then Chief of Police in 1901-2 and again in 1907-10. After his term as Fire Chief, he remained with his dairy job until a few weeks before his death in 1940. At the age of 82, looking a spry and wiry 65, he attained a Pacific Coast Fire Chiefs' Convention to be acclaimed as the oldest Fire Chief west of the Rockies.

There was also a new City Manager in 1918 —W. C. Bailey. On November 9, he wrote a letter to Chief Hobson praising the department's work at the Smith fire, adding: "I personally appreciate the way in which you and your men have taken hold of the influenza situation and helped out the street department and other departments of the city.

Civic leader Jay McCabe's World War I victory celebration was exuberant to a fault. A passerby tossed his coat containing war bonds onto the bonfire. The flames scored the trolley lines and McCabe was cited for destroying the street.

The flu epidemic would have crippled some of the city's operations, had not the Fire Department rendered "mutual aid" city-wide. One of the tasks was to wash the streets down nightly during the epidemic, presumably to help 'disperse the contagion.'

The tragic course of the disease was forgotten two days later, when once again the Market Street bell rang out, along with everything else in town that would make a noise, to signal the end of the war. Jubilant throngs went wild on First Street. Hat store proprietor Jay McCabe cleaned out all the old cartons from the nearby Arcade and other stores, to build a gigantic bonfire in the middle of the street. "The flames went above the buildings," he recalls with a chuckle, "It burned the trolley wires, and made a 25-foot hole in the pavement."

McCabe's rival fire buff, former Commissioner Louis King, was outraged. He summoned the Fire Department, then swore out a warrant for McCabe's arrest on charges of destroying the street. But street car manager Frank Chapin told Jay he'd square the rap. During the celebration, one over-excited bystander threw his coat into the flames; in the pockets were a pair of $100 Liberty Bonds!

Hobson Makes Improvements

Now that the attention of war-weary San Joseans was returning to domestic affairs, Chief Hobson let no grass grow under his feet. Inspections were made throughout the city to uncover hazardous condition. In 1919, it was announced that State firemen's associations credited San Jose with having "some of the fastest fire companies in California." We had come a long way, boasted the local press, from a few years earlier when San Jose (with Fresno) was condemned by insurance companies and Underwriters as the worst "firebug center" in the state.

Engine 1 on test, 1920; North San Pedro Street. This was the second—and last—Seagrave pumper ever to see service here. Notice the old Hook & Ladder house still standing, with flagpole, in the left background.

Actually, of course, it was bad construction practices, lack of sprinklers, and other safeguards, that caused poor fire records—just as it is today. Considering that the citizens of San Jose were spending only 50c per capita per year on their Fire Department (vs. $10 today), the record wasn't half bad.

Hobson took a pioneer step towards reduction of water damage. To get streams with more power and unlimited capacity compared to the feeble squirts from the chemical wagons, yet still save the wholesale flooding caused by 2½-inch lines, the Chief bought dividers to break the big lines down into 1½-inch hose. It was a radical idea then; now, every engine company is so equipped. Another improvement, an outgrowth of wartime de-velopment, was the first use of gas masks by San Jose firemen.

Final elimination of the steamers also came during Chief Hobson's administration. First step in this direction was in 1919, when — satisfied at last with the operation of the 1914 machine — San Jose ordered another Seagrave "combination pump and hose engine" of 750 GPM capacity. It arrived early in 1920 for assignment to Engine 1.

By the end of the fiscal year, it was easy for Hobson to win sympathy for his improvement ideas. He was able to officially report what has turned out to be the lowest fire loss in the half century of existing Fire Department records.

Missing from the center background of this December 1919 photo is one of downtown San Jose's best-known landmarks: the Bank of America Building, not constructed until 1928. In the foreground: ruins of the Rutherford Building on San Fernando near Second, after the fire was out.

There was only one serious fire. Sunday night, September 22, 1919, the Chartier Building burned. The old wooden structure had been a lumber mill for years, with a basement full of combustible rubbish, and was then used as an auto paint shop — perfect setup for a bonfire. A small basement blaze had been put out only two weeks earlier.

Covering most of the block bounded by Post, Vine, Westminster, and Orchard Streets, the building ignited from "unknown" causes and was fully involved when firemen arrived. They toiled valiantly—the Chartier Building was a $15,000 loss, but several nearby buildings were saved with minor damage. A householder at 227 Westminster escaped from his burning home carrying only a trunk and a canary. Captain William Sterling, just returned to duty from 8 months' sick leave, was knocked out when a 500 volt line fell into a pool of water in which he was standing.

Unappreciative of San Jose's fire protection bargain, next day's newspapers praised the firemen's conduct " . . . handicapped as they are by a lack of engines to supply the requisite number of streams of water with sufficient pressure to accomplish much against the fire." It was not considered cricket to editorialize on the lack of automatic sprinklers, or to wonder why the basement full of rubbish had not been cleaned out.

A much greater loss of about $50,000—and just as preventable — occurred one frosty December morning in the Rutherford Building at the southwest corner of 2nd and San Fernando. Earlier fires there, in 1902 and 1908, had given the place a bad name with the Fire Department. At 42 East San Fernando, the building housed the Enterprise Grocery and Gold Nugget Ice Cream Parlor downstairs, with the San Fernando Hall upstairs; at 44 East San Fernando was the Owl

Shoe Repair Shop. On the corner was J. W. Dixon's harness store, with A. and E. Schladt's flower shop adjoining at 119 South 2nd.

There had been a dance in the hall Sunday night, the 14th. Shortly after it ended at 1 a.m., someone in the street saw smoke curling under the eaves. As firemen summoned by Box 31 ascended ladders to the second floor, flames broke through the roof to threaten nearby buildings. A second alarm was pulled.

It was 8 hours before the fire was out; two of the twelve hose lines used were left at the scene until Tuesday afternoon. The entire second floor was burned out, including the regalia of three lodges which used the hall. Downstairs, water damage was heavy, but a neighborhood conflagration had been prevented.

"A Measure of Justice"

Forced to remain on duty, without rest or reserves, through the long hours of fighting fires like the Rutherford, firemen felt the time was ripe for a change. Early in February, 1920, the Richard Brown Club called a special meeting to organize a new group— the "Two Platoon Club." Officers of the new club were: President, Captain Walter Page; Vice-president, Captain R. D. Clearwater; Recording Secretary, J. F. Dwyer; Treasurer, Captain Bill Tennant; Campaign Committee, Captain John Gilleran, Bill Mason, and Fred Hambly.

Its purpose was to use the municipal elections in May to force division of the Fire Department into two shifts or platoons, only one of which would be on duty at any one time. Many other cities were beginning to operate this way. Not only would it give everyone a reasonable amount of time at home; it would provide some reserve force which could be called on to cover the rest of the city while the on-duty shift was occupied with a major fire.

A vote of the people was required because the City Charter called for firemen to be on duty 24 hours a day; no two-platoon system would be possible without a charter change. The men first proposed that they get 12 hours off on "certain days of the week," juggling assignments in some way so the city would have to hire no new personnel.

This turned out to be unrealistic. As it finally went before the voters on May 3, 1920, the system was this: Men would work an average of 12 hours a day 7 days a week, with no time off for meals. The average was made up something like this: Work two 10-hour day shifts, with nights off, the third day spend 24 hours on, then work two 14-hour night shifts with days off; every 6th day, 24 hours off. At that, it was a simple routine compared to schedules followed today.

This was an 84-hour week. Previously, every man worked 24 hours a day 6 days a week, with 3 hours daily off for meals, plus two days off once each month. This was roughly a 114-hour week. Thus, to provide the same force on duty at any given time under the new system required about ⅓ more men. Those off-duty would still be on call for serious emergencies.

In campaigning for two platoons, the Committee assured voters that lowered insurance rates from increased manpower would offset the cost to the city. (The 1920-21 Fire Department budget did take a startling jump, up to $124,055; $2300 of this was for payments on the new Seagrave engine.) In a final plea two days before election, firemen cried out for the change "as a measure of justice for the mens' families"; the firefighter was then the only class of city employee required to put in more than an 8-hour day.

Voters approved the change, 5 to 1. It took six months, until November 29, 1920, to work out the details and hire the new men. At the same time, San Jose was able to re-activate Chemical No. 4, which had been closed for some time as an economy measure.

Only two serious fires intervened, one of them in Chinatown. The other wiped out part of the O. A. Harlan Packing Company at 4th and Margaret Streets, with a $30,000 insured loss, shortly after midnight on August 24. Some other news items for 1920: the deeding of Backesto Park to the City of San Jose, groundbreaking for San Jose Technical High School, and two cases in one week of an errant automobile breaking off a fire hydrant. San Jose's District Attorney Arthur Free agreed with a U. S. Ambassador's statement that war with Japan was "simply unthinkable."

Then on a cold winter evening near the end of the year, San Jose firemen took one of their worst beatings in the first real test of the two-platoon system. At 5:46 p.m. December 7, a telephone alarm came in for fire in the 60-year-old F. W. Gross and Sons 3-story department store at 52 South First (the building housed Berg's in 1964). The first arriving companies took one look at the heavy smoke pouring up from the Gross basement and called for a general alarm. Soon all the men from both shifts were on hand.

Taking terrible punishment from smoke, firemen first tried to work into the basement from the sidewalk freight elevator. Forced back there, they cut holes in the first floor through which to direct streams. To get at the rear, lines were taken over roofs from 2nd Street and holes were breached in an 8-inch brick wall behind the Gross Store.

For three hours flames raged out of control. A score of firefighters dropped out of action, overcome by noxious fumes against which the early gas masks were useless. Half a dozen were hospitalized, some being loaded on hose wagons to be driven the few blocks to the old Columbia Hospital on Market

Fred Hambly of Chemical 1, whose promising career was cut short by the Gross fire in 1920.

Street. In the dark, Jack Wentzel fell through a skylight on an adjoining roof, breaking three ribs; Charles Madel was struck on the head by a nozzle when the line got away. Next door, the Metropolitan store manager kept his clerks busy for the evening, making coffee and serving doughnuts to the weary firemen.

Groping among the piles of stock in the hot, poisonous, and pitch-black basement, Acting Captain Fred Hambly of Chemical 1 was caught in a sudden flareup as the first floor began to collapse. Against the glare of flames, Captain Page of Chemical 5 saw Hambly drop and dragged him to the street.

Several firemen injured at the Gross store fire were taken here by hose wagon — the Columbia Hospital at Market and Auzerais. Still there today in use as apartments, it was the central city's only hospital until 1923.

This rare photo, one of the first ever made at night using "available light," shows the destruction of Grant School, December 8, 1920.

Unconscious for hours, Hambly then rallied and seemed to recover. But within a few weeks he was dead, his lungs burned out by superheated gases.

Only 24 hours after the Gross fire was finally put out by flooding the entire basement, a 2-alarm fire of unknown origin destroyed most of the Grant School at 10th and Empire Streets. Fifteen classrooms were burned out. Low water pressure handicapped the firefighting; to get water up to the second floor firemen had to siamese two lines into one. As the roof began to fall in, Chief Hobson had to restrain the enthusiastic efforts of a group of "old grads" who were busily rescuing school trophies, a clock, and an organ from the building. The loss exceeded $40,000.

This fire temporarily settled the argument as to which school in San Jose could boast the toughest kids — Grant or Longfellow. While Grant was being rebuilt, many students from there were transferred for the time being to Longfellow, thus giving that school the "honor."

The New Organization

In this trying time, the Chief declared himself well satisfied with the working of the two-platoon system. However, there was the problem of adequate leadership for both shifts. Each fire company was still headed by only one officer (the Captain), and when he was off duty, someone else had to be in charge. So a full slate of Lieutenants had to be created. Second in command to the Captains, but serving on alternate shifts, the Lieutenants were paid slightly less, and were not responsible for the station, equipment, company records, etc. The Captain remained the company boss, to be appealed to in matters of discipline. Several promising men were made Acting Lieutenants until the ranks were filled and proper promotional examinations could be given.

Recruiting began in earnest late in 1920 and continued into the following year. Much

Latest thing in manpower squads, 1920—San Jose's Model T, driven by James O'Day (a police officer for years after he left the fire service). Left, Asst. Chief Dominic Cavallero. On the rear, Carl O'Dell, later Captain of Engine 7.

more was involved, under the new Civil Service, than the simple furnishing of a health certificate. Besides meeting US Army health standards of 1916, candidates for both Police and Fire Departments now had to meet a minimum weight requirement (150 pounds), be able to carry 125 pounds of sand up a 40-foot ladder and back down, then run a quarter mile in three minutes. This and other physical tests proceeded under the watchful eye of YMCA physical director Fred Saxon. Psychological testing was administered by Dr. Leroy Stockton of the Normal School, colleague of the pioneer in intelligence and personality testing, Professor Lewis Terman of Stanford. By the end of 1920 they had processed three groups totalling 45 candidates. In August 1921, 21 men were qualified to take the exams for promotion to Lieutenant.

But even if all authorized Fire Department positions had been filled (which they seldom were), the companies remained shorthanded. This was especially true of the two-man chemical rigs, which had hose beds so they could be described as "equipped as hose wagon," yet had only a driver and officer to use that hose.

Therefore Chief Hobson established Squad Company No. 1, responding to all alarms to furnish additional manpower. Assistant Chief Cavallero and two men were assigned to it. Originally, the apparatus was a cut-down Model T fitted with chemical tanks. Old-timers recall that its front wheels rose off the ground if more than one man stood on the rear step! Within a few years a larger and heavier chemical wagon was used instead. Eventually coming to specialize in rescue work, as the "pulmotor" and other life-saving

92

San Jose's 1922 Stutz as it looked when assigned to Engine Co. 7 in 1937. Left to right: Fireman Frank Wysocki, Driver Larry Campbell, Lieut. Gilbert Stewart.

equipment was introduced, Squad 1, remained the department's "elite" for the next 30 years.

To keep one Assistant Chief available for duty on each shift, Charles Plummer was promoted to the rank of Second Assistant at the end of 1920. With only minor interruptions, there have been two Assistant Chiefs ever since, although their functions have changed considerably.

In 1922, San Jose purchased its one and only Stutz pumper—a 750 GPM right-hand drive machine for service at Market Street. This moved the 1920 Seagrave to Engine 2, where it replaced the last steamer on active service. Thus the successor to Empire, first fire company to have a steam pumper, was also the last company to operate one.

What happened to that last steamer? Nobody seems to know. One steam engine was in reserve at Engine 3 for at least 11 years. When World War II broke out, the Fire Department got some good publicity by firing up an old steamer for civilian defense emergencies But which rig it was, or where it is today, remains unknown.

The Stutz Company was new to the fire apparatus field, having built its first engine in 1919. San Jose got long service from theirs — almost a quarter century — but never bought another; the firm gave up the ghost long ago. Other new equipment acquired in the early '20's included replacements for the primitive Federals of Chemical 1 and Hose 1, featuring improvements not standard in the original rigs, such as the self-starter. Some apparatus was being equipped with sirens,

bells no longer being adequate in automobile traffic.

For the next couple of years the city enjoyed low fire losses. On October 22, 1922, a $30,000 fire destroyed the brick and corrugated iron plant of the California Pine Box Company, on Terraine Street across from the John Bean plant. Unable to get inside because of heat and heavy smoke, firemen were further hampered by lack of openings in the brick exterior walls. "We need a water tower," said the newspaper stories. Ladder pipes were called for, but the flimsy wooden aerial we then had could not be adapted to such use.

It took two hours to control the fire, which wasn't extinguished until after dark. During that time, the change of shifts brought in fresh manpower to relieve those who had fought the blaze all afternoon. This was hailed as a further justification for two platoons.

Lack of window openings and suitable ladder equipment complicated firefighting at the California Pine Box fire.

Downtown, John Stock & Sons' pioneer hardware firm at 71 South First Street bore the brunt of a $25,000 fire early on February 1, 1923. John and Francis Stock, founders of the business, had both been volunteer firemen in the early days, but their successors evidently weren't very fire-conscious — the 1923 fire began in a trash burner inside their store. Spreading to the rear of C. W. Dore's pharmacy, the American Trading Stamp Company, and Columbia Outfitting, flames for a time threatened the entire block. The alarm was given at 2:04 a.m. by telephone operators who discovered the fire from the rear of the Market Street exchange building.

Even more serious was the burning of L. S. Seeley's clothing store in the 2-story Doerr Building at 182-188 South First in February 1924. Firemen arrived shortly after dark in response to a box alarm, to find the store filled with smoke and fire extending through rear walls into the St. Paul Apartments upstairs. Fortunately, all the tenants fled to safety; the only casualty was in the Alton Hotel next door, where the manager's pet canary was asphyxiated by smoke. Burning in concealed spaces, the fire burned most of the night. Damage to two stores, a bakery, and the apartments was estimated at $50,000.

Just a week later, at 6:30 in the morning, a telephone alarm sent firefighters to the Smout Building at 63 West Santa Clara Street.

The top floor was well alight when they got there. Having burned a long time before discovery, the fire swept through a massage parlor and several office suites upstairs, while water and smoke damage was severe downstairs. A tangle of hose lines tied up streetcar traffic for hours. Praised for a good stop, the Fire Department acknowledged that only a brick fire wall prevented heavy damage to adjoining buildings on the west.

Out in the packing house district, on Montgomery Street near Cinnabar, firemen had won a hard battle in 1913 to save the buildings of the J. K. Ormsby Company, from flames which destroyed adjacent plants. Several years later, the Ormsby firm was absorbed by the newly-organized California Packing Corporation. The CPC night watchman there made his last rounds at 6 a.m. April 19, 1924, without noticing anything out of the ordinary.

At 6:45, when the plant foreman arrived to open the doors, he was greeted by a roaring fire. Within minutes, flames burst through the roof. Inside were 600 tons of dried fruit, plus hundreds of sacks of sulphur and huge stocks of box shook and paper cartons. Only ten feet away across an alley was Plant No. 2 of the Richmond-Chase Company.

Although CPC was technically outside city limits, nearby exposures (including Richmond-Chase) were San Jose territory. So

Burning of the California Pine Box Co., October 1922, near San Pedro and Bassett Streets.

95

while the valiant crews from the Southern Pacific roundhouse brought hose lines to bear on the flames, an urgent appeal was made to City Manager Goodwin for help from San Jose. He consented, but it was too late to do more than save other structures. The CPC plant was a total loss, along with a boxcar on the plant siding, totalling $75,000.

A competitor of CPC in the dried fruit business was the California Prune and Apricot Growers Association. This co-op had taken over the former Chilton property on North First at the SP tracks. As the J. W. Chilton packing house, the place had played an important role in the tragic drama of 1906. Its management suspended operations and turned the building into an emergency hospital for earthquake victims—of which there were many, especially from the shattered structures of Agnews State Hospital and O'Connor Sanitarium. One floor was used to

care for injured and burned refugees from the ruins of San Francisco, brought down by train.

About midnight on October 16, 1924, during a steady downpour of rain, the watchman saw fire in the boiler room at the rear, and before firemen could get into action half of the two- and three-story building was involved. In spite of the rain, trees in adjacent Ryland Park caught fire, while burning paper cartons descended on the surrounding neighborhood. Hundreds of spectators braved the weather, attracted by a glow visible for miles.

Machinery in the front of the building was saved. In the rear, the major loss was a thousand tons of prunes valued at $180 per ton; total damage was $200,000. The CP & AGA, though hard hit by two previous fires elsewhere that year, announced that fruit packing would resume in ten days. Almost as an afterthought, the Association also stated that

This fine shot by J. C. Gordon dates back to 1924. Squad 1 poses at Market Street, with Chief Herman Hobson (left). On the rig, left rear, young Lester O'Brien (later Chief 1944-1957) and Jim O'Day. Up front, Asst. Chief Cavallero and driver Ivor Jones.

the rebuilt plant would have the boiler room detached from the rest of the structure. That feature in itself, however, didn't save the building in 1955, when a two-alarm fire wrecked everything.

West Side Story

San Jose has met little organized opposition in expanding its boundaries to the east, the north, or the south. The real annexation battles have been on the near west side. In recent times, the Bradley Manor annexation — settled only in the courts — is a case in point. Decades of campaigning have failed to bring Burbank into the fold.

During the 1920's, controversy raged around the Hester-Hanchett district. Settlement of this large territory, ranging north and west to Park Avenue and the Santa Clara city limits, had begun as soon as San Jose was founded. The tree-lined Alameda, with its stately mansions, the brewery and car barns, the College of the Pacific (later Bellarmine College Preparatory), Hester School, plus the beginnings of several commercial developments—all these lay outside San Jose's boundaries.

By 1923, the 15,000 residents — many of them well-to-do and influential — had chosen sides for the final struggle. Victor Benson headed the forces favoring annexation to San Jose; Hiram Blanchard, president of the College Park Improvement Club, led the opposition. Once that year, then twice more in 1924, Benson's side lost annexation elections. That of February 1924, lost by a 2 to 1 margin,

was marked by "high feeling" on both sides. A fourth vote was scheduled for November 1925.

Fire protection was a major need of the Hester-Hanchett area, which was much too spread out, with too wide a variety of hazards, to be adequately covered by any home-grown fire department the residents might have scraped up. Since the first meetings of the Alameda Improvement Club 14 years earlier, no solution had been found. Unable to wait any longer, residents voted on November 10, 1925, to join with the Burbank and Sunol districts to form "Fire District No. 1"— which still covers the latter two neighborhoods today.

The same month, however, the fourth annexation election carried by a slim margin of 408 votes, and San Jose made its richest expansion to date. To cap their victory, the new San Joseans turned in a fire alarm after touching off a roaring bonfire in the middle of a vacant lot on The Alameda owned by the defeated Mr. Blanchard. No doubt alerted to be at their best, firemen from Market Street headquarters bounced over the car tracks and rattled to a stop at the Blanchard property in just four minutes. Acknowledging the cheers of an enthusiastic throng, the boys then toured the Hester District in a triumphal procession.

When the cheers had died away, clearer heads realized that the suburb needed protection closer to home. On December 18, 1925, according to a plaque still displayed in Fire Station No. 7, Chemical Co. 7 was established

Making good its boast to furnish Hester District fire protection, San Jose shows off the suburb's Chemical 7— March 25, 1926. Among the dignitaries: City Councilmen "Doc" Denegri, standing on the rig at left, and Joe Brooks, driving. Standing in front are City Clerk John Lynch, left, and City Manager Clarence Goodwin, right. The officer is Chief Herman Hobson.

Market Street, 1924. Left to right : Engine 1, 1920 Seagrave, with Louis Volonte and Capt. Siebuhr; Hose 1—Firemen Harry Miller and Walter Napolitano; Chemical 1—Capt. Nick Berryessa and Fireman Peter Consolacio; Chief Hobson's roadster; Squad 1—Asst. Chief Page, Firemen Ivor Jones and Merle Rhyne; Truck 1—Firemen C. "Peachy" Mills, Capt. Harry Dennis, Fireman Sal Bernal. Most of these men are now dead.

with a crew consisting of Captain L. M. Lunsford, Lieut. Ed Powers, and drivers John Gossett and Harvey Davis. First located at 1125 The Alameda, the company soon moved to 1187 Hester Ave. Their "firehouse" was the old Benson garage, behind which sleeping quarters were fitted up for the men.

There is no record of what the first apparatus was, but the following March local politician and auto dealer Henry Artana sold the city the last of its hose-chemical combinations—No. 7, a jaunty little 4-cylinder Reo carrying two 35-gallon chemical tanks.

The chemical engine was definitely past its prime as metropolitan fire apparatus. Yet San Jose, at this late date, was operating seven of them. San Francisco had never had more; Chicago, which was an "extensive user" of chemical wagons twenty years earlier, employed only 13; New Orleans, another major user, had 11. The Underwriters had a poor opinion of them. Without manpower or pumping capacity to be anything but "first aid" appliances, they were classed only as "hose carriers" for rating purposes.

Fire protection expert Jay W. Stevens, then State Fire Marshal and president of the International Association of Fire Chiefs, was pessimistic about San Jose's future with such equipment. Speaking before the local Kiwanis, he made business leaders squirm in their seats by blasting the San Jose Fire Department from top to bottom. "Within a year," he thundered, "you are due for a serious conflagration...this city has made little advance in fire protection and prevention." (This was hardly fair to Hobson.) His listeners did not, however, feel sufficiently alarmed to try to salvage the bond issue for fire alarm system improvements, which voters had just rejected.

Chief Hobson disagreed with the pontifical Stevens, whose prediction was premature, but his case was weak. The Chief had to admit his department did need 100 men rather than 64, four pumpers instead of three, and a second ladder company. Before all those needs were met, twenty years would have to pass.

Charles Plummer Takes Over

Fire and Police Department salaries made news during 1926, as the men set out to gain for themselves a share of the growing national prosperity making itself felt in San Jose. In March, firemen petitioned the City Council for raises averaging $20, which would result in this monthly salary schedule: Chief, $270; First Assistant, $215; Second Assistant, $205; Captains, $190; Lieutenants, $182.50; firemen, to start at $160 and rise to $175 after three years. The Council agreed to let the voters decide the issue in the May election, because only by increasing the tax rate from $1.25 to $1.40 could the money be provided.

On May 16, the ordinance establishing the new salaries was narrowly approved at the polls. Chief Hobson praised the voters, acknowledging the campaign help of the David Scannell Club of the San Francisco Fire Department.

Firemen soon had a chance to earn their new rates. At 3 a.m. June 13, a passerby on West San Carlos Street thought he saw a grass fire off to the south. Grass fires in the small hours of a Sunday morning rang no bells in his mind, so he went about his business. An hour later, however, he came that way again and realized the fire was bigger. A box alarm finally brought firemen at 4:05 a.m., to the U. S. Products cannery at Race and Moorpark, which was ablaze from end to end. The frame building was destroyed with an $80,000 loss, just before opening of the busy canning season.

The discoverer of San Jose's next major fire acted with more determination. He was "Pep" Young of the Mercury staff. Walking home from his night job at the newspaper office, at the corner of 3rd and Santa Clara Streets, Young saw that the 2-story Alliance Building was on fire. He sprinted up 3rd Street to the firehouse and pounded on the doors to rouse the men of Engine 2 (though it might have been quicker just to pull the alarm box on the front of the building).

Responding at 2:17 a.m., firemen found the Standard Tire Company fully involved, flames apparently spreading from a vulcaniz-

Chief Hobson stands beside his official car during the early 1920's.

ing machine. Rising through non-firestopped walls to sweep through music studios and offices upstairs, the fire burst through the roof, remaining uncontrolled for two hours. Most of the ground floor stores were saved except for water damage.

Owners and tenants of the Alliance Building lost about $75,000. San Jose lost a Fire Chief. Herman Hobson contracted pneumonia from soaking and exposure at the Alliance fire, and on October 7 he died at the age of 54. A one-time sign painter, the native son of valley pioneers, Hobson had enjoyed a steady rise in his profession since joining the department in 1908. Among his pallbearers were two future Chiefs—Henry Lingua and Arthur Gilbert—together with Captains Page, Gilleran, Welch, and Dennis.

City Manager C. B. Goodwin appointed Charles Plummer to fill the vacancy on October 19, 1926; both of these men were to hold their respective offices until almost 18 years later, longer than anyone else has ever held them in San Jose.

Plummer had started out as driver of Hose 1 in 1904, later being reduced to extraman after expressing some intemperate political opinions. Reinstated in 1918, after the call men were stricken from the rolls, Plummer became Captain later that year, then Second Assistant Chief on December 31, 1920.

Only the morning after Plummer's appointment, the new Chief had a serious fire to handle. It wrecked the frame and sheet iron building of the Pacific By-Products Company

On Santa Clara Street, near Market, about 1926, the former Hose 1 (chain drive Federal) supports an early cleanup campaign. Left to right, the firemen are Louis Volonte, Harry Dennis, and Harry Miller.

on Sunol Street at Auzerais, which produced charcoal from fruit pits. Some $20,000 damage to stock and machinery resulted from the 4:30 a.m. blaze. The place must have been a fire inspector's nightmare; it was reported that charcoal dust covered "every portion of the interior."

More disastrous, though outside San Jose's jurisdiction, was the October 25, 1926 burning of the Santa Clara Mission. A treasure house of Spanish missionary history, the twin-towered wooden church was no match for the flames. In desperation, the overtaxed Santa Clara volunteers appealed to San Jose for help.

Firemen were dispatched to Santa Clara, though it was too late to save the building. The Mission Fathers, however, did not forget their help. In January 1927 they gave a banquet at the University for San Jose firefighters in appreciation of their services the previous Fall.

The last fire of 1926 broke out about 7 p.m. November 8, in the large garage of contractor Earl Heple on William Street just around the corner from Delmas. Although two-thirds of the city's fire force was summoned, there was no saving the uninsured structure—with five busses, nine autos, two trucks, and a tow car, for a total loss estimated at $100,000.

Fires made no headlines the following year. Only once during the next 37 years did San Jose's fire losses dip lower than in 1927. Instead, the future growth of the city was foreshadowed by the emergence of an influential rival to the southwest.

While San Jose was a drowsy hamlet squatting in the mud around its plaza, a rutted country road far to the west was becoming a well-travelled route for cattle drives from the Almaden Valley to the Alviso docks. As the years passed, orchardists moved in, a few merchants set up shop along the road, and San Joseans seeking a rural life began to settle nearby. Certain swampy tracts in the neighborhood, overgrown with young saplings, are said to have given this area its name: "The Willows." Further settlement came when the interurban electric line of the San Jose and Los Gatos Railway Company was built in 1905, right down the middle of that dusty road which had become Lincoln Avenue.

Such were the beginnings of Willow Glen, which was incorporated as a city in 1927. Civic leaders like the late Oscar Bradley, proud of their community and wishing to fend off absorption by San Jose, worked hard to create the new city. They formed a volunteer fire department which within a couple of years boasted a pumper newer than any in San Jose.

Our town needed some new equipment rather badly. Automotive developments of more than a decade had left far behind the 1915 Federal trucks, with their oversize radiators and undersize motors. In 1927 two new hose wagons (Reos) were put in service with Engine Companies 1 and 2; Chemical 2 got a new chassis the next year.

Another creaking anachronism was the Knox-Martin tricycle tractor still pulling Hook and Ladder 1. Says retired fire officer Ed Powers, "We used to steer those tractors on Santa Clara Street by catching the front wheel in the streetcar tracks so we could go

Around 1916, San Jose's newly motorized Fire Department looked like this. Left to right: Chemical 3, Capt. M. Narvaez and driver Fred Salas; Engine 1, driver either Billy Mason or Tim Sullivan, Engineer Art McQuaide; Hose 1, firemen Araby Damonte and Reno Bacigalupi; Chemical 1; the Chief's car with Chief Ed Haley and Asst. Chief Hobson; Engine 2, Chemical 2, and Truck 1.

in a straight line." His brother John, also retired as a Captain, recalled earlier troubles at the rear wheels, when the rig was much newer: "I had the tiller once responding to an alarm at Lowell School. Rounding the corner of First and Reed, with Chief Haley riding the running board, the tiller wheel stuck for want of grease. I hollered for them to stop; the wheel was tearing my arm off. We finally got her stopped, took the wheel apart and greased it. Fortunately, the truck wasn't needed at the fire!"

Other old-timers recall that a favorite trick of the tricycle tractor was to "fold up and lie down" whenever that front wheel was cramped too hard against a curb. Chief Plummer tells the consequences on one occasion during the late '20's: "We couldn't get repair parts any more; the Knox people had been out of business for years. Once the front fork broke, and the rig was out of service for weeks while we made our own patterns from the broken parts so we could cast a new fork."

Big Fires, Small Pumpers

Unfortunately, San Jose was falling into the habit of replacing such relics only after a serious fire caused an outcry at City Hall. Three such blazes, just before and after the onset of the Depression, pointed up several deficiencies in equipment and manpower.

The Shaw Family cannery on Patterson Street at the SP tracks was preparing for the opening of their jam and jelly packing season in the Fall of 1928, when a "flying spark" from a locomotive or nearby bonfire lodged in the roof of one of the plant warehouses. At 1:10 p.m. September 8, a still and box alarm rang in to send firemen on the way through heavy Saturday crowds of downtown shoppers—which delayed the response. Meantime, a stiff breeze fanned the flames into an inferno. Leaping from roof to roof, throwing off clouds of embers, the fire rapidly involved two warehouses, two garages, the wood frame cannery itself, and several other buildings. Thousands of spectators gathered to see the conflagration — and to obstruct firemen in their work.

No idle watchers were the employees of adjacent exposed industries. A block away, Libby workers formed a bucket brigade amidst a rain of sparks. Six men beat out

spot fires on the roof of the Charles Vith Packing Company, across Patterson Street. An automatic roof sprinkler went off to save the roof of the Beech-Nut cannery at 249 Margaret. Next door to the flaming Shaw plant were the Williams and Russo coal yards, where employee Al Gomez climbed to the roof and tore off burning shingles with his bare hands to save the buildings. Half a block of homes on the east side of 3rd Street were endangered. One of them, No. 756, caught fire and the upper floor was destroyed before firefighters could reach it.

The Shaw Family alone collected over $120,000 in fire insurance (a year later, a second blaze on the same spot cost several thousand more). One of San Jose's more notorious visitors was apparently not in town for this occasion. He was Willie Fisher, firebug *par excellence*, eventually to be known nationwide for his spectacular pyrotechnics. Responsible for $4 million worth of California fires in 1928, including a $500,000 San Rafael hotel blaze, he was brought to San Jose that summer in the custody of Oakland police and Underwriters investigators. Here he freely admitted setting five fires in and around the city during 1927 and 1928, none of them serious. The 18-year-old Fisher "quivered with excitement" at Market Street headquarters when apparatus roared out in response to a still alarm.

Another demonstration of the conflagration hazard faced by San Jose's inadequate fire force came on June 22, 1929, along "Auto Row"—which by now was moved from North First Street to West Santa Clara between Delmas and Montgomery. Shortly before 2 p.m., a five gallon can of rubber cement exploded in the Wellmaid Tire Shop, upstairs in the old Red Star Laundry Building. Two alarms in quick succession brought almost the whole Fire Department, only 14 men being left to cover the city.

One tire shop worker sprained an ankle when forced to jump for his life. Fire quickly spread to the next-door Maurer Building with its upstairs rooming house, bordering Los Gatos Creek.

Delmas Avenue, shaded from a broiling sun by the pall of smoke, was jammed with people as throngs flocked to the scene. One group of "volunteers" rolled a bar and root beer barrel from a downstairs soft drink

The 1914 Seagrave in service as Engine 3, about 1915. Captain Lou Lunsford stands at right; driver is John Gossett.

Rear view of the 1914 Seagrave in the 1930's, before she was rebuilt, showing the massive pump with its inlet and outlet connections.

emporium in the Maurer Building, to stage "several impromptu drinking parties in the creek bed." It was a thirsty day, with 100 degree temperature and a brisk northwest wind.

At the height of the blaze, flying sparks ignited dry grass on the creek bank. Scores of men and boys left off their imbibing to lend a hand against this new emergency. But within minutes the grass fire swept under the bridge to destroy Mike Hammer's barn at 15 Delmas. This in turn ignited a neighboring barn at 25 Delmas.

Lacking additional apparatus to deploy, firemen dropped a hose line over the bridge rail, then slid down it into the creek to douse the grass and wet down the Delmas Ave. properties from the rear.

On the vacant strip of ground in front of the Red Star Building, flames damaged many autos in the used car lot of the National Auto Sales Company. Slightly injured in helping move one of the cars to safety was bystander G. L. Tonkins, of 373 N. 8th Street—probably the same man who had been Fire Chief in 1905-1908.

Several firemen were also hurt. Casualties might have been heavier had not a P. G. & E. crewman succeeded in cutting off power in the neighborhood only seconds before several high voltage lines collapsed into the wet street.

During the afternoon, San Jose was forced to exhume its oldest reserve apparatus. The only remaining tractor-drawn steamer was brought out of storage at Engine 3, steamed up, and placed on standby at Market Street. At least one alarm, for a small fire on The Alameda, was answered by Santa Clara firemen. Mopping up late that night, San Jose firefighters could count three buildings destroyed and several damaged, for a loss of $75,000.

The last straw for the City Council was a bad fire downtown. At about the spot where flames had broken out in Ah Toy Alley to level the Chinatown of 50 years earlier, stood the 3-story brick building of the San Jose Hardware Company, at 54 West San Fernando Street. The hardware firm occupied the ground floor and basement, while above was the Carroll Hotel. Proprietress Mattie Carroll, asleep upstairs, was roused by smoke before dawn on January 25, 1930. Going into

the hall, she found more smoke and phoned the Fire Department at 6:35 a.m.

After breaking in the rear door of the hardware store, firemen found the seat of the fire in the rear of the basement, full of stored paint and almost inaccessible. Though a city ordinance required "hose openings" into such basements, none was provided; so water could be gotten onto the fire only by breaking holes in the brick walls. During the early stages, with a cool nerve which went almost unnoticed in the newspaper accounts, Lieut. Thomas Higgins (wearing a gas mask) had himself lowered into the basement through a hole cut in the first floor, to inspect the fire's progress. While a squad of men searched every upstairs room to find and bring down all the hotel tenants—two of whom were almost unconscious—lines were taken to the roof next door to cover exposures.

Both shifts were called in to operate a dozen hose streams as fire ate its way through the largest paint and hardware stock between San Francisco and Los Angeles. Firemen were eventually forced entirely out of the building. As the last four men descended ladders from the second floor—Assistant Chief Page, Captain Bob Foley, Lieut. Higgins, and George Vitek—the roof and both upper floors collapsed with a roar, bulging out the front wall. It was Chief Page's second narrow escape that day; earlier he was "badly affected" by smoke and had to be led from the building.

Not until late afternoon was the fire controlled; for another 24 hours firemen stood by the smoldering ruins to guard against another outbreak. During this time, offers of outside help were made (which Chief Plummer refused), and again the old steamer was brought out of retirement to fill in at Market Street.

Faced with a loss estimate of a quarter million, the City Council conferred among themselves and with fire officials concerning the Fire Department's "adequacy." Unfortunately, with the shadow of the Depression already on the horizon, there was little money to supply remedies.

In fact, no reasonable expenditure of funds could make up overnight for the city's failure to enforce existing fire laws and enact new ones needed, or its years of clinging to the comfortable illusion that neighborhood fire stations housing 2-man chemical companies represented real fire protection.

The fire-retarding qualities of composition roofing are demonstrated, about 1930, in a vacant lot off East Santa Clara Street near 4th. Fire officers are (left) veteran Captain John Gilleran, acting Fire Marshal, and Chief Charles Plummer.

As political bodies do when confronted with such a situation, the Council compromised. Its Public Health and Safety Committee recommendation was adopted, calling for new chassis on which to mount the apparatus of Chemicals 1, 3, 4, and 5—two of which were nearing 20 years of age. At least three of the four should, of course, have been replaced by engine companies. On February 24, 1930, contracts totalling $7100 were let for a 1½-ton Dodge chassis, a 1⅓-ton Reo, a 2-ton GMC, and a 2-ton Federal. Purchase of 3300 feet of hose was also authorized.

Councilmen ordered a "study" of possible sale of Market Street fire headquarters. The money saved by moving to a cheaper site elsewhere could be used to buy new apparatus. Nothing came of this pipe dream, however, for there was no cheaper site acceptable to the Underwriters.

For use on basement fires, three cellar pipes were belatedly ordered. Another "study" was launched to see that downtown buildings actually had the basement hose openings they were supposed to have.

Not for a generation would San Jose have another serious basement fire, but there was no letup in blazes above ground level. Automatic sprinklers would have squelched the first one, which destroyed the G. W. Clanton & Company auction house and the adjoining Lion's mattress factory and furniture finishing shop. When the fire was discovered in the Clanton building at 132 South 3rd, about 11 p.m. on April 24, 1930, it had been quietly smoldering for hours. Employees of Brehm Bros. garage nearby had smelled smoke since 8 p.m.

A brick wall equipped with firedoors helped firemen keep the $50,000 fire from spreading to Lion's furniture warehouse, or the Lick Garage from which 200 stored autos were hastily removed during the hour it took to bring the flames under control.

The early Depression years brought the end of some old San Jose institutions. With the decline in rail travel and general prosperity, the elegant Vendome Hotel could no longer exist. During the summer of 1930 it was torn down. The firm of Stull and Sonniksen (like the Vendome, survivors of a disastrous fire) sold out, to end almost 50 years in business. Also gone was the F. W. Gross store.

A good start was made towards wiping out another center of business — the trade in Oriental art goods centering on South 2nd Street near Santa Clara. During the last evening of 1929, the throng of New Year's celebrants downtown got some unexpected excitement when the Mikado Company store burned at 57 South 2nd. Cause of the $12,000 fire was a mouse gnawing on a carton of matches!

On the second floor of the Mikado's brick building was the Richmond apartments, where a tenant's dog discovered flames and barked for his master. The alarm came in at 7:18 p.m. While firemen went into action, an elderly lady residing on the second floor wasted no time in forming a one-woman bucket brigade with two "huge kitchen utensils." While one was filling with water at the sink, she rushed with the other to the back door to pour water down upon the fire below.

Unfortunately, Charlie Guy, living in a rear lean-to behind his 2-story Pekin Art Store at 16 South 2nd, owned neither a dog nor the necessary kitchen utensils. At 4 a.m. July 22, 1930, he was forced to run for it when flames burst from his store into the lean-to, then spread into Allen's Emporium at 18 South 2nd. Firemen arrived on a still and box alarm, too late to save either of the flimsy frame buildings. The Wardrobe clothing store, at the corner of Santa Clara, suffered smoke damage, as did two other nearby firms, for a total loss of $25,000. One suspects Mr. Guy's housekeeping practices — he had owned a similar store at 39 South 2nd until 1929, when it too had burned.

Several other lives were almost lost in the Fall of 1930. On West San Fernando Street at the SP branch line tracks, the railroad company owned the old one and two story Griffin & Skelley warehouse which was leased to Markovits & Fox for old newspaper storage. The place was also commonly used as sleeping quarters by vagrants.

About ten p.m. on October 13, the railroad crossing flagman at Santa Clara Street stopped a passing beat patrolman to tell him something appeared to be "wrong" at the

Inspection: March 1932. Left to right: Louis J. Urzi, unknown, Lawrence A. Campbell, Carl Odell, Kenneth Squibb, John Matranga, Phineas Fuller, Merle C. Rhyne, John Gossett, Captain John Humburg, Walter Humburg.

warehouse. Investigating, the officer found a huge pile of newspapers ablaze inside the building. He turned in a fire alarm, then ran upstairs to find two tramps passed out in a drunken stupor. With the help of three other passersby he got them out, through thick smoke, plus five more discovered later. Engines 1 and 2, Truck 1, and Chemicals 3, 5, and 7 got the fire out after most of the building was wrecked.

Blamed for the fire was careless smoking by the tramps, who (as the Mercury reported next day) "owe their lives to the presence of mind and courage of a young patrolman of the San Jose Police Department." This heroic officer we shall call Officer P---------; he must remain anonymous in this account, and we shall see how he became the center of a tragic drama that was to involve the Fire Department over a period of months.

Back downtown, in the Purity Baking Company's plant at 288 South Market Street, a crew of nine bakers smelled smoke while turning out the next day's bread in the small

hours of February 9, 1931. They found flames sweeping through an upstairs stockroom, apparently starting from a faulty oven flue. A still and box alarm, then a general alarm, brought out San Jose's entire fire force which battled for three hours but saved only office records and the building's brick shell. Only half an hour after discovery of the fire, the roof and part of the north wall caved in, pitching Captain John Humburg of Engine 3 from a ladder.

San Jose's old City Hall housed the fire department's alarm system.

Court House Fire Stirs Council

While other fires have risked more lives, or cost more dollars, for sheer spectacle no fire in San Jose's history — at least before 1955 — can match the burning of the Santa Clara Court House on May 18, 1931. Designed by a former volunteer fireman, the imposing structure had been a downtown landmark for over 60 years.

During the hot, humid afternoon, fire started somewhere in the upper reaches of the old building; Chief Plummer believed the source was among janitorial supplies in the attic. Apparently the blaze was simultaneously discovered by four people. The first alarm was called in by an office worker a block away in the Bank of Italy, who thought

Before the fire, the Courthouse looked much as when it was built in 1868.

108

Down she comes! Firemen and bystanders scurry to safety as the impressive facade of the County Courthouse begins to collapse. The May 1931 blaze threatened Hotel St. James (left) where San Jose's St. James Branch Post Office stands today.

the St. James Hotel was afire (it adjoined the Court House, on the site of the present-day Post Office Building).

About the same time, County Purchasing Agent Sam Lowe attacked the fire with a hand extinguisher, while custodian Tom O'Brien turned in another alarm. Attorney Gerald Chargin rushed into Judge Gosbey's courtroom to warn the judge and spectators. The Board of Supervisors, meeting in executive session, were routed out by heat and falling plaster as flames roared through the attic overhead. County Clerk Frank Hogan calmly finished issuing a marriage license, collected the $2 fee, then left the building after seeing to it that the Great Register of Voters was safely removed.

Meanwhile Chief Plummer was on his way from Market Street with three fire companies. Within half an hour a general alarm was sounded, bringing every piece of fire apparatus in the city and calling in the entire off shift. Without proper ladder equipment or water towers, the department could not reach the spreading blaze which soon began to work its way down from floor to floor.

At the street level, troops of volunteers were recruited from a watching crowd of 5000 that gathered in St. James Park. Passing the ponderous volumes from hand to hand like a bucket brigade, this group brought out records from the Hall of Records to the north, connected directly to the blazing Court House by an enclosed corridor. At the rear, 74 prisoners were hastily removed under guard when it appeared flames might spread to the County Jail. Later, a recount turned up four extra "prisoners"—they were innocent bystanders caught in the shuffle!

Clouds of smoke and embers rose over downtown San Jose, setting fire to 6th and 7th floor awnings on the Commercial Building a block away, and drifting a mile and a half of the south. Recalled Chief Plummer, "I had to send one of the chemical companies to put out fires starting for blocks around."

To cover San Jose's vacated firehouses, equipment was rushed in from Santa Clara, Burbank, and the Willow Glen Volunteers. Even Chief Brennan of San Francisco stood by to offer assistance if needed. Firemen took lines to the Jail roof, and the St. James Hotel,

A hopeless task: alongside the burning Court-house, firefighters aim heavy streams from the ground against flames raging upstairs.

After the Courthouse fire, a strangely truncated structure resulted from the rebuilding, which added a third story but omitted the dome.

cutting off spread of the fire in those two directions. Others made a successful last-ditch stand at the entrance into the Hall of Records. But the Court House itself was doomed.

Slowly the burning building began to come to pieces. At the front, falling cornices forced firemen to retreat into First Street, which had been closed to all traffic. The flagpole dropped, narrowly missing one firefighter. Standing at the edge of the roof about 3 p.m., Captain Harry Dennis and a volunteer barely escaped with their lives as the great dome collapsed into the basement with a roar heard for miles. Several men were treated for minor injuries.

By nightfall the flames were under control. It was a gloomy report that the tired Chief took with him to the City Council meeting that evening. Destroyed were irreplaceable records dating back to 1854. Water damage

in the Hall of Records was heavy. The loss that could be assessed was over $200,000.

The disaster stung the Council into action that very night — the purchase of a new pumper. By a happy coincidence, there was available in the area a 150 horsepower 1000 GPM Mack "demonstrator," which the Council voted to buy at once. Priced at $12,500, a small fortune in those days, it was still a bargain; seldom has the city owned a more reliable piece of apparatus, with more pumping capacity than any other engine previously used here.

Hopes were high for a new Civic Center as an outgrowth of the destruction of the Court House — even then the old County Jail and City Hall were eyesores. However, it was no time to spend that kind of money. Once authorities determined that the walls were sound, rebuilding of the Court House began on the spot. It was converted from two stories to three, but the dome was gone forever.

111

One month to the day after the Court House fire, the new pumper passed its acceptance tests with flying colors. Pumping into four hose lines connected to the hose wagon monitor nozzle, it threw a 2-inch stream of water more than 500 feet. Put in service as Engine 1, the Mack displaced the 1922 Stutz to Engine 2, the 1920 Seagrave to Engine 3, and the 1914 Seagrave to Engine 4 at Spencer Ave. "In those days," said Chief Plummer many years later, "whatever we didn't want downtown, we sent to Spencer Avenue."

The Mack's first fire service was at the $2000 Beauty Box blaze, 17 East San Antonio, which threatened the Curtis Hotel upstairs. A more severe trial came in November. Using standpipe connections fed by a 4-inch main into the building, firemen had won a hard fight to save the 3-story St. James Hotel during the Court House fire. But their efforts were wasted; it burned anyway, six months later. The St. James was due for razing to make way for the new Post Office, and during the Fall of 1931 the last guests moved out of its 100 rooms. Sole occupant when fire

broke out downstairs, late Wednesday night November 25, was the wealthy owner, Joseph Basile.

A sound sleeper, Basile barely escaped after being aroused only by firemen crashing through the supposedly empty building. He grabbed a gun and charged into the hallway to rout what he thought were linen thieves— to be confronted by smoke and fire extending upward from the Crystal Laundry on the first floor.

After two hours, a general alarm assignment, operating twelve lines, had the flames beaten down. At 4 a.m. the fire was struck out; loss exceeded $10,000. The cause was never determined, but delay in discovering the fire was the contributing factor to its spread. Two employees of a downstairs print shop had smelled smoke four hours before the alarm was given, but found nothing amiss on the premises and failed to notify the Fire Department. Not until 12:10 a.m., after the fire had worked up through the walls to the roof, was an alarm turned in by Deputy Sheriff Hicks at the nearby Jail.

Purchased after the Courthouse fire of 1931, this 1000 GPM Mack served the city well for almost 30 years. In this June 1931 photo are Firemen Arthur Gilbert (left) and Walter Napolitano.

Besides the new pumper, Chief Plummer was able to wangle two minor apparatus improvements during 1931. Another new Reo "hose wagon" was bought for Chemical 6, and dealer George Peterson sold the city a 3-ton White 4-wheel tractor for the ladder truck, to replace the last tricycle tractor.

Lean Years Begin

These were the last gasps of prosperity. San Jose now possessed the four pumpers it had needed in 1925—but the city was one-third larger than it had been then. It had some reliable motive power for its ladder truck—but was still unable to use it as a water tower, something hoped for by Chief Tonkins 25 years earlier.

So, as the Depression tightened its grip on municipal finances, accompanied by a rising tide of public apathy, the stage was set for the Fire Department's slow decline. In 1956, 25 years after San Jose had been hailed as having some of the fastest fire companies in California, a disgusted reform Councilman could condemn the department as "the lousiest." An undeserved slur on the men themselves, his remark was a fair overall assessment which, happily, is far from true today.

Pictured in 1932 were Bill Ogden, Merle Rhyne, Peter Segard and Henry Lingua.

Journey Into Obsolescence
1932-1945

To residents accustomed to the sight of growth, new building, and a booming economy on every hand, the condition of San Jose in the early '30's should come as a shock. Except for a handful of public buildings, from limited injections of New Deal government funds, there was no major new building construction in the city for a decade. No schools, no theaters, no department stores, no subdivided tracts of homes—nothing. The ancient Knox Block at First and Santa Clara Streets, the foul County Jail, the City Hall—yes, and the 1908 firehouses—were condemned as outmoded eyesores by a procession of municipal critics. Each had his own solution; none had any money. During the years 1931-42, only two new pieces of fire apparatus were purchased, a record unmatched before or since in the history of the paid Fire Department.

When San Joseans speak of the good old days—these weren't the days.

An Unsolved Mystery

From the middle of 1932 on into the Fall, downtown San Jose was plagued by a series of highly suspicious fires. Department records show a neat black question mark inked in alongside the report of each of these blazes. The mystery of these fires was never fully unravelled; what is told here has never been told before.

Each fire broke out at night, during the week. Most of them originated in closets, basements, or otherwise unoccupied areas. Several were obviously arson. And the majority were discovered by one person: Patrolman P--------, hero of the 1930 Griffin-Skelley warehouse fire.

The first two outbreaks both threatened the same building the same night, in June. About half past eight, as Patrolman P-------- passed the old 2-story Knox Block, he reported that a man rushed downstairs shouting "Fire!" Leaving this stranger to disappear on the street, P-------- (now joined by another officer) ran up the stairs and found flames in a janitor's room. Closing the door again, the two officers called firemen who extinguished the blaze with chemicals. A "live cigarette" or similar source of ignition had burned a cardboard carton on which rested a 5 gallon can of flammable cleaner; as the box collapsed, the cleaner spilled to spread the fire.

Several hours later, as P-------- and another patrolman were going off beat, they smelled smoke, again from the Knox Block. Investigation this time disclosed smoke pouring into the upstairs hallway above an unoccupied store at 31 West Santa Clara. Again the flames were put out promptly, having apparently started in a closet full of trash.

The following week, fire No. 3 was reported at 9:12 p.m. June 14, in the Boomer Block at 193-195 South First. Two alarms were pulled in quick succession as flames spread from a second floor beauty shop via the two foot cockloft. Fireman James O'Day, overcome by smoke, was carried from the building by Assistant Chief Page. Eight firms in the building were damaged by flames, smoke, and water.

We find no mention of P-------- this time. Workmen remodelling at 195 South First had found a "smouldering waste can" upstairs, carried it out to the street, and on returning upstairs discovered the second floor in flames.

Tuesday night the 28th, at 10:26 p.m., Patrolman P---------- reported the fourth fire in the rear of the old Brassy Building, built in 1890 on the Market Street site where wood Chinatown had burned in 1887. Upstairs was a rooming house, where the fire broke out at the rear of a corridor. Downstairs, the building housed the Sherman-Clay sales room and warehouse with $25,000 worth of musical instruments.

Responding to P----------'s telephone alarm, firemen found the entire top floor involved. Only a firewall saved the adjacent San Jose Hardware warehouse; to the south, several exposed garages were wet down. The loss was about $20,000.

By now, Fire Marshal Lingua had called in investigators from the Board of Fire Underwriters. But the worst was yet to come. Early in the morning of Tuesday July 25, P---------- saw smoke pouring from the J. S. Williams clothing store at 227 South First, and phoned in another alarm at 4:20 a.m. The loss here was held to less than $10,000 by fast work of the firemen, for which Chief Plummer and Assistant Chief Page were praised. Gas masks had to be used to get at the source of the smoky blaze, which was found to be among paraffin-coated candy boxes in the deserted basement of O'Brien's candy store next door.

At exactly the same hour next day, P-------- reported another fire, the 8th in a month, in the Security Building at First and San Fernando. Offices and three ground floor stores were damaged to the extent of $17,000. Chief Plummer reported flatly, "This fire was set." Kerosene and excelsior used in the process were found around the elevator penthouse where the fire began. It was further reported that the attic leading to the penthouse was unlocked; the key had been "missing" for a week. Captain John Gilleran added that he had inspected the building two weeks before the fire and found it "one of the cleanest in town."

Early Monday morning, August 1, the series continued. Patrolman (later Chief of Police) Ray Blackmore did the honors this time. Flames caused $5000 worth of damage to the Palm Garden Dance Hall on South Market Street. Firemen summoned by Blackmore were able to confine the fire largely to its area of origin in an unoccupied back room full of old crates and floor decorations.

West Santa Clara Street's Auzerais Building was damaged after midnight on October 3. A passing motorist saw smoke inside, alerting firemen who contained the blaze in the 3rd floor rear of the building, where it had started in two vacant rooms.

All these circumstances were suspicious, to say the least. The prominent role of Officer P---------- in discovering downtown fires had not gone unnoticed; most of them were on his beat, during his duty hours. Was it possible that the young patrolman, his head turned by the praise he earned at the 1930 warehouse blaze, was trying to add to the lustre of his reputation?

Intensive investigation was without result. Night after night, among San Jose's darkened streets and alleys, Fire Marshal Lingua silently shadowed P------- as the officer made his rounds. But no evidence was obtained.

Finally, Chief of Police J. N. Black called P-------- into his office, with the Fire Marshal present, and accused him to his face of setting the fires. P---------- hung his head and wept, but would admit nothing. Lacking any basis for bringing the officer to trial, Chief Black then fired him, for the good of the department. Soon P-------- left the area, never to be heard from again in San Jose.

Was he guilty? Was an innocent man simply overwhelmed by the accusation, aware that he had no resources with which to fight the case? Was it all a remarkable series of coincidences, exploited by firebugs working with local property owners to beat the Depression by collecting on their fire insurance? We will never know.

At any rate, arson in downtown business buildings soon ceased to trouble the Fire Department. Elsewhere in town — visions of bearded anarchists and the Red Menace were called up by a destructive fire at the Herbert Packing Company. Located at the northeast corner of 6th and Empire, the wooden structure had been the Anita Packing Company owned by Mrs. Heinrich Haas of Hamburg, Germany. The Alien Property Custodian had seized the plant during World War I and its German owner had never regained possession.

Fog shrouded the neighborhood early January 11, 1933. A nearby resident thought he saw the light of a torch through the mist,

San Jose's "Style Center" of the depression years—Max Blum & Co.'s downtown depart-ment store. This was the Second Street side before the disastrous fire of January 1933.

about 6 a.m., but took no further notice. An hour later, two alarms brought firemen to what was now clearly visible; the packing house was fully involved, and burned to the ground with a loss of $55,000. Nearby box-cars were damaged, while other rail traffic was held up for some time by hose lines laid across the tracks.

What caused investigators to see "Red" was a series of three obvious arson attempts at other packing houses later the same day. At Bassett and Terraine Streets, a fire in box shook at the Earl Fruit Company was extin-guished with minor damage. A kerosene "trailer" was found beneath a loading plat-form at the Warren Dried Fruit Company, 100 Ryland Street. In the same area, a pile of debris was pushed against a warehouse wall and touched off, but died out before doing any harm.

Altogether, there were four arson convic-tions in San Jose courts during 1933. There seems to be no evidence, however, that a fire-bug was responsible for a tragic fire which still holds the dubious distinction of being the most spectacular downtown blaze since the Court House.

The Blum's Disaster

One of San Jose's more fashionable down-town women's stores for generations was M. Blum and Company, at 26 South First Street. Most recently, it was actually two separate buildings . . . the rear one fronting on South 2nd Street containing a book department and clothing specialties on the ground floor.

In 1933, this rear building or annex housed a new experiment in local retailing—a self-service supermarket or "groceteria" as it was called. On the second floor were offices and

116

storerooms. Above this was the Raymond Hotel, having only one exit via stairway leading down to the street.

Sometime early Thursday evening, January 19, fire broke out in the groceteria, to spread rapidly upward within the walls. Box 24 was struck at 6:50 p.m. Up on the third floor, as firemen were arriving, 16 hotel lodgers managed to squeeze through a ceiling hatch and escape over the roof to the adjacent Royal Hotel from which they made their way to safety. By this narrow margin a catastrophe was averted.

Still, rumors flew through the gathering crowd below that a woman was trapped upstairs. Rushing to the rescue up the single stairway, Captain Pete Segard of Chemical 1 was caught in an explosive flareup as both upper floors burst into flame. His helmet afire, Segard staggered back down calling for a general alarm. Radiant heat was now igniting the cloth tops of cars parked along Second Street. Chemical 1's rig had to be hosed down, then driven off to a safe spot.

Segard went to the hospital with face burns that scarred him for life. Driver Ed Terry of Chemical 4 was also burned; Lieut. Sal Bernal of Chemical 4 was overcome by smoke and hospitalized for days.

Towering flames soon lit up the business district as fire went through the roof. Firefighters kept the blaze from involving buildings to the north and south; the main Blum's store was cut off by fire doors, and it too survived, though there was damage in the basement.

For the second and last time in San Jose history, outside help came in to the downtown area, from four neighboring fire departments: Burbank, Santa Clara, Willow Glen, and the private Hedberg Volunteers. Their pumpers stood by to cover the city while San Jose's entire fire force toiled through the night at Blum's, where Second Street was a maze of hose lines and apparatus.

After collapse of the roof and third floor late that night, firemen were able to get the upper hand. Next day, they began to search the ruins for possible victims, for by now it had been confirmed that at least one lodger, William Bean, was unaccounted for.

His body was found in the rubble of the second floor. Ironically, Bean had not been in the building at all when the fire started, but was having supper in a nearby restaurant. When firemen rolled in on the first alarm, he rushed back to the hotel and dashed inside to save his belongings, unnoticed in the general confusion. By then it was too late to escape.

Blum's annex was left a hollow shell by the $175,000 fire; the groceteria was not rebuilt.

In earlier times, the Blum's disaster might have bought the Fire Department some new equipment. Not so in 1933. Prosperity was far out of sight around the corner. Breadlines, soup kitchens, whole families sleeping under the bridges—this was the Garden City's daily news in 1933.

"Fire College" training did have a brief beginning, directed by State Instructor J. F. Baker of the Bureau of Industrial and Trade Education. Firemen participated in 46 three-hour classroom sessions on "Use of Fire Equipment," "Care of Quarters," and related subjects.

Communications, never at their best since the alarm system troubles of the 1880's, were improved by installation of a telephone center in an upstairs room at Market Street headquarters, for which two permanent operators were detailed in March 1933.

But except for 500 feet of 2¾-inch hose purchased for Hose 1 to use with its monitor, apparatus itself was neglected. The critics of Chief Plummer who became so vocal in later and more prosperous years would have done better to review his 1933 report to the Council, in which he warned that San Jose was falling far behind other Northern California cities of comparable size—such as Berkeley, Stockton, and Fresno—in manpower, in pumpers, and in ladder trucks. It should be no reflection on Plummer that the deficiencies he spotlighted at such an early date were not remedied until after he was forced to resign.

That bewhiskered crank with a grudge against packing plants struck again on June 7. In Santa Clara that afternoon, he stuffed hay inside some empty fruit boxes at the Pratt-Low Cannery, then touched it off; damage was minor. At San Jose's Richmond-Chase plant on Stockton Avenue, a huge pile of boxes burst into flame just before midnight.

While the Fire Department was busy there, still another fire started in the yard of the M. Doane Lumber Company at Pleasant and Julian Streets, where the FMC plant later stood. Shorthanded, the San Jose department

Before December 1935, San Jose High School's Auditorium looked like this, on San Fernando Street at 5th. It was never rebuilt after fire destroyed it that month.

called for help from Santa Clara and Burbank. A water curtain set up on Pleasant Street saved the huge frame Guggenheim packing house, though its walls charred and steamed in the heat. Twenty trucks were hastily evacuated from the nearby San Jose Transfer Company. When it was all over, three buildings of the lumber company were in ruins.

That was the last major fire for almost two years. During the respite, on December 10, 1933, firemen took advantage of the more favorable attitude towards organized labor to form the first firefighters' union in San Jose—a group which ultimately wielded far more influence than the Richard Brown Club, or the Herman Hobson Protective Club of the late '20's, which were its predecessors.

Meeting on March 10, 1935, the City Council finally got down to business concerning

Chemical 7. Having been housed in one garage or another since its formation ten years before, the company was sadly in need of permanent quarters. The Council finally agreed on a lot at the corner of Laurel and Emory Streets, for which it was prepared to offer $1400. Not for another year, however, would the availability of WPA funds make it possible to put up a building.

Two Years of Heavy Losses

Lack of money for needed public buildings was further emphasized in the wake of a fire that gutted the 30-year-old San Jose High School auditorium before daybreak on the gray morning of Thursday, March 14, 1935. Set far back from the street, in a lightly travelled neighborhood, the frame and stucco structure was fully involved, with fire

118

through the roof, when firemen arrived in response to two box alarms. Ornate cupolas and colonnaded walls of the mission-style auditorium soon collapsed.

The two center wings of the school itself, flanking the auditorium, were saved with only minor damage in four classrooms. As crews were wetting down the ruins about 7 a.m., teachers and other staff members opened the cafeteria to make coffee and breakfast for the firemen. Chuckled one by-stander, "I've been attending meetings in there for 25 years, and it's the first time that place has been warm!" Disappointed students among the crowd of spectators soon learned that classes would be held as usual that day.

Although the $75,000 loss was covered by insurance, the replacement cost would have been much higher. So San Jose High did without an auditorium for the remaining twenty years of its life. Only the stage and slanting floor remained, becoming known as "The Quad" and used for open air student body gatherings in good weather.

Even before the fire the overcrowded facilities had been inadequate. Afterwards, Board of Education members made headlines by suggesting sale of the outmoded school to the adjacent State College. Since the College had no money to buy, nor the city any money to replace the buildings, there was no deal.

Simultaneous fires overtaxed the Fire Department on Sunday, December 1, 1935. First to be discovered, about 9 a.m., were flames in the Wellman-Peck grocery warehouse near the west end of Bassett Street. One fireman was hurt when tossed 35 feet by an exploding ammonia tank; others escaped injury when a large porch came down with a crash.

About 20 minutes after the first alarm, Captain Reno Bacigalupi, dispatched back to Market Street for extra clothing, saw flames erupting from the roof of the Lambert Marketing Company warehouse only a block to the east of the first fire. Assistant Chief Page rushed to the new outbreak with one engine company, to find fire already spreading to the adjoining plants of California Pine Box and California Spray Chemical. These exposed buildings were saved, but the Lambert warehouse walls collapsed, injuring fireman William Malpass. Six more hose lines were laid here, as additional alarms brought in the entire department plus the off-shift. Chief

Plummer, at his Santa Cruz summer home for the weekend, was called back to direct the 74 firefighters.

Out of control for five hours, the two blazes caused a combined loss of $200,000 (later adjusted downward). Two of the three sections of the Wellman-Peck warehouse were destroyed, with $100,000 in canned goods.

One month later to the day, as the temperature dipped toward freezing, another industrial area fire destroyed the ancient two-story brick plant of the San Jose Ice and Cold Storage Company, at 10 Center Street. Shut down since the previous February, the firm was due for remodelling and reopening during 1936. Meantime a "resident watchman" was on the premises—but not all the time; the building caught fire while he was away for his evening meal. Firemen fought the "incendiary" blaze most of the night. (Center Street, incidentally, ran north from San Augustine to Julian Street along the east side of the SP tracks. Reduced to an alley by rail line changes when the present depot was opened in 1935-6, it has since disappeared from the City maps.)

Helping to boost the 1936 fire loss to the highest point in ten years was the $40,000 damage to the top floor of the Stratford Shop clothing store on South First Street, starting at 5:30 a.m. April 5. It was easy to spot the cause of this one—a forgotten pressing iron, which burned its way down through the ironing board, then dropped to the floor and touched off the building. Discovered by the janitor of the First National Bank next door, the fire caused a hot air explosion when firemen opened the building, then spread out of control for three hours. Water damage was heavy downstairs.

119

Next to go, early on April 16, was the Goodwill Industries building at 131 South Third Street. Again it was a "delayed discovery," seen by two policemen only after there was enough fire to be visible four blocks away. Downtown water pressure was lowered by the firefighting, enough to set off a pair of finely adjusted sprinkler alarms at the Civic Auditorium.

The new auditorium was one result of the shot in the arm being given to San Jose's economy by the massive Federal measures taken to relieve the Depression. Another was the new Post Office, with consequent remodelling into a library of the old Post Office at Market and San Fernando.

Still another, of more concern to the Fire Department, was the construction of the long-awaited quarters for Chemical 7. San Jose had just gone through the longest period in its history—23 years—without getting any new firehouses. The new No. 7 was a handsome building, done in residential style to harmonize with its neighborhood; the first one-story fire station of this type.

It was also the first one of reinforced concrete design. Total cost was just under $17,000, of which the city had to pay only $6738, the balance coming from WPA funds.

During the construction, fires kept the men on the jump at the other side of town. Fanned by a brisk wind, a $5000 blaze hit the 50-year-old Centella Methodist Church, Second and Reed Streets, on the afternoon of July 6. In mid-August, $40,000 in tires and equipment was lost in the burning of Ray Fair's Tire Service at First and San Salvador —later rebuilt into the Gay Theater.

These continuing serious losses finally resulted in the decision to purchase a new pumper. Three of the existing four engines were now outmoded and dangerously aging. Chief Plummer's 1936 annual report is missing from the municipal archives, but there is no doubt that he again warned the Council against the consequences of continued deterioration of his equipment.

By way of adding to the Chief's problems, San Jose—for the second and (so far) the last time — annexed an incorporated city in October 1936: Willow Glen. It was a close

vote, 928 to 871, with violent opinions on both sides. But the suburbanites reluctantly agreed that Willow Glen on its own could no longer resist such indignities as San Jose's allegedly influencing the Southern Pacific to reroute its relocated main line through Willow Glen territory instead of through San Jose.

Because it was the natural nucleus for residential expansion, Willow Glen was readily assimilated, and has since become larger in size than the original San Jose which absorbed it.

There were no funds to buy fire apparatus for the new territory. So San Jose took a unique action by absorbing, as Engine Company No. 6, the 1929 American-LaFrance 500 GPM pumper of the Willow Glen Volunteers. Equipped with a new motor in 1940, it remained in service until 1946 when it was sold to the city of Capitola. Willow Glen's firehouse was taken over also. Located next door to the former Town Hall, it served its purpose until 1948 when a new combination firehouse and branch library was erected in a more traffic-free location.

Choice of the number "6" for this fifth of San Jose's engine companies showed that Chief Plummer was well aware of the need for another engine, logically to be called Number 5, in the Second Ward. But this was still years away.

Unfortunately, as far as the Fire Underwriters were concerned, little No. 6's limited pumping capacity entitled it to be rated only as a "hose company."

The Hedberg Volunteers

Charles Plummer was unpleasantly surprised that summer to learn that he wasn't the only Fire Chief in town. The other man claiming the title was not, however, after Plummer's job—he had his own personal fire department!

He was J. N. Hedberg, founder and owner of the Hedberg Mfg. Co., makers of the nationally-advertised Hedberg "long roll" coaster sirens. Pattern maker, mechanic, and inventor, Hedberg reportedly went into the siren business in 1920, when he got a speeding ticket for failing to hear the siren on an officer's motorcycle. He made the officer a better siren, thus creating a demand for the product.

The Hedberg Volunteers in 1936: Chief J. N. Hedberg stands on the rear of the chief's car at left. The pumper was one of the few Pierce-Arrow fire engines that ever existed.

Ideal motive power for his siren, Hedberg discovered, was the Wagner starting motor used in some early models of Studebaker automobiles. Without any load on the shaft, these motors turned over at 10,000 RPM. Hedberg kept his shop supplied with motors, which he rewound before using, by ransacking junkyards in search of old Studebakers.

The siren was made "free-wheeling" by a small solenoid which lifted the brushes free of the commutator when the motor was not energized, this almost eliminating friction drag. At one time, fire departments throughout the West used Hedberg sirens. San Jose had many, and at least one was still in service recently on Hose 6. They had a beautiful tone, and when fitted with a suitable "bell" to project the sound forward the Hedberg siren could be heard for miles.

Within a few years, Hedberg's association with the fire service led him to branch out. He got into apparatus and pump manufacture, once equipping an old horse-drawn aerial ladder with a gasoline tractor for the Modesto Fire Department.

As a community service, as well as to publicize his business, Hedberg conceived the idea in 1930 of forming his own volunteer fire department, not to serve in San Jose but to offer some protection to the unincorporated rural areas around the city. Prior to formation of the County Central Fire District, such areas had no coverage at all.

Hedberg's own employees living near his shop became the first volunteers. They built their own pumper, in the Hedberg shop, which lasted about six years; it had to be dragged to its last fire! Its replacement was another Hedberg hybrid, one of the only Pierce-Arrow fire engines ever built (Milwaukee had one for some years during the 1920's).

For many years, rural fires on San Jose's outskirts were fought by "The Hedberg Volunteers," who oftentimes arrived too late to do much good, but nonetheless became a local institution.

In 1936, the Pacific Coast Fire Chiefs met at convention in Seattle. Chiefs were given red badges as identification; other guests received blue ones. One day in the convention hall, Plummer and Hedberg met face to face —each wearing a red badge reading "Chief, San Jose, California."

Plummer saw red in more ways than one. Hedberg felt justified; after all, he *was* from San Jose, and he *was* a Chief. But the wrathful Charlie Plummer took the convention floor to denounce his "colleague" as an imposter. The executive secretary of the Association thereupon stripped Hedberg of his badge. When he returned home, Hedberg complained to the City Council—with little effect. Presumably the hard feelings subsided, because two years later the Hedberg firm built for Plummer a beautiful little squad wagon, on a Mack chassis, that was the showpiece of the department for years.

Since then, the Hedberg Volunteers have disappeared from the local scene. The old man himself died in 1955, and his decaying shop buildings on the Guadalupe Creek at 321 West Reed Street became overgrown with weeds and vines.

New Rigs and Old Problems

In January 1937, San Jose's newest pumper went into service as Engine 1. It was a 1000 GPM American LaFrance, with the pump up front between engine and driver's seat — a novel arrangement at the time. According to Chief Ron LeBeau, this rig was one of only four of its kind that were built.

The 1931 Mack went over to Engine 2. The Stutz went from 3rd Street to replace Chemical 7, henceforth to be known as Engine 7. A second monitor nozzle was purchased, so that both downtown hose wagons now had them. And, Truck 1 was presented with a new "ladder nozzle" (though apparently it was never used).

Field trials for the new LaFrance began Monday night, May 10, 1937, with the $40,000 destruction of the First Christian Church at 80 South 5th. Custodian Frank Horn had checked the 28-year-old building at 4:30 p.m., and all was well. But at 10 p.m. neighbors were aroused by crashing glass as hot gases blew out the third floor windows. Fire had begun around the basement oil heating system, spread through an unprotected vertical shaft to the attic, then burned through the roof.

Firemen, battering their way in through locked doors, found the entire rear of the church well involved. One crew was assigned to try to save the $5000 organ, but were soon forced out by imminent collapse of the roof and bell tower. Within 45 minutes after the alarm was given, the flames had gutted the 500-seat church auditorium, destroyed the organ and 8 pianos, razed furnishings, ruined valuable books and church records, and left what had been one of the city's most beautiful houses of worship a mass of smoldering debris amid a charred shell of walls. District Chief George Vitek, veteran of 43 years' service, recalled this as one of his worst fires.

His morale was boosted in the Fall, when the City Council granted wage hikes in both Police and Fire Departments averaging $15 per month for most ranks. Not for almost ten years had there been a general salary adjustment for San Jose firemen. The new monthly rates were: firemen, starting at $160 and reaching $190 in three years; Lieutenant, $200; Captain, $210; Assistant Chief, $300; Chief, $350. Although only about 63% of what the employees had requested, the increases totalled $22,000 per year.

This left little in the municipal kitty to take care of other needs. On November 24, 1937, only a day after announcement of the raises, an Underwriters rating report was released (superseding that made in 1932) which really raked San Jose over the coals.

Its findings were: the Fire Department was "seriously undermanned," stations "in-

One of only four units of its kind ever built, this is the 1000 GPM LaFrance Engine 1 purchased in 1937, now in reserve.

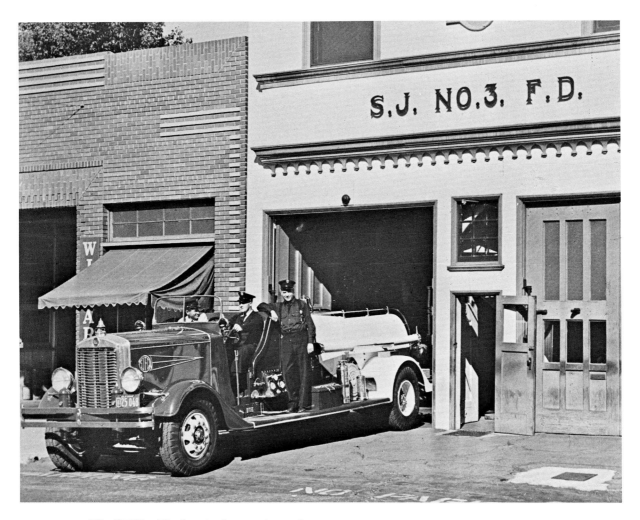

The "White Elephant," about 1945, with Lieut. Wm. Malpass and Firemen Wehner and Urzi. Engine Co. 3 occupied this South First Street site for 66 years.

efficiently placed," promotions were "not strictly competitive," drills were "infrequent" (and there was no drill tower or comparable facility), equipment was poor, discipline only fair, the alarm system "poorly maintained and inadequate." Among the concrete recommendations was removal of the alarm headquarters from the City Hall; for 25 years or more, officials had recognized the need of a separate building for this, but nothing had been done. More boxes were needed. Certain of the "hose" (chemical) companies should be converted to engine companies.

These things weren't news to the Fire Chief. For years Plummer had vainly asked for more men; he dutifully recommended to the Council that they hire the dozen new firemen the Underwriters asked for. But he didn't get them. Next Spring, he weathered Council criticism by pointing out that he had tried, and failed, to secure improvements before the adverse report was issued.

He did get some more new apparatus. On October 1, 1938, Chemical 1 and Squad 1 were both replaced by a 500 GPM "squad car." Built on a small Mack chassis by J. N. Hedberg, with a racy red-and-white color scheme, the new Squad 1 was an eye-catching sight. It was seen often, too, for it responded to all alarms or rescue calls anywhere in the city. This was the first piece of fire apparatus to be radio-equipped—the only one for almost ten years—and it carried a powerful floodlight plant, resuscitator, pre-connected 1½-inch hose lines; even sported a rear windshield for protection of the men riding on the back step.

If We Can't Buy, Let's Build

Some other equipment was fixed up so it at least looked like new. Between 1938 and the war years, several old pieces of apparatus were refinished in the distinctive two-tone paint. Unable to wangle an appropriation to

Engine 7's Stutz after extensive rebuilding in 1940.

replace the 1914 Seagrave pumper, Plummer did get permission to save a few thousand dollars by spending some $6300 to rebuild the rig. Considering how little they had to work with, and the advancements in motorized pumper design since World War I, it was remarkable the rebuild produced anything workable.

The job was supervised by the late Captain Louis Gurgiolo, the department's automotive expert at that time. Actually, very little of the original Seagrave was used in the rebuild except the pump and its connections. Somewhere Gurgiolo got hold of a ten ton chassis intended for a school bus, sent it off to the Hall-Scott factory in Oakland, and had the "new" pumper assembled on it there.

Trimmed in glittering chrome, with a camel's hump on its back where the huge pump casing projected upward, the "White Elephant," as it came to be known in the department, was tested at the end of August and officially became Engine 3 on October 13, 1938.

Encouraged by the outcome of this project, the city "modernized" a second unit two

years later. The 1922 Stutz got a new Hall-Scott motor, new wheels, water tank and booster line, and a streamlined two-tone body at a cost of $4500; it went back in service December 5, 1940.

What made these few progressive gestures look good was a conspicuous absence of large fires. Between July 14, 1938, when a spectacular night fire gutted a large section of the Lion's Furniture warehouse on South 4th Street, and the Spring of 1942, San Jose had only one really costly blaze.

This was a two-alarm worker which started in the paint shop at San Jose Technical High School, occupying about half the block south of San Fernando Street between 7th and 8th. Today, the entire area—including South 8th Street along which the fire broke out — is covered by buildings of the San Jose State College Engineering Department.

It was a Saturday afternoon, March 11, 1939, so there was no one to notice the fire in the unsprinkled one-story structure until flames broke through the roof of the east wing about 2:30. Engines 1, 2, and 3 responded, with most of the rest of the depart-

The Technical High School fire, March 12, 1939; Squad 1 in foreground. Poor water supply and limited Fire Department resources contributed to a heavy loss.

ment, controlling the flames after four more shop sections were burned. Collapse of portions of the heavy tile roof endangered firefighters, two of whom were injured.

The loss was $40,000. Low water pressure handicapped operations, in spite of booster pumps started by the Water Works; mains and hydrants in San Jose's old Wards were gener-

ally inadequate and have since been largely replaced. Besides, the undermanned Fire Department needed too much time to get into action. Engines today carry as much as 1500 feet of hose, hose wagons as much as 2000; in 1939 the average figure was 800 to 900 feet. Companies manned by 4 to 6 men today had 2 or 3 men in 1939.

San Jose Gets a Drill Tower

It was no wonder, then, that Chairman Glenn Bagwell of the Junior Chamber of Commerce Fire Committee complained that there were too few hose lines operating in the early stages of the Tech High fire, and asked for an "investigation." In retrospect there seems little excuse for the city's neglect of its fire force. In 1939 and again in 1940 San Jose finished out its fiscal year with a cash surplus exceeding $30,000; in 1940 the bonded debt was cut ten per cent.

But—if more men could not be provided, at least steps were taken to improve the training of those available. During 1941 a four-story drill tower was erected in the yard behind the North 3rd Street firehouse. The steel frame underlying the wooden tower structure was cleverly designed with bolted joints to facilitate its removal to a more favorable location when such a site might be available. How useful a feature this was became clear in January 1952, when a new drill yard was developed; the entire tower was easily moved across town, one story at a time, and re-erected in 2½ days.

Now it was possible to drill firemen in ladder evolutions, net handling, work with standpipes and fire escapes, etc., at the department's convenience. The position of

Another view of the 1938 Mack squad in action: burning of the Donn Refrigeration Co. on South First Street, November 1941.

Armistice Day Parade, 1931. Marchers include (left to right) Chief C. Plummer, L. Volonte, G. Murphy, Lt. Stewart, W. Malpass, G. Vitek, Lt. Fischel, J. Gossett, J. Wehner, I. Jones, J. Powers, A. R. Lunsford, F. E. Conyers, C. Kimball, Lt. Curin, E. Miller, T. Higgins, Sr., S. Bernal.

"Drillmaster," with the rank of Captain, was revived in 1940. Up till then, the function had been informal. Life net drill might consist in jumping from a firehouse roof. When Tim Sullivan had been in charge of drills back in 1915, the four-story Rea Building at Market and Santa Clara Streets was used for net exercises, along with the old Eagle Brewery. Each New Year's Eve, firemen had staged a jumping display at the Montgomery Hotel.

As war clouds gathered during 1941, and Americans watched the dramatic struggle of London firemen to cope with the blitz, fire protection problems were increasingly in the public eye. In April, the issue before the Council was a change in the platoon duty hours from 10 and 14 hours day and night shifts to 24 hours on followed by 24 off. After much argument, the Council abided by a vote taken among the firemen themselves; 25 favored a change, while 45 preferred the old way.

At the same time, the whole city's attention was drawn to a thornier problem. A tragic fire just a few yards outside the city limits raised the old question of Fire Department response beyond those limits. The blaze destroyed a home on the south side of Moorpark Ave., just west of Northrup, in Burbank Fire District territory. For some reason, Burbank apparatus reportedly took nearly three-quarters of an hour to arrive. Because the jurisdiction was in doubt at first, San Jose firemen were also dispatched, arriving much

sooner. Squad 1 parked across the street to watch as flames consumed the little frame house—and the two young children trapped inside.

There was nothing firemen could have done. Rescue was out of the question when they got there. Nevertheless, the tragedy made San Jose and its Fire Department look pretty bad to suburban residents. "Provision should be made to protect life anywhere," was the cry in the May 28 City Council meeting. That body's Committee on Public Health and Safety urged "extension of the fire limits" to authorize outside-city responses.

The only trouble was that no one could agree on how far to extend the line. After another month had passed, further reports were in from City Attorney Bowden on the question of liability, and the Moorpark Avenue children were forgotten. At issue instead was the effect on San Jose's economy of the loss of an industry just outside the city. Councilman Bradley raised this concern, and proposed including schools, churches, and hospitals as well as industries. Clyde Fischer (a Councilman even then!) thought the County Almshouse should be protected.

For the time being, however, Bowden's counsel prevailed. Should fire apparatus be involved in any outside-city accident, or should fire damage within San Jose result from the absence of firemen on an outside-city run, the city could be sued. And so the controversy faded out, until 1944.

Spring 1942—the Auxiliary Fire Department poses in front of the Civic Auditorium with its converted WPA apparatus. Captain Art Gilbert, one of the group's organizers, stands near the right end of the line.

On the Home Front

During the final week of November, 1941, in the face of national emergency, Fire Chief Plummer called for volunteers for the duration, to serve in a newly-organized auxiliary fire department. Deputy State Fire Marshal Charles Smith appeared in San Jose December 10, to warn City officials: "It is time to stop dillydallying around — war conditions mean a multiplicity of fires—some by incendiary bombs, some by saboteurs . . . " He exhorted San Joseans to sweat and effort, with little glory. It was great stuff.

Two weeks later, the City Council ended its own dillydallying by ordering a pair of new American LaFrance pumpers at $8835 each. In January, a modern 65-foot aerial ladder truck was ordered on the strength of almost $13,000 in ready cash—in spite of City Man-

ager Goodwin's cautious warning that the money might instead be needed for the "war effort."

Just to help things along, pessimist Jay Stevens (now 9th Corps civil defense director) stopped in with caustic comment on San Jose's fire force. He was particularly critical of the aging Market Street firehouse, saying, "I've been coming here for 25 years and headquarters was terrible when I started, and it hasn't gotten any better . . . " Perhaps he was unduly harsh; the building had been only 8 years old on his first visit.

The apparatus purchases came a little late. We did get in under the wire on the ladder truck order, and it was delivered from Seagrave in August 1942 at a cost of $17,363. But new pumpers required a higher priority than San Jose could show; they were in heavy demand for the vast network of military camps and bases springing up around the country and overseas.

So veteran Captains John Humburg and Peter Segard once more fired up the last remaining tractorized steamer, brought out of retirement to serve as "backup" during the war emergency. The auxiliary got going in earnest during January, with nearly 800 members among employees of local industry, headed by "Chief" Captain L. A. O'Brien and "Assistant Chief" Captain Arthur Gilbert. For apparatus, they had a remarkable collection of old WPA trucks and similar castoffs, whatever would still run and carry hose and ladders, spotted at strategic locations around town.

On April 10, 1942, San Jose managed to "borrow for tryout" a pair of experimental high pressure fog trucks made by the local John Bean Division of the Food Machinery Corporation. The trial soon attained permanent status, and one of the two rigs—the last ones, incidentally, to use the red-and-white colors—went into service as Chemical 2. The other replaced Hose 1.

Both new trucks got their first workout about sundown on May 8 when fire destroyed the Standring Tire Shop at 375 West Santa Clara Street. Wartime rubber shortages, rather than sabotage, were in the minds of thousands of San Joseans witnessing the "tragic black funeral pyre." Within five minutes after proprietor W. O. "Bill" Standring had closed up for the night, a nearby gas station attendant saw flames in the building. The fire roared out of control two hours, under a mile-long pall of greasy black smoke. Hundreds of irreplaceable tires were destroyed with the shop and its equipment—a loss of $75,000.

Twelve pieces of San Jose apparatus answered the alarms. As firemen drove flames back from the front stockroom (using Hose 2's monitor nozzle more effectively than in 1933), volunteers crept in under the smoke to roll out every tire they could reach. "The oldest pumper in the force," probably first-due Engine 4, blew a valve midway through the battle and had to retire. Said the Mercury next day, "Fire Chief Plummer emerged from

the gutted structure, his face smoke-blackened and his uniform soaking wet, to say he had no idea how the fire had started."

Bridgeman's Bowling Alley later occupied the site; then Valley Bowl and Downtown Bowl. Along Guadalupe Creek bank, the dead skeleton of a eucalyptus tree testified for 20 years to the Standring fire's intense heat. The Downtown Bowl itself was destroyed by a multiple alarm fire in August 1969.

Despite the dire predictions, San Jose suffered only one fire directly traceable to its war effort—and it wasn't too serious. One of the hasty (and since much-criticized) decisions of those responsible for West Coast safety was to evacuate to the interior the thousands of Californians of Japanese descent. Many lived in the San Jose area; most were native-born American citizens. There were some sad days in the Spring of 1942, when trainloads of them pulled slowly out of the old depot yards near San Pedro Street, headed east—many never to return to their homes.

While these people were being relocated, some place had to be provided to store the goods they could not carry with them to the

internment camps. Authorities selected the old Brodel Building at 560 South First Street, which after the fire of 1918 was occupied for a long time by Hennessy Drayage, then stood vacant except for the "Treasure Gardens" flower show.

A new roof was needed before the building could be used. The roofing crew set up their tar pot inside the building, instead of outside where it belonged; when it exploded, shortly before noon on May 21, fire was thrown throughout the structure. Three workers were trapped on the roof and had to jump for it. Half a dozen hose lines brought the flames

under quick control, but the new roof was a total loss.

Other Wartime Casualties

It was just about the last call for 71-year-old Walter Page, a firefighter since 1907 and an Assistant Chief for 16 years. In August, 1942, he was hospitalized by a heart condition. For two months he improved slowly. Then, on November 1, he suddenly died at his home. In the thick of the fight at every fire, Page was a fireman's fireman—courageous and conscientious. Time and again he was cut, knocked out, or overcome; led away to safety, he returned to direct his men. He was a religious man—one old-timer recalled that Page didn't miss church once in 34 years —and a Catholic convert. Characteristic of the man was his reaction to a new fireman who wore the Masonic emblem. Glaring at

May 21, 1942—the second fire in the Brodel Building on South First St. Hose 1, only a month old, at right.

Captain Walter Page, later Assistant Chief from 1926 until his death in harness near the end of 1942.

the luckless recruit, Page growled: "So you're a Mason. Well, if you're going to be a Mason, be a good one!" His job, but not his place, was taken by Henry Lingua the following Spring.

During 1943, the Goodwill Industries shop, which had moved to North Market Street after the 1936 fire, was again burned out. Almost across the street from fire headquarters, it was a total loss nonetheless. Part of the rear of the building was used as storage by a local cheese firm, and in the aftermath of the fire they suffered some losses of their own. As firemen were overhauling in the Goodwill store, several men backed a truck up to the building and began loading it up with cheese. Thinking they were agents of the cheese company trying to salvage the stock, firemen made no move to interfere. Much later, the men were discovered to be thieves!

As winter came on in 1942, with the beginning of wartime crowding in many small and makeshift apartments, there was a series of deaths caused by unvented gas heaters operating in closed rooms. The issue had sparked weeks of debate in the City Council chambers, resulting in a March 1943 ordinance banning the use of such heaters. However, unless a complaint was issued or attention otherwise called to an illegal installation, there was really little that could be done to enforce the law.

Such heaters could be a fire hazard as well, as events of 1943 proved. One was believed responsible for San Jose's second highest all-time fire death toll, early on the morning of October 30. The blaze originated in a ground floor room of an old 2-story frame "apartment" at 432 South 3rd Street. Although the tenant claimed to have turned off the heater a couple of hours earlier, fire started in that area about 4 a.m. and swept rapidly upstairs.

Escaping from his burning room, the occupant tried to call the Fire Department from a hallway pay phone, only to discover he had no nickel! Another resident was called on for funds, and eventually firemen arrived to extinguish the relatively minor blaze.

But on the second floor, four persons had died—a couple in their 60's, plus two elderly pensioners. Eight others were homeless. Except for the quake-caused fire that took seven lives in 1906, the previous fatality record had been held by the North Market Street rooming-house blaze that killed three in the Spring of 1907.

At its November 1 meeting, the City Council ruled that "housing permits" then needed to permit use of old homes as rooming houses would henceforth have to be approved by the Fire Chief, who could then deny the permit if he found such hazards as the outlawed heaters on the premises.

As 1944 began, a mysterious fire at Grant School (not so bad as that of 1920) burned out the attic and four classrooms after rising through the walls from a basement lavatory. Assistant Chief Cavallero took a little too much smoke, and was put out of action; the consequences were to be far-reaching.

Another momentous event was on tap the 1st of May. At long last, San Jose's priority number had come up, and on that day the first of the two 750 GPM pumpers ordered way back in 1941 finally arrived. She was a wartime design—gleaming brass and chrome replaced by gray paint or black oxidized finish—but was new, powerful (200 HP), and reliable, with a 250 gallon water tank. The $8700 rig easily passed Underwriters' tests and was assigned to Engine 4, dropping the 1920 Seagrave down into reserve status.

"Coffee Bill" McCarthy would have been pleased. Since his Fourth Ward firehouse had been built almost 30 years before, only the castoffs of the department's apparatus had

D.E. Cavallero
Ass't Chief

Chas. Plummer
Chief.

W.A. Page.
Ass't Chief

been used there. Now, the tables were turned. It was a wise decision, for during the following years Engine 4 became one of the city's hottest companies, first-due at many major blazes and a second-alarm company at most others, making more runs than anything else except the Squad. Never again was there a winter like 1943-44 when Engine Co. No. 4 went 59 days without a single run on either shift.

Reformers Make a Clean Sweep

As far as the Fire Department was concerned, San Jose's simmering political stew finally came to a boil over the flames of the 40-year-old Garden City Pottery Company at 560 North 6th Street.

The complex of old frame and stucco buildings occupied most of the block between Empire and Jackson Streets, eastwards towards the SP tracks. Ten minutes after the night watchman had finished a round at 6:30 p.m. May 11, the plant was seen to be afire. Engine and Hose 2, Squad 1, and Chemical 4 responded to the still alarm with four officers and six men (these details got front-page publicity six months later, when the handling of this fire was used as a case study of the Fire Department's deficiencies).

When these first companies arrived, fire was rapidly extending from shop buildings to a frame warehouse containing $40,000 worth of finished clay products. Assistant Chief Cavallero called for a box alarm at once, bringing Engine and Hose 1, Truck 1, and Chemicals 2 and 3, with four more officers and seven men. Engines 3 and 7 were special-called by radio. All that remained to cover the city were eight men, with the new Engine 4, the undersized Engine 6, and Chemical 6.

Clouds of heavy smoke attracted a great crowd, many of whom assisted firemen in manning six hose lines and in rescuing the firm's records before the office burned. Several exposed residences were wet down. Cause of the $100,000 fire was never found, although the FBI routinely investigated because Garden City Pottery was working on "war orders."

The initial still and box alarm assignment of seven fire companies, that took half an hour to get all their lines into operation on the fire perimeter of over a city block, had a complement of only 20 men—including pump operators not available for firefighting. An equivalent assignment today would bring 31 men. City Manager Clarence Goodwin, facing a swelling tide of criticism of his Fire Department, stood squarely behind Chief Plummer. The newly-elected Council slate, however, clamoring for Plummer's scalp, then

The fire that finally brought action to rebuild San Jose's fire defenses was this $100,000 blaze at the Garden City Pottery Co., May 11, 1944; Chemical 2 at left.

turned their guns against the Manager. On May 22, a group of four Councilmen confronted Goodwin with a demand that he resign.

Goodwin did so, and his replacement, John J. Lynch, forthwith requested the resignations of Fire Chief Plummer and Police Chief Black. Although obviously being made a scapegoat for years of municipal neglect, Plummer was getting old after 40 years in the fire service, and was no longer disposed to fight for his job. He stepped down, and the following day, May 23, 1944, Captain Lester O'Brien was appointed to replace him. It was an ignominious windup to a long career of public service.

Nor was this the end of the Fire Department's troubles. In selecting the new Chief, the administration had passed over both Assistant Chiefs. Dominic Cavallero, 61 years of age, was ready for retirement, and in poor health; his throat and lungs had been damaged by smoke inhalation at the Grant School fire in February, putting him on sick leave for two months. Cavallero retired effective December 1, 1944.

Second Assistant Henry Lingua, however, above O'Brien on the eligibility list, was nowhere near retirement age. Thus it came as a surprise when, on November 22, 1944, Lingua tendered his immediate resignation. In the department since July 1922, Lingua

In front of the downtown General Paint store after this 1944 fire were a number of department notables: Chief Charles Plummer, Asst. Chief Cavallero, behind him Fireman Gene Sawyer, Capt. Ralph Jennings, and Brownie, ready to return to quarters.

was promoted to Lieutenant in 1933, Captain in 1939, and Second Assistant Chief in 1943. One of San Jose's most able and promising fire officers, he had been Fire Marshal since 1930 and an outstanding student in outside fire training courses.

Lingua gave no reason for quitting. It is worth noting, however, that he later enjoyed a long successful career as the first Chief of the postwar County Central Fire District, prominent in statewide firemen's organizations, retiring with honors in 1963.

Thus, within six months' time, the Fire Department's entire top leadership was gone. To add to that, two veteran Captains were outraged by the City Manager's selection of a man below them on the eligible list as Lingua's replacement. Manager Lynch refused to give ground, claiming that absences of some officers on military leave affected his interpretation of eligibility standing. In December, one of the protestants, allegedly backed by the Civil Service Commission, confirmed his intention to seek redress in the courts—which was of no avail.

Arising out of all these gloomy developments was one piece of good news. The late Fred Watson, for years a senior member of the City Council, rose up to sponsor a $406,000 improvement program for the Fire Department. He got the Council to appropriate $56,000 in available funds for new fire apparatus, then started a campaign to float a $350,000 firehouse bond issue for 1945.

In the Fall of 1944 most of San Jose's oldest retired fire equipment—some of it superseded for six years or more—was sold at public auction. Unfortunately, even if wartime ceiling price rules could have been waived, the obsolete rigs were of little value except as collector's items. It is a matter for everlasting regret that at least one of them could not have been tucked away somewhere for preservation as a museum piece.

First to go, on August 9, 1944, was the old Hook and Ladder truck with its 3-ton White tractor. There were five bidders, including J. N. Hedberg and retired fireman Harry Miller. Low bidder, at $725, turned out to be a Santa Clara fruit grower named George T.

Peterson, who as a White dealer in 1931 had originally sold the tractor to the city. Peterson announced his intention to use the tractor as a farm truck in his orchards — *sic transit gloria mundi.*

Shortly before noon on Friday, October 6, a few curious passersby wandered into the paved courtyard behind the Market Street firehouse to watch City Manager Lynch personally wield the hammer as an oddly assorted group of relics went on the auction block. The two 1927 Reo hose wagons were knocked down for the ceiling price of $205.59 each. Chemical 7's graceful little 1926 Reo was sold, along with Chemical 3's 1929 Dodge, eight old chemical tanks, and a hose reel. For this priceless set of museum displays, the City of San Jose collected the magnificent sum of $1109.

While the sale proceeded, Chief O'Brien was submitting to the City Council a proposed Fire Prevention Code. A product of long, hard labor by O'Brien, both Assistant Chiefs, and Captain William Ogden, the Code would re-peal or supersede practically all existing city ordinances relating to Fire Prevention, dating back at least as far as 1908. Included was the plan for a new agency within the Fire Department: a Fire Prevention Bureau. There had been a Fire Marshal for many years, but his primary concern was with arson investigation.

Without fanfare, the new Code was adopted; the new Bureau opened for business August 17, 1945. As that year began, Fred Watson's bond drive went into high gear. Publicity was the first order of procedure. Two simultaneous reports burst upon the front pages to reveal to a startled citizenry just how bad things were behind the sagging doors of their neighborhood firehouses. At the City Council meeting of January 22, Chief O'Brien laid his report on the department's condition before the city fathers. An entire page of text and photos in the January 28 Mercury highlighted such gems as these:

Chemical 3's old rig, with a top motor speed of 2700 RPM, had been equipped in 1944 with

The Market Street headquarters from 1908 to 1951, taken June 11, 1944. Left to right: Engine 1, Lieut. Frank Basile and Fireman Fred Luhring, (later Chief of the Central Fire District); Squad 1, Fireman Ted Parker, Capt. Ralph Jennings, and Lieut. Ron LeBeau; the Assistant Chief's car; Hose 1, Firemen Sam Scarpace and Simon Garcia; Truck 1, Firemen Ed Robinett, Capt. Henry Anderson, Fireman George Batti.

a 500 GPM front-mounted pump, loaned to the city by Civilian Defense authorities, requiring 3300 RPM for proper operation. In December the power takeoff to the pump had failed in service. Chemical 4 was a dandy; the 30-year-old Pope-Hartford chemical apparatus leaked, the hose was porous, the 1930 chassis couldn't be pushed beyond 30 miles per hour, and the tires had dry rot.

The remaining old hose wagon, No. 2, also having a top speed of about 35, was liable to be left at the post by the much faster Engine 2. One of its front wheels had come apart and been welded back together; altogether in 14 years the city had spent over a thousand dollars to keep it going. Engine 3, the rebuilt 1914 Seagrave, had an "unreliable" pump— and such a long turning radius it couldn't turn around between intersections. The rebuild itself wasn't the bargain it had seemed to be, for it cost over $8400 if one included $1600 for Gurgiolo's lost time while supervising the work in Oakland. Besides, maintenance on the rig had cost almost $900 more since 1938.

Engine 6, in Willow Glen, got another rebuild job. The work cost $1963, followed by over $460 in upkeep. Engine 7's 1922 Stutz, rebuilt in 1940, was becoming dangerous to drive. Its single rear wheels skidded on turns, unable to hold traction against the side sway of the water in its tank (inside which the baffles had rusted out). Repair parts were hard to find; the Stutz firm had been out of business for years.

Firehouses themselves were as bad or worse —damp rot at Chemical 6; no alarm system tie-in at Engine 6; at Market Street, the department's telephone nerve center, only voice link between stations, was located in a "small, poorly-lighted, poorly-ventilated and noisy room . . . between the apparatus floor and the dormitories . . ." Market Street, like most of the others, was over 35 years old, its haymow and other features of horse-drawn architecture glaringly evident. The painful facts of San Jose's Fire Department manpower, administration, and salary schedules were apparent from the table below.

Submitted to the Council with O'Brien's report was another from the Underwriters. Lacking proper fire prevention regulations and enforcement machinery, without up-to-date building codes, San Jose had three downtown blocks considered to be extreme conflagration hazards. The 1937 recommendations for more men, better station locations, and modern equipment, were repeated with added emphasis. Specifically, the report asked for at least five new engines and two new aerials.

Mutual Aid Begins

This time, Councilmen reacted with enthusiasm and speed. On January 29 they called for bids on three 750 GPM pumpers, one 1000 GPM, and a 75-foot aerial. Two weeks later there were some mild repercussions as both Seagrave and Mack representatives appeared to protest award of all four rigs to the high bidder—American LaFrance, at $56,351. The city countered charges of bad faith by pointing out the importance of an offer by LaFrance of a five year guarantee, plus past service by the LaFrance people.

Also, explained City Manager Lynch, the department planned to standardize on LaFrance apparatus to minimize its spare parts inventory. That plan has since been consistently followed through the administration of three Fire Chiefs over a 20-year period.

There was still the priority system to overcome. In April, Lynch appealed to local Congressmen for aid in giving San Jose higher fire apparatus priorities; nevertheless, it was to be nearly a year and a half before any of this batch of new equipment arrived.

How San Jose's Fire Department Compared with Other Northern California Cities
January 1945

City	Area Square Miles	Population	No. of Hydrants	No. of Alarm Boxes	No. of Firemen Recom.	No. of Firemen Actual	Salary	Chief's Aides	Assistant Chiefs	Chief Salary
Sacramento	14	123,334	1855	520	191	188	$195-225	5 BC	2	$400
Stockton	10.3	60,000	917	208	128	118	185-215	2 Sec.AC	1	360
Fresno	10.37	75,000	1429	212	142	142	160-200	2 Pl.Ch.	2	350
Berkeley	9.5	100,024	1343	241	140	140	208-230	1 AC	1 Dep.	434.5
San Jose	14.5	80,000	776	120	162	81	180-210	0	2	320

However, some additional manpower—the auxiliaries—became a permanent adjunct to the Fire Department in February 1945. Officially termed the "San Jose Plant Protective Fire Auxiliary," this group had been hastily formed just before Pearl Harbor; besides Captains O'Brien and Gilbert, its only professional staff was a paid secretary. First civilian "chairman" of the auxiliary was the late Morris Turner of American Can Company.

Purpose of the group was not civilian defense in the popular sense, but the establishment of a trained firefighting force within the city's industrial plants. In the event of disaster or sabotage, such a force could be counted on to control fire on the premises pending arrival of the Fire Department.

A total of 776 auxiliary firemen were recruited in 38 factories. During the war years, when there was always the chance that the auxiliaries might have to fight fire entirely on their own, a ragtag collection of makeshift apparatus was gotten together for their use.

The work of these men was not to be scorned. In its first three years, the organization was called on to handle 239 industrial fires, extinguishing 95% of them without San Jose Fire Department help — a record that was maintained for many more years after the end of the war. Auxiliary firemen received many hours of training, and still put

in hundreds of annual man-hours of classroom and drill work with professional firefighters. At many major fires, auxiliaries have proved their worth in assisting the regular fire companies in both salvage and firefighting operations.

So successful did the program become that Sacramento, Stockton, Watsonville, and Fresno established similar groups. Governed by a board of four directors, under Chairman Louis Sorenson of Food Machinery, the auxiliaries became a permanent branch of the San Jose Fire Department in 1945. Since then, membership and plant coverage have declined about a third, but the auxiliary is still a key factor in San Jose's industrial fire protection.

Voters passed the firehouse bond issue in May 1945, but construction of new stations was even further in the future, following a long process of site selection, approval by Underwriters, purchase of property, preparation of plans, etc.

Long-overdue settlement of another Fire Department headache moved closer with the signing of San Jose's first mutual aid agreement on March 5, 1945. This agreement removed the threat of damage suits against the city arising from outside-city responses, for the city could not be liable if firemen crossed the borders in response to a call for help by proper authorities of another municipality.

Again, as in 1941, death by fire in the Burbank District brought the problem forcibly to community-wide attention. Early on December 2, 1944, a garbled report had reached San Jose Fire Headquarters of a barn afire on the grounds of O'Connor Sanitarium (then located just outside the city at Race and San Carlos, where Sears is now). No apparatus was sent.

But the "barn" turned out to be the outbuilding residence of two Sanitarium employees; one escaped with injuries, the other was burned to death. Again the hue and cry

went up. After all, San Jose firemen had responded to a $100,000 blaze beyond the city limits which wrecked the Gambord Meat Company. Chief O'Brien pointed out that he would have sent his men to O'Connor also, except for the report that only a barn was involved. Again he reminded critics of the danger of lawsuits. But the four area Fire Departments — San Jose, Santa Clara, Burbank, and Cottage Grove — did promise to meet "to discuss ways of working more closely together," and the March agreement resulted.

After the formation in 1947 of the County Central Fire District, all of San Jose's environs were covered by their own fire services, making mutual aid effective throughout. Today, although problems still arise (as we shall see), San Jose firemen work smoothly with adjacent departments; when alarms reach either City or County Communications centers for fire close to either side of the city limits, two or as many as four Fire Departments may be dispatched. Whichever arrives first goes to work on the fire regardless of jurisdiction.

Handicapped from the beginning by the circumstances of his appointment, praised by some as having launched the rebuilding of the department, and damned by others as having wrecked it, Lester O'Brien had his troubles. One of his ideas in assigning personnel was to periodically move men around from station to station to familiarize them with the territory and operations of other companies. Regardless of the merits of the idea, which provoked a storm of controversy when he applied it wholesale a few years

Chemical 3, South 8th Street, 1945. Note front-mounted pump. Left: Captain Earl Conyers, Sr.; right, Fireman Jack Stanley.

later, it added nothing to Chief O'Brien's popularity in the department.

One of several men transferred in apparently routine fashion by O'Brien in 1945 was Captain C. W. Martin, a fireman since 1924, who was moved from Engine 7 to Engine 4. He protested, allegedly in profane terms, to both O'Brien and Assistant Chief Gilbert. After a public hearing on charges of "Insubordination and unofficer-like conduct," City Manager Lynch fired Martin September 14, 1945.

Overshadowed by the "exposés" of the Fire Department's condition, as well as by the approaching end of World War II, fires themselves were in the background during 1945. There were a number of them: April 9, Dan's Tire Shop was destroyed at Santa Clara and Montgomery Streets; May 16 there was a threatening blaze at Bellarmine School; May 25 a storage building of the Salvation Army was razed; June 7 the Individual Laundry burned on Almaden Ave. Captain Gilbert Stewart of Engine 4 was badly burned when caught by falling debris at a $25,000 fire in Bachrodt's feed and fuel warehouse on Lincoln Ave., Saturday September 15. Fireman Brad Jones of Engine 6 was overcome by smoke from tons of sacked barley, walnuts, and alfalfa hay. Both the San Jose and Burbank Fire Departments turned out for this one, discovered about 8 p.m. and going strong when firemen arrived.

Second of the new pumpers ordered almost four years previous was tested at Ryland Park on October 18, 1945, delivering a maximum of 1150 GPM before a crowd of interested spectators. In most respects almost identical to Engine 4, this one boasted a little more brasswork. It was assigned to Engine Co. 6, thus freeing the 1929 LaFrance—still labelled "Willow Glen Volunteers" — for a stint at Chemical 4.

Last major fire of the year was an $85,000 loss at the Farnsworth and Callahan auto supply store, 266 West Santa Clara. A passerby gave the alarm at 10:40 p.m., November 21, as a hot air explosion blew out the front windows. Firemen under Second Assistant Chief Ed Powers were hampered by heavy smoke and fumes from burning lacquer and insulation.

What Next?

At the end of World War II the San Jose Fire Department had reached its lowest ebb. Political upheaval had rent the city government, forcing the Fire Chief out of office. One Assistant Chief retired, the other quit. Promotions made to fill the vacancies were challenged in court by those passed over in the selection process. The new Chief, incurring unpopularity that would soon lead to his resignation, had fired one of his officers who recklessly protested against the new order of things. Ugly headlines, and uglier rumors, darkened the department's image in the community.

Although new equipment had been ordered, the public was exposed—long after it should have been done—to full-page newspaper features on the literal and figurative decay in their fire protection. Slow, decrepit apparatus, a patchwork of makeshift rebuilding, had just about reached the end of the road. And yet, even here, a priceless opportunity to save some of the old rigs for posterity, as museum pieces, was lost with the 1944 auctions — which brought such a pitiful financial return.

What else could happen? From now on, the road led upward.

Santa Clara St. at 17th, 1945; the site now occupied by Station 8. With the 1930 GMC chemical wagon are Lieut. Malpass (left) and Fireman Everett Lyda (later the city's recreation director).

Up From The Depths 1945-1963

In 1939, San Jose's annexation of 40 acres was important enough to be mentioned prominently in the Fire Chief's annual report. Less than 25 years later, the city was nonchalantly absorbing chunks as large as 40 square miles.

Today, each of San Jose's several District Chiefs is alone responsible for as much territory, and almost as much fire equipment and manpower, as the Chief of the entire department was in 1946—the year when San Joseans saw the first tangible progress toward today's fire forces.

Changes in the Charter

Once the new apparatus was ordered, the administration turned to the firehouse problem. Some of the sites took many months to pin down. In its meeting of February 18, 1946, the City Council approved spending $63,000 for three properties—only one of which was ever used. This practice continued for years, but even when land was bought and its use proved infeasible, in the postwar boom it could usually be re-sold at a profit.

Sites selected in February were: 100 x 192 feet, northwest corner of Market and St. James, for $43,000; northwest corner of 15th and Julian, 125 x 137 feet, for $5000 (never used); northwest corner of 35th and Santa Clara, 110 x 125 feet, for $15,000 (earmarked for Engine 8, but never used). The Market Street location was approved by Underwriters in March as a new headquarters site. Still another lot, near Alma and Almaden, was under negotiation but never purchased.

Last big fire to be fought by the old rigs broke out early July 16, in the Eggo Food Products mayonnaise and potato chip factory at Julian and San Pedro. Stocks of oil and waxed paper spread flames throughout the unsprinklered building in a short time, while a salad oil tank explosion rocked the neighborhood. The $200,000 loss might have been reduced if the passerby who discovered the fire had used the alarm box only a block away, instead of running the four blocks to the Market Street firehouse to give the alarm.

A week later, Chief O'Brien had to cut his 1946-47 budget request from $458,790 to $406,030. His major sacrifice was the creation of the full staff of Battalion Chiefs for which he had been campaigning ever since he took office. He also had to drop the proposed addition of two new squads and a ladder truck. These cutbacks resulted from a recent election in which voters had approved a "salary adjustment" consisting of reduction in firemen's work week hours from 84 to 70. The extra cost was $34,530 annually; 18 additional jobs were created.

Many other changes in governmental machinery arose from Charter amendments passed in the 1946 election. A Board of Administration for the Police and Fire Department Retirement Plans was created, along with a mandatory retirement age of 65 for municipal employees. At its first meeting on September 30, the Board approved retirement of over-age Captain Louis Siebuhr—a fireman since 1903.

Another innovation was the post of Personnel Manager. At the end of 1946, this office had to oversee two minor revolutions in the Fire Department. First, the work week change finally superseded the 10 and 14 hour day-night shifts with 24 hours on and 24 hours off. Secondly, authorities now felt that there was no essential difference between the duties of the Captain, on one 24 hour shift, and those of the Lieutenant, on the other shift. Accordingly, the rank of Lieutenant was abolished on December 31, 1946, and most of those holding that rank became Captains.

Meanwhile, the new pumpers were arriving. Engine 5, 750 GPM, came at the end of July, to replace Chemicals 2, 3, and 4. Engine 8, a duplicate, also arrived to replace Chemical 6. By September, Engine 3 (1000 GPM) and Engine 7 (750 GPM) were in town. The "white elephant" went into reserve, and Chemical 2, second of the two 1942 fog trucks, was converted to a hose wagon for Engine Co. 2. On Wednesday, September 25, under the watchful eye of Underwriters engineer Herbert Raines, Superintendent of Equipment Manuel Maral put the re-vamped department through its paces in a day-long test.

Like Engines 4 and 6, the new arrivals carried 250 gallon tanks. During Fire Prevention Week in October, all six of the department's new pumpers, plus the "1898" steamer and two other "old engines" otherwise unidentified, appeared in a downtown parade to show San Joseans what had been accomplished. A minor fire alarm pulled two engines and the squad out of the parade, but they soon returned, and "slid back into the parade line with a loss of only seven or eight minutes." Truck 1, a 75-foot cab-ahead aerial, arrived December 13.

Once again the auction block was dusted off, this time at the now-abandoned quarters of Chemical 3 on South 8th Street. At 3 p.m., Monday October 14, 1946, the city received a total of $4985 for six old rigs—any one of which would be worth more than that today. Sold to the City of Capitola was the old 500 GPM LaFrance from Willow Glen, at $3000, to be "recommissioned" and see several more years of firefighting service. The 1922 Stutz, the 1920 Seagrave, and three 1930 hose and chemical wagons—Dodge, Federal, and GMC —went for an average of $500 each (wartime price ceilings had been lifted.)

Inevitably, some residents became concerned about their fire safety when the neighborhood firehouse closed down. The same day the auction was held, residents of the Second Ward appeared in force before the Council to protest abandonment of Chemical 4. Debate lasted an hour. People feared long trains on the SP's line from Milpitas might cut them off from the Fire Department. Chief O'Brien pointed out that "the protection given by an obsolete chemical truck and two men was largely imaginary." Officials had tried, and failed, to get one of the new pumpers through the doors of Chemical 4's little house. O'Brien had put the old Willow Glen engine there some 8 months previously, but still could give it only a two man crew because there wasn't enough living space in the house to accommodate more men.

So the place was closed. Later it was used for meetings by Boys' City, then was taken over by the North Star Social Club, and remains in good repair today — oldest of the four retired firehouses still standing in San Jose.

All these improvements resulted in the long-awaited step up in insurance classification. In December 1946, San Jose rose from Class 5 to Class 4, saving residents an estimated quarter million dollars annually in fire insurance premiums.

Chemical 4 poses in 1946 with Fireman George Fusco. This former Willow Glen volunteer equipment was stationed here only temporarily.

June 1947: the James Transfer warehouse at 230 Bassett Street goes up in smoke; Hose 2 at right.

Changes in Command

Banner headlines on Saturday, June 7, 1947, told the city that Fire Chief O'Brien had resigned. In explanation, he blamed a "malicious smear campaign, detrimental to the welfare of the city and to his personal health." Rumors had been "systematically initiated and spread throughout the community," charged O'Brien, in the form of anonymous calls to his wife, and unsigned communications mailed to Councilmen. The Chief was not a well man — ill and hospitalized frequently during his tenure in office, he was at the time under a doctor's care.

Lack of a thoroughly experienced replacement would not have troubled the city administration in 1908. But that day was past. On Thursday, June 19, 1947, ex-Chief O'Brien was persuaded to meet with City Manager Campbell to discuss O'Brien's possible return to duty. As they talked, the drama of the mid-afternoon conference was heightened by receipt of the news that a general alarm fire was raging in the Bassett Street warehouse area.

A James Transfer Company truck driver had heard an explosion in the small paint shop adjoining the James Warehouse at 230

Bassett. Running to investigate, he found flames in the warehouse, "shooting in all directions." Feeding on tons of stored combustibles, including huge rolls of scarce newsprint, the $100,000 fire involved the entire building before firemen got six hose lines in operation to cut off spread of the blaze to exposed industrial buildings crowding in on every side.

Both Campbell and O'Brien rushed to the scene. Next day, it was announced that O'Brien had withdrawn his resignation, to return to command the following Monday. "However," he warned, "I'm still under my doctor's care, and his permission for me to return to work was contingent on my taking it easier." Campbell agreed, "O'Brien has been working too hard." Heartened by what he termed his first vacation in six years, the Chief put behind him the "rumors" threatening his career saying "...it's all over and done with. I'm not holding any grudges or ill will..."

Campbell's concern for delegating more work to junior officers, leaving the Chief with a lighter load, pointed up the need for better definition of the roles of all department officers. The organization's rapid growth, without experienced top leadership since 1944, was complicated now by the division of company authority between two Captains — one on each shift. Some old-time firemen deplored the removal of the Lieutenants. Said one, "There used to be a cleancut line of command. The Captain was in charge of the company and the house, whether he was on shift or not. The Lieutenant was always the second in command, taking over only in the Captain's absence. Now, with a Captain on each shift, there are two separate departments, and the men don't understand it."

Another controversy was sparked by the newly created post of Battalion Chief, restored to the department budget. During June, 23 of the 29 Captains petitioned the Civil Service Commission to require 15 years instead of 2½ years service as Captain prior to further promotion. The Commission studied practices in other Fire Departments, then declined to change the rules; on July 2, examinations were set for the end of the month, to select permanent replacements for the three "temporary" Battalion Chiefs on duty.

All this left many firemen disgruntled. It was not surprising, therefore, that 15 of those who failed to pass the exams later brought suit against the Commission and the City Manager, alleging several irregularities in the testing procedure.

A Fiery End for Chemical 1

Except for the "White Elephant," about the only remaining piece of obsolete fire apparatus was tucked away among the trees up in Alum Rock Canyon. Once the city's busiest fire company, first unit to get a fully paid crew, the elite of the department, Chemical 1 had been turned out to pasture since 1938.

Replacement of the chemical tanks by a flat water tank and front-mounted pump, under Lou Gurgiolo's supervision during the early '30's, had been only mildly successful; the pump was later removed. Taken out of service when the Mack squad was received, Chemical 1 was further revamped and turned over to the Parks Department to protect the Alum Rock buildings.

She was housed in a shed next door to the Park blacksmith shop. About 2:45 a.m., Saturday July 5, 1947, the shop caught fire. Within a few minutes the shed also was burning furiously, making it impossible to rescue the fire truck.

Units summoned from San Jose joined forces with three State Forestry crews to control the $15,000 blaze that left the two buildings in ruins. Only a charred, rusty hulk remained of the old chemical wagon; hauled back to San Jose, it languished in the Corporation Yard for a time, then was junked.

Chief O'Brien announced a plan, on July 16, worked out with the local Jennings Radio Company, to put three-way radio equipment in each piece of fire apparatus. In August, orders totalling $11,000 were placed with Motorola for 19 sets of FM mobile transmitter-receiver sets, to be delivered before the end of the year. Only a few Pacific Coast cities had such a communication system, which, explained O'Brien, would for the first time permit assignment of fire rigs to roving inspections without taking them out of service. One by one during the Spring of 1948 each engine and truck company reported to the Fire Department "shop" on South 8th for installation and checkout of its radio equipment, under direction of City Radio Technician Henri Kirby. The work was completed in mid-April.

Throughout the city, during the Fall of 1947, Public Works crews stencilled all hydrants with identifying numbers. Next, a flow test was made on each hydrant. Complete records of numbers and capacities were set up at Fire Headquarters. Then, beginning in January 1948, the top of each hydrant was painted a distinctive color—red for flow of 500 GPM or less; orange for 500 to 1000 GPM; green for above 1,000 GPM. Thus, company officers could tell at a glance what to expect from a hydrant before hooking up to it.

Still recuperating from his ailments, Fire Chief O'Brien left his sickbed September 24, 1947, to direct operations at a $50,000 fire which wrecked the 3-story frame Pine Chateau Hotel at Stockton Ave. and Clinton Street. The elderly man in whose room the fire broke out had long been known to local police as a habitual drunkard; badly burned and clothes aflame, he leaped to his death from a top floor window before firemen arrived. One firefighter was injured during the blaze. Afterwards, the 60-year-old landmark —once a private school—was torn down and soon forgotten.

Another San Jose landmark, of greater sentimental value, also disappeared during the fall of 1947. This was the old wooden grandstand of the Graham Field baseball park, which stood on Willow Street at the foot of Prospect. Home of many semi-pro ball teams, summer softball leagues, and site of a bocci ball court popular with the neighborhood's elderly Italians, Graham Field commemorated well-known local sportswriter Jack Graham, who had died some years earlier.

Late in the evening of October 21, fire started in trash under the right-field stands; soon there was nothing left. Nominally only $20,000, the loss to old-time San Joseans was not readily measurable. Graham Field was never rebuilt. Eventually, the Willow-Keyes Street connection was cut through where second base had been, and apartments covered the rest of the site.

One of the first postwar firehouses: Engine 2's quarters at 6th and Julian.

New Firehouse vs. Old Temple

On February 16, 1948, the City Council was finally able to award the first firehouse contracts. Total contract price was $184,695, covering new quarters for Engine 2 (6th and Julian), Engine 5 (6th and Taylor), and Engine 6 (1161 Minnesota Ave.). Construction was to start at once; ground was broken for No. 2 on March 6.

This silver lining for the Fire Department was not without its cloud for San Jose taxpayers; on February 24, 1948, the Council had to enact a permanent municipal sales tax ordinance to help pay for capital improvements.

Members of San Jose's AFL Firefighters Union No. 873 were likewise concerned with financial matters. After long debate, the City Council declined to back a proposed Charter amendment requiring "review" of firemen's wages and hours twice a year, such wages not to be less than the average of other Bay Area Fire Departments on the date of comparison.

Faced with Council refusal to put the issue on the May ballot, for fear of granting firemen "preferential treatment," the union began circulating initiative petitions to force a citywide vote; the drive was successful. Arguments advanced, as the election date neared, ran like this: "Your firemen put in longer hours and get less pay than firemen in the average Bay Area city of over 50,000 population . . . It merely sets a fair and flexible standard of which San Joseans need

Engine Co. 5, 1955. Rig at left is High Pressure 5, one of the revamped 1942 Bean fog trucks. This building at 6th and Taylor Sts. was remodelled into Public Works Department offices after Engine 5 moved to North 10th Street.

never be ashamed." Countered the opposition: "Firemen now get a basic $273 per month plus $22 pension contribution for not more than 14 24-hour days each month, plus . . . other benefits. This is a result of three salary increases in the past 18 months. The initiative . . . would mean $310 monthly for firemen . . . It would cost an extra $57,767 . . . each year for fire department salaries alone."

Adding bitterness to the issue was the prolonged case of Fireman John P. McLaughlin, fired in February for allegedly leaving the city without permission and failing to report for duty February 21. McLaughlin's attorneys claimed throughout lengthy hearings that his Union activities were the real reason for his ouster. Weeks of charges and denials finally resulted in the Civil Service Commission's upholding the dismissal.

On the same day, April 5, Superior Judge John Foley ruled against the 15 firemen who had sued the city administration to set aside results of the July 1947 officers' promotional exams. All six of their legal objections were found invalid by the Court. Another blow fell on May 17, when San Jose voters turned down the salary plan initiative by a two to one margin.

But construction of the firehouses proceeded apace. A $40,000 contract for Engine 8 at 17th and Santa Clara, only one of the new stations to occupy the site of an old one, was awarded in May. At the same time, dis-

trict inspections by radio-equipped engine companies began in the residential areas. Engines 5, 6, and 7 covered their territories during successive weeks.

One of the new houses, No. 5 at 6th and Taylor, came in conflict with a historic remnant of old Chinatown, and in the march of civic progress the firehouse won out. Right next door to it, overlooking the dormitory area, was the 1888 Chinese joss-house or shrine known as the "Temple of the Five Gods." Neglected for years, its ownership the subject of argument, the old 2-story brick temple was falling apart, with visible cracks in the outside walls. Chief O'Brien feared its collapse onto the firehouse.

It was estimated that over $5000 would be needed to restore the building inside and out. Before the war, public opinion had acted to save the joss-house when it was to be sold for delinquent taxes, and the city had retained the title since 1942. Only two such temples now remained in the entire state, from the days when over 4000 Chinese had lived in San Jose alone.

But now, the tiny remaining Chinese population could muster neither public nor private support to preserve the historic building, with its thousands of dollars worth of religious furnishings, the gilded altar, and statues of the five gods themselves. It was torn down in May of 1949. Ironically, the location of the next door firehouse, which brought the destruction about, was only temporary. Within 11 years Engine 5 had been moved to still another site.

"New Deal in the Fire Department"

One of San Jose's last ventures in homemade fire apparatus got under way about the middle of May, when a pair of 1½-ton GMC truck chassis arrived in town. Costing $3700 altogether, the two rigs were built into new hose wagons by Master Mechanic Cecil, aided by Captain Ron LeBeau and Fireman Joe Bonnell.

Because the South 8th Street "shop" was serving as quarters for Engine 8 during construction of 8's new station, the work was done in the old Lion Stables on St. John near 4th Street. Also kept in the stables during this period was the "white elephant" reserve engine, officially taken out of service by Chief O'Brien in 1948.

Taking over as Hose 1 and Hose 2 near the end of the year, the new wagons carried 2000 feet of hose in beds having four compartments so that as many as four lines could be laid simultaneously.

Headlined "'New Deal' in Fire Department," a Mercury editorial in July 1948 claimed that "In all the years of its history it is doubtful if there has ever been a time when as many and as important changes were being made in the San Jose Fire Department as are taking place today."

One of our more unusual fires taxed the department on August 21. Sparks from a nearby rubbish burner, or perhaps a passing locomotive, touched off a block-long pile of bagged cans in the storage yard of the Continental Can Company, 357 East Taylor Street. Paper shells and liners of 15,000 bags burned for four hours, fed by the pockets of air within the cans themselves—three million of them. Fire and water combined to ruin the whole works, for a loss approaching $100,000. No buildings were involved. Plant workers saved other nearby piles by moving them away on fork lifts, while firemen gradually drowned the blazing bags with streams directed from atop boxcars.

Another resident arose in November to protest the Second Ward firehouse relocation. Making Engine 2's well-publicized move sound like a mystery thriller, he complained, "I understand on good authority that plans have been laid in secret to move it within the next few weeks . . . If so, it would be a terrible calamity . . . Suppose a fire should break out in a downtown office or commercial building or in a large hotel . . . could not great loss of life and property be had in the extra time it would take to go the additional 6 blocks . . ."

Despite the "secret" plans, on February 23, 1949, 200 visitors, including reporters, showed up for dedication ceremonies at the new station, sponsored by the North Star Social Club. Longtime fire protection booster Fred Watson, then San Jose's Mayor, had the satisfaction of delivering the principal address.

The only new firehouse of 2-story design, requiring a brass sliding pole, No. 2 inherited one — said to have been 50 years old — from the abandoned Chemical 2 house, vacated February 5 when Engine 5 moved to its new location.

At the same time, No. 5 became a two-piece company. Marking a final break with the old days, the high pressure fog truck that had been Hose 2 was repainted solid red, and assigned as "High Pressure 5" to run with Engine 5; the other Bean rig became "High Pressure 3."

Towards the end of February, Engine 6 moved to its new building, handsomely faced with brick and housing the Willow Glen Branch Library in its east wing. A dedication was staged by the Willow Glen Lions Club on the 18th, at 8 p.m. Next was Engine 8, moving in on March 25; that evening, the East Santa Clara Street Improvement Association put on a gala reception with music (the Roosevelt Junior High Glee Club) and speakers (Chief O'Brien and Mayor Watson).

Still another dedication ceremony on February 1, in a truck farm along the Guadalupe Creek, launched a San Jose enterprise which would someday require its own fire station— the San Jose Municipal Airport. The Municipal Band, Councilmen, and a handful of spectators braved the wind to bring the air age to San Jose, out among the cabbage fields; officials managed to have one plane on deck for the occasion.

Phantom Fire Boxes

When Chief O'Brien had announced the three-way radio plans, two other communications changes had been associated with it. Throughout the summer of 1948, Captain (later Chief) LeBeau toiled at the details of one of those changes — the "phantom box" alarm system. Its key feature was assignment of a "box number" to each of the city's

Complete crew at Station 5 (Sixth and Taylor). Left to right: Gene Germano, Loren Gray, Coy Harris, Capt. Larocca, Capt. Conyers, Tony Sapena, Joe Wehner, Bill Lennon, Theron Connett, Severo Garcia, Joe Carlino, George Fusco.

Built in the Fire Department shop during 1948, Hose 1 and its twin Hose 2 were the department's first heavy artillery. Both are still in service.

1700 street intersections. Captain LeBeau, appointed to take charge of the installation, began by intensively studying systems in use elsewhere in Northern California. Assignment of numbers in an orderly pattern, and making up the necessary eight sets of new running cards for each "box," took many months of effort.

Meantime, the other new wrinkle in fire communications was being ironed out. Into a revamped City Hall Communications Center went a Gamewell "Vocalarm" intercom system linking all fire stations. Communications was made a unified department, under Police Department control, but serving fire and other needs as well.

Costing $9000, the new alarm transmitting equipment, expected to trim two minutes from the department's average response time, went into operation February 11, 1949. Upon receipt of any telephoned fire alarm, City Hall operators quickly found the correct "phantom box" number for the nearest street intersection in their files, set up the number on the four dials of the transmitting console, then pushed a single button to send the number out to all stations via telegraph. Simultane-

ously, each firehouse got the address over the intercom. Additional information, or recall of companies if the first arrivals found the alarm false, went out by radio.

Contributing to 1949's status as a banner year in Fire Department history was a series of major fires, one of which set some new records. The first of these, at 11:40 p.m. January 31, was the 2-alarm blaze which wrecked the 2- and 3-story offices and workrooms of the Volunteers of America, at 311 Auzerais Ave. The 40-year-old building, with no fire protection of its own, was a $20,000 loss.

A night watchman, asleep on the premises, was awakened by the crackle of flames just in time to escape. Firemen surrounded the place to set up water curtains protecting exposed residences on all sides, and were later praised by the Volunteers' building owners for fast response and quick work in confining the fire.

Another good stop was made February 24 at the Sainte Claire Club, 2nd and St. James Streets. Beginning in a grease-laden, substandard kitchen vent, fire swept up into a second floor bar and third floor cardrooms.

One of California's oldest private men's clubs, the Sainte Claire was fortunately occupied by only one guest when the fire was discovered at 5 a.m. He escaped safely as masked firefighters moved into the upper floors via ground and aerial ladders, under a pouring rain. Loss was $37,000.

Firemen faced an unprecedented challenge on the night of April 4. Either a dust explosion or an electrical failure touched off the seventh floor of the Wieland's (now Falstaff) Brewery malt house on Cinnabar Street. Startled residents miles away, hearing the repeated hoarse blasts of the brewery whistle, looked out to see the night sky lit by a gigantic bonfire more than a hundred feet in the air.

Engines 4 and 7, Squad 1, and Truck 1 responded on the first alarm, 8:07 p.m. A second alarm was pulled immediately, bringing Engines 1 and 2 with both hose wagons. Groping through the darkened building with the guidance of 50 plant workers called from their homes by the whistle, firemen cut off downward extension of the flames to save $35,000 worth of malt and barley.

The fire itself could be reached only by aerial ladder. For the first time, both San Jose's aerials were raised for use as water towers; Truck 2, on Cinnabar Street, had only limited reach, so could do no more than wet down the surroundings. Truck 1 operated its ladder pipe through the seventh floor windows to knock the fire out. Lost along with fan and elevator machinery was rooftop

equipment used to boost County and Highway Patrol radio signals. Although this $22,000 "fire in the sky" was far from the most costly, it was one of the city's most spectacular.

Climax of a Record Year

Worst of 1949's fire losses was a blaze outside the city limits by just 18 feet; however, San Jose firemen were among the 60 firefighters called in from four departments. It all started when rays of the late afternoon sun, Saturday June 18, fell upon two glass jugs of paint thinner in a window of the Joy Manufacturing Company, Park Ave. and McEvoy Street.

Heat focussed through the glass exploded the jugs, sending the plant's owner and one employee fleeing for their lives after a futile attempt to douse the flames with a hand pump. Burbank firemen were called at 5:15, and immediately sent for all the help they could get. The half block long frame and stucco building, crammed with wickerware, was ablaze from end to end in a few minutes.

Teams of volunteers rushed into adjacent apartment buildings, directly in the path of wind driven flames, to bring out furniture. Embers showered over a two block area, adding to the troubles of firemen coming in from Santa Clara, the Central Fire District, and San Jose. Another problem was the narrow street, cut off to the east by railroad tracks, which was the only access to exposures.

Heavy streams, including Hose 1's monitor, eventually got the fire under control. Chief O'Brien's concern was the sprawling General Box lumber yard across Park Avenue to the north, but a favorable wind spared the yard —this time. Loss at the Joy building, where only one wall remained standing, was $120,000, with an additional $40,000 in the next-door apartments.

Playing no favorites, fire which had struck the Continental Can Company the preceding summer turned against the rival American Can Company on July 1, 1949. Ten pieces of apparatus responded to two alarms at the old paper and carton storage shed across South 5th Street from the main plant. Although the night watchman had seen no sign of fire in the shed at 8 p.m., twenty minutes later it was fully involved, and burned to the ground. Flying sparks on a stiff north wind set a minor fire at the Old English pet food factory down the block. An open incinerator apparently caused the $35,000 blaze.

With all this activity, it was a good thing firemen were keeping in shape with plenty of off-duty athletic activity. The Starr Hilton Club, named for a fireman killed on duty in 1930, and the latest in the long succession of fraternal-social groups within the department, was active in local bowling leagues (by 1952, league-leading Fire Department teams were in the 7th annual State Tourney in Los Angeles). On the softball diamonds, firefighters were doing equally well. Veteran pitcher Ron LeBeau, then a Captain on Truck 1, hurled a no-hit no-run game on August 10, chalking up 15 strikeouts as his team swamped the losers 9-0. Donkey softball in September pitted policemen against firemen; so did handball, in which the Fire Department won for the third straight year.

Plans for a new Fire Headquarters were finally under way during the summer of 1949. Money raised by the 1945 bond issue didn't leave quite enough for the last and biggest of the fire stations provided for, so some financial "juggling" was necessary before a

$159,559 contract could be awarded on March 6, 1950. One big help was transfer from the general fund to the firehouse fund of money for the library wing of Engine 6's quarters. Altogether more cash went for fire protection improvements during 1949 than in several preceding decades combined. And this was over and above the Fire Department's annual budget, itself risen to $559,000—an increase of more than a third in only two years.

Engine 6 was temporarily a two-piece company. Annexation of "South Willow Glen No. 5" in June, where there were no fire hydrants, led Fire Chief O'Brien to shift High Pressure 3 (with its 400 gallon booster tank) and one extra fireman to run with Engine 6. It remained there until the following April.

There was still no decision about building the alarm center, a building first proposed almost 40 years earlier. For administrative reasons, it had to be near the City Hall, but as yet no definite location had been chosen for that. Meanwhile the Council busied itself with adoption of the Uniform Building Code —an important step in fire prevention.

Unfortunately a building code was of no help against fires in lumber which was not yet part of a building. In 1949, one of San Jose's largest lumberyards sprawled over most of a city block between Park Avenue and San Fernando Street, just west of the SP tracks. Here, General Box Distributors had nine huge stacks of 2 x 12 planks, piled 20 feet high, 50 feet wide, and as much as 200 feet long, separated by narrow passageways

The "McCarthy House" on Spencer Ave., Engine 4 out front (San Jose's first "postwar" pumper). Notice the W over M initials formed by the front door panels.

Inferno at General Box Company, December, 1958. Fire followed this company through several locations.

sometimes only a foot wide. The box firm had also operated a factory and yard on the nearby southwest corner of Park and McEvoy, in Burbank territory, but this burned in a spectacular blaze in 1938.

Seldom have San Jose firefighters had a rougher time than during September 24-25, 1949, when fire of unknown origin broke out in this piled lumber. When discovered by employees at 4:20 p.m., flames were rolling in all directions along the tinder-dry planks. Responding to phantom box 4312 were Engines 1-4, Hose 1, Truck 2, and Squad 1. As these units rolled in, fire and smoke were already visible for miles.

At the time, there was no hydrant at Park and McEvoy; one has since been installed. Engine 1 had to hook up at Park and Sunol, more than a thousand feet away. To fill out the long lines, a second alarm was pulled at 4:27, calling for Engines 2-7, Hose 2, and Truck 1. Assistant Chief Gilbert arrived to take charge, and sent in the general alarm (signal 5-5-5-4312) at 4:44 p.m., followed by a call for assistance from Burbank and the Central Fire District. Five lumber stacks were now involved, with flames moving steadily against the wind through the narrow aisles and between the boards.

High Pressure 6 was special-called to extinguish spot fires along Park Avenue; Burbank and the County sent half a dozen units, laying lines from Engines 3 and 5 and working at the scene until late that night. Climbing atop the stacks on all sides, a hundred firemen (including 57 of San Jose's off shift) operated heavy streams on the fire for almost 8 hours before containing it. Each of the eleven 2½-inch lines used averaged 1000 feet in length. Once isolated, the blaze had to burn itself out; heart of the fire was completely inaccessible to water streams.

151

Late in the evening, a Salvation Army truck appeared to supply refreshments to weary firemen—most of them on either shift had missed their supper. More lumberyard employees arrived too, bringing large fork lifts from the main box plant several blocks away, to unpile the outermost stacks so hosemen could work in closer. For an hour, in virtual darkness, these trucks shuttled back and forth, each load of charred lumber being doused by firemen before removal to a far corner of the yard. Eventually, a truck spilled its load in the way, after hitting one of the many obstacles, and ended this operation. But by then the fire was controlled.

The long hours of capacity pumping—unmatched before or since—pushed fuel supplies dangerously low before shop personnel could cope with the problem. Engine 4's tank went dry during the evening, but luckily Engine 2 was standing by to take over. Later, a shuttle gas service was organized. All night, curious crowds, attracted by the fire's glow, thronged the surrounding streets.

Eight firemen, including two from the county, were treated for minor injuries. The total loss, first estimated at $90,000, was scaled down later by salvage of many timbers. Next morning, 8 lines were still working as overhauling began. Engines 2, 3, and 5 stayed most of the day, Engine 3 not picking up until 24 hours after the first alarm—a record pumping stint. About the same time, crews digging through the lumber came upon a 30 cubic foot pocket of live coals—untouched by almost 3 million gallons of water.

Sorting out the tangle of fire equipment at the scene proved the value of an identification scheme initiated that Fall by Chief O'Brien. Stripes of paint were used to "color-code" all the nozzles, hand tools, and similar portable equipment of each fire company; red for Engine 1, black for Engine 2, yellow for Engine 7, etc. When there got to be too many companies for one color each, combinations

were used. Later the system fell into disuse because of the frequent shifts of apparatus from one company location to another.

Almost a month later another hectic day began, this time involving three separate fires; total loss: two lives and over $100,000. The sequence began at 4 p.m. October 23, when the pilot of a light plane buzzing the neighborhood crashed into the roof of a house at 1127 South 10th—killing him, and setting the house afire. Firemen quickly extinguished the flames, but were there for hours mopping up.

No sooner was Engine 3 back in quarters that Sunday evening than another call came in from the 25,000-square foot Barron-Gray cannery warehouse buildings on Patterson Street at the old SP tracks on San Jose's south side. Consisting of several connected structures, once a packing house, the complex was fully involved along Patterson Street when four fire companies arrived on the 7:45 alarm. A second alarm followed at once, bringing two more engines; High Pressure 5 was special-called. Flames were visible for 20 miles before firemen controlled the blaze about 9 o'clock. Sixteen extra police were rushed in to handle a crowd of 3000 that swarmed into the area.

Inside the warehouse, exploding like giant firecrackers, 40,000 cases of fruit cocktail at $6 a case were the major loss—later reduced by salvage efforts. Firemen manning 11 lines

Backbone of the city's fire protection for a decade were four of these LaFrance pumpers with one-man suction hookups. All have been replaced since this photo of the early 1950's.

hit the fire from all sides, cutting it off from two warehouse buildings to the north, and homes across an alley on the east. Of the involved areas, mostly frame and chicken wire, plus a large stock of cartons, nothing was left; total damage was $90,000.

Before overhauling was complete, weary firefighters were turned out at 4:45 a.m. next morning by an alarm from the 75-year-old Derrick Broom Factory at 4th and Washington. Roused by cries for help from an aged pensioner living on the second floor, neighbors found the factory ablaze, its doors locked on the inside. The old man died of suffocation before Captain LeBeau and Fireman Boyarsky of Truck 1 could reach him. Most of the building was burned out, including 4 tons of broom straw. Chief O'Brien had begun studying possible condemnation of the place only a week earlier.

Santa Claus Wears a Fire Helmet

Altogether, just about every fire company in San Jose got a workout during the 24 hours. This was a fitting climax to a year of the highest fire losses since the conflagration of 1892. Two other records had been set; the month of June logged an unprecedented total number of alarms—174—more than half of them grass fires. Then one day in August, 24 hours passed with no alarms at all.

During November and December, San Jose's Exchange Club joined with the Fire Department in the first annual "Toys for Joy" campaign to gather and repair used toys for donation to needy children.

Firemen have always had a soft spot in their hearts for the youngsters of San Jose. Beginning in the Depression year of 1929, the late Captain Carl O'Dell enlisted the help of the P.T.A. and Kiwanis clubbers to gather and mend discarded toys for poor children. He kept up the work for years. In 1934, O'Dell repaired the wagons and playground equipment at the San Jose Day Nursery. Working with American Legion Post 399, he built a quarter mile miniature railroad system, with four operating trains, for the children at the County Preventorium.

Highlight of the 1949 campaign was a free children's movie at the California Theater on December 3, with one toy as the price of admission; 4000 toys were collected that day

Lawrence A. Campbell, retired Battalion Chief, has been of great assistance in preparing this history. Chief Campbell opened his files and offered expert consultation. He also assisted in the "Toys for Joy" program for many years.

alone, of the campaign total of 30,000. Other playthings were left at firehouses, where firemen spent their free time repairing them. Thirty children in County Hospital, others in the tent camps of migrant workers, and many more on welfare, had a happy Christmas because of the efforts of firemen and clubmen, and their wives, in 1949—when "Santa Claus wore Firemen's Blue." The successful toy drive became an annual, then a year-round event during the next few years. Expenses for paint, parts, and material were met by raffling off a full-size "doll house" donated by local lumber firms.

Christmas spirit was forgotten, however, when the two opposing sides squared off in January, 1950, to fight out the Bradley Manor annexation. The Fire Department was involved only insofar as fire protection and insurance rates under San Jose's jurisdiction was one of the bones of contention.

Bradley Manor, a postwar residential area with some business buildings, covered a quarter of a square mile south and west of Stevens

Creek Road at Bascom Ave. Between San Jose and this new tract lay Burbank, with a long history of vigorous, successful resistance to annexation by San Jose—a stand which might have been weakened had Bradley Manor joined up with San Jose to virtually surround Burbank.

Average annual home fire insurance cost in Bradley Manor would drop about $3 if San Jose took over; furthermore, the City Council assured residents that a new San Jose firehouse would be built in the vicinity whether or not annexation succeeded (Engine 10's quarters today are only a few blocks away). On January 16, the Council set aside $7500 for purchase of land.

An annexation election in Bradley Manor was set for February 23. During the intervening weeks, publicly and privately, both sides battled to convince the voters. After the balloting, San Jose emerged victorious—or so it seemed.

But even as acting City Manager Harold Flannery announced extension of police and fire protection to the territory, pending completion of "formal" annexation in April, opponents vowed a finish fight in the courts to overturn the election. (City Manager O. W. Campbell had left San Jose for a similar post in San Diego—to be replaced by City Manager A. P. Hamann.)

In a stunning blow to San Jose boosters, Superior Judge Avilla ruled on April 4 that the vote was illegal, because the City Council had allowed the election in the first place only by striking some 52 names from anti-annexation petitions in January.

San Jose decided to appeal, stopping its fire coverage meanwhile. But San Francisco's District Court of Appeals also ruled against the city. As far as the Council was concerned, that ended it—at least for 10 years. To this day Bradley Manor, along with Burbank, remains County territory.

Peacetime Civil Defense

As in the grim days of 1941, San Joseans were rudely awakened during the summer of 1950 by the menace of a new conflict—the Korean War. The almost forgotten rigmarole of Civil Defense was once more added to the Fire Chief's worries.

At the end of August, City Manager Hamann ordered Chief O'Brien to enroll 20 auxiliary firemen in each of ten "Civil Defense Districts" around the city, to be on call for major disasters. Air raid sirens, stored away in mothballs for years, were dusted off and installed at seven firehouses. Assistant Chief Gilbert was temporarily put in charge of personnel recruitment for the San Jose Disaster Council, to gather a force of air raid wardens for the emergency.

O'Brien, seconded by Underwriters Engineer Herbert Raines, began urging further improvements in his department. Not only was it necessary to prepare for attack; the city kept on growing, and once more the Fire Department was falling behind. At a July 18 meeting with the Manager, Raines, and Council members, the Chief asked for $65,000 for two new squads, 20 alarm boxes, and a bomb-proof communications building. Two weeks later, the request swelled to $264,000 covering four new firehouses, a new shop, four other pieces of apparatus, and 12 more men. The idea was to re-organize the department into two separate divisions, capable of independent operation.

Engine 7's residential firehouse, 1955.

154

Such improvements were to raise San Jose to Class 3, saving taxpayers $150,000 or more annually on fire insurance premiums. Officials hopefully suggested an "underground" communications center at Park and Almaden Aves., after it became known that the city was finishing the fiscal year with a quarter million dollar surplus. But it didn't pan out; the only action of 1950 was the ordering of two squad chassis in the Fall, for $18,000, assembly work to be done by the shop.

Just one serious fire intruded, keeping 1950's loss at the lowest level in six years. At 7:05 a.m. July 6, a passerby turned in the first of two alarms for a $100,000 blaze in the offices and shop of the Kurze Electric Works, 562 West San Carlos. Evidently burning for hours before discovery, flames so gutted the interior that the cause could never be determined. Thirty-five firemen controlled the blaze in an hour, and extinguished a spot fire in a church across the street, ignited by flying scraps of burning roofing.

The threat of war intruded even on the festive Firemen's Ball in October. Recognizing that "close co-operation of all fire departments in this area is a major factor in civilian defense preparedness," those in charge made special effort to invite members of neighboring departments to the dance.

A brief lapse in the "close co-operation" was recorded in November, 1950, when units from San Jose and Burbank hurled insults at each other from opposite sides of the dividing boundary. "Innocent cause of the departmental ruckus," explained the San Jose Mercury, "was a fire . . . shortly before midnight on October 14 at 195 Topeka . . . Burbank firemen clanged to a stop on the west side of the street a bare two minutes before San Jose's 'best' hauled up on the east side."

"San Jose firemen were chagrined," the account continues, "when they discovered their Burbank rivals had 'hogged' the water supply by attaching their lines to all the nearby fire hydrants. Not that it made any difference. For, while the two departments were racing to the scene, neighbors put out the blaze. It was the look of things."

"To show their displeasure, the San Jose laddies lined up on the east side of Topeka St., their rivals claim, and hurled insults at the Burbank firemen who lined the opposite sidewalk."

And so a trace of the spirit of Torrent and Empire Engine Companies survived, after all. The Secretary of Burbank Fire District No. 1 made huffy complaint to the San Jose City Council, which dutifully placed his letter on file.

It was all smoothed over in September 1951, when San Jose fire units stood by to cover for Burbank volunteers during Burbank's worst fire—the $500,000 destruction of the Larson Ladder factory in the orchards along Moorpark Ave., about where the White Front store stands now. Burbank's Chief Frank Mileham sent the City Council another letter after that, this time one of appreciation.

Meantime, in district after district, the new Civil Defense organization was staging disaster drills to check out their planning. South Willow Glen came first, on January 20 between 8:30 and 9:30 a.m. In spite of marked civilian apathy, the drill was considered a satisfactory demonstration of the readiness of fire, police, and medical services. A larger scale test on the west side in February involved a simulated A-bomb blast, calling out 14 fire rigs and ambulances.

New headquarters at 201 N. Market Street, 1951. Rigs are Squad 1, Hose 1, and Truck 1. Fireman Gene Sawyer is second from left.

Facelifting on Market Street

On February 21, San Jose's Planning Commission finally ended months of discussion by deciding where the Fire Department's drill tower should go. Chief O'Brien had suggested 6th and Taylor Streets; however, planners preferred a location near a creek for easy drainage of water from hose streams. Therefore a site was chosen along the Guadalupe Creek at Home (later W. Virginia) Street.

Big news in the Spring, however, was the opening of the new Fire Headquarters at Market and St. James, completed in March, the scene of a day-long Open House on April 30. The Chamber of Commerce turned out, along with the San Jose High School Band, civic officials, veterans' groups, and 500 school children. Among the many speakers was Jay Stevens, on hand to bid farewell at last to the old station he had labelled "terrible"—it was demolished a few months later.

The new building, complete with administrative offices only recently outgrown, was the first of San Jose's "drive-through" stations, arranged so apparatus could be driven in from the rear instead of having to back

in from the front. In its 10,000 square feet of floor space was even a "guest bedroom" for visiting fire officials, as well as a 40-bed dormitory for regular crews. Its hose tower could process almost a mile of hose in a few hours.

No sooner did he occupy the building than the Chief began to campaign vigorously for more improvements. "O'Brien Warns City Growth Outstripping Fire Department," one headline ran. And well he might, for San Jose had almost doubled its area between 1940 and 1950; since 1950 it has redoubled three times over!

The inevitable friction with other communities in the path of the city's expansion often generated more heat than light; controversy has involved even the State Legislature, where San Jose and other County cities have been at odds over proposed changes in legal annexation requirements.

Santa Clara was miffed, for example, by rumors that the San Jose Fire Department might cancel its mutual aid agreements if the Mission City continued to try to obstruct San Jose's growth. "That's all right with me," retorted Santa Clara's Fire Chief; his city's Underwriters classification depended only on its own resources, which were more than adequate. As if to prove it, Santa Clara did get a Class 3 rating years before San Jose did! Defending Santa Clara's attempts to protect her own interests, Mayor Toledo dismissed reports of his city's inability to protect such hazards as the University, and Pacific Manufacturing, by saying, "All this talk is childish."

Working relations between the two Fire Departments continued good, nevertheless, and many fires along the fast-growing residential fringe of San Jose — in the Kaiser-Bascom Gardens area—have been handled by firefighters from both sides.

O'Brien got his two new squads in mid-1951, but still wanted more manpower. Warning that his department was "seriously short of men and equipment," that the new rigs were idle for lack of men, the Chief disclaimed responsibility for the city's continuing to annex new territory without providing for its fire protection. Only four new firemen, he pointed out, had been added since 1946. Fred Watson, still on the Council, chimed in with his fear that the city was in danger of "reverting to a former error" of neglecting its Fire Department.

In the end, O'Brien got five more men. Faced with a united city employee demand for a 5.7% raise (which took effect in January 1952), the City Council went as far as they thought possible during the August budget hearings. The axe was wielded heavily in other areas to give the Fire Chief the benefit; even at that the tax rate went up 17½ cents. Total Fire Department budget for 1951-2 was $657,800.

By re-arranging some personnel, the Chief got Squads 1 and 2 into service, and set up new Battalion Chief positions to split the department into two operating Districts. Squad 1 responded to all alarms roughly north of San Carlos Street; Squad 2 covered everything to the south. Actually, the Squads were 750 GPM pumpers, using the first of FMC's new line of volume pumps. Other features included 300-gallon tanks with preconnected 1½-inch lines, 1500 watt electric plants, backpack cutting torches, and electric saws.

As this was being organized, one of the new rigs was used to replace Engine 2 while the old Mack was updated with a new motor and transmission. Its replacement GMC power plant gave it a top speed of 80 miles per hour!

A New High in Monthly Fire Loss

San Jose's worst fire since 1949, like that year's General Box blaze, hit a lumberyard on Saturday afternoon. This time it was the Cheim Lumber Company—1400 The Alameda at Lenzen Ave. On the Cheim property were four parallel lumber sheds and mill buildings almost a block long, with an office at the front. Adjoining the yard on the south were the old frame and sheet iron streetcar barns abandoned in 1938 by the San Jose Railroads, later used by Cheim for additional lumber storage.

A janitor discovered fire among piles of waste paper and scrap wood in the mill, about 3 p.m. August 25. He ran to phone the Fire Department, then dashed back with a water bucket — only to find the blaze far out of control, fed by four carloads of newly-arrived lumber, tons of hardboard and exotic plywood plus large supplies of creosote and tar paper. Fanned by a brisk northwest wind, raging flames rapidly spread the length of the yard, throwing off billows of black smoke; intense heat ignited trees and power poles across Lenzen Ave.

Sixty firefighters responded on the general alarm, including 25 of the off-shift. Aided by fire auxiliaries manning a monitor nozzle atop the Wieland's Brewery fire tower, they saved the car barns (though one wall was scorched) and brought the flames under control by 4:15. Engine 4 protected exposed residences along Lenzen Ave.

The yard itself was a $150,000 loss. Last to go was the Cheim office, from which volunteers had removed records and office furniture. A crowd of 6000 gathered to watch, swelled by patrons of the nearby Towne Theater which was darkened when utility crews cut off power in the area.

In October, Fire Chief O'Brien urged expenditure of $180,000, for stations, rigs, and a dozen new men, to save over $200,000 annually in insurance costs. On the 26th he met with Underwriters Engineer Herbert Raines in San Francisco, along with other San Jose officials, to map out a campaign for Class 3.

Raines agreed that if the city properly spent only $110,000 it would be "in an excellent position to apply for the new rating."

City Manager Hamann claimed there was money in the treasury to pay for the needed improvements.

The City Council, however, was also facing wage increase demands. A 5.7% raise was granted, to take effect January 1, 1952, and cost $162,000 annually. This left only enough to cover one of O'Brien's recommendations: purchase of 100 new alarm boxes for $27,000, mostly as replacements for old Gardner-type boxes in the downtown district.

At the end of the year, Councilman George Starbird explained how San Jose stood in the ratings. At the last classification in 1946, the city had 1744 "deficiency points." For Class 3, the total had to be 1500 or less. At the moment, the unofficial total was 1656 points. An additional truck company would wipe out 77 of these; the new communications center, 40; drill tower relocation, 27. Starbird added that, as in 1945, San Jose's fire protection trailed other Northern California cities such as Berkeley, Stockton, and Fresno — they were already Class 3.

In January 1952, the last-named change was made; a $30,000 drill yard was completed at Sycamore and Home Streets. With ample space for all kinds of company evolutions, the yard featured a 35-foot deep re-circulating drafting pit. The tower itself, designed for just such an eventuality, was dismantled floor by floor and moved across town by Bridges Construction Company.

Plagued by a recurring stomach ailment, Fire Chief O'Brien went on indefinite sick leave April 4, 1952, leaving Assistant Chief Gilbert in charge. O'Brien had been undergoing special treatment off and on at the University of California Medical Center. His physical condition had been worsened by carbon monoxide poisoning incurred at a small but punishing fire set by an arsonist at the Western Cold Storage Company, 44 North 4th Street, on February 25. Some combination of burning insulation and chemicals produced fumes that knocked out 13 firemen, some of whom were hospitalized in serious condition.

Rumors of O'Brien's imminent retirement were scotched by his July 1st return to active duty. Six weeks later, a pair of general alarm fires celebrated the occasion. The first, late in the evening of August 4, did $30,000 damage to the Western Metal and Export Company at 220 Ryland.

The second one, on August 17, destroyed Pacific Gas & Electric Company's big service garage at Stockton and Lenzen Aves., with damage exceeding $350,000. An employee, spending a Sunday morning cleaning up oil spills on the floor, was driven from the building when the solvent he was using ignited, spreading fire to walls, roof trusses, and parked trucks. Leaping from truck to truck as gas tanks exploded, unimpeded by any fire breaks inside the structure, flames speedily involved the entire garage.

Three alarms between 9:15 and 9:20 a.m. brought Engines 1, 2, 4, 5, and 7, both aerials, two hose wagons, Squad 1, and High Pressure 5. Using eight 2½-inch lines, 70 firemen knocked the fire down within half an hour. But only a gutted shell remained of the garage and the 60 trucks inside.

These two blazes pushed San Jose's insured loss for August 1952 to a new record for any one month — $394,727.48.

Wages and Hours Make News

Firemen sought a further salary increase in the summer of 1952, as budget hearings drew near. Along with a public employees' group representing some other city workers, Local 873 of the Firefighters' Union got Council assurance that their requests would receive special attention at budget time.

This had serious repercussions. At the request of city officials in 1945, a loosely organized "Municipal Employees' Council" (MEC) had been formed as a single unofficial "bargaining agent" for all city workers, for the City Council to deal with on salary matters. The MEC was outraged, now, to have such important segments as the Fire Department taking wage requests direct to the City Council. On July 26, the MEC made a "surprise" demand that all 800 employees represented by it receive the same 5.7% raise asked by firemen.

The ruckus just about tore the MEC apart. "We are at a loss to understand how the new City Council can find justification in bypassing us in favor of minority groups," complained MEC President Al Boyarsky—himself in an unenviable position, as a member of the Fire Department.

In mid-August the wage request was rejected. For a while, it looked like the controversy would evaporate; however, the news was soon out that firefighters, seeing the

Headquarters of District 2, Third and Martha Streets, 1955.

wind blowing against them, had emphasized their departure from MEC aims by switching their support to a compromise proposal for an across-the-board $20 monthly raise. After a heated three-hour debate on the 18th, the $20 increase was granted by the City Council, and within a few weeks 70 members dropped out of the MEC—including President Boyarsky. In spite of the turmoil, firemen had gained a raise; the Starr Hilton Club sent Councilmen a grateful letter in behalf of Local 873.

Other Council action in August involved scheduling of a November 4 bond election for $1,200,000 worth of civic improvements. Included was $250,000 for four firehouses: replacements for No's. 3 and 4, plus new houses for South Willow Glen and "West Side" areas. That was almost all the Fire Department got, for the time being, in spite of the Fire Chief's continuing pressure on the Council; on August 5 O'Brien complained that he was "dangerously short of men and equipment" to cover the 23 square miles now within city limits—including the latest expansion into "South

Willow Glen No. 10." Fire protection booster Fred Watson provided some solace by getting his fellow Councilmen to raise the department's contingency fund (to cover apparatus repairs or replacement) from $15,000 to $20,000. A Fire Department budget of $759,-790 was adopted, but rising property valuation allowed a 3.8¢ cut in the tax rate.

The 1952 bond issue carried 3 to 1, yet it was two years before any money was spent. Meanwhile, personnel problems held the spotlight. "Outside jobs" or "moonlighting" had first become a problem in the spring. Too many people, some officials believed, held outside jobs which interfered with their regular work in many municipal departments. This was particularly bad in the Fire Department, because having every other day off a fireman was very likely to get such a job. The Civil Service Commission granted permits to employees to hold second jobs, but in April had cancelled them all pending review of the entire situation which was "getting out of hand." They finally gave new permits to about 40 firemen.

Chief O'Brien was unsympathetic. In October, he delivered a withering blast against the outside job practice, asking the Commission to abolish it entirely. That body sidestepped the issue neatly by citing legal opinion that its jurisdiction was limited; the matter was passed on to the City Council. Periodically, it has continued to crop up since.

O'Brien was particularly miffed because his regular department strength was badly depleted by September vacations and sick leave; he claimed that some of those apparently able to hold two jobs were turning up on sick leave! He asked that 20 men, including himself, then eligible for retirement but still on the active list, be first to get physical exams when the Commission's examination program began. Such checkups, complained the Civil Service group, though called for by the City Charter and Municipal Code, had never been given because of lack of appropriation by the City Council.

In November 1952, the Chief went further with his personnel ideas by ordering "mass transfers" in the Fire Department. In the first phase, 52 men were moved from one station or shift to another, including half the captains. "We've had men assigned to the same houses for 10 or 15 years," said O'Brien. "Some of them don't know anything about fighting fires in any part of the city but their own." No disciplinary action was involved in the moves, which sooner or later were to affect all firemen.

Common elsewhere, and recommended by Underwriters, the shifts were fully backed by City Manager Hamann and the City Council, although there was some grumbling at first in the department.

The Herschel Conflagration

Despite worries expressed as far back as Fire Chief Haley's time, the "new age" of motorized, high speed fire apparatus had never resulted in a traffic accident fatal to a civilian—although Fireman Starr Hilton had been killed at the wheel of his rig in 1930. This safety record was tragically broken on Friday afternoon, May 8, 1953, when Engine 6 went out of control while responding to an alarm and killed a 7-year-old girl on the lawn of Willow Glen School.

Providentially, about 40 other children standing at the curb had boarded an outgoing bus just before the first unit of Engine Co. 6 rounded the corner of Lincoln and Minnesota Aves. en route to a minor blaze which, ironically, was not only outside the city limits but was put out before any firemen arrived.

One theory was that this rig spilled some booster tank water on the street. When the following pumper hit the water it went into a skid. With its driver desperately trying to avoid a parked truck, and unable to straighten the wheel, the rig grazed another parked vehicle and a curbside tree, then bounded onto the school lawn to roll another 200 feet before smashing to a stop in a chain-link fence. En route, it struck down two little girls, the wheels straddling one child who escaped injury, but killing the other.

Fire losses, low in 1953, skyrocketed again the following year, beginning with a $125,000 blaze May 11 that destroyed much of the old Central Block at First and San Fernando Streets. Shortly after lunch, the proprietor of the Blouses Preferred store at 108 South First saw smoke curling around wall joints in the rear, and ran next door to warn jeweler Ben Hecker, who opened his storeroom door to be met by a wall of flame. Sprinklers saved two adjoining ground floor shops, but most upstairs offices were burned out. A force of 32 firemen held damage to the one building. During the four hour battle, Captain Ralph Jennings fell and sprained his shoulder; two other officers and three firemen suffered minor injuries.

Biggest fire of 1954 was the towering conflagration which swept through five buildings of the Herschel California Fruit Products Co. on Lincoln Ave., north of Moorpark, Thursday June 24. The fire broke out in a small shed next to a three-story former packing house on Lincoln, sold to Herschel in 1952. Temporarily leased by General Petroleum Corp., the shed served as office space and storage for parathion insecticides. At 5:17 p.m., a passerby gave the first alarm, bringing Engines 4 and 6, Truck 2, and Squad 2. By the time these companies laid two lines down Lincoln Ave., a stiff breeze had spread the fire into the huge empty packing house, with its wood frame construction built around massive redwood timbers. The structure literally exploded in towering flames, forcing abandonment of the lines as hose caught fire in the street.

Fireman Jim Mitchell filled his lungs with refreshing oxygen after being overcome by smoke inhalation during the 1958 Pabco Paint fire. His boots, trousers, and coat are paint-splattered from the blaze.

A second alarm for Box 4411 registered at 5:22, Engines 2 and 7 responding; three minutes later the general alarm brought Engines 1 and 3 with Truck 1. Other apparatus was special-called later. Meantime, because of the plant's location, Burbank volunteers responded to lay lines to cover exposures—by far the most dangerous of which was the bulk oil plant of General Petroleum, directly across Lincoln Ave. and already smoking in the radiated heat. Engine 2 attempted to operate a monitor stream down the street as a water curtain, but low hydrant capacity made it impossible. Only a desperate and dangerous stand by San Jose firemen with hand lines, their backs to the intense heat, surrounded by high voltage lines whipping into the street with spectacular arcs, prevented ignition of 45,000 gallons of gasoline and Diesel fuel.

Behind the blazing packing house, accessible only by narrow plant alleyways and the SP right-of-way, were four more Herschel buildings, including two smaller warehouses, one containing 9000 cases of tomato paste and five million can labels. One by one, they were all involved, before Engine 1 could stretch in three lines from Moorpark Ave., and Hose 1's monitor went into action to sweep walls and roof of the last building to burn.

The two high-capacity hydrants closest to the fire, unfortunately, were so close to the packing house that both were untenable until after the fire was well under control at 6:45 p.m.

Within an hour from the first alarm, the packing house was levelled to the ground. A firedoor cut off extension of the blaze to a concrete warehouse directly to the south, and the worst was over. There was a scare along the railroad tracks, when radiated heat touched off a large pile of wooden pallets piled just outside the older section of the U.S. Products Corp., fronting on Race Street. At the moment, neither firemen nor apparatus could be spared to deal with this new outbreak. Volunteers and USP workers poured into the building nearest the burning pallets and discharged a marvelous number and variety of hand extinguishers and garden hose, with little effect. Eventually a County rig pulled into the USP yard and connected a 2½-inch line to the plant water system. But there was no water! So more hose was stretched from a city hydrant on Race Street, after which the pallet fire was speedily doused.

San Jose Fire Captain Kunze and Fireman Don Bernardo were slightly hurt; four other San Jose firemen were made ill for a short time by deadly parathion fumes, which their masks would not filter out. Throughout the evening, exploding cans of tomato paste popped off like firecrackers.

After dark, Lincoln Ave. was a wild scene of floodlighted confusion as half a dozen San Jose fire companies were joined by a mob of Pacific Telephone personnel working frantically to repair a large cable burned in two during the fire's early stages. Four of the total of 17 2½-inch hose lines remained in use throughout the night, though most of the 120 firefighters were released after a few hours. Altogether, 14 city rigs worked at the

Herschel fire, plus half a dozen more from Burbank and the County. The total insured loss was $134,000, much below original estimates.

On the opposite side of the Burbank district from Herschel's San Jose's west side area was growing fast, and in need of new fire protection. A brand new 4-story O'Connor Hospital had just opened, out among the pear orchards west of Bascom Ave., replacing the old red brick "Sanitarium" at Race and San Carlos. Nearby, the rural site of the 54-store Valley Fair Shopping Center was annexed to San Jose in 1954.

To cover these new hazards, the first of the city's "temporary" fire stations opened, a block from the hospital at 161 O'Connor Drive, in June of 1954. All trace of it has vanished today, for it stood squarely in the eventual path of a freeway off-ramp on Highway 17. The concrete block building was uniquely designed to serve as a firehouse with later conversion to an office building. It was leased by the city for $140 monthly. Stationed there was a new fire company, Engine 10, using one of a pair of 1000 GPM Coast pumpers assigned to San Jose that summer by the Office of Civil Defense.

Second of the two new rigs went to Engine 2, retiring the Mack to reserve status. In addition, two more 750 GPM pumpers similar to Squads 1 and 2 had been purchased; one replaced High Pressure 3, the other was used for some months to fill in while Engine 4 was repaired—it had collided with a loaded fruit truck at Delmas and Auzerais while answering an alarm August 2.

Three months later came San Jose's costliest downtown fire in a generation. About 4:20 a.m. September 22, Patrolman Don Moore, on routine check of the area, discovered smoke seeping from doors and windows at Robinson's Furniture, 500 South First at William St. One of San Jose's leading firms for many years, Robinson's occupied a two-story concrete building, 140 feet square, that had once been an auto agency. Inside was a quarter million dollars worth of quality home furnishings.

Two alarms and a special call brought Engines 1-2-3-4 plus the Mack reserve, Trucks 1-2, Squad 2, and two hose wagons. At first, firemen's efforts were concentrated along the William Street side of the store, at the rear of which the fire had evidently started; Hose 1's monitor and several hand lines were operated through display windows. Heavy smoke and heat made it impossible to work inside the building.

Both aerials were raised to the roof where truckmen attempted to ventilate. However, fire soon burst through all the downstairs windows on the First Street side, forcing hasty relocation of Truck 2. Here, Engine 4 operated a deluge set from the street, driving back the flames so that shortly after 5 o'clock firemen could enter both floors. Other lines, of the 13 used altogether, were taken atop the next-door San Jose Supply House to cover the exposure and work into Robinson's rear windows upstairs. Overhauling began at dawn. The loss, mostly in stock and furnishings, was $255,000.

In October 1954, the City Council opened bids on two new firehouses—replacements for the 1908-model quarters of Engines 3 and 4. A site for Engine 3 at Third and Martha Streets, large enough to include a shop, had been acquired in August for $28,500. Construction began there without incident.

San Jose vs. the Scharff Sisters

But there was nothing routine about Engine 4's relocation. In the first place, it took a good many years for the city to decide where the station should be. Chief O'Brien once proposed rebuilding on Spencer Ave. In 1950, the chosen spot had been at Montgomery and Lorraine Streets. A lot in the Gardner District had been chosen decades before that. First one place, then another got the nod; the final site at 456 Auzerais Ave., corner of Minor, was picked only because the Emergency Aid Station (originally intended for the property) was switched to another lot donated to the city.

The Auzerais Ave. property had been sold to San Jose in the Spring of 1954 for $10,191 by the guardian of its two elderly owners, Frieda and Elise Scharff, to raise cash to settle delinquent taxes and meet the sisters' living expenses. These sheltered ladies had lived in a small, 90-year-old house on the property all their lives, alone together since their father's death in 1950. With its jungle-like yard, sagging porch, wood-burning stove and other quaint furnishings, the place was the only home they had ever known. "Oblivious to the ever-increasing pace of life outside their now shaky walls," wrote a Mercury reporter, the sisters stayed on in the house which was "rapidly falling apart, sorely in need of paint and creaking with every wind."

Suddenly, in late October, city officials woke up to the fact that the firehouse contractor was waiting to start work, but not only had the Scharff sisters never moved out —they refused even to acknowledge the validity of the sale! Here was a human interest yarn of the first magnitude, and squirming officials found it confronting them almost daily in the morning paper. City Manager Hamann complained, "We've had this place for six months and have to get going. The house must be torn down within 30 days." To which the sisters replied vaguely, "We haven't sold this property, you know." Reluctantly, the City Attorney prepared an eviction order, while glumly forecasting that the Scharffs would simply squat on the sidewalk for the rest of their lives.

In desperation, the administration sought help from a San Francisco relative — who tartly refused, with a scathing denunciation of the luckless estate guardian. Assuring a sympathetic public that the sisters would not be evicted without some place to go, the harassed City Manager was finally — in December—able to announce that the guardian's attorney had found a new home for the ladies in Burbank.

The next problem was to get them into it. On December 19, Sheriff's deputies, reporters, attorneys, and anxious city officials descended en masse on the old home. "From the moment the Scharff sisters saw the mob coming and slammed the door tight until a deputy sheriff gently buffeted the old lock loose it was anyone's guess . . . how the great departure would be made." After a touch-and-go discussion in the old parlor, a sheriff's matron succeeded in talking the two ladies into taking a ride just to see the new home. They were escorted away, as all present heaved a sigh of relief —and moving crews began transferring the Scharffs' possessions, while deputies changed the door locks, just in case.

At the Burbank house, the sisters soon lost themselves in discussion of the merits of their new gas heater, and the drama was over. On December 14, after the Alken Construction Co. had been delayed three days, a bulldozer wrecked the old Scharff house with one tug on a steel cable.

Wanted: Firehouses to Rent

While construction proceeded in the Third and Fourth Wards, San Jose launched a unique experiment in South Willow Glen. The unforeseeable speed and patchwork nature of city growth in that direction, plus the increasing controversy over trends in commercial development of annexed areas (which within ten years would tear the city apart in a Council recall election), made it impossible to locate permanent firehouses in the best spot to serve new territories. Said Chief O'Brien, "We've found that in building station houses without future planning, some of them have proved too small to take care of the territorial development which followed."

Years later, Chief Ron LeBeau pointed out the opposite possibility: "Suppose you annex an area where a big commercial development is planned, and build a $150,000 station. Maybe in a few years you find the developer's plans didn't work out, and the area has grown in a different way so all you really need out there is a single engine company. Then where are you?"

A solution was the temporary firehouse, located so as to be adequate coverage for a suburban area until the development pattern dictated its relocation elsewhere. So the city commenced a program unheard of among nationwide fire protection authorities — the use of leased single-family dwellings as temporary fire stations. For rentals averaging $120 a month, the Fire Department used the homes until a permanent site could be properly chosen and permanent quarters built on it. At that time, the home could be quickly restored to its residential status and the lease terminated—leases have customarily included a $500 bond covering the restoration.

Generally, fire engines were too large for the residential garage, so a temporary apparatus garage costing $1000 to $2000 was moved onto a corner of the lot. When the site was vacated, the extra garage was easily moved away.

In March 1955 the City Council approved the $125 monthly rental of a house at 1787 Foxworthy Ave. in South Willow Glen. Engine Company No. 9 opened for business there on April 17, using one of the newer 750 GPM GMC-FMC pumpers.

Cheim Lumber Company and Pacific Hardware and Steel Company fire and explosions, 1400 The Alameda, on April 15, 1955. The fire was started by small boys, 7 to 8 years old, playing with matches. It was fanned by high winds as firefighters poured 3,750 gallons of water (15 tons) on the fire every minute. Glass on the instrument panel of Engine 4 cracked and the paint blistered and peeled from the intense heat.

Overshadowing this development was a more dubious distinction. April 1955 brought San Jose its highest single monthly fire loss in history—plus the largest insured loss for one fire, beyond even the conflagration of '92.

Hester District Holocaust

In a back corner of the vacant lot on The Alameda where the Cheim Lumber mill and yard had stood prior to the fire of 1951, there remained a small shed, still used by Cheim

for unpacking and storage of window glass. Late in the afternoon of April 14, a nearby resident at 1046 Lenzen saw that this shed was on fire. She ran in the house to call firemen; simultaneously a boy on traffic patrol at Hester School saw the blaze and turned in a box alarm.

Right beside the little shed was the rear of the huge old carbarn which had barely been saved in the 1951 fire. This time, it was beyond saving. Within minutes, flames billowed through the cavernous spaces above the

164

Pacific Hardware & Steel Company. Firefighters vainly try to stop the spread of the fire which started in the rear of the Cheim Lumber Company yard, spread to the Pacific Hardware & Steel Company store, and gutted the Prime Rib dining room.

stored lumber inside, leaping across the wooden rafters coated with half a century's accumulated grease and sawdust.

Eleven minutes after the first 4:05 p.m. alarm, the general alarm was in; both squads, both trucks, Engines 1-2-3-4-5-7, and four hose wagons, plus reserve apparatus, were in action inside of a half hour, laying 17 hose lines under the direction of Chief O'Brien, Asst. Chief Gilbert, and Battalion Chiefs Vitek, Jones, and Ogden.

The heat radiated across The Alameda was intense. A gigantic spout of flame shot from the front of the carbarn as from a blowtorch,

melting a streetlight electrolier like wax, scorching trees and cracking store windows across the 80-foot street. Truck 1's ladder pipe and deluge sets went into operation, while at the northwest corner of the fire Hose 1 and 2 started up their monitors to break up the heat.

But the fire was simply too much for them. Two lines feeding Hose 2 were burned through, and replaced by others from Engine 4, hooked up at Shasta Ave. Almost directly across the street from the carbarn, Engine 4 had a rough time of it too, its engineer forced to crouch down behind the pumper to escape the furnace-like heat. Soon the rig itself was put out of action—its windshield and instrument dials cracked, paint blistered, and fan belt afire. Squad 2 pushed the dead engine out of the way to take over its lines.

Under a brisk wind, the fire moved south into the other half of the one-time San Jose Railroad's property, the car shops and offices at 1344 The Alameda, occupied by the Pacific Hardware and Steel Company. Working in a tangle of burned and discarded hose, firemen in the middle of the street got another deluge set going to prevent flames from involving Franco's grocery store across The Alameda.

At 4:31 p.m., after employees had warned authorities so police could clear the area, cylinders of compressed acetylene inside the hardware firm went up in a series of thun-

A dramatic picture of Truck 1's ladder pipe in action at the Cheim Lumber Company blaze.

derous explosions heard for miles, shattering the remaining windows in the neighborhood and bowling over several firefighters.

Flames then spread through an unprotected attic window opening in a brick wall into the dining room of the Prime Rib restaurant, adjoining Pacific Hardware on the south. Several lines from Engines 2 and 7 were on hand there to stop the fire before it could reach the Prime Rib's cocktail lounge —which remained open throughout the afternoon, its patrons undisturbed by the comings and goings of firefighters or the hose lines and water-soaked debris cluttering the foyer.

Looming up over the mass of smoke and flame were the towers and turrets of the Falstaff Brewery (formerly Wieland's). Firemen took three lines from Engine 5 into the brewery yard, and with the help of 20 auxiliary firemen among the Falstaff employees were able to prevent any damage to brewery property.

By five p.m., as the Prime Rib involvement was being mopped up, nothing was left of the lumber and hardware buildings except a few charred columns rising starkly from a half-block expanse of blazing rubble. Closing of The Alameda caused a colossal traffic jam reaching clear downtown until late in the evening. Several fire companies remained on the scene all night, unpiling and wetting down stacks of lumber;; not until 6:30 p.m. next day did the last rig return to quarters.

Of the 77 firemen who fought the blaze, including 33 of the off-shift, half a dozen were hurt. Capt. Wm. Malpass and Fireman Ray Jones were burned; Jack Stanley was hospitalized for smoke inhalation.

In spite of the million gallons of water poured in, the ruins smoldered for weeks, recalling firemen repeatedly to the property. On July 6, the Fire Department summoned a bulldozer to rip into the masses of debris and get at pockets of live coals. But the dozer itself came to grief, breaking open buried containers of calcium carbide, which ignited to envelop the driver in flames! He escaped with second degree burns as firemen turned their hoses on him.

Total insured loss in the Cheim-Pacific conflagration was $472,900—a San Jose record for many years. Investigation revealed that the excelsior-littered glass storage shed, where it all started, had been touched off by

three 7-year-old boys with matches stolen from Franco's.

Pacific Hardware took note of the "hazardous conditions" Cheim permitted to exist in the glass shed, which had not been kept locked, and sued Cheim Lumber for $204,000 damages in November 1955. The litigation dragged on for years.

Only a matter of hours after the Alameda fire was controlled, firemen were called to another San Jose landmark which had survived flames several times previously. This was the old Chilton-CP & AGA packing house at 405 North First Street, used in 1955 as a scrap paper warehouse. A general alarm blaze finally wiped out the two- and three-story frame building at 4:11 a.m. April 16. Truck 1's ladder pipe saved the front wall; otherwise, the warehouse was a $32,000 loss. Ten 2½-inch lines were used. At 4:37, Engines 4 and 7, Squad 2, and Truck 2 were detached to knock down a threatening fire in the projection room of the downtown California Theater (now the Fox).

A week later, Box 4121 was pulled for fire in the basement hobby shop of the Boy's Store, 321 South First. Engines 1-3-4, both trucks, and Squad 2 responded shortly before 10 p.m. Firemen, advancing small lines down the stairs, driven back at first by heat, were able to confine the $60,000 fire to the basement. Clothing in Appleton's store next door suffered considerable smoke damage.

It was a far cry from the downtown mercantile fires of 40 years earlier, when basement flooding was the order of the day. The Boy's Store owner had nothing but praise for firefighters whom he had "never seen work like those boys did. They didn't turn on the water until they found the fire, instead of breaking in and hosing down the place." He marvelled at the careful mopping up of his premises after the fire was out.

Similar tactics brought Fire Chief O'Brien a grateful letter in June, from the Martinous Rug & Upholstery Cleaners. The owner wrote, concerning a fire there, "I was amazed when I saw your men grab a broom and a shovel to clean up the mess they made. I wouldn't have believed it if I hadn't seen it myself."

Such praise helped ease the pain when it was revealed that the total April 1955 fire loss was $566,557—two thirds of the loss for the entire year!

Brownie Answers His Last Alarm

Three new "members" of an unprecedented sort were added to the Fire Department in May of 1955. Under auspices of Firefighters' Union Local 873, and its President Ralph Bernardo, three official chaplains were installed during an evening dinner meeting at Market Street Headquarters. Receiving their special badges and certificates before a large group of city, county, police, and fire officials were Father Paul E. Duggan, assistant pastor at St. Patrick's, Dr. James H. Strayer of Calvary Methodist, and Rabbi Joseph Gitin of Temple Emanu-el.

Major duty for the chaplains, besides fulfilling "other functions relating to their professions," would be to participate in the dedication of new firehouses (though not a great deal ever came of it.) Two more stations did open that year, No. 3 in July and the $70,000 No. 4 on September 3.

Upon the opening of Station 3, with its adjacent shop facilities, the Fire Department was formally reorganized into two operating districts. The city's south side became District 2, under a Battalion Chief at Station 3. District 1, based on Market Street, covered the north side. With improvements in apparatus, particularly the addition of resuscitators to outlying companies, it was no longer necessary to operate the squad companies as special units, so in 1955 these were offically converted to engine companies in order to strengthen the city's Underwriters rating. Squad 1 became Engine 11 at Market Street, while Squad 2 went to Third and Martha Streets to serve as Engine 13. High value district first alarm response then became three engines and a truck.

"Brownie" in full uniform, ready to roll — the department mascot of the 1940's. His favorite perch was here on the Mack squad wagon.

Ordered in March, a new $35,000 100-foot American-LaFrance aerial arrived in November, freeing the older 75-foot unit for a new Truck Co. No. 3 at Station 3. Engine 4's 1944 pumper was retired to various fill-in assignments, its place taken by the 1000 GPM Coast rig formerly at Engine 10. This was only the beginning of a juggling of apparatus from station to station that eventually became almost impossible to keep up with, and cannot be detailed in these pages.

The department also lost one of its more esteemed members that year. "Brownie," the purebred mongrel mascot of the 1940's, died of throat cancer at the ripe old age of 14 or 15. He had wandered into the old Market Street station about 1942, and soon attached himself firmly to the personnel of Squad 1. Springing to the seat at the sound of the gong, riding the squad wagon to alarms all over town, he was a familiar and beloved figure for a decade.

Occasionally, recalls Judge Marshall Hall, "There was some rivalry between the two platoons . . . One group said he liked them best, and he would go home with somebody on that shift and not return till that shift went on duty again."

At last, Brownie got too old for the strenuous life of a fireman. But he never ceased trying to respond to the call; fearing that the aging animal would be hurt, firemen finally had to hold him back whenever they could, until the squad was out of sight. Poor fellow! Though the spirit was ever willing, he came to realize his flesh was weak, and suffered himself to be banished to a quiet life at the department shop.

L. A. O'Brien

Chief O'Brien Bows Out

In the summer of 1955, Lester O'Brien again complained of "a serious shortage of personnel," requesting that his force of 160 be increased by 10 firemen, 5 captains, and a new Battalion Chief. Primary reason for the request was the activation of Truck 3. The City Council went him a little better; since the truck wasn't due to arrive till November anyway, they gave him 12 men starting November 1 instead of 10 men at the September 1 opening of the budget year. As adopted, the final 1955-6 Fire Department budget was $962,580.

Finances were very much in the news throughout most of the following year. Effective September 1, 1955, the Council granted a 5.7% raise to all employees, and also agreed to a new health-accident insurance plan. Before long, the city sales tax was increased to 1% to cover rising costs. Next April the

Council was asked by Attorney John Thorne — representing police, fire, and "public workers" unions—to appoint a citizens' committee to study revision of the "antiquated" Police-Fire Retirement Plan; a "skeleton" plan adopted April 20, 1914, and amended by a formula for retirement fund contributions in October 1916, had been changed only slightly by Charter review in 1946.

Thorne himself was made chairman of the 9-man committee, appointed April 16 by Mayor George Starbird. In July of 1956, they came up with a new plan similar to Oakland's, which the Council agreed to consider for the November ballot (a Charter change was required). More about this issue presently.

Meanwhile, Fire Department shop personnel built three new Ford hose wagons, featuring booster tanks and reels with separately powered high pressure pumps. In January 1956, the first two went into service with Engine Co.'s 3 and 5, replacing the 1942 model "High Pressure" rigs. Two months later Engine Co. 6 got the third new wagon.

Another piece of new equipment assigned to the Fire Department came in handy on September 4, 1955, when a violent earthquake caused widespread damage in Willow Glen. This was the Reo OCD rescue van. It stood by along with five fire companies while firefighters and others pulled down scores of damaged chimneys. Civil Defense wardens themselves reported in for duty, but casualties were too few to require their services.

Salvage drill, Engine 4 and Truck 2, 1954. Captain Malpass, John Schaar, David P. Miller, Corneal Tollenaar, Tony Gomes, Orville Keyser, Howard Overhouse, Captain F. Earl Conyers.

Above and left—Pacific Truck Service, Inc. explosion and fire (Park Avenue and Montgomery Street), March 3, 1956. Firefighters S. Ciraulo, G. Wallace, and Capt. F. E. Conyers, Sr. direct cooling streams of water on nearby propane storage tanks to prevent them from overheating and exploding.

171

When budget hearings rolled around again in mid-1956, another 5.7% wage increase was included, along with funds to lease a second residence as a temporary fire station — this time on Saratoga Ave. — and five men to staff it. The total Fire Department budget would have topped a million dollars for 1956-7, the first time in history, except for a fiscal year change made at this time. Instead of running from September 1 to August 31, the 1957-8 year and those following would run from July 1 to June 30. Thus the 1956-7 budget ($893,440) covered only ten months. It was the last budget request Fire Chief O'Brien was to make. He announced his intention to retire, after years of poor health, at the end of 1956.

The new 1524 Saratoga Ave. station, near the site of the present-day Westgate Shopping Center, held open house in October, occupied by Engine Co. No. 14. San Jose's city limits were spreading toward the western foothills, miles beyond the reach of fire companies downtown or even near Valley Fair. In fact, some of the distant suburbs were still being covered by the Central Fire District until such time as San Jose could provide its own fire protection. In August, 1956, the City Council had voted to continue a $15,000 annual contract with the County for such coverage.

Another leased residence took over as the temporary Station 10 about this time. The proposed West Side freeway, Highway 17, cut right through the existing quarters on O'Connor Drive, so the company was moved two blocks away to a house at Forest and Genevieve, costing the city $135 a month. Located to the west of the freeway for unrestricted access to Valley Fair, Engine 10 remained there for several years.

On the east side, at 3:45 a.m. October 19, Box 2114 at 5th and Santa Clara Streets was pulled for the only serious fire of 1956 — a $72,000 loss at the unlucky Lucky Market, 182 E. Santa Clara. Battalion Chief Campbell radioed in a general alarm on arrival at 3:50, bringing 65 firefighters from both shifts with Engines 1-2-3-4-11-13, three trucks, and three hose wagons; Engines 5-6-7-10 relocated into vacated stations. Ten 2½-inch lines, with one monitor nozzle, were used to knock down fire which ruined the store's mezzanine floor. Lines were taken to adjoin-

Typical of the rented firehouse era in San Jose's rapid expansion was the first home of Engine 19 in this carport alongside a rented dwelling on Vesuvius Ave.

ing store roofs, preventing any extension of the blaze.

Chief O'Brien directed operations, along with Assistant Chief Arthur Gilbert. It was O'Brien's last fire; two weeks later he began a 60-day disability leave, with final retirement to take effect January 6, 1957. As O'Brien departed for San Francisco to have the State Industrial Accident Commission certify the extent of his disability for pension purposes, City Manager Hamann appointed Gilbert to replace him.

Garage at right sheltered Engine 15 during the years the company occupied these temporary Bollinger Road quarters.

Chief Arthur Gilbert

Gilbert was the same age (61) as O'Brien —he couldn't hold office very long. But after what had happened in 1944 Hamann was not of a mind to step outside the line of succession. Squelching rumors that he was promoting Gilbert only to increase the officer's pension upon retirement, Hamann said, "If I appointed Artie Gilbert, it wouldn't be for the financial compensation involved, but for prestige and for all of these years he has served..."

Battalion Chief and OCD head Russ Lunsford became Acting Assistant Chief until the Civil Service Commission could set up exams creating a 7-man eligible list from which two Assistant Chiefs could be chosen. Actually, according to the Charter, only one of the two had to be picked by competitive exam; the other could be arbitrarily appointed by the Manager.

Forlorn Hopes for Burbank

Hamann first busied himself with a successful campaign to put across a $23,400,000 bond issue, to be retired from sales tax receipts, which he had proposed to the City Council in March. Bonds were to be sold at the rate of about $4 million worth annually. Prominent in the issue was a $1,750,000 "public safety package"; once more the aim was a Class 3 fire rating. All the expenditures made so far had been insufficient, because the city was growing faster than the improvements could be made!

Eight new 3-door fire stations accounted for half of this package including relocation of Engines 5, 6, and 7 — the latter to go to the expanding Municipal Airport. Alarm system improvements at $350,000 and $200,000 worth of hydrants were relatively minor items, though each in itself represented more money than had gone for a decade of Fire Department improvements only a few years earlier. New apparatus costing $150,000 was added later, raising the total package to almost $2 million.

One of the proposed firehouses reflected a vain hope. It was to be a multi-company house somewhere near San Carlos and Dana Aves. —to cover the Burbank district; then, as now, staunchly opposed to union with San Jose. In those days, however, San Jose officials still had hopes.

The original idea was to establish an Engine Co. 12 as a "backup" unit at the Auzerais Ave. station, much as Engines 11 and 13 were used. When this was ruled out as unnecessary, No. 12 was reserved for Burbank, if and when annexation succeeded; this was held out as bait in subsequent efforts to entice Burbank's residents into the fold.

During the latter part of 1957, another try at annexing Burbank-Bradley Manor ran its dismal course. In response to questons from the Westside Improvement Association, City Manager Hamann said that if the annexation succeeded, "those members of the Burbank district fire department as are available will be hired and taken into the City's civil service system." Fire insurance rates would drop ten per cent—but he was forced to admit that property taxes would go up. At a meeting of 100 Burbank residents in January, 1958, Battalion Chief LeBeau assured them a firehouse would be built in the vicinity of Shasta and Dana (Engine 12 again).

But, with such bitter comments as "Twenty years ago, when we were mudholed, you didn't want us," Burbank spurned San Jose's blandishments to remain in the County. Eventually, Engine 12 was established elsewhere.

Two major fires occurred in the meantime. A general alarm at 7:48 p.m. July 7, 1957, did $30,000 damage to both floors and the roof of the 70-year-old Centella (St. Paul's)

Methodist Church at 2nd and Reed Streets. Salvage covers were spread to save the organ, while crews of ten fire rigs knocked down flames upstairs. Captain Russ Batten of Engine 3 was overcome by smoke.

At 644 Stockton Ave., a $100,000 two alarm blaze gutted offices and garages of the Garden City Disposal Service and J. C. Bateman Co., on August 10. Engines 1-2-5-7-11, Trucks 1-2, Hose 1-2-5 operated ten 2½-inch lines to control the fire quickly and prevent involvement of the Moore Machinery Co. next door. Large quantities of truck parts and tires were destroyed, sending up a column of smoke visible for ten miles.

Even without absorbing the reluctant West Siders, San Jose was now caught up in a genuine boom. Assessed valuation in the city reportedly increased some $7 million in a year's time, sending Attorney John Thorne before the City Council with impassioned pleas for further wage increases covering a large group of city employees. A three per cent raise, backed by the Civil Service Commission and City Personnel Director MacRae, was granted on June 24, 1957—pushing the 1957-58 Fire Department budget up to the $1.25 million mark. Firemen's salary range just prior to this raise was $381-$476 monthly.

Thorne continued, with unflagging zeal, to appear at City Hall asking for more increases; the wearisome regularity of his visits led Councilmen to groan, "Oh no; here comes that man again!" Every year or two, Thorne succeeded. However, he had less success with the "thorny" problem of pensions and retirement.

For a year, Thorne's Citizen's Committee had been looking over the "outdated" retirement system, concluding that it needed a complete overhaul. By October 1957, he was asking for a measure on the next election ballot to revise the system completely by Charter amendment. The City Council turned him down, 4 to 2, upon which a referendum attempt was immediately forecast; Thorne said, "I couldn't hold the men back."

City Manager Hamann's staff brought out their side at an acrimonious discussion of the issue in January 1958: "How are we going to finance it?" (Added annual cost to the city was expected to average $150,000); and "How do we justify creating this additional disparity between what we do for policemen and firemen, and what we do for our other employees?" Firefighters could answer the second question by pointing out that the hazardous, nerve-wracking nature of their calling entitled them to a special scale of benefits. They could point to the short life expectancy of the average retired fireman.

But the first question was tougher. Attorney Thorne was riding the "increased valuation" horse into the ground. The Council finally compromised in January by agreeing to put the issue on the May 13, 1958, ballot as Proposition F. With a wary eye on the record of Thorne's salary requests, however, they deleted a controversial "escalator clause" tying proportionate pension increases to future salary hikes.

Beginning of a Bad Year

San Jose suffered the highest per capita fire loss ever, during 1958; the total loss topped $1 million for the first time. Except for the increased size and effectiveness of the Fire Department the loss would have been far worse.

Thirteen hose lines were needed, with two ladder pipes, to subdue flames that did $150,000 damage to the Healey Motor Company, 477 S. Market Street, on January 28, 1958. After having smoldered so long that 14-inch beams were burned almost through, the fire was seen by a passing motorist at 6:30 a.m.

Beginning somewhere in the rear repair shop, flames were through the roof when firemen arrived. The first alarm response to Box 4154 included Engines 1-3-4, Truck 2, Hose 1-3; second alarm brought Engines 2-5-13, Truck 3, Hose 2-5; third alarm Engines 8-11. Fifty firefighters controlled the blaze after the roof collapsed.

There followed a deceptive lull, during which the headlines proclaimed a rush of developments. In March, after field tests conducted for the California Optometric Association by Dr. Arthur C. Heinsen, Jr., San Jose firemen were adding yellow stripes to their turnout coats, intended to improve nighttime visibility.

Of five entrants in the February exams for Assistant Chief, two men passed. Leader in both written and oral tests was John Jones, army reserve officer, former paratroop jump instructor, 19 years a fireman, and in 1947 (at age 30) one of the youngest Battalion Chiefs in the nation. The other, also with 19 years' service, was Battalion Chief Ron Le-Beau. Both men were appointed Assistant Chiefs February 28, 1958.

Soon thereafter the entire department administrative setup was changed. Chief Jones, given the "unclassified" post not under Civil Service, took over the line organization — in charge of firefighting. Chief LeBeau headed the staff — equipment and repair, budgets, and records, water supply, etc. Arthur Gilbert was to concentrate on personnel problems and fire prevention.

A decision was made at the same time to change the rank of firefighting Battalion Chief to "District Chief." The 40 Captains and 140 Firefighters were split into District 1 (north side), under District Chiefs Gerald Murphy and Larry Campbell, and District 2 (south side), under District Chiefs George Vitek and John Knapp.

District 2 was an enormous entity, sprawling from San Jose's eastern limits across the valley almost to Cupertino—more than ten miles. Near the new district's western extremity, Engine Co. No. 15 went into service on March 24. This was another residence temporarily in use as a firehouse, at 6590 Bollinger Road, leased by the city for $160 a month.

Apparatus for Engine 15 was one of two brand new rigs of a pattern destined to become a San Jose standard: American-La-France pumpers built on tilt-cab short-wheel-base commercial chassis. They could turn on a dime—a feature just as useful downtown as on country roads in the West Valley. Each carried a 500-gallon water tank.

At Last: A Fire Alarm Headquarters

With few nostalgic tears, the San Jose City Council held its last meeting at the old Market Street City Hall in mid-March of 1958; decades of dreams had produced the reality of a new Civic Center. Squatting unobtrusively behind the sparkling glass-and-brick arc of the $2,500,000 City Hall (which some wag had suggested building on a turntable during the months of argument about which direction it should face) was a smaller building of vast importance to the Fire Department.

This was the Communications Center, 171 W. Mission Street. Inside this $165,000 bomb-proof municipal nerve center was another $70,000 in equipment—since expanded considerably. Here, San Jose became the first Western city to house all its emergency communications services (and routine telephone circuits as well) under a single roof. Towering above that 16-inch concrete roof, which covered 8000 square feet of floor space, was

Second of the city's light units, built in the department shop.

175

Two tall antenna towers and the new microwave dish mark San Jose's modern Communications Building in the Civic Center, 1962; the City Hall in background.

a pair of 140-foot radio antennae. Baffled entrances to exclude blast shock waves, and an outside sprinkler system to wash down radioactive contamination, protect the center from nuclear attack.

It was a far cry from the generation of makeshift arrangements which had gone before. No more would the identity of those calling in false fire alarms be a mystery, for with new equipment the voice could be recorded. In later years, at least one arsonist was caught with just such evidence. No more would there be any guesswork about what time firemen were dispatched; new recorders would automatically fix the time on the register tapes.

Centrally located in the building is the fire dispatching console, surrounded by the rows of alarm circuit panels. To the dispatcher's left, in a separate, glass-enclosed cubicle, are three switchboards serving the hundreds of Civic Center telephones. Nearby is the police and Civil Defense emergency switchboard. Further on, offices of the City Radio Technician and his staff, plus restrooms, kitchen, and repair shops, take up the building's west end. At the east end, OCD headquarters include plotting board, desk space for emergency service directors, and facilities for amateur radio operators. A 60 kilowatt stand-by generator keeps the center on the air if commercial power fails.

For years, the city's communications system had been held together by little more than hard work and dedication, starting with the first police radio in 1931—not made two-way till 1938. All routine and emergency calls went through two overloaded switchboards in the basement "broom closet" under the old City Hall; equipment and power supplies were located in dank basement corners. Repair and maintenance were handled in a rented building across the street, once a telephone company service garage. The Fire Department's own internal phone service was based for years in a corner of the Market Street firehouse above the apparatus floor.

Although the Communications Center remained in overall Police Department control, the Fire Department could well be proud of the new facilities. It was a long step ahead.

Thumbs Down on the Retirement Plan

Despite the best efforts of police-fire campaigners, headed by Fireman Joe Fries and including Ralph Bernardo (9 years President of Firefighters Union Local 873) and Leonard Marks (graduate of the USC School of Fire Administration), the proposed retirement plan revision was defeated in the May election by the lightest turnout of voters in 14 years. A committee of 80 business and labor leaders also plumped for Proposition F, arguing that firefighters and police officers weren't covered by Social Security—although other city workers had been thus protected since 1957. While agreeing that survivors' benefits ought to be provided, somehow, the San Jose Mercury vaguely editorialized that "There is reason to believe that the City Council can

by ordinance provide survivors' benefits..." (This was in fact done several years later when Firefighter Don Carrera was killed in a training accident — but the procedure was hardly one the unfortunate survivors could bank on.)

Committee Chairman Frank Callisch said "the people are not living up to the times," and that voters had simply put off the inevitable. He was right.

A cut from 70 to 63 hours as the Fire Department work week, twice recommended by the Civil Service Commission, was tentatively set for the 1959-60 fiscal year, the Council meanwhile granting another 2.7% raise, across the board. Ten more firemen were authorized for the latter part of 1958, to be trained and ready for arrival of another new aerial truck.

Then fires began in earnest. August 14th, 1958, a 6:35 p.m. phone call started a two alarm assignment on the way to the 101 Plating Works at 953 Chestnut Street. Forty firemen made a good stop in preventing more than minor damage to the adjoining plant of Pillar Case Goods Mfg. Co. One of the two plating works buildings was a total loss.

Box 4119 routed downtown firemen from their sleep at 3:04 a.m. November 22, and as companies left headquarters they could see the glare from the burning Glazenwood Hotel at 189 S. 3rd. The front of that ancient 2½ story frame rookery, housing 36 residents in a maze of 27 small rooms and 5 apartments, was fully involved on the arrival of Engines 1-2-11, Hose 1-2, and Truck 1. A second alarm brought Engines 3-4, Hose 3, and Truck 3. Eight 2½-inch lines were laid. Engine 7 was special called for a resuscitator.

Neither fire escape nor rear exit existed for evacuation of residents, mostly elderly, who were rescued via ladders—some from a roof next door where they had managed to flee. Six of them were on crutches. Again, quick action by firefighters, directed by Chiefs Gilbert, LeBeau, and Parker, prevented heavy damage in the crowded neighborhood. Although 7 persons were hurt,

Closeup of the 1958 Communications Center after addition of the microwave transmitter, showing the water piping around the roof for washdown of radioactive contamination in case of atomic attack.

The last of three disastrous fires covering a span of ten years, this one put the General Box Company out of business.

including Firefighter Larry Sammaron, no lives were lost. Source of the $28,000 blaze was a gas heater in a basement apartment.

Lumber Takes a Beating

San Jose's westside lumber business, responsible for more record-breaking fires than any other single occupancy, provided the balance of 1958's unprecedented losses. After work on November 26, employees of the Georgia-Pacific Company, relaxing in a nearby tavern, saw fire spouting from the firm's 14,000 square foot plywood warehouse at 345 Sunol Street. Rushing to the building, they rescued two trucks before heat and smoke drove them back; one employee, overcome by smoke, was dragged out unconscious.

Meanwhile, someone phoned in the alarm, and Box 4323 was struck at 6:38 p.m.; Engines 1-4-10, Hose 1, and Truck 2 responded. Engine 4 wet down the high-piled lumber in the Cheim yard across Sunol St., while a monitor nozzle and two deluge sets went into action with the help of Burbank and County firemen arriving on mutual aid call.

Flames shot 80 feet in the air as Engines 2-3-7 rolled in on the second alarm. The fifty

firefighters on hand, using 14 hose lines, succeeded in saving the adjoining Marin Dell Milk depot, but the warehouse itself—loaded to the roof with plywood—was a total loss. Mopping up the $240,000 ruins took days. Sunol Street, blocked by giant piles of rubble, was closed while a Public Works crane, two forklifts, and a bulldozer tore apart masses of smoldering plywood for firemen to wet down.

This was only a curtain-raiser for Sunday, December 21, 1958—a day many San Jose firefighters will not soon forget. At 1:48 p.m., an alarm came in for fire in piled box shook along the Julian Street side of the lumber yard operated jointly by S. H. Chase and General Box Distributors, occupying most of a square block from Montgomery Street west to the alley (once known as Center Street) along the S.P. main line. The south and west sides of the yard were occupied by old, tinder-dry frame storage sheds loaded with box shook.

This was a threatening blaze, but a two-alarm assignment soon knocked it down with seven hose lines. Responding were Engines

178

Visible for twenty miles, this General Box Company fire threatened the natural gas storage tanks shown in this picture and closed rail traffic on the nearby mainline.

1-2-7-11, Hose 1-2, and Trucks 1-2. Some four hours later, most of the companies had been released and were either returning to quarters, reloading hose, or otherwise getting back in service. Engine 11 was ready to leave the scene, when a dark sedan occupied by three men drove up; the men reported a second, apparently unrelated fire in the rear of the same lumberyard.

"We drove around to investigate," reported Engine 11's Captain, "and saw a large shed completely involved and spreading rapidly." Radioing Battalion Chief Murphy for help at 5:59 p.m., Engine 11 dropped its last few lengths of hose and went to work.

Fire apparatus converged from unexpected directions in the mad scramble that followed. Engine 4 was at Market Street and responded from there. Its first line into the southwest corner of the yard was burned up before water could be turned on. A second alarm at 6:03 and the general alarm at 6:07 eventually brought Engines 1-2-3-4-5-6-7-10-11, all five hose wagons, and all three aerials, leaving only five first-line engine companies to cover the city throughout the evening.

Truck 3, moving to fill in at Market Street on the second alarm, was called to the fire by radio while still en route. Truck 2, pulling into the rear of the Market Street station to refuel, also got the radio call and drove right through the station, out the front, and back to the fire scene — to the astonishment of bystanders.

Twenty 2½-inch lines were used to surround the raging blaze, which for a time threatened the P. G. & E. storage tanks only 50 yards away, containing four million cubic feet of natural gas. Police under Chief Blackmore ordered the area evacuated while utility crews patrolled the tanks in search of leaks. Firefighting operations were under Chief Gilbert's personal direction.

For an hour and a half, heavy streams including a deluge set and two monitors played on flames visible for 20 miles. Four firemen suffered minor burns and cuts. Fire spread from the blazing sheds into a large pile of used tires in the rear of Harold Johnson Distributors at 211 North Montgomery, destroying large numbers of them. Several trains were held up because of the main line's proximity to the fire; the crack "Coast Daylight" northbound from Los Angeles was finally rerouted via Campbell to Palo Alto, on the rusty old branch line.

Overhauling began late in the evening, and continued for 24 hours, with the help of a bulldozer to break up charred piles of box shook, and the Salvation Army to provide coffee and sandwiches to tired firefighters. Total loss in the devastating blaze was $355,000. While the cause was never determined, suspicion naturally focussed on the three men in the dark sedan. This slim lead petered out, however, when the license number hastily recorded at the time proved to be non-existent.

Thus ended the local General Box Distributors operations, punctuated by three disastrous fires at ten year intervals. San Jose has had no further serious lumberyard fires since 1958.

Meanwhile, Back at City Hall...

In December of 1958 the city received its first 1250 GPM pumper—a cab-ahead American-LaFrance unit, replacing the 1937 Engine 1 which went into reserve. Also retired from service was the 1938 squad wagon, which at the end of 1958 was auctioned off; but there were no takers, and not for another year was Hedberg's pride actually sold.

Next to arrive, in rapid succession: January 1959, a 100-foot American-LaFrance aerial for Truck Co. 1, bumping existing trucks down the line until the 1942 Seagrave was available for a new Truck Co. No. 5; in February, a 1000 GPM pumper for Engine 2, similar to the new Engine 1. The OCD pumper from Station 2 was moved over to Station 8, because recently annexed built-up areas along Alum Rock Ave. required greater pumping capacity. A new $110,000 Station 5, with engine and truck companies, opened for business on March 5 (its $15,000 site on N. 10th Street had been purchased in November 1957). D. Tomacci & Sons received a $108,936 contract in February to build permanent quarters for Engine 10 on Monroe Street.

For several months, San Jose school officials — public and private — acted to abate school fire hazards, many of them of very long standing, "discovered" following the tragic Chicago parochial school blaze that took almost a hundred lives in December 1958. Thousands of dollars were spent in January 1959 for additional panic hardware for San

Jose schools. In February, the Board of Education dipped into school bond funds, without a dissenting vote, for immediate spending of $58,000 to bring half a dozen old schools up to snuff by enclosing boiler rooms, installing basement sprinklers, and the like.

Six months later, the City Council approved a $16,800,000 capital improvement budget submitted by A. P. Hamann, including three new firehouses for $334,000 to be built on sites already bought. Final official approval was also given to a change in title for San Jose Fire Department personnel; henceforth, they would not be known as "firemen," but as "firefighters."

John Thorne made his regular visit at this time, to remind Councilmen about that 63-hour work week. It was approved, effective July 1 — later postponed to September 1, at Chief Gilbert's request, to allow training time for the 28 new firefighters needed. Thorne also kept the heat on about the retirement-pension plan, pressing his case before the Citizens' Charter Review Committee.

Newly-appointed Fire Captain Leonard Marks announced on September 8 that survivor's benefits would again be the chief issue, and that Thorne (with his insistence on a formidable package of other issues as well) would no longer represent firefighters concerning retirement plan changes.

Instead, Marks himself became spokesman. Under the existing plan, disability pay (accruing to survivors in case of death) was nil for a recruit, rising gradually to half pay after 20 years service. Arguing persuasively before a sympathetic City Council on September 14, Marks claimed that "this tends to force the young men to avoid being hurt. But they are the ones who take the most chances . . . . We aren't asking for a free ride for the disabled, but protection for our families." Eventually, the Council offered to give disabled or survivors half pay regardless of length of service. The fire and police unions, however, complained it would cost them too much in contributions, as compared to what employees covered by Social Security were paying.

The retirement plan arguments dragged on for two more years, getting so bogged down in confusing detail that the city's best legal actuarial brains had a tough time making sense out of it. Obviously, there could be no repetition of the 1958 popular vote on a new plan; if officialdom couldn't understand the ramifications, how could the voters? Therefore, the Council agreed to police-fire requests

Captain Leonard Marks took over as union spokesman for the San Jose Firefighters in 1960. Ten years later Battalion Chief Marks received his doctorate in Public Administration (the first earned by a fireman in the United States) at the University of Southern California. Now Deputy Chief under John Jones, he has led the effort to collect antique fire equipment for the eventual display at the San Jose Historical Museum.

to put a Charter revision—Proposition A—on the April 1960 ballot; if approved, it would empower the Council to enact a new plan by ordinance without another election. Proposition A passed, and the Council quietly began working out the endless details.

An Embarrassing Episode

First, however, Councilmen had to deal with an unfortunate breakdown in the city's communications system. Fire officials had been far from unanimous in approving the principle of Police Department control of the system; the events of March 20, 1960, caused them to grumble openly.

What happened was a major fire along the Santa Clara-San Jose border, followed by the appearance of a neighborhood resident before the Council to ask pointedly why the San Jose Fire Department didn't get there until 15 minutes after the alarm—well after arrival of Santa Clara firefighters.

Subsequent investigation brought out this story: Two passing newsboys (who later received trophies for "outstanding community service" from the California Newspaper Foundation) discovered flames inside the rear of the Lucky supermarket, Bascom and Heatherdale Aves., at 5:20 a.m. Few people, the boys included, ever thought of locating the store in terms of the obscure little side street of Heatherdale. So when one boy dashed to his nearby home to phone the San Jose Fire Department at 5:25, he naturally identified the store as being at Bascom and Newhall — the major intersection nearby, center of the shopping center of which the Lucky store was the prominent landmark.

The corner of Bascom and Newhall, unfortunately, was 60 yards outside the San Jose city limit, though the store itself was about six feet *inside*. The Civic Center dispatcher receiving the call—which, like all such "fire" calls, did not go directly to any fire station or official—passed the alarm on to County Communications on San Jose's southern outskirts. There it was relayed to Santa Clara police for direct line transmission to Santa Clara Fire Headquarters.

In response to this fifth hand information which took 12 minutes to reach them, Santa Clara firemen rolled out of their stations into a dense fog. Not until their three engines actually reached the scene could they confirm

that the fire was out of their territory. Nevertheless, they set to work with a will.

Meanwhile, the newsboys had gone back to the Lucky store, to find the whole interior now filled with smoke. Hearing no fire sirens, the boy who'd given the alarm returned home to have his father, Charles Moore, call once more. Telling the skeptical dispatcher, "I know it's in the city, I live here. The fire's getting bigger and you'd better get somebody out here," Moore banged down the phone. Santa Clara firemen were then radioing back the official location of the blaze, and San Jose logged the first of three alarms at 5:41 a.m. Nine pieces of apparatus and 36 firefighters responded. Fire was through the roof, its fitful glare invisible a block away through the fog, by the time the tardy San Joseans got into action.

Nothing was left of the store but the four walls; a total loss of $269,000. An incensed Charles Moore went before the next Council meeting to demand an explanation of the foulup.

The Fire Department was blameless; through no fault of theirs, the alarm simply didn't reach them promptly. Complained an "unnamed" fire official, "An experienced man would have called us right away. That's what we want ... " Fire dispatchers, he felt, should be firemen, trained in fire equipment operations as well as in city geography.

The Police Chief admitted that his dispatcher had violated a long-standing rule to notify the Fire Department District Chief in any such borderline cases. Defending the Communications Center operation, City Manager Hamann admitted the need for "better training" of the dispatchers.

A Mercury editorial suggested "metropoliton government" as a solution—not without merit, although a couple of telephone circuits would have been cheaper and less of a political issue. It is regrettable that the dispatcher's conduct was allowed to completely obscure the remarkable length of time it took for the alarm to reach Santa Clara firemen after it did leave San Jose, as well as the curious lack of direct telephone lines to Santa Clara Fire Headquarters from either San Jose or County Communications.

The snafu also obscured the smooth-working co-operation between the Fire Departments themselves. Santa Clara had gone to work on the Lucky fire without question, later being warmly commended for its efforts; San Jose would have done the same.

This is one aspect of mutual aid which has gone far toward easing the Santa Clara Valley's growing pains. Repeated examples could be cited: The $6000 garage-shed fire, Sept. 26, 1958, at 253 Brooklyn Ave., in San Jose territory—extinguished by the nearby Burbank volunteers before San Jose firemen arrived; the co-operation of Burbank and San Jose on the $40,000 fire three days later which wrecked the California Popcorn and Peanut Supply, 349 Lincoln Ave. — in Burbank territory; the shed fire at 502 Sunol Street in July 1954, outside the city, extinguished by joint efforts of 13 rigs from three departments; and many others.

There is constant close working with County firemen. Hazards in some of the rural areas of overlap are out of the ordinary; in August 1963, a 40-acre grass fire in the Almaden Valley disturbed a horde of rattlesnakes which kept San Jose and County firemen stepping livelier than usual!

The other aspect of mutual aid is the call for assistance from another department, where jurisdiction is not in doubt. Having the area's largest firefighting agency, San Jose seldom calls for help — but has never hesitated to answer such a call, beginning with the April 16, 1894, dispatch of fire companies to Santa Cruz where a downtown conflagration threatened the entire Surf City. When the unprecedented tornado wreaked heavy damage to Sunnyvale in January 1951, San Jose responded. When a $400,000 fire in January 1959 threatened the huge Libby cannery in Sunnyvale, San Jose sent Truck 2 (Sunnyvale then had no aerials). Sunnyvale's mayor wrote an appreciative letter to San Jose's mayor Solari, saying "This further proves that co-operation between cities . . . pays dividends." When a December blaze that same year did $500,000 damage at a Milpitas wood products plant, San Jose's Engine 2 worked alongside Milpitas and County crews.

More Expansion, and a New Chief

Keeping pace with the 10,000-home Tropicana Village development and associated growth in business on San Jose's far southeast side, a $97,000 multi-company firehouse

was opened in March 1960 at King Road and Cunningham Ave. Engine 16 held open house there on April 2-3.

Main direction of the city's expansion was not to the east, however, but to the south and west. "Fringe areas," to which San Jose simply could not give fire protection, were still covered by the Central Fire District, at a cost (fortunately on the decline) exceeding $200,000 annually. For the 1960-61 fiscal year, the Council acted to cut the bill by putting two more city fire stations in service —Engines 17 and 18—using 25 additional firefighters authorized on June 6.

During the same month, Fire and Police Unions asked for raises ranging from 11 to 14%; the Council granted an average 8%, following Civil Service Commission recommendations. Soon afterward, at a meeting involving the Council, the City Attorney, and police-fire representatives, chaired by Police Chief Blackmore, "general agreement" was reached on a new retirement plan. Higher survivorship benefits were a key provision. Other details remained to be resolved.

Fire Chief Gilbert's brief tenure ended in the Fall, for his 65th birthday, on September 16, made retirement mandatory. City Manager Hamann puzzled for some time over his replacement, although it was certain to be one of the two Assistant Chiefs. Said Hamann, "It is not often I have an appointment made so easy because of the candidates' qualifications, and so difficult because they are so close in ability."

Chief Ron LeBeau

On September 6, he announced his decision. The new Chief was Ron LeBeau, 48, appointed at a monthly salary of $1038. Chosen over the somewhat younger John Jones because of "greater experience in the department's administrative affairs," LeBeau was the first Chief in 50 years on the scale of Dick Brown—6 ft. 3 inches tall, and heavily built. Born in Duluth, Minnesota, he was a top-notch softball pitcher in the 1930's and '40's. Entering the Fire Department in 1939, he was promoted to Lieutenant during the war; Captain in January 1945; Battalion Chief July 1951, and Assistant Chief in February 1958.

LeBeau's stature caused chuckles in 1963 when he and "shortie" Ralph Bernardo disputed "the case of the shrinking fireman" before the Civil Service Commission. LeBeau asked the Commission in April to raise the height limit for new firefighters from 5' 8" to 5' 9", after discovering some recruits were cheating; one man, checked at 5' 8" and hired, was re-checked three months later and found to be a half inch shorter. About to be fired, he appealed for a new measurement. On the appointed day, he arrived at the City Health Department in an ambulance, prone on a stretcher—and measured 1/16 inch over the minimum. It was presumed that he had some chiropractic help in bringing his height up to snuff. Another applicant had been known to knock himself over the head with a board, only to be found out next day when the lump went down!

Bernardo, two inches shorter than the minimum, protested with tongue in cheek that some of the force's best men wouldn't be there if the new standards had been followed. Nevertheless, LeBeau won the argument.

Another bond package of capital improvements was proposed by the City Manager in October, 1960; almost $27 million worth, including $965,000 for fire protection, went on the ballot for February 7, 1961. By this time almost half the 1957 bond funds were spent. The city was buying equipment in unheard-of quantities; on one occasion the City Council seriously debated acquisition of a storage warehouse to facilitate carload purchase of hydrants, which were being installed by the hundred.

Ride 'em, Cowboy!

No history of the San Jose Fire Department could be complete without the story of what has become one of this area's most colorful entertainment events—the Firemen's Rodeo. It's a story that deserves to be told all in one place, because the Rodeo was so largely the work of one man.

Creator of the first modest show in 1954, president of the Rodeo throughout the early years which saw it grow into a nationally known attraction featuring top stars and drawing huge crowds, the late Captain Gene Sawyer was active in Fire Department fraternal and recreational affairs throughout much of his 18-year career—terminated by his sudden death on December 12, 1960, at the age of only 40.

The Firemen's Ball, for many years the principal support of the department's Widows and Orphans Fund initiated in June 1918, was no longer a big drawing card in postwar San Jose. A dance alone, without other attractions, was rather tame fare. By 1949 it was necessary to encourage attendance of non-dancers by adding a variety show to the program. Other forms of public entertainment were tried; the "Hollywood Ice Parade of 1947" was one experiment—however, the brief attempts to revive San Jose's Ice Bowl, first built in 1941, had no lasting success.

Furthermore, the increasing size of the Fire Department meant steadily mounting

Gene Sawyer

demands on the Fund ($12,000 in benefits was paid out in 1961). Something new was needed, something that would be a major area attraction.

Gene Sawyer's answer was a rodeo. Western tradition supported a lot of enthusiasm for horsemanship in the Santa Clara Valley. And, since the war, the magnificent grandstand-track development at the County Fair Grounds beckoned invitingly during the 11½ months of the year that the Fair was not in operation.

The 1954 show that Gene organized was a small one, but it showed promise. None was held in 1955, and when the second rodeo rolled around in 1956 it starred "the cream of the nation's rodeo riders." An entire week late in May was designated "Rodeo Week" by the City Council, to focus attention on events including the Queen's Ball on May 19. The next Friday, a 7 p.m. downtown parade of horses and riders, led by veteran horseman and former fireman Tim Sullivan as Grand Marshal, was followed by the Cowboy's Dance at the open air Fair Grounds pavilion. Official rodeo host was Fire Chief O'Brien.

In three performances on Saturday and Sunday the 26th and 27th, over a hundred of the country's top saddle stars pitted their strength and skill against equally determined specimens of horseflesh and cattle that came charging from the chutes. Almost $4000 in prize money, besides entry fees, awaited the lucky winners. The crowd of 6000 was "nearly triple the attendance of our first rodeo," said Gene Sawyer, the show's proud director.

Before 1957's rodeo, Sawyer was nominated in February to be an officer of the nation-wide Rodeo Information Commission, representing some 600 United States rodeos. Bit by bit, the show grew larger, the parades more colorful—featuring such units as Camp Cooke's pre-Civil War cavalry troop, the U.S. Pacific Marine Band, and the drill team from San Francisco''s Fire Department.

The queen contest was a big thing as well. By 1958, the girl received over $1000 in merchandise, awards, and travel, plus a $500 scholarship and a chance to become Miss California Rodeo; then a chance at the national finals in Las Vegas. Later, an annual "Tim Sullivan Memorial Trophy" award was established for the Santa Clara Valley teenager judged to have done the most for the horse or rodeo world during the year. Fire Chief Gilbert posed proudly in May 1958 with a copy of the State Senate resolution congratulating his department for bringing rodeo back to San Jose for the first time since the days of the Spanish Dons.

In 1959, Sawyer resigned from the rodeo presidency to become its general manager; Assistant Chief LeBeau replaced him. The rodeo that year again set attendance records, leading the directors to expand the show to a 3-day run for 1960, with five performances. The parade, now a daytime affair, promised for 1960 to be "one of the largest here in the past 20 years."

Then, on December 12, 1960, after putting in a day of final arrangements for the rodeo "award banquet" scheduled for later in the week, Gene Sawyer complained of chills. His wife drove him to the nearby San Jose Hospital, where he died of an apparent heart attack before he could be admitted.

For years, the soft-spoken Sawyer had been driver of Squad 1, B Shift, when the company was San Jose's busiest. A native San Josean, one-time Los Gatos High School athlete, he was five times president of the San Jose Unified Widows and Orphans Association, new title of the former San Jose Fire Department group which earlier in 1960 had merged with the County Central Fire District Association. He had been chairman of a firemen's committee in the 1952 "Toys for Joy" drive.

Chief LeBeau termed his death "Premature —and a great shock to the department." At the December 26 banquet, which went ahead as scheduled, guests observed a moment of silence in memory of this man who built the rodeo into a modern San Jose institution— the second largest outdoor rodeo in the State.

Captain Joe Paradiso was named to succeed Sawyer at the helm. Since then, many changes have been made as interest and attendance continued to rise. Starting in August 1961, an annual "horse show and gymkhana" began at the Santa Clara County Horseman's Grounds, with over 150 entries in 16 different events—barrel races, keyhole races, a pole bending contest. Year by year rodeo attendance has swelled, topping $20,000 in 1963, with a new record that year of $13,725 in prize money.

Although others have carried on Gene Sawyer's work, and done it well, San Jose's Firemen's Rodeo was properly a monument to the memory of this one man.

Blowup on the West Side

San Jose's temporary firehouse program was going strong as 1960 ended. Engines 9, 14, and 15 were located in leased residences. Explaining selection of the houses, Chief LeBeau said, "We look for a 3 or 4 bedroom house in the 1500 square foot class, located on a corner for quick response in as many directions as possible."

A fourth temporary station was replaced by permanent quarters on November 14, when Engine 10's multiple company house opened at 511 S. Monroe. Like its first home, 10's second temporary station was immediately moved away to make room for freeway development. A new Third District was now established, with District Chief quartered at

Monroe Street, to cover the West Valley and reduce District 2 to reasonable size. District 3 contained all the temporary stations.

Also in November, Station 10's place in the temporary ranks was taken by a new company—Engine 17, occupying an $18,500 residence at Ridgewood and Dent Aves. in the Robertsville area. Location and nature of fire protection needed there was in doubt for a long time pending decision by the University of California on a possible Almaden Valley campus (eventually it went to Santa Cruz County).

Engine 17's quarters were not leased, but purchased outright by the city. Being "stuck" with such property, when a permanent station was eventually built, didn't worry officials; there seemed no end to the steady rise in property values. And the Fire Department maintained the premises in good order, making it easy to resell at a profit when it was time to move.

Land once bought for relocation of Engine 6, at $11,500, and unused because a better site was found, was sold a few years later for $13,000. As for older properties—the abandoned quarters of Chemical 3 on S. 8th Street, representing a municipal investment of perhaps $5000, were sold by San Jose for many times that amount. A jury awarded the last owner $26,611 when San Jose State College condemned the place in 1960 for campus expansion.

Hopeful now of making Class 3, San Jose requested a new Underwriters rating survey in January 1961. Two weeks later, the latest fire protection bond issue, providing for ten more permanent fire stations, and 1800 hydrants, passed by a vote of 4 to 1. Maps prepared for election publicity wistfully showed one of those new stations in Burbank; to no avail. However, San Jose's spectacular growth in other directions continued unabated — a hundred people a day, fifteen square miles annually; there was talk of passing up San Francisco within a decade.

District 3's baptism of fire, literally, came along in February. First-due Engine 10 led a two alarm assignment in making an excellent stop of an "explosive" $100,000 blaze which wrecked much of Lou's Village restaurant and night spot, 1465 West San Carlos. Only quick action by the first arriving com-

Sherman Oaks Bowl explosion, February 22, 1961.

panies prevented loss of the entire building, according to Assistant Chief Jones. Cause of the early morning fire on February 2 was never determined. Three of the 36 firefighters were injured: John Diquisto, Nick Mayers, and Ed Silva.

Later, Captain Larry Cunningham was cited for merit in his initial handling of the fire. At Headquarters ceremonies, he was presented with a certificate reading, "Demonstrating exceptional achievement . . . your aggressive attack on the base of the fire prevented its spread and a major loss."

Engine 10 was also first-due at a major disaster on Washington's Birthday—the ex-

plosion of the $750,000 Sherman Oaks Bowl, 920 San Jose-Los Gatos Road. The block-long concrete block structure was completely demolished by the 8:39 p.m. blast, felt by nearly 200,000 San Joseans over a ten mile radius. For blocks around, windows blew out, doors flew open, and residents were lifted out of their chairs. Miraculously, there were only three minor injuries and no deaths; the bowling alleys were closed for refinishing at the time.

Three blocks away, one eyewitness reported "The flames were cresting with a big, red mushroom top . . . the cloud was dotted with flaming bits of wreckage...like a big Christmas tree." Said another, "The whole roof of the building seemed to fly up and blow away in pieces. The walls went sideways . . ."

Flames of three-alarm proportions then swept through the 24 bowling lanes, billiard room, bar, and restaurant. Third District Chief Ted Parker heard the blast at Station 10, three quarters of a mile away. Seeing fire in the sky in the direction of the nearby County Hospital, he immediately started for the scene with Engine 10, radioing Headquarters that he was checking an unreported explosion and fire. When still several blocks away, he realized it was a major structure beyond the hospital and radioed for a second, then a third alarm. By this time, countless phone calls were swamping switchboards of all emergency services, radio stations, and newspapers. Thousands of motorists converged on the area, requiring a score of police cars to control traffic.

When Assistant Chief Jones arrived, Chief Parker's men were proceeding with the pre-fire plan worked out for the building two years earlier. A dozen fire units also responded from the Central Fire District, and from Burbank, which had received a report that the County Hospital had exploded. Within twenty minutes, flames had been knocked down by eleven 2½-inch lines, a ladder pipe at the side of the building, and a deluge set at the rear. Thirty-two city firemen responded with seven engines and two trucks.

Across the street from the rear of the Sherman Oaks Bowl, at 919 Del Mar Ave., the blast left the Del Mar Apartments a shambles of broken glass, strewn furniture, and crushed timber. Ten families were made homeless. Broken cables cut off hundreds of West Side telephones; electric power was off for an hour, forcing both County and O'Connor Hospitals to go on emergency power. Damage to the bowling center and two apartment buildings was estimated at over $800,000. Thirty-nine other buildings and eight automobiles were damaged.

Joined by Underwriters investigators and P. G. & E. crews, plus representatives of 9 insurance companies, Fire Prevention Chief William Ogden ran down every clue to the blast's origin without much result. The alleys had been closed for lane cleaning and refinishing; however, flammable paints and lacquer thinners were found intact in a separate stor-

age area. Furnaces and water heaters in the building were virtually undamaged. After more than four years, suits and countersuits involving insurance carriers, the building owners, and the bowling center operator remained unsettled in the courts, while the empty shell of the ruined structure still stood untouched.

The Sherman Oaks Bowl fire was not a "general" alarm, because by 1960 three full alarm responses no longer depleted the fire force enough to call in the off-shift.

During the early 1900's, alarm response assignments had been haphazard. There was no central dispatching; box alarms sounded the big Market Street bell to alert the extramen. Running cards in the firehouses told which companies were to respond — usually two engines downtown, one elsewhere; the hook and ladder; and one or more of the chemical wagons. "Still" or telephone alarm response depended on the circumstances. For a time, each firehouse had its own phone—one didn't call the Fire Department, but simply phoned the nearest firehouse.

Anything too big for one box alarm assignment automatically became a "general alarm"; there is no mention in the records of a "second alarm" as such until the 1920's.

In 1947, the standard response was: first alarm, two engines, the squad, one truck; second alarm, usually two more engines; third or general alarm, one or two more engines and the other truck. Then in 1955, with abolition of the squads, first alarm assignment in high value areas became three engines plus one or two trucks.

By 1963, San Jose was a 5-alarm town. So far, there have been no 5-alarm fires here, but running cards are set up for it without tying up much over half the city's apparatus. The phantom box numbers themselves have used up all the four digit combinations, and now extend into the 12,000's.

In May, 1961, the City Council approved a call for bids on two 1000 GPM pumpers, and the first of a new breed of firefighting units: an 85-foot elevating platform or "Snorkel.' First adopted on a large scale by the city of Chicago, where as many as five of the crab-like monsters have been used at a single fire, the snorkel swept the country within a few years. (There was only one obstacle to its use in San Jose; when Snorkel 1 arrived in 1962,

The heartbreak in every fireman's life—District Chief Harold Parker uses mouth-to-mouth resuscitation in a vain attempt to revive 5-year-old Mike McKechnie, suffocated with his mother in their burning Willard Ave. apartment on June 11, 1961.

189

the Market Street apparatus room ceiling was a few inches too low for it. Some beams had to be notched out to solve the problem.) Several other new fire companies were scheduled to go in service during 1962, for which the Fire Department budget of $2,335,000 included 28 additional firefighters.

Fire Hazards, from Weeds to Ward

Once that was settled, the Council turned to the first of three legal headaches—involving, of all things, weeds.

With its long dry summer, San Jose is plagued with grass fires from June to October. At one time, vacant lots were not too numerous within the city limits, but when those limits began to expand by leaps and bounds, things got out of hand. Especially bad were areas like the North 10th Street industrial district, where large tracts of vacant land were dotted here and there with factory or warehouse buildings. There was a 2-alarm grass fire in July 1956, covering several blocks of that district.

Included in the 1945 Fire Prevention Code was provision for the Bureau to abate the dry weed hazard by having contractors burn off the ground at a cost of $6 to $8 for the average residential lot. Lot owners got the bill.

By 1953, lots were instead being disced or ploughed up, at slightly higher cost. In about March of each year, the city was surveyed to locate dangerous tracts—totalling as many as 2000. After notification, the owner was obliged to have the land cleared or face misdemeanor charges.

Even this wasn't good enough. In July 1961 the City Council passed an "emergency" ordinance empowering the Fire Chief to have lots cleared and put the cost on the owner's tax bill. An estimated 7000 lots were involved, making abatement one of the department's major tasks. A full-time Abatement Bureau, headed by an Abatement Officer, began in 1961 to handle an increasing flood of neighborhood complaints not only about weeds, but rubbish and other trash. Hundreds of properties were cleared, with a marked drop in grass fire calls resulting—in 1962, more than

$68,000 in abatement charges were assessed against property owners.

The 1961 ordinance still had to allow for the Fire Department's burning off some lots which were too full of trash to disc. Said Chief LeBeau, "We will have to burn off some lots which have become dumping grounds... The owner, of course, will be asked to clear away the rubbish after the weeds are burned."

Not all the "rubbish" was to be found in vacant lots. The headaches incurred by the Fire Prevention Bureau in abating other types of hazards were epitomized by the celebrated Ward affair.

On July 29, 1961, a relatively minor fire put an end to this long and colorful running battle between the Bureau and a private citizen; rancher William B. Ward, scion of a pioneer family of Agnew area orchardists, frequent pleader before local political bodies in a host of causes, and would-be antiquarian. The July fire destroyed a 2-story house on South 11th Street where much of Ward's antique treasure trove was stored, in violation of several fire regulations.

His troubles began as far back as 1955. He had hopes of saving the Morrison mansion on Julian Street between 5th and 6th, and purchased the huge old home for $1400. The land itself, however, remained in other hands. When its developer was ready to clear the ground for new buildings, Ward had no money to move the huge, decaying mansion elsewhere.

Diversified duties: Gene Stenzel, Harold Richardson, and Philip Wunderlick handle bicycle registration, 1964.

A fireman's jobs are varied. Here Robert Crowder aids in voter registration program, 1964.

But he did buy much of the interior woodwork from the wreckers, storing it at 470 S. 11th in an otherwise empty residence he owned there. Not only did he pay for the material with a rubber check (later made good); he immediately ran afoul of Fire Prevention Chief Ogden.

Repeatedly warned to remove the 11th Street fire hazard, Ward ignored condemnation orders issued in May 1959. Ogden finally hailed him into court; trial was set for August 31, 1959, on 35 separate charges of fire code violation. Only a few days before the trial, the second floor of the house (once the showplace home of Superior Court Judge George Welch) was gutted by a mysterious fire—Ward alleged vandals had done the mischief, while fire officials muttered, "We told you so." Surrounded by apartments and boarding houses in the heart of "Fraternity Row" near San Jose State College, the place was literally crammed with antique furniture.

In December, the 54-year-old rancher was convicted and given 60 days to avoid a jail term by removing the hazards. When he hadn't complied by the end of February 1960, he was handed a 90-day jail sentence.

Stalking angrily from the courtroom, Ward shouted, "I'd rather die first," and took a melodramatic dive from the third floor landing of the Hall of Justice. Escaping serious injury, he passed a psychiatric examination at Agnews State Hospital and soon went off to County Jail to serve his time.

But the 11th Street house still stood—what remained of it. Finally, in July 1961, the place caught fire again; this time it was totally destroyed. Only quick work by San Jose firefighters prevented spread of flames to adjacent apartments.

So, as the San Jose Mercury reported, "The house of Ward—object of a half dozen court hearings—stands a charred skeleton today, offering mute evidence of the repeated warnings of San Jose fire officials."

The remains disappeared later that summer, after the defeated owner had taken out a wrecking permit upon receipt of still another demolition order from the city. San Jose's newly adopted Housing Code provided that if Ward failed to comply this time, the city could do the work itself and attach a lien on the property for wrecking costs.

School Days for Firefighters

The summer of 1961 brought fruition of the San Jose Fire Department's plans for the area's first Oil Fire Control School, an outgrowth of attendance by Battalion Chiefs Tony Sapena and Tom Higgins and Captain Richard Hall at a similar school in Bakersfield in March. These officers returned to San Jose convinced that all firefighters, not just a select few, should have such training.

Supported by Chief LeBeau and Assistant Chief Jones, they formed a committee including Santa Clara and County officers, then polled all 11 San Jose area Fire Departments to see who might be interested in an oil fire school here. The results were astounding—all 11 departments wanted to enroll their entire memberships! On a percentage basis, men were picked from each organization to form two 125-man classes. Each class was to work through an 8-hour day, including demonstration and participation.

State fire training supervisor Tom Ward helped with the planning. Earl Hancock, secretary of the Western Oil and Gas Association's fire safety committee secured a gift of 3000 gallons of gasoline; 1000 gallons of crude oil and the same amount of LP gas were also rounded up. Safety engineer D. M. Johnson of Standard Oil advised on safety measures to minimize danger to those taking part. Location for the school, scheduled for August 16-17, was open land at the lower end of William Street Park, where a natural amphitheater was available for observers.

The 240 officers and men "graduating" from this first Bay Area school received completion certificates from Mr. Ward. In addition to this group, 260 others from 33 Fire Departments watched from the sidelines as students went through extinguishment of all kinds of petroleum blazes, including tank truck fires. So successful was this program that it was repeated in 1962, when over 100 San Jose firefighters were enrolled, plus 175 from other departments.

The oil fire school, gaining nationwide publicity, was only one facet of a vastly expanded training and education program for San Jose firemen. Formal class work actually began here more than thirty years ago, but was slow to become a vital part of the department's training. State instructor J. F. Baker, formerly of the Los Angeles Fire Department, taught three courses in the latter part of 1933, totalling nearly 140 hours.

This was a pioneering effort. Baker was the first teacher hired by the state in a program begun during 1931, and was the only such teacher until 1935. During the late 1950's, after casting an admiring eye at the

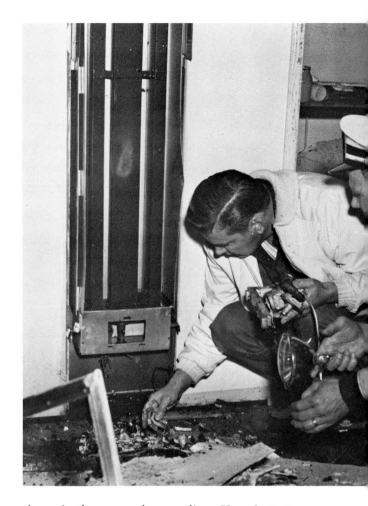

Arson is the cause of many fires. Here Inspector Michael Devitt and Capt. Ernie Anderson investigate an explosion, 1964.

success of San Jose State College's Police School, City Personnel Director Donald MacRae set his sights on a similar setup for firemen. It took a long time, a lot of letters, and many meetings to get the project off the ground, but by the end of 1957 school was in session.

MacRae opened his fire college campaign with a questionnaire to all Fire Chiefs in Santa Clara and San Mateo Counties. The Peninsula Fire Chief's Association backed the plan, as did the League of California Cities. San Jose State later became interested, but, pleading lack of facilities, encouraged MacRae to approach San Jose Unified School District.

Working with Joe Bellenger of San Jose Unified, chairman of a Fire Training Advisory Committee, MacRae saw his plan become a reality at San Jose Junior College. First two courses offered were "Basic Fire Hydraulics," created and taught by County Battalion Chief Ed Severns, and "Fire Control Strategy," under San Jose's Drillmaster Shannon. Two hundred firemen, almost half of all those in Santa Clara County, showed up for enrollment. Classes were specially scheduled to fit the 24 hour on and off duty hours of the students.

By the end of 1961, six courses were offered and two others were in preparation, with still another five being planned. The program led to the degree of Associate in Arts; students not completing all the degree requirements got a "Certificate in Firemanship." The expanded faculty included Captain Charles Crabtree of Sunnyvale, Chief George Maxwell of Campbell, and County Fire Marshal Bruce Wiggins. A hundred and fifty San Jose firefighters have completed City College work in such subjects as "Hazardous Materials," "Codes and Ordinances," and "Fire Department Administration."

Within the San Jose Fire Department itself, courses began in 1959 on advanced first aid, specialized fire rescue techniques, resuscitation, and artificial respiration. In classroom sessions at the drill yard, company officers have been taught courtroom procedure, external cardiac massage, emergency birth delivery, and radiological monitoring.

Because most of the firefighters' everyday instruction comes from their own company officers, a 30-hour course in instructor training was given to 44 San Jose and 14 County fire officers during January and February 1959. The State Department of Education sent Instructor Carl Kistle down to spend ten days on the fine points of lesson planning, teaching methods, occupational analysis, etc. Subsequently, 40 officers from San Jose completed a one-semester course in Municipal Fire Administration, taught by Dr. Wilton Cook, the city's consultant in education. One group of 16 Captains and District Chiefs scored straight A's, an achievement unmatched by any other Fire Department.

All of this is a long way from the one-time "on the job" training consisting of learning how to hang onto a hose line!

At the old Fire Department Training Center, West Virginia Street: Truck 5 during a drill session.

Besides the classroom work, and the company or tower drills (currently totalling 30,000 man-hours annually), newly appointed firefighters underwent a 180-day probationary period followed by a stiff exam, then another 6 months of concentrated training. All department personnel spend four hours twice a month at the drill tower. The probationary period was later changed to one year.

Retirement Recap

After Ron LeBeau's elevation to top command, one of the two Assistant Chief's posts remained open for some time. On September 6, 1961, City Manager Hamann announced the selection of 43-year-old John F. Knapp to fill the vacancy. Knapp got the job, over close contenders Tony Sapena and Tom Higgins, because of seniority (20 years' service) plus an edge in administrative experience—he had initiated San Jose's Junior Fire Marshal program and the 1949-1951 "Toys for Joy" campaigns, and had spent two years in OCD liaison work.

Captain Jim Westerhouse and the crew of Engine 1, checking out the rig at the drill yard.

Other events of late 1961; Chris Shannon was officially named Drillmaster, freeing Chief Russ Lunsford for full-time Civil Defense management. Veteran Fire Prevention Bureau Chief Ogden was due to retire soon, and John Gerhard was chosen to replace him. New permanent stations for Engines 9 and 18 went out to bid, while Architects Kress and Winston were hired to design quarters for Engine 19.

The big news, though, was the second and by far the knottiest of the legal issues faced by the City Council during the 1960's — a "final" solution to the Police-Fire Retirement problem. One confusing development followed another in an atmosphere of comic opera, not without repercussions to this day.

In the late summer of 1961, after a year's negotiations between the City Council's finance committee and Police Chief Blackmore's fire-police pension group, a new retirement plan had been submitted to the Council. Increased survivorship benefits—pensions payable to families of deceased retirees — had been agreed upon, but were so costly the city couldn't afford to put them into effect immediately. Therefore, the rates were "escalated" —rising 25% per year for four years until the new rate (half pay) was reached. At the end of the four years the city's contribution to the benefits would total $400,000 annually.

One of many bones of contention was the plan's requirement for a Council vote during each of the four years, to carry out the escalation process. The pension committee, understandably, preferred future Councils bound to escalate without a vote.

Realizing that these things were going to take some ironing out, Blackmore's committee on July 30, 1961, asked the Council to postpone adoption of the plan until "later in the year." Instead, some $220,000 in pay raises was requested. All city employees did get a 2.9% increase effective October 6.

Then, a month later, the Council enacted a 90-page ordinance — the fruit of years of work by a host of officials and committees. Besides the survivorship benefits, provision was made for 20-year veterans to retire at 55 on half pay, and for similar retirement for any service-connected disability.

It looked good, at first. Then the Santa Clara County Taxpayers' Association rose in protest. "Hold off for a while," urged Association president Joe Levitt, seconded by

Counsel Mel Hawley. Levitt said merely that "The ordinance is lengthy, and has just been printed; we're not opposing the plan—we just need some time to study its implications."

Hawley wasn't so non-committal. It looked to him like the new scheme would cost taxpayers almost as much as the Proposition F defeated in 1958. Officials estimated the city's share of the bill would about double the half million dollars budgeted for the existing plan.

Mayor Paul Moore readily granted a delay for further study. After the Association spent a month trying to figure out the details, it requested further cost data from the city. "It's a bit rich," admitted City Manager Hamann, acknowledging that the program could eventually cost the city $2000 per employee per year.

By a 6 to 1 vote on December 11, the Council tossed the hot potato back to its Finance Committee. That group bogged down in a lengthy, heated session punctuated by frequent clashes between Fire Captain Marks and Joe Levitt. After another day, the ship of state all but foundered on the shoals of confusion. In desperation, the Finance Committee tried to pass the buck on to a newly created "Citizens' Financial Structure Study Committee."

That group washed its hands of the matter, saying loftily: "If the appropriate municipal authorities have already been fully satisfied as to the propriety of the benefits offered, the cost to the City and the source of revenue from which such benefits are to be paid, the committee sees no reason to comment either for or against the plan."

So the Finance Committee wearily started over again. Fire-police organizations reported shortly after Christmas that a 300 to 0 "vote of confidence" had authorized their negotiating teams to strike a "final bargain" with the City Council on pensions. The same day, the ponderous ordinance, within a hair's breadth of final adoption only a few weeks earlier, was junked; an alternative proposal built around $\frac{3}{8}$ instead of $\frac{1}{2}$ pay was given preliminary approval in January 1962.

Calling for an actuarial expert to verify costs, Taxpayers' Counsel Hawley declared, "This program will . . . bankrupt the city!" Charges and counter-charges of "political deals" flew through the air during the ensu-

Typical young fireman Dennis Madigan trains for a Sunday Drill. Following in the footsteps of John Cunan and Larry Campbell, Madigan's scrapbooks unofficially record the deeds of the San Jose Fire Department for the use of future historians.

ing days. But there was little argument on the plan itself—it was too complex for anybody to argue about. In a feature editorial, the San Jose Mercury claimed that "After diligent search, the Mercury-News has been unable to find out what the newly amended pension plan will cost this year, next year or for the next century. Nobody knows. We don't know; the staff personnel at City Hall don't know . . . Much more study and many more answers are needed."

Nevertheless, the Council unanimously adopted the final ordinance January 8, 1962 —in a form which left future Councils free to disapprove the remaining steps of escalation. Then the next blow fell. Necessary publication of the 24,400 word ordinance in a local legal newspaper was invalidated by partial garbling of the text, requiring repetition of the entire adoption procedure!

While this was being done, Captain Marks continued to pledge fire and police efforts towards still further pension benefits, noting that the disputed legislation was only a "small step, but definitely in the right direction."

The controversy is far from ended, even now. Councilmen didn't enact the second escalation step during 1963. Furthermore, a couple of deaths since 1962 have shown inadequacies in the very survivorship benefits which were so long debated. When Firefighter Donald Carerra was killed in October 1963, his widow was unable to collect city death benefits until her state workmen's compensation payments were used up at a pro-rated monthly amount which could have lasted 17 years. A sympathetic City Council changed the law to eliminate this problem. Other special legislation was passed in April 1964, to aid Gene Sawyer's family.

Then in mid-1964, when retired veteran Wiliam Ogden died, Chief LeBeau appeared before the Council to point out the plight of Ogden's widow—subsisting on $77 monthly. Said LeBeau, "The Council has a moral obligation to augment this survivor benefit." Agreed Councilman Hathaway, "It's a disgrace to the city . . . that widow had to apply for welfare to get along." And so another administration "study" was ordered.

Closing in on Class III

On the last day of 1961, San Jose experienced an event which would have been a rarity in any city's history — a 3-alarm fire involving a single private residence. Forty-seven firemen and 17 pieces of apparatus took 3 hours to subdue the flames.

The 50-year-old Leet mansion was, of course, no ordinary residence. It stood on a wooded, 8-acre plot at 1550 The Alameda, developed in the 1850's as the estate of Judge Craven P. Hester, from whom San Jose's Hester District took its name. Built at a cost of $175,000, and boasting 17 bedrooms, the rambling, tile-roofed mansion had stood vacant for a decade — prey to vandals and vagrants.

Alarms at 11:12, 11:17, and 11:25 a.m. were followed by calls for more water pres-

A fireman's job is facing danger. A training accident cost the life of Firefighter Donald Carerra at this spot in 1963.

sure, as firefighters used half a dozen hand lines plus a ladder pipe to get the fire under control. Most operations were from outside the building as the heavy tile roof threatened to collapse. Firefighter William Meyers was hurt by falling bricks when a towering chimney collapsed.

During the next few months, fires were few, but additions to San Jose's fire force came in rapid succession. To serve fast-growing south side areas, such as the Seven Trees subdivision, stretching to the IBM plant on Monterey Road, a temporary Engine 18 was established in January, operating from a garage in a new branch Corporation Yard at Monterey and Snell Roads.

Coverage for Piedmont Hills, northeast of Berryessa, was provided by another leased residence firehouse — No. 19. Not even a garage was used for the apparatus here; Engine 19 was sheltered by a carport alongside the house at 3432 Vesuvius Ave.

In February, 1962, out towards Cupertino, a permanent 2-door drive-through station was completed for Engine 14 on Saratoga Ave. opposite Doyle Road. In March, "Snorkel and Ladder 1," with its 85-foot elevating platform and 220 feet of ground ladders, replaced Truck 1 at Market Street. Once again all the aerials were reshuffled, the 1946 75-footer winding up as a new Truck Co. No. 4 at Station 10.

Snorkel and Ladder #1 has performed Herculean duty since its arrival in 1962. Here it is used by the crew at the ALCO-Paramount fire, February 12, 1970.

At Left, when the Snorkel-Ladder truck arrived in 1962, the beams of the Central Fire Station had to be notched to get the equipment through the building.

In the basket of Snorkel and Ladder No. 1, Capt. George Bradford and Engr. Jess Cordoni douse the Western Prepack blaze, a four alarmer, October 1970.

It isn't only the older rigs that need shop attention. In this 1964 photo, the two-year-old Snorkel 1 gets a clutch overhaul.

198

By July of 1962, this microwave antenna had been installed at Engine 17 for the Mt. Chuai fire alarm link.

The microwave relay antennas at the Mt. Chuai station. Top dish transmits and receives between the mountain top and downtown; bottom dish handles the beam to the outlying firehouse 17.

During the Spring and Summer, plans for permanent stations 6 and 15 were approved, and bids were received on a permanent Station 18. The 1962-63 Fire Department budget topped $2.5 million, with the addition of 3 Captains and 7 Firefighters to the 299-man force. Proposed capital improvements for San Jose, totalling $14 million, included $207,000 for fire equipment and expansion of the department shop.

All these improvements pushed San Jose ever closer to the goal of a Class 3 fire rating —a goal seemingly within reach year after year, only to fade as the city's growth outstripped every firefighting advance. In 1962, it looked like there was a good chance to make the grade; one reason was a unique addition to the fire alarm system.

Fire Alarms Take to the Air

Having taken one unusual step that drew nationwide fire service attention, by its leased-residence temporary fire station program, San Jose scored another "first" in 1962 —the development of a microwave radio system for fire alarm transmission to outlying firehouses.

The city could not justify permanent municipal telegraph alarm circuits to its temporary stations, as far as ten miles from downtown. In most of the newly annexed suburban neighborhoods it would be years, if ever, before street box circuits would go in. The alternative — leased wires — was expensive, and rapidly becoming more so. For example, Engine 17, seven miles from alarm headquarters, needed three communications circuits: Vocalarm, telegraph, and a control circuit for a branch transmitter handling heavy police radio traffic (squad cars out that way were near the practical limit for radio transmission direct from downtown). Leasing these three wire circuits cost $150 monthly. Stations still further out required toll cables at higher cost.

Engine 18's temporary quarters also needed extra communications channels, including radio traffic for road repair and other work crews operating out of the branch corporation yard. Engine 19, in the east foothills, was also a natural for microwave.

The radio system put into operation in July 1962 uses a 6000 megacycle continuous wave signal, beamed from alarm headquarters to an unattended relay station 18 miles away atop 3600-ft. Mt. Chuai near Loma Prieta peak. From there, the signal bounces back down to an antenna atop the firehouses—Engine 17 was tied in first, later Engines 18 and 19.

This beam is modulated by equipment permitting simultaneous transmission of as many as 600 2-way conversations, or a mixture of voice communication with many other types of signals. Sending the fire alarm telegraph signals to the conventional register tape receiver at the firehouse consists simply of converting the electrical impulses to a set of tones, which go out on the microwave beam. At the station, similar converting equipment reverses the process. Fully transistorized except for one transmitting tube, the compact sending and receiving units only require 200 watts of power at each station; the mountain-top relay equipment draws 500.

For reliability, a separate transmitter at the firehouse feeds each received alarm automatically back downtown via the same beam (transmission and reception can occur simultaneously!). There, it bangs out on a register tape right alongside what was originally sent out—while that original is still being transmitted. Dispatchers can immediately spot any disagreement between the two.

Battery power backs up commercial electric lines to keep the equipment working at each location. On Mt. Chuai, a propane-fueled standby generator starts automatically if power fails. Trouble lights at headquarters are triggered via microwave whenever trespassers open the relay station doors, battery voltage falls too low, or other troubles occur. The trouble-free operation of the system has been a tribute to its design and installation.

Equipment for Engine 17's initial link cost $38,000, plus another $13,000 for the fireproof relay station. Land for the latter was leased for $100 monthly. With only Engines 17, 18, and 19 tied in, the equipment would pay for itself in 25 years. However, with continuing city growth and use of microwave channels for non-fire use, the investment should be justified sooner.

Another new one — Engine 9 at Hillsdale and Ross Aves., Oct. 1963.

Station 10 on South Monroe Street, mid-1961.

Engine 15's quarters on Blaney Avenue at Rainbow Drive, October 1963.

200

It was Project Engineer Dick Moore, now in charge of all city communications, who originally "sold" the use of microwave in 1960. His idea was for the radio beam to serve many municipal needs with fire alarms as a specialty. His reason was: "Firehouses are the natural terminals for this relay system, because of their strategic locations around the city. Some of them are being built on the same property with branch libraries and other outlying city offices, which also need communications facilities that my department will have to supply." (An example was Engine 9; its $108,000 permanent quarters at Ross and Hillsdale Aves., sharing a site with a new branch library, opened in August 1962.)

Because of the many information channels in the beam, selective fire alarm transmission is readily accommodated. In this system, adopted in mid-1963, only those firehouses due to respond to an alarm actually receive that alarm.

Underwriters' acceptance of the microwave scheme was in doubt. Experts who visited San Jose to look over the system withheld any comment. Chief LeBeau, however, was optimistic, saying, "The new microwave relay will make a big difference in whether or not we get up-graded. What held us back before was a Class 5 rating in two areas, one of which was Communications."

When the Underwriters' survey results were published in November 1962, LeBeau's optimism was justified. From a total of 230 deficiency points in the alarm system, San Jose dropped to only 91 points; overall, points dropped from 1624 to 1334—and the coveted Class 3 rating was achieved at last. Commented Underwriters Assistant Chief Engineer Carl A. Weers, "I am amazed that a city growing as fast as San Jose could improve its rating when, during such a period, it is difficult even to maintain one; the city is to be complimented."

The Fire Zone Squabble

While the microwave system, new fire companies, and apparatus like the four 1000 GPM LaFrance pumpers ordered in November 1962 for $79,859, had tipped the scales in San Jose's favor, there was another significant rating area where we looked much worse in 1962 than we had in 1955—the matter of building laws.

Permanent home of Engine 14, at Saratoga Road & San Tomas Aquino Road, 1962.

Chemical 4's old house at 2nd and Jackson as it looks now. Not city property today, it is now a private club.

New Station 18 nears completion on Monterey Road; Spring 1963.

This pointed up the third legal problem which occupied the City Council. Basic to a community's regulation of building fire hazards is a definition of the high value areas where fire danger is most severe, where the most stringent building construction and maintenance practices must be followed. Beginning with the primitive fire ordinances of 1847 and 1850, this definition had always been the "fire limits" or "zones" setting the downtown area apart as the highest hazard. It was within this one district, the "Fire Zone 1" of the 1945 Code, that concrete walls, sprinkler systems, "basement hose openings," fire escapes, and similar measures had been required by law.

But in postwar San Jose, extremely high value, congested, multi-story commercial districts were going up in outlying neighborhoods far removed from downtown—and from Fire Zone 1. One good example was Valley Fair. What was even worse, entirely through oversight the city's latest Fire Prevention Code, adopted in March 1962, completely omitted any fire zones at all!

When the Underwriters rating staff arrived in the summer of 1962 to re-survey the city, they pointed this out to fire officials. On August 6, the City Council hastily passed an emergency ordinance to reinstate the zones, taking the opportunity to add suburban commercial areas so as to double the size of Fire Zone 1.

There arose an immediate storm of protest from contractors and builders, faced with costly revisions to make work in progress conform to the new requirements. Backing off, the Council rescinded the new zones August 13 and reinstated the old, pending public hearings and other review. That brought a cry of alarm from Fire Prevention Chief Gerhard, who said the delay could jeopardize the city's upgrading in the Underwriters' survey.

However, Assistant City Manager John Knofler wangled a 3-week reclassification delay to give San Jose time to adopt the revised fire zones. As public hearings were scheduled, there was dark muttering that the expanded Zone 1 was a "plot" to hinder outlying commercial competition with downtown through higher building cost. Flooded by complaints from suburban developers, Councilman Joseph Pace called for the proposal to be "studied

very carefully," adding that "It's possible we can't afford this much in fire prevention."

As the deadline neared for a final vote, pressure continued to mount against the change, despite the valiant efforts of fire officials and the City Manager's staff. Finally, on September 11, the Council rejected the expanded zones by a 4 to 3 vote, going along with the view of the Stevens Creek Boulevard Association that the changes would "seriously hamper huge developments and threaten millions . . . already invested."

That didn't end the issue, even though the Class 3 rating was reached. A "City Fire Zone Committee," appointed to study the problem, recommended a compromise plan in April 1963—omitting such controversial areas as Town and Country Village from Fire Zone 1, but putting all the city's commercial construction in a less restrictive Zone II. It was June 1964 before this finally became law.

Downtown Disaster

In spite of shortcomings in building codes, San Jose's firefighters chalked up impressive performances during a rash of multiple alarms in the early months of 1963. Only 32 minutes into the New Year, a hot 2-alarm fire destroyed the Delta Sigma Phi fraternity house — fortunately empty at the time — at 124 S. 11th. Nearby dwellings on the crowded block were saved by fast work of 31 firemen. The owner of an adjacent student residence called the "Halls of Ivy" praised firemen for saving his property, and for cleaning up the mess made in operating hose lines from his windows.

Next, at 9:48 p.m. January 17, was a 2-bagger originating in a defective heater at 340 Little Market Street, controlled in ten minutes, but causing a $97,000 loss to the Western Manufacturing Co.

Lumber company fires have always plagued San Jose. Here the Willow Glen Lumber Company fire burns at Willow and Bird Avenues, September 24, 1966.

At 3:20 a.m. January 21, the first of three alarms sent Engines 3-13 and Truck 3 to the Sun Garden Packing Co., 1582 S. First, where they found flames pouring from a 40,000 square foot warehouse. Second alarm response was Engines 1-4, Truck 2; Engines 6-11 came in on the third, followed by a call for Salvage-Light Unit 1. Truck 2's ladder pipe kept fire from spreading either to the roof of the adjoining cannery or across a 25-foot driveway to a stack of 100,000 fruit boxes. Exposures to the south were guarded by hand lines and a monitor stream. Cause of the $337,000 blaze, which completely destroyed the one story warehouse, was never learned.

March was even rougher. Three alarms were sounded early on the morning of the 11th for a stubborn, smoky fire that did $152,000 damage to the gymnasium, shower and locker rooms at Camden High School on the far southwest side. Believed to have been burning for two hours before a passing patrolman discovered it at 3 a.m., the blaze was controlled by 38 firemen in 45 minutes, but took all morning to mop up. Responding were Engines 4-6-9-10-13-17, Trucks 2-4; four 2½-inch lines were used, each almost 1000 feet long.

Arson was the obvious cause. Empty beer bottles at the scene, plus office files and other debris in the swimming pool, pointed to vandals as the firebugs. Within a few days, two brothers aged 11 and 13 confessed setting the fire accidentally with paper torches they were using while looting the locker room. Eventually, their confession led to roundup of a major juvenile crime ring in the Cambrian area.

Worst trial of the year for firemen, however, involved no fire at all, but a disastrous downtown boiler explosion. Three persons were killed outright and 71 injured, of whom two later died. Damage totalled several hundred thousand dollars. The blast occurred March 22 in the basement furnace room of the 3-story concrete and steel J. C. Penney building at First and Santa Clara Streets, at 4:49 p.m. Scores of rush hour shoppers and office workers in and around the building were knocked over like tenpins. A 900 square foot hole was ripped in the floor of the Thrifty Drug Store directly over the furnace room.

The 16-year-old boiler itself was one of a pair in the building's central heating system. Its safety valves were set to "pop off" at a maximum pressure of 30 psi and temperature of 250 degrees. In charge of the installation was an attendant who that same afternoon had been told by Penney's management that boiler maintenance was henceforth to be contracted out, and that his services would no longer be required. This employee admitted later that he then left the store, about 4 p.m., after locking wide open the boiler's fuel and blower controls. However, criminal charges against him were dropped when it became impossible to prove that his actions caused the explosion.

In his own defense, he claimed that the boiler's automatic controls had not functioned properly for several days. Similar trouble had occurred with the companion boiler, then shut down for repairs.

Penney floor manager Raymond Mauss went downstairs shortly before the blast for a last minute checkout with the attendant, but couldn't find him. Opening the boiler room door, he saw the room filled with escaping steam. At once, he telephoned the San Jose Fire Department, then ran through the basement shouting for everyone to clear the building.

San Jose Communications dispatched a full first alarm assignment at 4:45 p.m.: Engines 1-2-11, Hose 1-2, Snorkel 1, Truck 2, and District Chief Gerald Murphy. At 4:49, as Engines 1 and 11 rounded the corner a block away, the boiler exploded. Firemen saw all the show windows along the sidewalk erupt across the street in a cloud of steam and dust; two hundred feet of glass "seemed to billow out for a moment and then mannequins flew out into the street."

As the companies pulled up, firemen streamed into the Thrifty and Penney stores to aid scores of injured—many of them cut by flying glass. Inside the darkened drug store, victims were trapped by timbers, pipe, and other debris. Some had fallen into the basement, from which the last body was not recovered for an hour.

Engine 11 radioed for all available ambulances; as many as 17 were en route at one time. Under the city's disaster plans, the four San Jose hospitals began calling in extra doctors to treat the flood of patients.

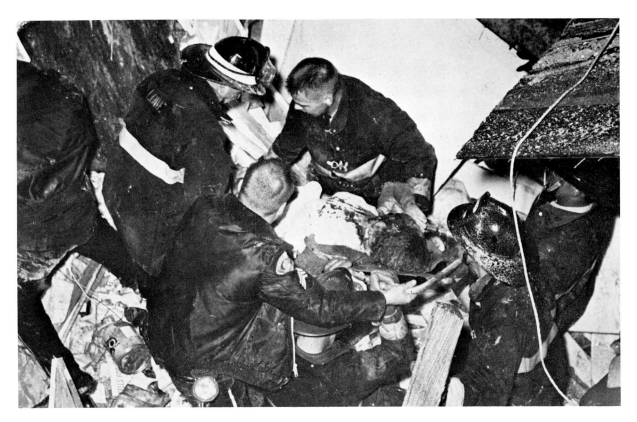

J. C. Penney explosion, March 22, 1963 — 5 dead, 71 injured. Firemen and police remove fatally injured victim minutes after the explosion.

When Assistant Chief John Jones arrived from Market Street, he ordered a third alarm to bring more manpower and equipment for prolonged rescue and overhaul operations. This summoned Engines 3-4-8-13, Hose 3, Truck 3, Chief LeBeau, and two more District Chiefs. Salvage-Light Unit 1 was special-called at 5:02 to floodlight the area, remaining at the scene for more than 24 hours. This unit also operated submersible de-watering pumps to clear basement areas flooded by broken mains and sprinkler piping before firemen could shut off valves.

The force of 50 firemen was aided by 120 police and sheriff's deputies in extricating blast victims from the basement via ladders and Stokes stretchers. Firemen administered oxygen on the spot to a number of the unconscious, and helped remove stocks of narcotic drugs from the store debris.

Despite drizzling rain, huge crowds of curious bystanders formed outside. Finally, streets were completely closed to vehicular and pedestrian traffic for several blocks, while nearby buildings were evacuated (at first it was thought that leaking gas from broken piping might cause further explosions).

Most fire companies were released by 8:30 p.m., after it was determined that no more victims remained in the ruins, but Trucks 1 and 3 continued overhauling chores most of the night. Five firemen suffered minor injuries, including Capt. William Lamb of Truck 3 who fell through the hole in the drugstore floor.

Investigation of the blast centered around failure of the safety valves to operate under the "forcing" of the fire with wide open fuel and air controls. Supervising Engineer A. I. Snyder of the California Division of Industrial Safety was called in to look at the valves, but they were so badly damaged that he could draw no conclusions. Laborious sifting of the basement rubble by firemen and police investigators produced a truckload of broken boiler parts, study of which was inconclusive.

A few weeks after the fatal explosion, safety experts from the International Union of Operating Engineers, meeting in San Francisco, called for stricter State controls on the many such boilers in California, terming them "virtual bombs of fatal destructive power." Local law required inspection of high pressure units, and licensing of attendants, but was silent concerning low pressure boilers.

New San Jose ordinances were soon drafted to plug this loophole, plus a new State law sponsored by local Assemblyman Al Alquist. The City's new boiler law was finally in full use six years after the tragedy.

The Penney store, its basement departments a shambles, was closed for two weeks. Thrifty Drug was a total loss. Though that part of the structure itself remained sound, the entire store interior had to be rebuilt.

Another aftermath of the tragedy was a total of over $9 million in damage suits by blast victims against owners and managers of the stores and the building itself; litigation dragged on for years, with a number of out-of-court settlements running as high as $400,000.

Ironically, the Penney building had been built in 1946 on the site of the ancient fire-trap Knox Block. A generation of prophets had foreseen a conflagration there, but after this eyesore at First and Santa Clara Streets had been torn down, the handsome modern structure which replaced it gave the city a far greater catastrophe than the old building ever had.

Keeping 'Em Rolling

On April 16, 1963, a $13,174 contract went to D. Tomacci & Sons for an addition to the Fire Department Shop adjoining Station 3. The work was completed late in the year. Since the days when Engineer Art McQuaide and his set of hand tools kept the department's vehicles in repair, or even since the 1948 construction of two hose wagons in an abandoned stable, the shop operation had come a long way — from the 18 rigs in the pre-war department, to 1963 when the total reached 100 vehicles ranging from motorcycles and jeeps to fork lifts and snorkels.

Still in charge after 16 years was the first civilian Master Mechanic, Darwin Cecil — a tall, taciturn automotive expert whose leisurely drawl was no clue to his ability to get things done. Aided by several firefighter-mechanics, part or full time, Cecil carried out an impressive list of annual accomplishments.

Besides routine maintenance and repair, the shop in recent years designed and built the beautiful ten-foot replica of a 1920-vintage pumper —"Engine ½"— which has delighted the city's youngsters at school visits, in parades, and other public appearances.

Captain Howard De Camp, Jr., points to the control assembly which failed in the Penny's boiler explosion which killed five and injured 71, March 22, 1963.

Powered by a Crosley engine, with an operating water pump, the little rig carries a load of scale model hose specially made by Oakland's American Rubber Co. Rebuilding of San Jose's airport crash truck, the reserve service ladder truck, grease and light trucks; installation of air horns on all rigs during 1963—these were some of the other projects carried through by Cecil and his staff.

Latest major shop job was conversion of a 1952 Reo military 6 x 6 truck into a 1000 gallon tanker to be quartered with Engine 18. Reason for the new rig—first tanker ever used in the San Jose Fire Department—was a controversial annexation adding 40 square miles of rural territory to the city's southern outskirts, which took place in September 1963.

As the need for shop space grew, so did the need for office space. The roomy administrative offices at Market Street were bulging at the seams by 1963, and officials cleared off a lot, next door to Station 2, for erection of offices which would more than double the space available. (It wasn't used — eventual shifting of other municipal functions freed the Carlysle Street Emergency Aid Station building for new Fire Department offices in November 1964.)

Paper work had multiplied, along with the budgets (risen 500% in 16 years), the number of vehicles, and the firefighting problems; as one example, the Chief's annual report, a single typed page until 1933, has since grown into a handsomely bound illustrated volume of 70 pages.

The Men from Mars — Engine Co. 20 at San Jose Municipal Airport, with the Crash Truck and Cardox Jeep; 1963.

Protection for the Airport

With property acquired and taxiways being extended, the San Jose Municipal Airport was preparing in 1963 for main runway lengthening to 8000 feet. Already, small jet and large conventional cargo planes were using the facilities—in addition to scheduled passenger service by feeder airlines. Takeoffs and landings topped 20,000 per month, more than at any other airport in the San Francisco Bay Area.

To keep pace in its coverage of the terminal, the San Jose Fire Department opened Station 20 in May, fronting directly on the taxiway between hangar-service areas and the new control tower.

The $100,000 station is of one story, 4-door design. Apparatus includes a 750 GPM pumper (Engine 20), the former Navy crash truck with foam turret, and a CO_2-equipped jeep.

Direct "hot line" telephones link the station with the airport tower controller, the administration building, and the city communications center. Station 20 also has a loudspeaker system for monitoring radio traffic between aircraft and the tower.

Special training in aircraft fire fighting and rescue for Engine 20 personnel began before the station was opened. In an out-of-the-way corner of the field, firemen set up an old bus body simulating an aircraft fuselage. "We place dummies in the bus, set fire to it and then practice getting the dummies and the fire out," explained Captain Jim Mitchell. An all-day training session, including a foam demonstration, was conducted for 40 San Jose firemen by the chief of the crash unit at Alameda Naval Air Station.

Alarm response to the airport includes Engine 7. In turn, Engine 20 answers alarms in a limited industrial and residential area adjacent to the airport, via the main access road leading out both ends of the property and passing right behind the firehouse. When Engine 20 does go outside, Engine 7 moves up to keep the airport covered at all times.

Next to open was the $90,000 permanent home of Engine 18, followed by Engine 19's $50,000 station on Piedmont Road. With a day long fete at Calabazas Park, and a 3 p.m. flag raising ceremony with a speech by Mayor Welch, Station 15 was dedicated on July 4.

Three weeks later, a $108,000 Station 6 was ready for use, on Willow Glen property acquired for widening of Minnesota Ave. As part of the week-long celebration sponsored by Willow Glen business and civic leaders for the station's opening, San Jose held its first real Fire Parade at 6 p.m., July 26, 1963. Its line of march extended southward on Lincoln Ave. from Coe to Minnesota, then west to the firehouse. Featuring an impressive display of equipment of all ages, from communities throughout the North County, the Willow Glen Fire Parade was a failure in only one respect—not nearly enough people turned out to see it.

San Jose's Fire Department color guard led the way. Then, with screaming sirens and flashing beacons, the rigs moved out, red paint and chrome trim glinting in the late afternoon sun. The brand-new 1000 GPM Engine 6 and Central Fire District's Engine 15 provided the most modern touches. Resplendent in white chief's cap with silver badge, Sunnyvale fire buff Len Williams drove his 1929 Ahrens-Fox piston pumper, formerly of Ocean Grove, New Jersey, and brought to California by ship through the Panama Canal. Santa Clara volunteers, Campbell clowns with their Model T, hand engines and hose reels, plus San Jose's Engine ½, delighted the small fry along the route; scatterings of candy sent the kids scrambling. For older observers, Miss Campbell of 1963 and her attendants provided an extra eyeful.

Windup of the week's festivities was dedication of Station 6 on July 28, with speeches by Fire Chief LeBeau and City Manager Hamann.

Arriving in town along with Engine 6's new apparatus were the other three 1000 GPM tilt-cab LaFrance pumpers ordered late in 1962. Each featured a front-mounted soft suction. These were assigned to Engines 4, 9, and 14. Still another new company—Engine 21—was put in service, but without a station of its own. Intended to cover the Mt. Pleasant area north and east of Evergreen, No. 21 operated out of Station 16 pending final agreement on a Mt. Pleasant firehouse site. Twelve new firefighters were budgeted for Truck Co. No. 6, to be activated at Station 9 early in 1964 when a new 100-foot aerial arrived.

Engine and Truck 5, North 10th Street.

Ready for business: Station 6, Cherry Ave. at Minnesota, in July 1963.

City limits reaching out towards Milpitas and Alum Rock Park necessitated activation of Engine 19; its Piedmont Road station is shown here shortly after its 1963 completion.

Equipment gets into position to battle this two alarm Brake Shop fire which threatened the surrounding area in November of 1964.

Above and left page: Two-alarm Brake Shop fire on South First Street, November 1964.

Other long range plans, as the year drew to a close, called for a second brush fire tanker at Station 21, and a third at Station 19. Engine Co. No. 22 was to be built in the Almaden Golf Course area, where the rolling, wooded countryside was rapidly filling with homes and apartments, its residents caught up in squabbles over commercial development; Engines 9 and 17 had runs of several miles to answer alarms there.

Where was the money coming from? Sales tax revenues and city growth held firm, de-

The old and the new, 1884 to 1964. These three pieces of equipment were acquired in 1964 by the San Jose Fire Department. The new piece is the American LaFrance 100 foot aerial ladder. Chief Ron LeBeau accepts the antique rig donated by Dick Levin of Levin Machinery and Salvage Company of San Jose. Originally horse drawn, the 1884 steam pumper was made by the American Fire Engine Company and was modified to be used with the 1904 three-wheel Knox Martin tractor. This equipment was originally sold to the San Francisco Fire Department and used in the 1906 earthquake fire. Extremely rare, this piece of equipment is currently valued at $38,000 for insurance purposes. The 1926 Seagrave pumper (center) has been completely restored and is on display.

spite cutbacks in defense industries so vital to the local economy. The eight fire stations provided for in the 1957 bond issue—No.'s 5, 6, 9, 10, 14, 16, 18, and 20—were now complete, but much of the 1961 bond money remained unspent. And San Jose had no trouble selling its bonds. On August 21, 1963, $4.4 million worth went at the "most favorable" interest rate of 3.004%, considered par for "prime quality" California municipal bonds. Included in the sum was a $195,000 fire protection item. The sale, commented the local

press, "reflects high respect the financial community holds for the financial solidarity of the City of San Jose."

As for the firefighters themselves—3 years of effort towards a 56-hour work week ended in failure at the polls in a bitter 1964 election. But no one doubts the eventual adoption of the short week. Meanwhile, the men continue, unhesitatingly, to risk their lives daily for the safety of the lives and property of their fellow-citizens, just as they and their predecessors have done for 115 eventful years.

Epilogue

Near the end of 1963, two brief news items looked forward to the future, and glanced backward to the past. One announced the Fire Department's organization of an Explorer Scout Post specializing in fire protection. The handful of such posts existing around the country represent an effort to impress upon a coming generation the importance of the fire service, its career possibilities, and the impossibility of its functioning without public support.

The other item reported the death of retired Fire Prevention Bureau Chief William Ogden, 40 years a fireman under five different Fire Chiefs, co-author of the city's first modern fire code, and first head of the Bureau. So passed one of the last of an older generation.

During a quarter century's explosive growth, not only the men themselves but almost every visible sign of San Jose's pre-war Fire Department has disappeared: the stations, all but one; the equipment (rigs still undelivered in 1944 have been superseded and sold already). The city itself, in its administration, its economy, and above all in sheer size, bears little resemblance to the community of 50 or even 20 years ago. Everything has changed.

The years of change since 1963 can be summed up in these terms: another 30 per cent in city growth; more and bigger fires; and the crunch of tight money plus taxpayer revolt. In the Appendix can be seen most of the Fire Department's expansion, with addition of seven new fire stations, seven engine companies, three truck companies, and a fourth District; nearly 200 additional men have been added. Airport crash protection has been revamped with addition of new and exotic firefighting chemicals and techniques.

The Department's annual budget now tops $5 million.

Other changes evident from Appendix VIII are the shifts of District Headquarters locations, and the renumbering of units so that all companies in one station bear the same number. This has long been the practice in Los Angeles County.

To match the new men and the new apparatus, other men and institutions have departed. Darwin Cecil retired in mid-1966 after 18 years' service, his place at the helm taken by Gene Germano. (Cecil's sudden death January 26, 1972, was a loss to his many friends.) Former Chief O'Brien died in September 1964; Charles Plummer a few months later; the following year Art Gilbert and Civil Defense Director Lunsford both died. On February 11, 1967, the oldest man in service in the Department died of cancer: District Chief George Vitek, age 63 and due to retire later that year after 43 years on the job. Another death in 1967 reflected a situation of increasing impact on San Jose and the rest of the nation — Firefighter Don Phipps of Engine 16, on military leave, was killed in Viet Nam. Finally, Chief LeBeau retired October 1, 1970, to be replaced by long-time Deputy John Jones.

The shop outgrew its quarters behind Station 3, moving in 1964 to the old Pacific Truck Service garage at Park Ave. and Montgomery Street. Expecting to lose the drill yard and tower site through extension of the Guadalupe Freeway, the city bought the Pacific property in early 1965 for relocation of the Training Center.

In May of that year, the Firemen's Rodeo drew record crowds. But behind the crowds lurked growing difficulty in making ends

Chief John Jones

meet. In a surprise announcement December 1967, after 13 years of operation, the Rodeo Association called it quits—the performances no longer made money.

More honorary firemen were created—longtime photographer and engine-chaser Rocky Santoro got the honor in July 1966. Maestro Arthur Fiedler, honorary member of 250 fire organizations, received his badge (plus coat and helmet) while here with a Pops symphony concert in July 1968. Following the lead of most of the nation's major cities, there is now even a "buff" club in the area—the Fire Associates of Santa Clara Valley, who among other things are doing a great job of coffee service to firefighters at greater alarms throughout the County.

The city's continuing growth didn't please everybody. After a hard four-month campaign, the Feb. 1968 annexation election in the bayside community of Alviso resulted in a vote of 189 favoring joining San Jose, 180 against. (Elections in 1961 and 1962 had rejected consolidation.) But the opponents refused to give up. While San Jose took over, establishing Engine 25 in the old volunteer fire hall during February while its crew lived in a nearby motel, challengers took the election to court where in March a judge ruled the vote was proper.

San Jose then built a permanent (remodelled residence) fire station during the Spring of 1969. But dissidents continued their fight. All the way to the California Supreme Court it went, where in September 1970 the high tribunal ruled the lower court's finding was invalid and ordered a retrial of the case.

After almost three years of city rule, then, the entire annexation fell under a legal cloud. "How do you unscramble an egg?" was one city official's reaction.

As for the fires—we haven't the space to recount them all. The mere second alarm blaze had become commonplace by 1967. During one 4-week period of 1970 alone there were three 4-alarm fires.

But let's look at the landmark blaze, at least—the first 4-alarm fire in San Jose's history, Sunday June 6, 1965, fittingly destroyed in spectacular fashion one of the city's most historic buildings: the Crest Theater, at 57 N. First Street.

It hadn't always been the Crest. Senator James Phelan built the theater (fifth one erected in San Jose) during 1898. When it opened its doors in February 1899, and for half a century thereafter, it was called the "Victory" in honor of the nation's recent triumph in the Spanish-American War. The land had long been in the Phelan family; the Senator's father at one time owned most of the block.

To the cream of Santa Clara Valley society, seated in its plush boxes, the great names of the American theatrical world played on its stage for a generation. Ethel Barrymore, Maude Adams, and Lillian Russell appeared at the Victory. Starring in its first production was a young actor named Harry Langdon, who later became one of the silent screen's brightest stars. Lew Dockstader's Minstrels entertained San Joseans at the old Victory, as did the legendary Sousa's Band.

With the years during and after World War I, vaudeville came to the Victory, and then went its way in turn as the movies took over. But even into the 1940's occasional stage shows were presented. By 1950 the boxes were removed; in 1964, the latest in a long series of remodellings was completed for $35,000.

Crest Theater fire, June 7, 1965. Firemen vainly play a stream of water on the building as flames devour an upper section.

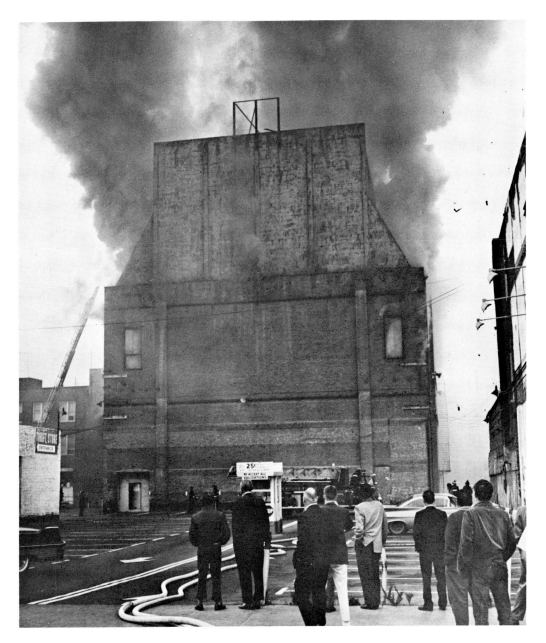

Spectators watch smoke from the Crest Theater fire.

On that final Sunday, a patrolman using a Market Street callbox happened to spot smoke curling from the eaves, beginning this sequence:

1st alarm Box 1111 8:57 a.m. Engs. 1-2-11, Hose 1-2, Trucks 1-2

2nd alarm 8:59 a.m. Engs. 4-13-3, Hose 3, Truck 3
(radioed by District Chief True as soon as he saw the building)
Transferring: Eng. 5 to 1, 18 to 3; Truck 5 to 1.

Special calls for Truck 5 and the reserve 1931 Mack were sent in, to get two 3-inch lines working into a ladder pipe at the rear of the theater.

3rd alarm 9:33 Eng. 8
Transferring: Eng. 16 to 8, 10 to 4, 14 to 10.

4th alarm 10:11 Eng. 5, Hose 5 (to check roofs downwind)
Transferring: Eng. 7 to 1, 14 to 7, 15 to 10.

Firemen at work on the Calvary Temple church fire, 1104 Kotenberg Avenue, April 10, 1965.

Truck (snorkel) 1 worked at the First Street front; Trucks 2 and 3 used ladder pipes at the rear north and south, and Truck 5 directly behind the building.

First-in Engine 1's Capt. George Lucchesi and his men took their line up the south staircase, but were stopped by heavy smoke. Said Lucchesi, "I checked the stair walls and they were starting to discolor. We opened up the wall and found the whole balcony floor going." A fog nozzle operated through the wall did no good.

Several firefighters working their way into the main floor narrowly escaped death as part of the balcony collapsed behind them; no sooner had they backed hastily into the lobby than the roof began to come down. Truck 2's

crew ventilating at the north side of the building left via exits as the floor there started to drop.

Although 53 guests were quickly evacuated from the adjoining Angelus Hotel, firefighters confined the blaze to the theater, which was a total loss. Its remaining walls were later knocked down by wreckers.

Also being demolished that year was a long tradition of easy bond financing for civic improvements. The bonds were still selling well. But voter resistance was beginning to materialize. City Manager Hamann proposed a $57 million capitol improvement issue in the Fall of 1965, which included nearly $1.9 million for the Fire Department—seven pumpers, an aerial, seven new stations, and many other

The aftermath of the Emerson Court explosion and fire, May 7, 1968. San Jose Senior Fire Inspector, James Friday, points to one of the locations where natural gas was detected flowing from house sewer vent. Below, damage was widespread to vehicles and other houses in the area.

necessities. Of the 12 measures on the ballot February 1966, however, only six passed, including the fire protection item. By fiscal 1968-9, the 1961 bond money had been used up, but though Hamann proposed $152 million in expenditures over the ensuing five years, less than half a million of that was for the Fire Department.

One of the things making it tough financially was the long-sought 56-hour work week for firefighters. After the refusal of the voters to adopt it in 1964, the Manager and Council worked out means to bring it about in stages over the next few years. By mid-1965, men were working only 60 hours while receiving 63 hours' pay. The final goal was reached January 1, 1969 when the work week was officially lowered from 58 to 56 hours.

Captain A. B. Jones, A. G. Anderson, and J. Spinler of Engine 5 and Truck 5 at Santa Clara Packing Company fire, February 4, 1969.

Another problem was the continuing difficulty of catching up to the growing city's needs. According to a Northwestern University study in mid-1967, Metropolitan San Jose was the nation's fastest-growing urban area. Chief LeBeau's budget request for 1966-67 sounded discouragingly like the complaints of Chief Plummer 30 years earlier, or of Chief O'Brien after World War II. "Fire Department too thin, understaffed" went the headlines.

Though 111 new firefighters were requested, even this was still 96 men short of the manning recommended by authorities. At least ten engine companies had only three-man crews. In outlying areas those three men might be all alone at a fire as much as seven minutes before help could arrive. Said Chief Jones, "It it just a matter of time until one of these undermanned companies will be unable to cope with the size of a fire . . . " (It was, in fact, a matter of just about three years' time, until an apartment house fire on the southern outskirts in Sept. 1970.)

This $500,000 blaze destroyed the Downtown Bowl August 19, 1969. Firemen using air masks on aerial No. 2 and the snorkel unit fought the stubborn fire with little success, but confined it to the bowling alley.

Said Hamann, "This is the toughest financial problem in my 16 years of administration." But worse was to come.

The City budget (over $68 million) and the property tax both set new records during fiscal 1967-68. In April of 1967, voters were asked to approve City Charter changes to allow a hike in the property tax rate—then at its legal ceiling. They turned thumbs down, leaving a million dollar hole in the budget.

Three years later money was even tighter. Aerospace cutbacks and a general recession shot down the Santa Clara Valley's high-flying economy. Unemployment in some areas hit 15 per cent. A utility tax bill, adopted in mid-1970 by the Council to ease the revenue pinch, was successfully challenged by initiative petition, and its fate is in doubt at this writing—threatening not just a hole, but a gaping $5 million void in annual income. New hiring has stopped.

By November 1970, even the fire protection bond issues weren't making it at the polls.

While some talk of "upturn" or "levelling off," hard times have arrived for a lot of San Joseans. Paradoxically, however, city growth continues, albeit at a somewhat slower pace. Population today is pushing half a million, sprawled over 128 square miles reaching from Alviso on the north to Morgan Hill on the south.

One thing is certain. Tomorrow's firemen, still better trained and equipped though they may be, will still need the interest and support of the people they serve. They will need morale, and tradition—which can only spring from some sense of past history. In its "forward look," San Jose tends to forget the past. Yet out of the service and the accomplishments of generations of men like William Ogden, Herman Hobson, Horace Damonte, Walter Page, Miles McDermott, John Cunan, Art McQuaide, and Gene Sawyer, must come the tradition and spirit that will sustain tomorrow's San Jose Fire Department.

⊰ THE END ⊱

Firemen disappeared into dense clouds of smoke to fight this difficult blaze at the Downtown Bowl, August 19, 1969. The only injuries were minor, suffered by Tom Schultz and Luke Goodrich.

220

FIRE DEPARTMENT—CITY OF SAN JOSE.

THESE ARE TO CERTIFY:

That *George Donner* was, on the *Sixth* day of *January*, 186*5* duly elected an Active Member of *Empire Engine* Company, No. *One*, attached to the

San Jose Fire Department,

and entitled to all the privileges granted by State and Municipal enactments.

C. P. Crittenden
President, Fire Department.

D. A. Leddy
Chief Engineer, Fire Department.

Jno. H. Gregory
Secretary, Fire Department.

San Jose, California, *March 23rd*, 186*6*

This fireman's certificate was awarded to George Donner in 1865. Donner was a survivor of the tragic Donner Party which was caught in the Sierra blizzards the winter of 1846-47. His namesake, Uncle George Donner, was the leader of the party who perished near Truckee.

George Donner II escaped with the "Forlorn Hope" party, and eventually made his way to San Jose, where many other survivors of the Donner party settled. He served with the Empire Engine Company during the middle sixties and is now buried in Oak Hill Cemetery in San Jose.

In Memoriam

Miles McDermott

Extraman, Eureka Hose Co.

Born New York State 1858

Killed Sept. 26, 1898

While manning a hose line with other members of his company on the second floor of the old Vendome Hotel on North First Street, shortly before midnight, Extraman McDermott was caught in the sudden collapse of the rear wall and three upper floors. Scalded and suffocated by steam, his body was not found till next day, under twenty feet of debris.

The general alarm fire in this showplace of the Garden City resulted in a $30,000 loss, causing injuries to several other firemen; fifty guests were safely evacuated.

McDermott's widow and three children were left almost destitute by his death.

❖

Paul Furrier

Foreman, Hook & Ladder Co. No. 1

Killed April 18, 1906

A member of the department since before its 1898 reorganization, Foreman Furrier (sometimes spelled Furrer) was on duty in the North San Pedro Street quarters of his company when the pre-dawn earthquake disaster of 1906 overwhelmed San Jose. Attempting to escape from the collapsing building, he was struck and killed by a falling section of brick wall.

Furrier was his widowed mother's sole support.

Chief Richard F. Brown

Born San Jose 1873

Killed Sept. 10, 1910

Perhaps the best-liked Chief Engineer the San Jose Fire Department ever had, Dick Brown was described as "a most zealous and efficient officer"; "a public official nearest the ideal"; "personally one of the most popular men in the city."

Son of an earlier chief of both the Police and Fire Departments in San Jose, Brown grew up in and around firehouses. Appointed Extraman of Franklin Engine 3 in 1896, he became Foreman in 1898. For the next three years he was a member of the police force, from which he was appointed Fire Chief.

Popular though he was, he was not without enemies in the rough-and-tumble ward politics of the day. Fired in 1904 for alleged abuses in department disciplinary procedures, he was restored to his post when a new city administration took over in July 1908.

Returning from the Coast Convention of Fire Chiefs in Stockton two years later, Brown detoured via San Francisco for the Admission Day Parade there. En route down the Peninsula in his Winton chief's car, accompanied by a local businessman, Chief Brown lost control of the vehicle near South San Francisco. It overturned, crushing him beneath it.

His funeral procession down San Jose's First Street, a mile and a half in length, witnessed by thousands, was unique in local history. A monument to his memory, paid for by popular subscription, is still to be seen beneath the shade trees of Oak Hill Memorial Park. Also liquidated by popular subscription was the mortgage with which his widow was left by his death.

In Memoriam

Acting Captain Fred W. Hambly
Chemical Co. No. 1
Born 1885
Died Jan. 21, 1921

Fred Hambly was a 15-year veteran of the fire service, when in November 1920 San Jose placed a two-platoon system into effect. During the resulting re-shuffle of assignments he was made acting Captain of his company.

On the evening of December 7, Capt. Hambly responded with Chemical 1 to a $250,000 fire in the F. W. Gross dry goods store at 52 South First Street. Groping through the darkened basement towards the seat of the fire, he was overcome by smoke and hot gases, and was dragged from the building by Captain (later Assistant Chief) Walter Page of Chemical 5.

Taken to O'Connor Sanitarium unconscious, Capt. Hambly rallied during the ensuing weeks. But late in January, after taking a turn for the worse, he died in Columbia Hospital from the injuries to his lungs sustained at the Gross fire.

❖

Fireman Peter Consolacio
Chemical Co. No. 6
Killed July 19, 1925

A large tree, its roots perhaps loosened by a minor earthquake, fell from an embankment in Alum Rock Park near the interurban car tracks, bringing down the trolley wire and an 11,000 volt feeder circuit which was broken at several points.

Sparks from the fallen wires started a ten-acre grass fire. Trying to put it out, two passersby were killed by accidental contact with the high voltage line. A fire alarm was turned in, and Chemical 6 responded from five miles away at 17th and Santa Clara Streets.

Unaware of the electrical hazard (the earlier victims having been removed by rescuers), Firemen Consolacio was using a chemical line on the fire when the stream contacted the downed wires. He was killed instantly. His widow later sued the city (owner of the park), as well as the power company, in an attempt to collect compensation for his death.

Chief Herman W. Hobson
Born San Jose Dec. 17, 1872
Died Oct. 7, 1926

During the early hours of September 16, 1926, much of the two-story Alliance Building at 3rd and Santa Clara Streets was gutted by flames that had evidently been smouldering for some time before discovery. Chief Hobson personally led the two-hour fight to control the $75,000 blaze.

The combination of his exertions, the cold night air, and the soaking spray from hose streams brought him down with pneumonia, from which he died within two weeks.

Herman Hobson's rise in the Fire Department was steady from the date of his appointment, December 31, 1908. The one-time sign painter, son of Santa Clara Valley pioneers, managed to escape the tribulations of so many fellow-firemen during those years. Soon he was a Captain, February 1910; Assistant Chief in January 1916; Chief in 1918. Hobson backed the successful effort to put his department on a two-platoon system, greatly improving morale as well as giving him reserves to call on during major emergencies.

One daughter survived him.

❖

Captain George Welch
Engine Co. No. 2
Born 1861
Died Sept. 18, 1929

Engine 2 received a midnight alarm of fire from a cottage at 430 North 4th Street. As the company arrived on the scene, Captain Welch "leaped from the engine as it stopped, took a few steps, stopped, and fell over," dead of a heart attack. Members of his company tried vainly to revive him, while the fire was easily extinguished.

Appointed Extraman in 1896, George Welch at his death was the oldest man in the department in point of service, having been stationed at North 3rd Street (Engine 1 until 1908, later Engine 2) for 33 years. He suffered a broken leg and head injuries in a porch collapse at the 1916 Gillespie Mill fire. In 1922 Welch became acting Captain, a rank made permanent a few months before his death.

In Memoriam

Fireman Starr G. Hilton

Chemical Co. No. 3

Killed Nov. 1931

Starr Hilton had planned to join the police force, but after passing his examinations in 1928 was instead assigned to the Fire Department.

He was driver of Chemical 3 (Capt. George Barber) when the company answered an alarm in the 4th Ward a few days before Thanksgiving, 1931. A car, either not hearing or not heeding the fire siren, drove into Hilton's path at the blind corner of Almaden and Grant Streets. Swerving in an unsuccessful attempt to avoid a collision, he was thrown from the driver's seat and crushed beneath the rig as it overturned.

Hilton's wife and family survived him. The fraternal Fire Department group, Starr Hilton Club, was later organized to perpetuate his memory.

❖

Fireman Donald E. Carrera

Engine Co. No. 10

Born San Jose 1932

Killed Oct. 13, 1963

Fireman Carrera, four years in the department, was taking part in hose evolutions during a company drill. In a freak accident, the end of a hose line whipped up to strike him in the forehead. He died that evening in O'Connor Hospital—leaving a widow and five children.

The City Council took special action during the following weeks to award full death benefits to Carrera's family, after these had been held up because of a conflict with state compensation payments.

The strain of battle: Capt. Merryle Wiese, Firefighter Hugh Smith, Capt. Dick Reimuth, and Firefighter Ronald Lane, Engine 5 and Truck 5, in action at the Place and Gera fire on E. Brokaw Road, July 2, 1968.

"Location of San Jose's fire companies in 1901."

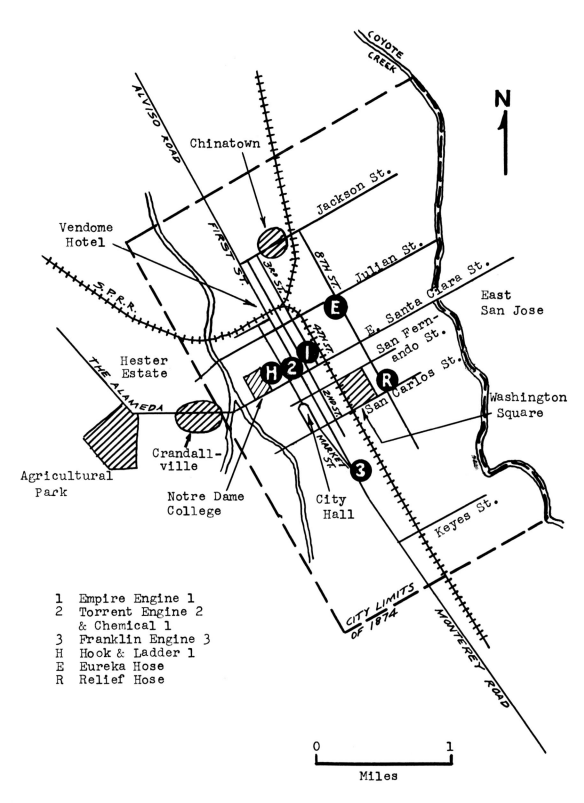

1   Empire Engine 1
2   Torrent Engine 2
     & Chemical 1
3   Franklin Engine 3
H   Hook & Ladder 1
E   Eureka Hose
R   Relief Hose

San Jose, 1901

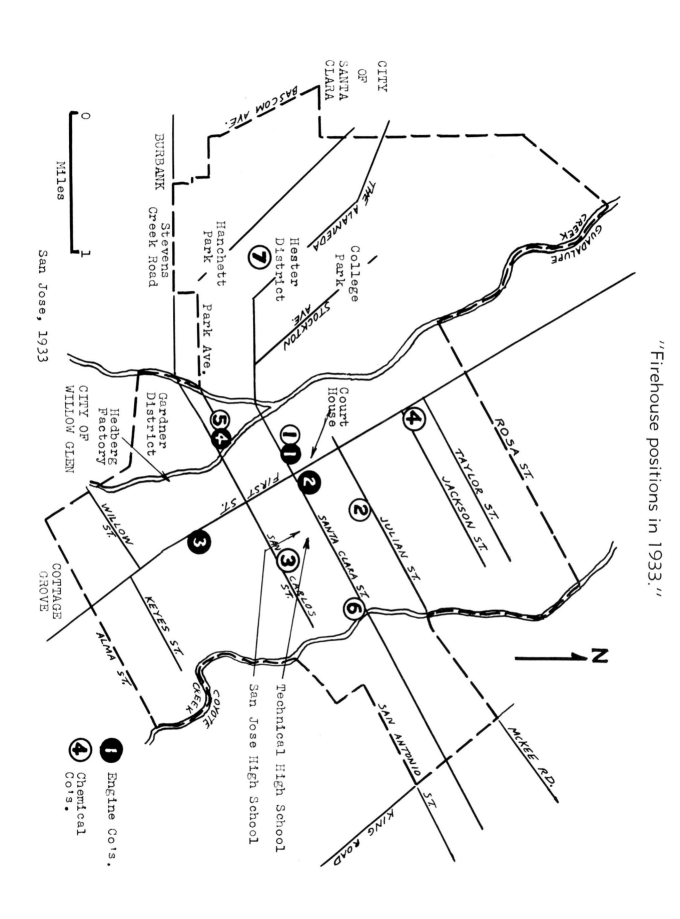

"Firehouse positions in 1933."

San Jose, 1933

227

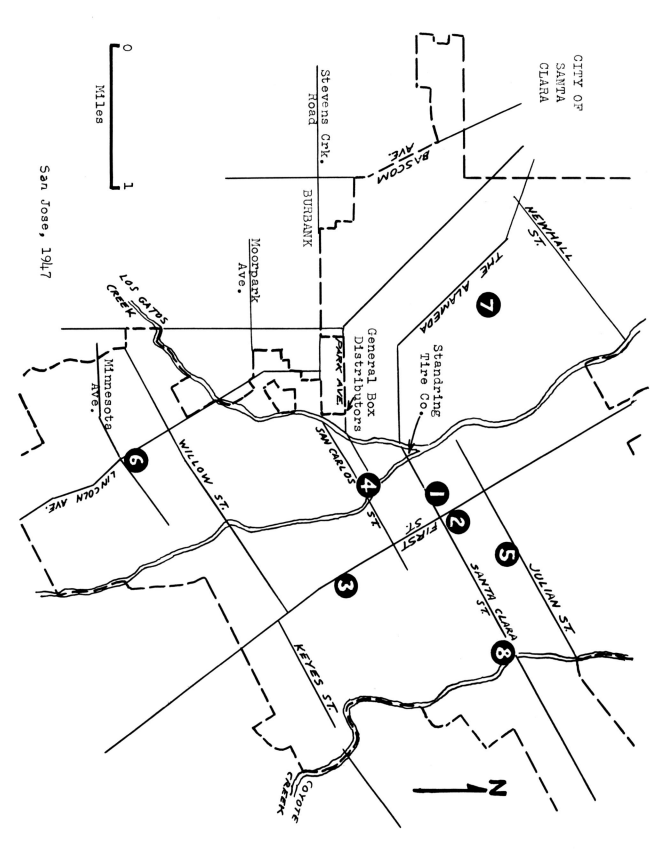

"1947 locations were not so very different."

San Jose, 1947

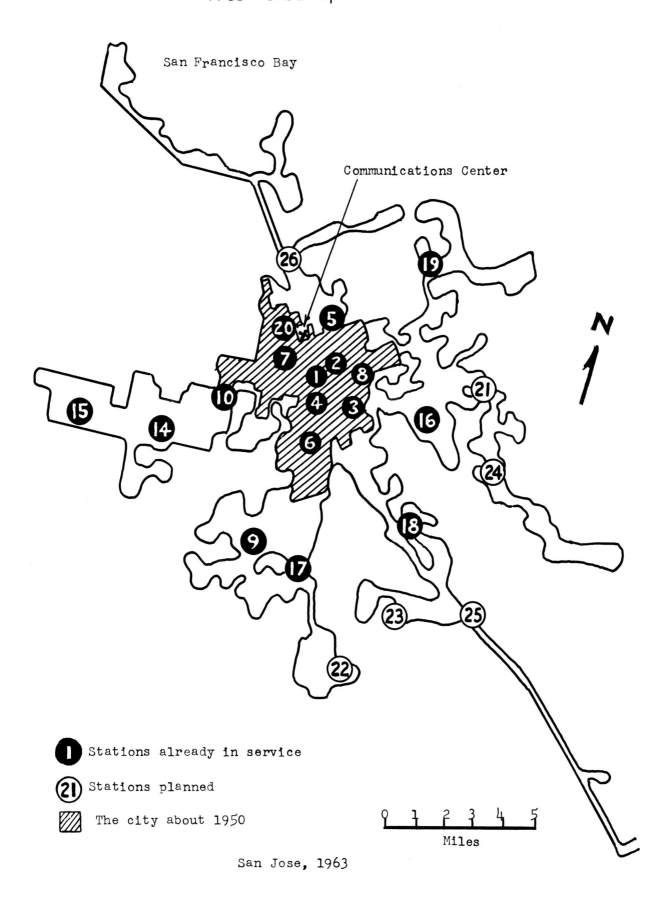

"1963 — Urban sprawl takes over."

San Francisco Bay

Communications Center

N

●1 Stations already in service

㉑ Stations planned

▨ The city about 1950

0 1 2 3 4 5
Miles

San Jose, 1963

"The big change, and still growing—city boundaries and fire stations in 1970."

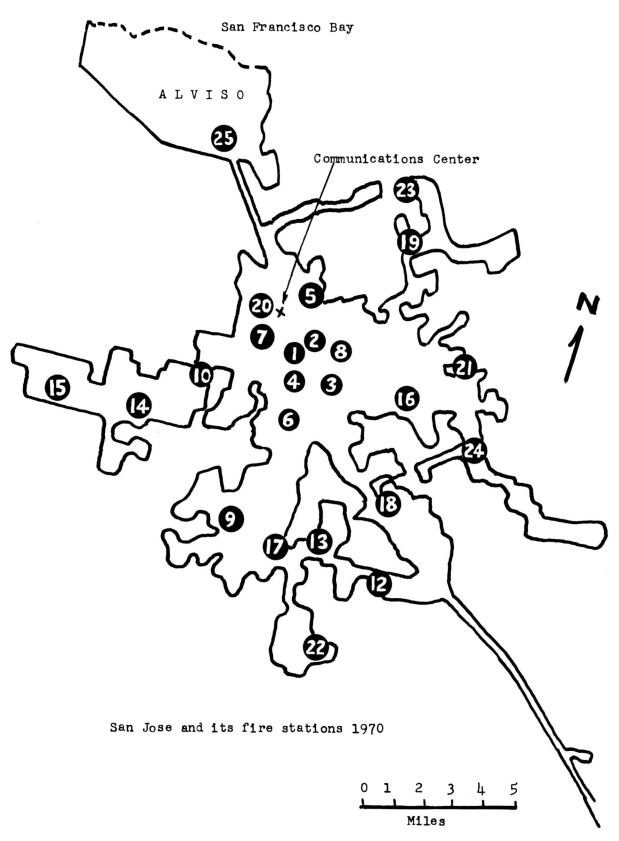

San Francisco Bay

ALVISO

Communications Center

San Jose and its fire stations 1970

0 1 2 3 4 5
Miles

Salon de Elegante Beauty Shop explosion and fire, 1093 Minnesota Avenue, January 25, 1970. Firefighters from Engine 6 prepare to put another 2½-inch hose line into operation on the fire following massive natural gas explosion which knocked out the front and rear walls.

APPENDIX I

Fifty Years of San Jose Fire Losses

Year Ending	No. Alarms	Bldg. Fire Loss	Population	Per Capita Loss
Dec. 31, 1914	184	$ 35,574.	45,000	$.79
Dec. 31, 1915	260	111,011.20	45,000	2.466
Dec. 31, 1916	280	83,130.37	45,000	1.847
Dec. 31, 1917	258	44,192.85	45,000	.982
Dec. 31, 1918		169,148	45,000	3.75
Dec. 31, 1919	346	25,448	45,000	.506(.566)
Nov. 30, 1920	343	84,406	45,000	1.875
Nov. 30, 1921	328	186,215	45,000	4.138
Nov. 30, 1922	324	66,070	45,000	1.46
Nov. 30, 1923	327	50,110	45,000	1.11
Nov. 30, 1924	320	193,028.07	43,000	4.49
Nov. 30, 1925	332	39,571.12	47,000	.84
Nov. 30, 1926	380	203,609.35	62,500	3.25
Nov. 30, 1927	404	54,151.40	62,500	.86
Nov. 30, 1928	410	178,490.34	67,000	2.67
Nov. 30, 1929	565	97,651.13	67,500	1.44
Nov. 30, 1930	444	160,308.81	60,000	2.66
Nov. 30, 1931	434	149,963.56	67,500	2.22
Nov. 30, 1932	507	165,331.15	62,500	2.64
Nov. 30, 1933	536	127,956	63,300	1.94
Nov. 30, 1934	486	47,780	63,300	.75
Nov. 30, 1935	530	99,506	64,849	1.52
Nov. 30, 1936	556	196,124	67,500	2.72
Nov. 30, 1937	665	55,267	75,000	.73
Nov. 30, 1938	556	58,357.50	77,000	.75
Nov. 30, 1939	652	81,532	77,650	1.05
Nov. 30, 1940	573	57,384	70,200	.81
Nov. 30, 1941	649	38,113	71,000	.536
Nov. 30, 1942	683	70,504	72,500	.972

Year Ending	No. Alarms	Bldg. Fire Loss	Population	Per Capita Loss
Nov. 30, 1943	531	$85,716	76,000	$1.12
Nov. 30, 1944	641	169,377.47	76,641	2.228
Nov. 30, 1945	653	177,122.91	78,687	2.25
Nov. 30, 1946	763	214,095.91	85,000	2.51
			(80,734)	
Nov. 30, 1947	747	180,534.35	85,000	2.13
Nov. 30, 1948	996	194,887.33	86,500	2.25
Nov. 30, 1949	1031	339,450.52	93,000	3.65
Nov. 30, 1950	968	126,019.49	95,020	1.33
Dec. 31, 1951	1107	289,277	98,520	2.94
Dec. 31, 1952	1179	518,540	102,148	5.07
Dec. 31, 1953	1476	204,487	104,448	2.00
Dec. 31, 1954	1348	640,548	107,000	5.99
Dec. 31, 1955	1328	869,597	135,000	6.44
Dec. 31, 1956	1602	290,535	137,000	2.28
Dec. 31, 1957	1847	231,439	140,000	1.65
Dec. 31, 1958	2379	1,142,989	158,600	7.21
Dec. 31, 1959	3094	669,607.78	190,000	3.52
Dec. 31, 1960	3911	985,589.37	204,000	4.83
Dec. 31, 1961	4847	1,351,180.71	250,000	5.40
Dec. 31, 1962	5604	772,043.30	270,000	2.86
Dec. 31, 1963	6312	1,975,292.00	310,000	6.37
Dec. 31, 1964	7450	1,248,923.96	320,000	3.09
Dec. 31, 1965	7816	1,666,252.24	342,000	4.87
Dec. 31, 1966	8907	1,574,503.90	380,000	4.14
Dec. 31, 1967	9219	1,540,536.21	400,000	3.85
Dec. 31, 1968	10,219	2,071,709.00	430,000	4.81
Dec. 31, 1969	11,533	2,535,415.00	445,000	5.70
Dec. 31, 1970	12,108	2,762,902.00	460,000	6.01

During the first 20 years of this table, there are occasional minor discrepancies between figures given in the Fire Department's record book and those in the annual reports. Note also the peculiar fluctuation in population figures between 1924 and 1942.

CHEMICAL 3 — 386 S. 8TH ST.
DEC. 26, 1947

234

APPENDIX II

San Jose Fire Department

Chief Officers

	Chief	Year	Assistant Chief
1.	C. E. Allen*	1854-	First Foreman of Empire Engine Co.
2.	J. B. Hewson*	1857-1858	First "Chief"
3.	Levi Peck*	1858-1863	
4.	J. C. Potter*	1863-1864	
5.	Adam Holloway*	1864-1865	
6.	Dan A. Leddy*	1865-1867	Jos. Ingham
7.	James V. Tisdall*	1867-1871	
8.	William Petry*	1871-1872	Jos. Ingham
9.	Barney Ward*	1873-1874	Geo. W. Zimmer
10.	J. Chris Gerdes*	1874-1876	
11.	J. Chris Gerdes	1876-1881	W. D. Brown, Jas. Brady
12.	William D. Brown	1881-1884	R. Hoelbe
13.	James Brady	1884-1888	J. Cunan, J. T. Moore
14.	Rudolph Hoelbe	1889-1892	John T. Moore
15.	James F. Dwyer	1893-1896	John T. Moore
16.	Henry Ford	1897-1901	Charles Brodie
17.	Richard F. Brown	1901-1904, 1908-1910	Joe McDonald, Frank Whiteside
18.	George E. Hines	1904-1905	
19.	George L. Tonkins	1905-1908	John Cavallero
20.	Edward Haley	1910-1918	F. Whiteside, H. Hobson
21.	Herman W. Hobson	1918-1926	C. Plummer, D. Cavallero
22.	Charles Plummer	1926-1944	D. Cavallero, Walter Page, Henry Lingua
23.	Lester A. O'Brien	1944-1957	A. J. Gilbert, E. Powers
24.	Arthur J. Gilbert	1957-1960	R. LeBeau, J. Jones
25.	Ronald B. LeBeau	1960-1970	J. Jones, J. Knapp
26.	John W. Jones	1970-	Leonard Marks (Dep. Chief)

*Volunteer. Note: The early records did not always distinguish between "Chief Engineer" and "President" of the volunteer fire department. Holloway, Ward, Leddy, and Tisdall were Chief Engineers; status of most of the others is uncertain.

ENGINE 8 — 802 E. SANTA CLARA ST.
NOV. 29, 1947

APPENDIX III

San Jose Fire Department 1901

Chief Henry Ford, Assistant Chief (Acting Chief) Charles Brodie

Acting Assistant Chief Claude Everett

Market Street Station (built 1855, remodelled 1868):
    Torrent Engine 2 with hose reel   Extramen:
        Captain Frank Hogan   Ben Connors
        Engineer H. R. Bates   D. Amador
        Driver Dan Durkin   H. McKee
        Hose cart Driver Charles Metzler   D. R. Knowles
        F. Hambly

    Chemical No. 1 (1894)
        Captain John Cavallero
        Lieut. John Kent (only such rank in department)
        Driver W. H. Farthing
        Fireman Frank Boronda

San Pedro Street Station: Extramen:
    Hook & Ladder 1   John Doyle
        Captain Wm. Sullivan   J. Lavin
        Driver George Hines   Frank Cox
        Tillerman Wm. Tennant   Alfred Bernal
        Claude Everett
        Paul Furrier

Third Street Station (built 1893):   Extramen:
    Empire Engine 1 (1898) with hose reel   Mike Zimmer
        Captain Jos. McDonald   D. McElwain
        Engineer Frank Munroe   John Gilleran
        Driver John Waibel   P. Narvaez
        Hose cart Driver George Welch   George Perry

North 8th Street Station (built 1874)   Extramen:
    Eureka Hose No. 1, reel   J. Carroll
        Captain D. Hayes   C. J. Walthers
        Driver E. Mangin   W. Fitzgerald

South 8th Street Station: Extramen:
    Relief Hose No. 2, 4-wheel wagon   Fred Salas
        Captain E. Salas   R. D. Clearwater
        Driver T. Kerr   W. McGinley
        R. Stillwell

South First Street Station (built 1889):   Extramen:
    Franklin Engine No. 3, with hose reel   Chas. Williamson
        Captain Wm. Basse   Jacob Walt
        Engineer H. Drexler   W. Cahden
        Driver Jas. J. Kell   J. Wilmer
        Hose cart Driver E. Frost, Jr.   A. Roberts

San Jose Fire Department, December 1920 *(2 platoons)*
Chief Herman Hobson, Assistant Chief Dominic Cavallero

Headquarters, 35 N. Market Street (built 1908):

Engine 1, 1920 Seagrave 750 GPM pumper

Hose 1, 1915 Federal chassis, 1½ ton, with monitor nozzle

Captain Louis Siebuhr	E. O. Stevens
Firemen William Mason	Harry Miller
Charles Madel	Jack Kent
C. C. Miramontes	R. H. Fishel

Chemical 1, 1915 Federal chassis, 1½ ton
Captain Fred W. Hambly
Firemen Reno Bacigalupi
Nicholas Berryessa
L. Rozzi

Truck 1, 1908 Am.-LaFrance 75-ft. aerial, 1915 Knox-Martin tractor
Captain Charles Plummer
Firemen A. Bernal
Robert Foley
J. Ryan
John J. Clunan

Squad 1, 1920 Model T Ford chemical wagon
Assistant Chief Cavallero
Firemen James O'Day
Carl O'Dell
Ed Terry
Gilbert Stewart

Station 2, 61 N. Third Street (built 1908):
Engine 2, 1908 Extra First Size Metropolitan steamer with 1914 Knox-Martin tractor
Hose 2, apparatus unknown, possibly 1915 Mitchell chassis

Captain G. Perry	George Welch
Firemen John Humburg	L. Horn
Sid Rainier	Peter Segard
George Sturges	M. F. Young

Station 3, 620 S. First Street (built 1908):
Engine 3, 1914 Seagrave 750 GPM pumper

Captain John Gilleran	G. H. Wehner
Firemen Lou Lunsford	John Gossett
John Wentzel	Thomas Higgins

Station 4, 254 Spencer Ave. (built 1908):
Chemical 5, 1913 Knox chemical wagon
Captain Walter Page
Firemen Theo. Haub
A. Bernal
Burnell Kunze

Station 5, 255 N. 8th Street (built 1913):
Chemical 2, 1915 Federal chassis, 1½ ton
Captain William Sterling
Firemen William Lennon
John Powers
Henry Anderson

ENGINE 4 — 254 SPENCER AVE.
NOV. 8, 1947

The fireman who raised the California Bear Flag upside down on November 8, 1947, will not be identified here, but he is now a Captain at Station 2. The drawings on pages 234, 236, and on this page are from the originals by Richard Nailen in the collection of Retired Captain Brad Jones.

Station 6, 386 S. 8th Street (built 1908):
    Chemical 3, 1915 Federal chassis, 1½ ton
        Captain Reuben D. Clearwater
        Firemen D. Curin
            Dean Hubbard
            F. Ballard

Station 7, 45 E. Jackson Street (built 1913):
    Chemical 4, 1913 Pope-Hartford chemical wagon
        Captain William Tennant
        Firemen L. D. Stewart
            C. Oxander
            F. Vacarrello

Station 8, 17th and Santa Clara Streets (built 1913):
    Chemical 6, apparatus unknown
        Captain Louis Bein
        Firemen Ed Powers
            Fred Salas
            E. Owens

APPENDIX V

San Jose Fire Department 1933

Chief Charles Plummer; Assistant Chiefs Dominic Cavallero, Walter Page
Headquarters, 35 N. Market Street:

Engine 1	1931	Mack 1000 GPM pumper
Hose 1	1927	Reo hose wagon with monitor nozzle
Chemical 1	1930	Reo chemical wagon, two 80-gal. tanks
Truck 1	1908	Am.-LaFrance 75-ft. aerial, 1931 White tractor
Squad 1	1920	Federal hose-chemical wagon

Station 2, 61 N. Third Street:

Engine 2	1922	Stutz 750 GPM pumper
Hose 2	1927	Reo hose wagon

Station 3, 620 S. First Street:

Engine 3	1920	Seagrave 750 GPM pumper

Station 4, 254 Spencer Ave

Engine 4	1914	Seagrave 750 GPM pumper
Hose 4	1930	Federal chassis, two 35-gal. tanks
(Chemical 5)		

Station 5, 255 N. 8th Street:

Chemical 2	1929	Dodge hose wagon

Station 6, 386 S. 8th Street:

Chemical 3	1931	Reo hose wagon, 60-gal. tank

Station 7, 1187 Hester Ave. (garage):

Chemical 7	1925	Reo hose-chemical wagon, two 35-gal. tanks

Station 8, 17th and Santa Clara Streets:

Chemical 6	1930	GMC hose wagon

Station 9, 45 E. Jackson Street:

Chemical 4	1930	Dodge Chassis; 1913 Pope-Hartford chemical apparatus

APPENDIX VI

San Jose Fire Department, 1947

Chief L. A. O'Brien, Asst. Chief A. J. Gilbert

Battalion Chiefs George Vitek, Gerald Murphy, John Jones

Headquarters, 35 N. Market Street:
Engine 1	1937 American-LaFrance 1000 GPM pumper
Hose 1	1942 Dodge-FMC high pressure fog truck with monitor
Truck 1	1946 American-LaFrance 75-ft. steel aerial
Squad 1	1938 Mack-Hedberg 500 GPM pumper-squad truck
Battalion Chief's Car	

Station 2, 61 N. Third Street:
Engine 2	1931 Mack 1000 GPM pumper
Hose 2	1942 duplicate of Hose 1

Station 3, 620 S. First Street:
Engine 3	1946 American-LaFrance 1000 GPM pumper

Station 4, 254 Spencer Ave.:
Engine 4	1944 American-LaFrance 750 GPM pumper
Truck 2	1942 Seagrave 65-ft. steel aerial

Station 5, 255 N. 8th Street:
Engine 5	1946 American-LaFrance 750 GPM pumper

Station 6, 1342 Lincoln Ave. (acquired 1936):
Engine 6	1945 American-LaFrance 750 GPM pumper

Station 7, 791 Laurel at Emory, built 1937:
Engine 7	1946 American-LaFrance 750 GPM pumper

Station 8, 17th and Santa Clara Streets:
Engine 8	1946 American-LaFrance 750 GPM pumper

Shop, 386 S. 8th Street:
Reserve Engine	1914 Seagrave 750 GPM pumper, rebuilt 1938

APPENDIX VII

San Jose Fire Department, December 1963

Chief R. B. LeBeau

Assistant Chiefs John Jones, John Knapp
District Chiefs Art McLean, Robert True, George Vitek,
Tony Sapena, Gerald Murphy, Thomas Higgins

District 1 (headquarters at Station 1); north of San Carlos Street, east of The Alameda

Station 1, 201 N. Market Street, built 1951:
Engine 1	1958 Am.-LaFrance cab-ahead 1250 GPM pumper
Hose 1	1948 GMC-SJFD hose wagon with monitor
Engine 11	1951 GMC-Hedberg 750 GPM pumper
Snorkel 1	1962 Van Pelt-HiRanger
Salvage 1	1951 Ford 1½-ton truck with skid-mounted generator
District Chief's Car 41, 1960 Ford station wagon	

Station 2, 304 N. 6th Street at Julian, built 1949:
Engine 2	1959 Am.-LaFrance cab-ahead 1000 GPM pumper
Hose 2	1956 Ford-SJFD hose wagon with monitor, booster tank and high pressure pump

Station 5, 1380 N. 10th Street, built 1959:

Engine 5	1954 GMC-Hedberg 750 GPM pumper
Hose 5	1955 duplicate of Hose 2, but without monitor
Truck 5	1942 Seagrave 65-ft. steel aerial
Reserve Engine	1946 American-LaFrance 750 GPM (former Eng. 7)

Station 7, 791 Laurel at Emory:

Engine 7	1958 Ford-LaFrance 750 GPM cab-over pumper

Station 8, 802 E. Santa Clara Street, built 1949:

Engine 8	1954 GMC-Coast 1000 GPM pumper (OCD)

Station 19, 1025 Piedmont Road, built 1963:

Engine 19	1960 Ford-LaFrance 750 GPM cab-over pumper
Reserve Engine	1937 American-LaFrance 1000 GPM (former Eng. 1)

Station 20, San Jose Municipal Airport, built 1963:

Engine 20	1954 GMC-Coast 1000 GPM pumper (OCD)
Crash Unit 1	1942 International 500 gal. foam (acquired 1957)
Cardox Jeep	1960 Willys

District 2 (headquarters at Station 3); east of Meridian Road, south of San Carlos Street)

Station 3, 98 Martha Street at S. Third, built 1955:

Engine 3	1961 American-LaFrance 1000 GPM cab-over pumper
Hose 3	1948 duplicate of Hose 1
Engine 13	1961 Ford-LaFrance 750 GPM cab-over pumper
Truck 3	1956 American-LaFrance 100-ft. steel aerial
Reserve Truck	1942 Seagrave service ladder truck (acquired 1962)
District Chief's Car 42, 1961 Ford station wagon	

Station 4, 454 Auzerais Avenue at Minor, built 1955:

Engine 4	1963 American-LaFrance 1000 GPM cab-over pumper
Truck 2	1958 American-LaFrance 100-ft. steel aerial
OCD Rescue	1954 Reo van
Ford-Hale trailer pump	
Utility truck	
Gas Truck 1	1943 GMC 750-gal. tank truck
Reserve Engine	1931 Mack 1000 GPM (former Eng. 2)

Station 6, 1386 Cherry Avenue at Minnesota, built 1963:

Engine 6	1963 American-LaFrance 1000 GPM cab-over pumper
Hose 6	1956 duplicate of Hose 2

Station 16, 2001 S. King Road at Cunningham, built 1960:

Engine 16	1960 American-LaFrance 750 GPM cab-over pumper
Chrysler-Hale 500 GPM trailer pump	
Engine 21	(temporary)

Station 18, 4420 S. Monterey Road at Snell, built 1963:

Engine 18	1946 American-LaFrance 750 GPM pumper (former Eng. 8)
Tanker 1	1952 Reo 1000-gal. tank truck with booster pump (acquired 1963)

San Jose Fire Department, 1963 *(Continued)*

District 3 (headquarters at Station 10); west of The Alameda, Meridian, and Almaden Roads; south of San Carlos and Foxworthy Avenue.

Station 9, 3410 Ross Avenue at Hillsdale, built 1962:
Engine 9   1963 American-LaFrance 1000 GPM cab-over pumper
Reserve Engine 1946 American-LaFrance 1000 GPM (former Eng. 3)
Reserve Engine 1952 GMC-Hedberg 750 GPM (former Eng. 9)

Station 10, 511 S. Monroe Street, built 1960:
Engine 10   1961 Ford-LaFrance 1000 GPM cab-over pumper
Truck 4   1946 American-LaFrance 75-ft. steel aerial
District Chief's Car 43, 1960 Ford station wagon

Station 14, 1201 San Tomas Aquino Road at Saratoga Avenue, built 1962:
Engine 14   1963 American-LaFrance 1000 GPM cab-over pumper
Lube truck   1961 Ford 1½-ton flat bed
Reserve Engine 1946 American-LaFrance 750 GPM (former Eng. 5)

Station 15, 1248 Blaney Avenue at Rainbow, built 1963:
Engine 15   1958 Ford-LaFrance 750 GPM cab-over pumper

Station 17, 1494 Ridgewood Avenue at Dent, bought 1960:
Engine 17   1951 GMC-Hedberg 750 GPM pumper

Overall size of department: 70 Captains, 221 Firefighters; 96 pieces of apparatus.

APPENDIX VIII

San Jose Fire Department, December 1970

Chief John W. Jones

Assistant Chief John F. Knapp

District 1 (headquarters Station 5) - northeast side
District Chiefs: Leonard Marks, William Murray, Robert True

Station 2, 304 N. 6th Steet at Julian, built 1949:
Engine 2   1958 ALFCO 1000 GPM
Hose 2   1956 Ford-SJFD hose wagon with monitor, booster tank, and high pressure pump

Station 5, 1380 N. 10th Street, built 1959:
Engine 5   1963 ALFCO 1000 GPM
Hose 5   1956 Ford-SJFD hose wagon with booster tank and high pressure pump
Truck 5   1965 ALFCO 100-ft. steel aerial
District 1   1966 Ford 4-door sedan
Reserve Engine 1951 GMC-Hedberg 750 GPM (former Eng. 11)

Station 19, 1025 Piedmont Road, built 1963:
Engine 19   1964 ALFCO 1000 GPM
Patrol Tanker 19 1953 Dodge ¾ ton, rebuilt 1964

Station 20, San Jose Municipal Airport, built 1963:
Engine 2   1954 GMC-Coast 1000 GPM (Eng. 4 prior 1963)
Rescue 20   1969 Dodge pickup
Tanker 20   1965 SJFD 1700 gal.
Light Water 20   1967 Ford-SJFD with Purple K and cab turret

Station 23, 1771 Via Cinco de Mayo, built 1965:
Engine 23   1965 Van Pelt 1000 GPM

Station 25, 1421 El Dorado Street, Alviso, built 1968:
Engine 25   1969 International 1000 GPM

District 2 (headquarters at Station 3) - near southeast side and east side

District Chiefs: H. Borch, Anthony Sapena, Russ Batten

Station 1, 201 N. Market Street, built 1951:
Engine 1   1958 ALFCO 1250 GPM
Hose 1   1948 GMC-SJFD hose wagon with monitor
Engine 101   1958 ALFCO 750 GPM (former Eng. 15)
Truck 1   1962 Van Pelt-HiRanger 85 ft.
Light Unit 1   1970 Chev.-SJFD 10 kw generator

Station 3, 98 Martha Street at S. Third, built 1955:
Engine 3   1970 ALFCO 1250 GPM Diesel
Hose 3   1948 duplicate of Hose 1
Engine 103   1958 ALFCO 750 GPM (former Eng. 7)
Truck 3   1964 ALFCO 100-ft. steel aerial
Reserve Engine 1945 ALFCO 1000 GPM (former Eng. 6, earlier Eng. 3)
Reserve Engine 1946 White 500 GPM
Gas Rig No. 1   1943 GMC 750 gallon
Light Unit 3   1952 GMC rebuilt 1965 7.5 kw generator
District 2   1969 Chev. 4-door sedan

Station 4, 454 Auzerais Avenue at Minor, built 1955:
Engine 4   1970 ALFCO 1250 GPM Diesel
Truck 4   1970 ALFCO 100-ft. steel aerial
Rescue 4   1954 Reo (OCD)
Reserve Engine 1931 Mack 1000 GPM (Eng. 2 prior to 1954)

Station 8, 802 E. Santa Clara at 17th, built 1949:
Engine 8   1967 ALFCO 1000 GPM

Station 16, 2001 S. King Road at Cunningham, built 1960:
Engine 16   1963 ALFCO 1000 GPM (former Eng. 4)
Patrol Tanker 16 1953 Dodge ¾ ton, rebuilt 1964
Reserve Engine 1951 GMC-Hedberg 750 GPM (former Eng. 17)
Truck 16   1942 Seagrave 65-ft. steel aerial (former Truck 2, Truck 5)

Station 21, 1749 Mt. Pleasant Road, built 1964:
Engine 21   1964 ALFCO 1000 GPM

District 3 (headquarters at Station 10) - near southwest, west, and northwest

District Chiefs: David Van Etten, Tom Higgins, Ted Klein

Station 6, 1386 Cherry Avenue, at Minnesota, built 1963:
Engine 6   1963 ALFCO 1000 GPM
Hose 6   1956 duplicate of Hose 2
Reserve Service Truck   1942 Seagrave (acquired 1962)

Station 7, 800 Emory Street (formerly 791 Laurel), built 1937:
Engine 7   1967 ALFCO 1000 GPM

San Jose Fire Department, 1970 (Continued)

Station 10, 511 S. Monroe Street, built 1960:
Engine 10	1961 ALFCO 1000 GPM	
Truck 10	1958 ALFCO 100-ft steel aerial (former Truck 2 which was then located at Station 4)	
Light Unit 10	1951 SJFD 5 kw generator (formerly called Salvage 1)	
Reserve Engine	1960 ALFCO 750 GPM (former Eng. 16)	
Reserve Engine	1954 GMC-Hedberg 750 GPM (former Eng. 5, Eng. 9)	
District 3	1966 Ford 4-door sedan	

Station 14, 1201 San Tomas Aquino Road at Saratoga Avenue, built 1962:
Engine 14	1963 ALFCO 1000 GPM
Truck 14	1946 ALFCO 75-ft. steel aerial (former Truck 1; Truck 4 which was then at Station 10)

Station 15, 1248 Blaney Avenue at Rainbow, built 1963:
Engine 15	1967 ALFCO 1000 GPM
Reserve Engine	1937 ALFCO 1000 GPM (former Eng. 1)

District 4 (headquarters at Station 13) - far south side

District Chiefs: Larry Cunningham, E. Anderson, E. Thompson

Station 9, 3410 Ross Avenue at Hillsdale, built 1962:
Engine 9	1961 ALFCO 750 GPM
Reserve Engine	1954 GMC-Coast 1000 GPM (former Eng. 8, Eng. 2)

Station 12, 502 Calero Avenue, built 1966:
Engine 12	1961 ALFCO 750 GPM (former Eng. 13)

Station 13, 4380 Pearl Avenue, built 1968:
Engine 13	1969 International 1000 GPM
Truck 13	1956 ALFCO 100-ft. steel aerial (former Truck 3)
Light Unit 13	1952 SJFD 7.5 kw generator
District 4	1968 Ford 4-door sedan

Station 17, 1494 Ridgewood Drive at Dent, bought 1960:
Engine 17	1960 ALFCO 750 GPM (former Eng. 19)

Station 18, 4430 S. Monterey Road at Snell, built 1963:
Engine 18	1964 ALFCO 1000 GPM
Tanker 18	1952 Reo 1000 gal. rebuilt 1963 (then called Tanker 1)
Reserve Engine	1946 ALFCO 750 GPM (former Eng. 18, Eng. 8)

Station 22, 6461 Bose Lane, built 1965:
Engine 22	1967 ALFCO 1000 GPM
Tanker 22	1952 Reo 1000 gal. (rebuilt 1965 - formerly called Tanker 2)

Station 24, 2525 Aborn Road, built 1968:
Engine 24	1967 ALFCO 1000 GPM
Patrol Tanker 24	1953 Dodge ¾ ton rebuilt 1968 (formerly called PT-7)

This antique fire equipment is owned by or in the possession of the San Jose Fire Department. It will eventually be on display when the San Jose Historical Museum at Kelley Park is completed. Because of the size of the collection, only a small portion of it is now on display at the Central Fire Station at Market and St. James Streets in downtown San Jose. Much of the equipment shown on the next four pages was collected through the efforts of Deputy Chief Leonard Marks (a member of the Historical Landmarks Commission of San Jose) and was restored by the fire department shop. Particular benefactors were the Levin Brothers, Captain Sam Seibert, Captain Joe Paradiso and Chief Marks.

This rare 1800 hand pumper is on display at the Central Fire Station. It was built by James Smith of New York and commonly called a piano box or squirrel tail pumper. It was used in New England and was acquired and donated by Captains Joe Paradiso, Sam Seibert and Chief Leonard Marks.

Hand drawn ladder truck now restored and on display at the temporary San Jose Historical Museum. It was donated by Richard and Sydney Levin who obtained it from the Palo Alto Fire Department.

Two horse steamer, vintage 1880, donated by the Levin Brothers who obtained it from the Tracy, California Fire Department.

1884 Steamer (American Fire Engine Company) pulled by a 1904 Knox-Martin water cooled tractor. Extremely rare, this piece of equipment is believed to be only one of two still in existence in the U.S. Donated by Levin Brothers to the City of San Jose in 1965.

1925 American-LaFrance 750 GPM pumper. Donated by Leonard Marks, it was originally used by the Westmorland Fire Department in Southern California.

1926 Seagrave 1000 GPM pumper, donated by Dick Levin who obtained it from the Palo Alto Fire Department. Now on display at the Central Fire Station.

1914 American-LaFrance wood aerial ladder (motorized) owned by Desmond Johnson, on permanent loan to the San Jose Fire Department.

1937 American-LaFrance V12 1000 GPM
pumping engine—used by the San Jose Fire
Department.

Engine ½. Built in the Fire Department
Shop, this midget fire engine is the delight
of children. See story on page 206.

1946 American-LaFrance V12 1000 GPM
pumper. Acquired after the end of World
War II, this pumper saw many years of
service in San Jose.

1946 Van Pelt-White 500 GPM pumper
acquired in the annexation of the town of
Alviso by the City of San Jose. The large
white object is a paper mache fireman's hat
used in some by-gone day parade.

Hand drawn hook and ladder awaiting restoration—acquired from the Lou Bohnett collection and believed to have been used by the City of Santa Clara.

1928 Bulldog Mack 1000 GPM pumper donated by Chief Leonard Marks who obtained it from the Burlingame, California Fire Department.

A portion of the collection of hand drawn hose reels and hand drawn chemical tanks awaiting restoration.

Equipment Soon To

Be Restored For

Eventual Display

This Ahrens-Fox 750 GPM pumper is owned by Fire Associates of Santa Clara Valley President Len Williams and is NOT a part of the collection of the SJFD. Pictured here with Williams is Fire Associates' Vice President Neil Carlson.

249

The Fire Associates of Santa Clara Valley serving coffee and food to weary firefighters April 18th, 1971.

THE STORY OF FIRE ASSOCIATES OF
SANTA CLARA VALLEY

Fire Associates of Santa Clara Valley is unique among the many civic and fraternal organizations in the greater San Jose area. The limited regular membership of the group is composed of men who are interested in all phases of fire department operations and the various principles of fire protection.

The nucleus of the group was comprised of local residents who were also members of a similar organization, the Phoenix Society of San Francisco. Believing that there were other individuals in the San Jose area with an interest in fire department operations, Leonard Williams and Fred Oehm approached the San Jose Fire Department with the idea of forming a group similar to the Phoenix Society.

Permission to form a group was granted and the fire department gave the organizers the names of individuals known to be friends of the department. Formative meetings were held in the late fall of 1969. The name was chosen and a state charter as a non-profit corporation was issued in early 1970.

The principal qualifications for membership are good character and an interest in some aspect of the fire department. Members' interests range from fire department history to fire equipment.

The members operate a canteen service that is available to requesting fire departments on a 24-hour basis. A vehicle for use in providing this service has been donated by the Palo Alto Fire Department.

Fire Associates of Santa Clara Valley is proud to present this book to the community. It will preserve the rich history of the fire department and give insights into many other historical aspects of San Jose's growth and development.

Acknowledgments

The Publisher appreciates the assistance of the many local people who were generous with their time and provided access to relevant material as Guardians of the Garden City was being readied for publication.

Chief John Jones made possible the active help of all sections of the Fire Department and use of all available records. Chief Leonard Marks made suggestions as to sources, loaned photos, and retired Battalion Chief Larry Campbell spent many hours going over his forty-year collection of Fire Department pictures and stories for background material. The cooperative spirit of the Fire Department proved to be operative in many dimensions— we even took pictures off the walls of fire stations all over the city for reproduction.

The Index, included in order to make the book a useful tool in the future, was done by Naomi Lockley.

The following persons have contributed greatly to the research and supply of photos for the publication of this book:

Clyde Arbuckle
Earl Conyers
John Gerhard
Judge Marshall Hall
Richard Hall

Dennis Madigan
Howard Overhouse
Sam Seibert
Richard Wells

Guardians of the Garden City is printed on Paloma Coated Matte paper, with Century body type and headings in Bodoni. All work was done by Smith & McKay Printing Company except the binding.

LEONARD McKAY
Smith & McKay Printing Company

Index

252

Index
(C O N T I N U E D)